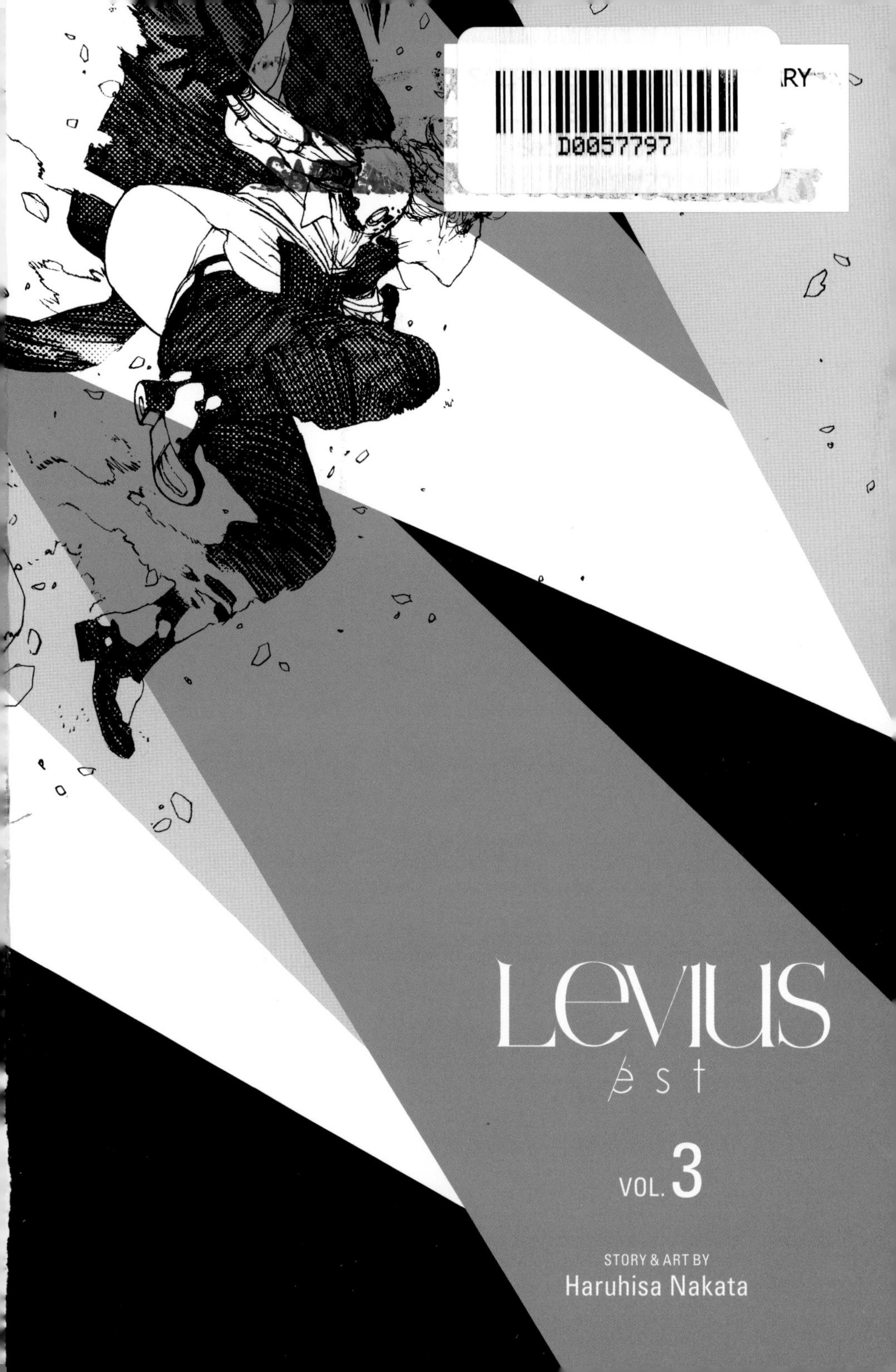

Levius est

VOL. 3

STORY & ART BY
Haruhisa Nakata

Levius/est
VOL. 3

Chapter 12

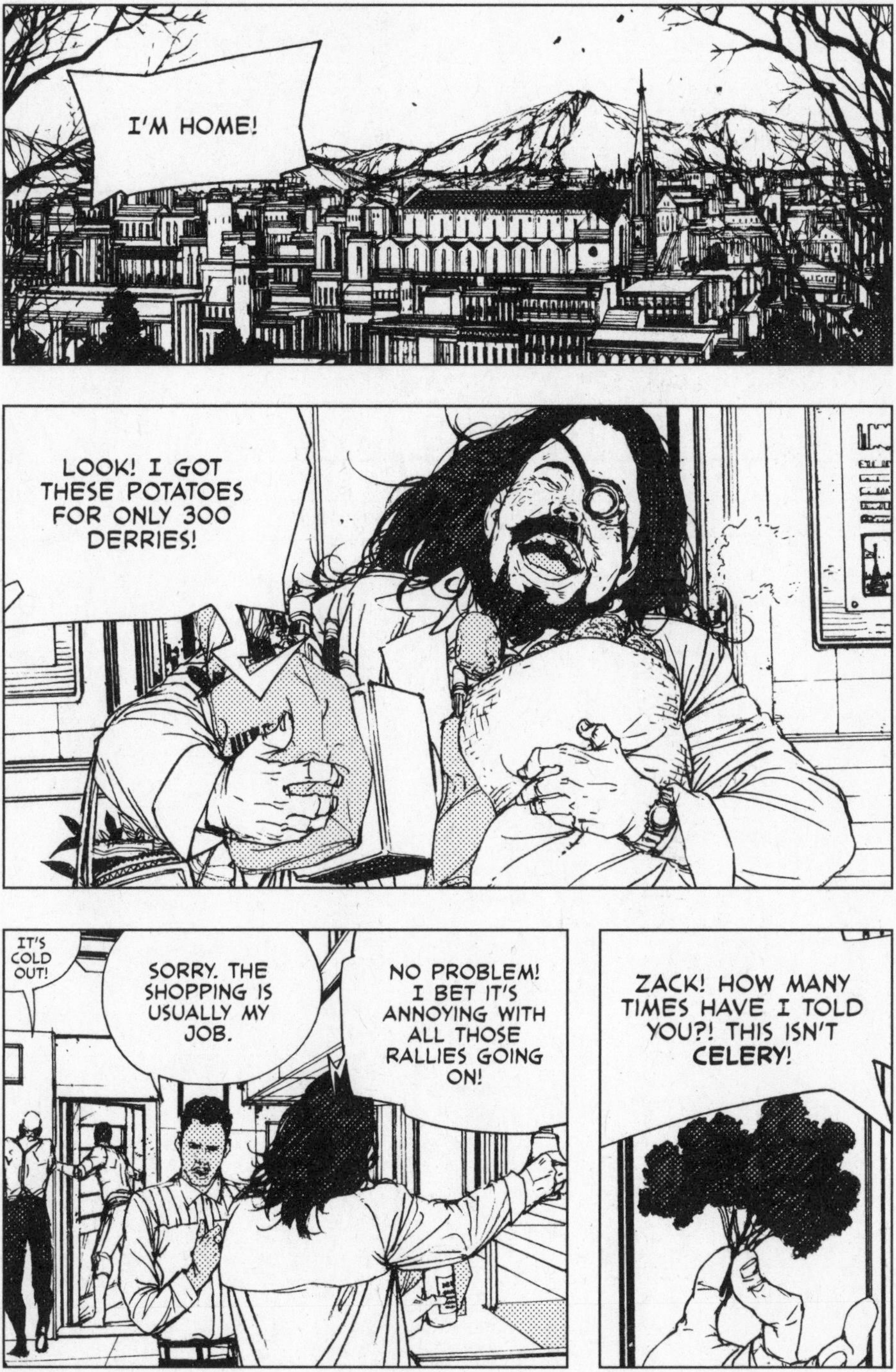
I'M HOME!
LOOK! I GOT THESE POTATOES FOR ONLY 300 DERRIES!
IT'S COLD OUT!
SORRY. THE SHOPPING IS USUALLY MY JOB.
NO PROBLEM! I BET IT'S ANNOYING WITH ALL THOSE RALLIES GOING ON!
ZACK! HOW MANY TIMES HAVE I TOLD YOU?! THIS ISN'T CELERY!

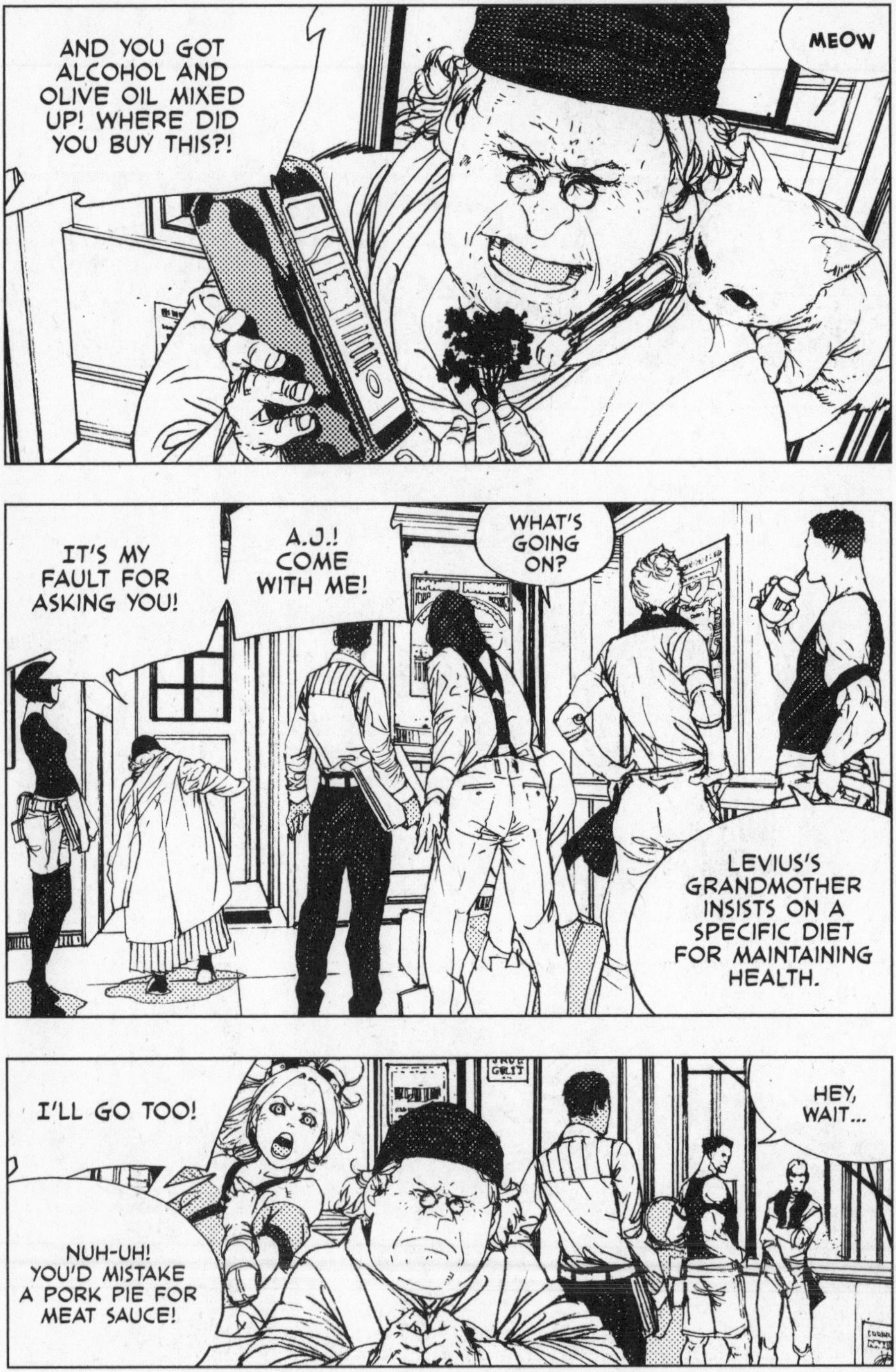
AND YOU GOT ALCOHOL AND OLIVE OIL MIXED UP! WHERE DID YOU BUY THIS?!
MEOW
IT'S MY FAULT FOR ASKING YOU!
A.J.! COME WITH ME!
WHAT'S GOING ON?
LEVIUS'S GRANDMOTHER INSISTS ON A SPECIFIC DIET FOR MAINTAINING HEALTH.
I'LL GO TOO!
HEY, WAIT...
NUH-UH! YOU'D MISTAKE A PORK PIE FOR MEAT SAUCE!

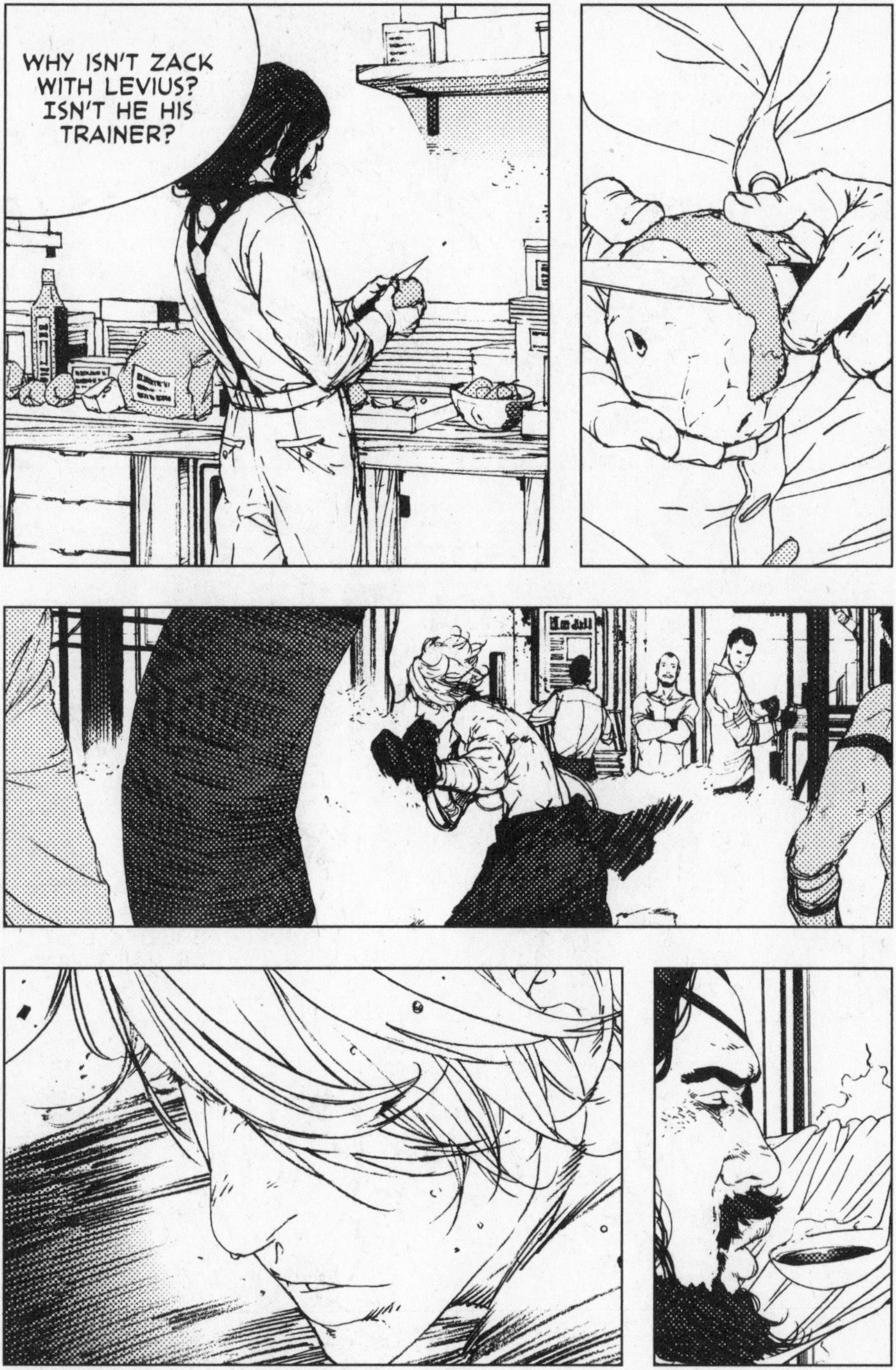
WHY ISN'T ZACK WITH LEVIUS? ISN'T HE HIS TRAINER?

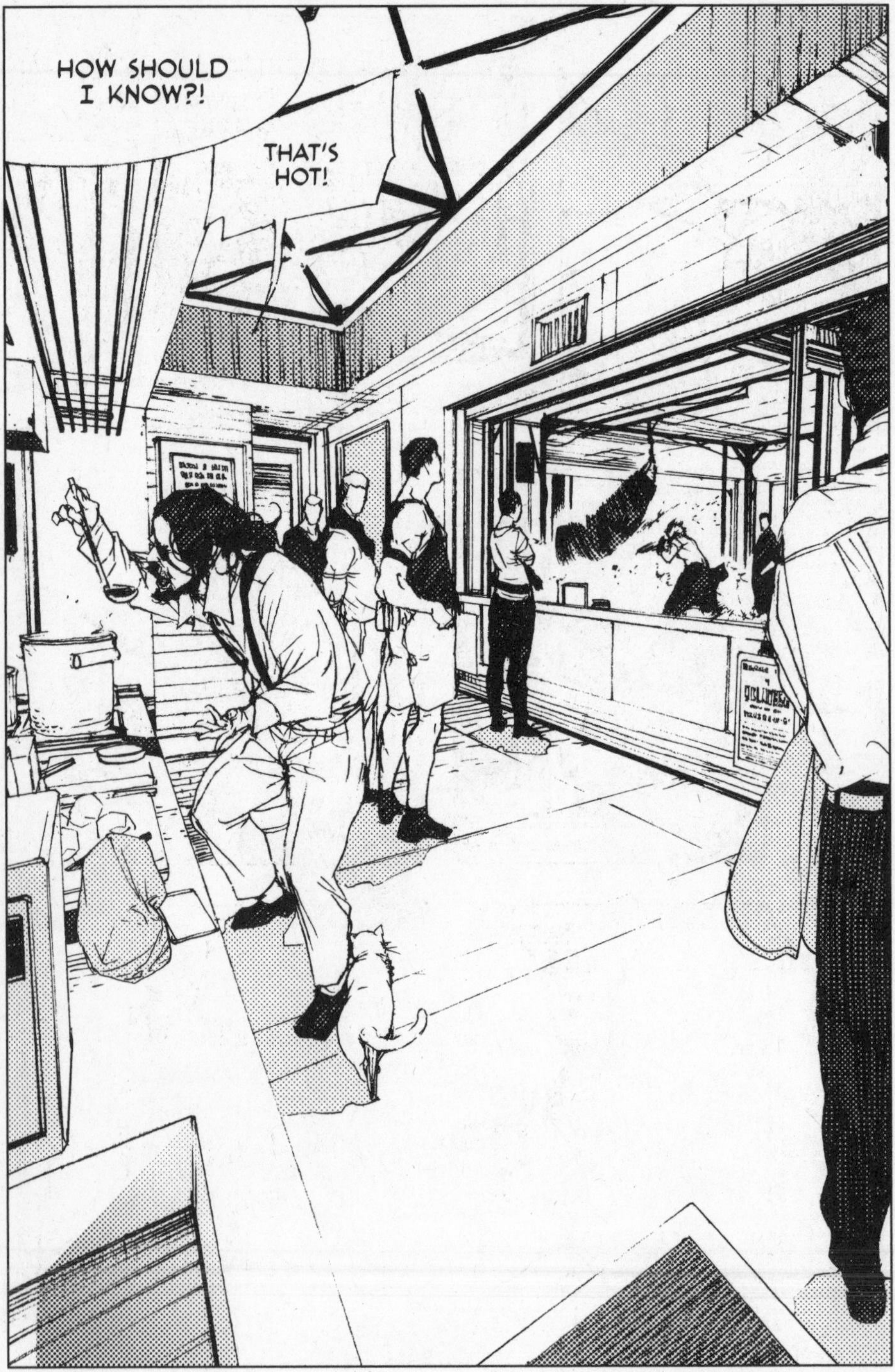
HOW SHOULD I KNOW?!
THAT'S HOT!

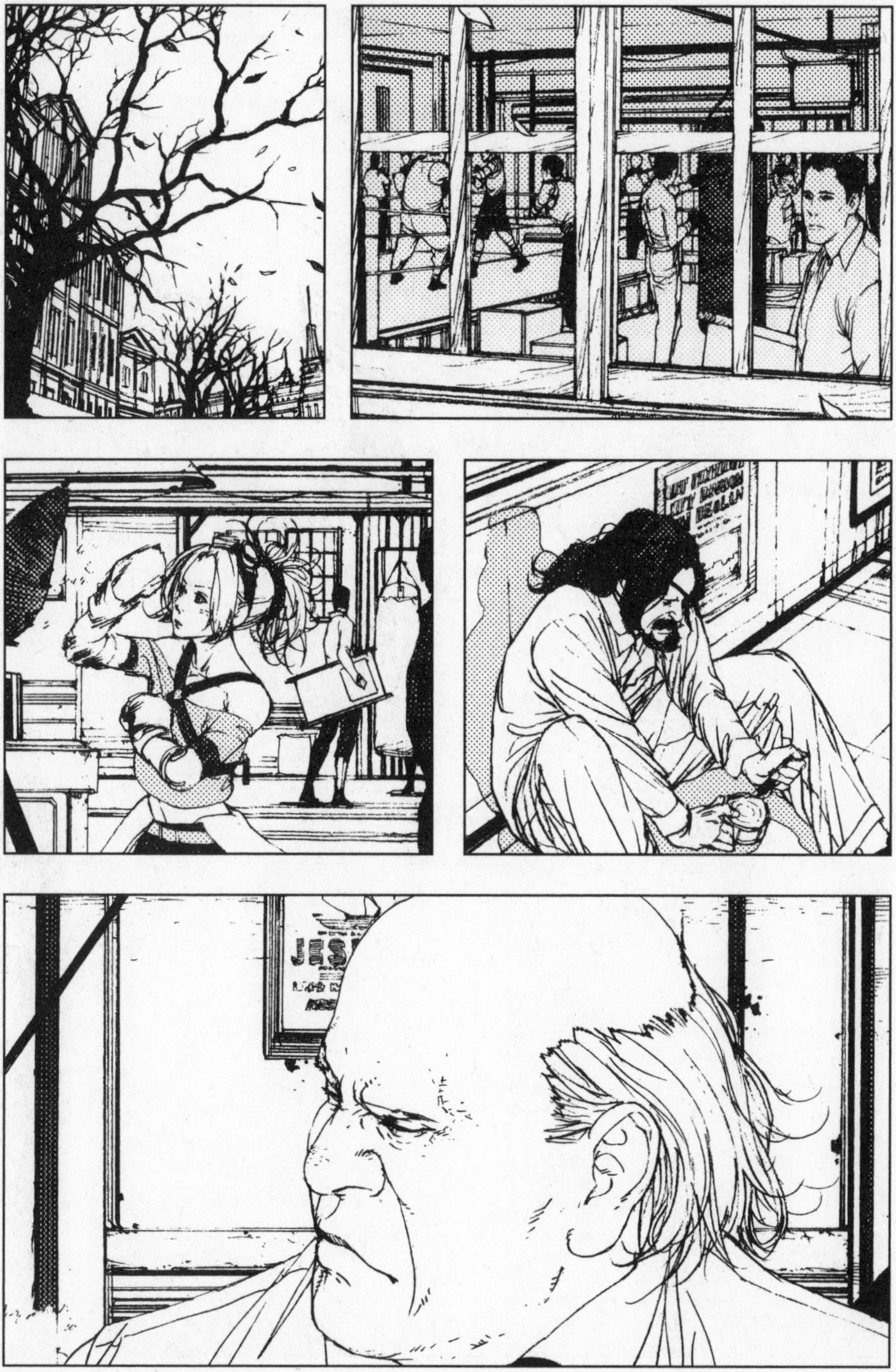

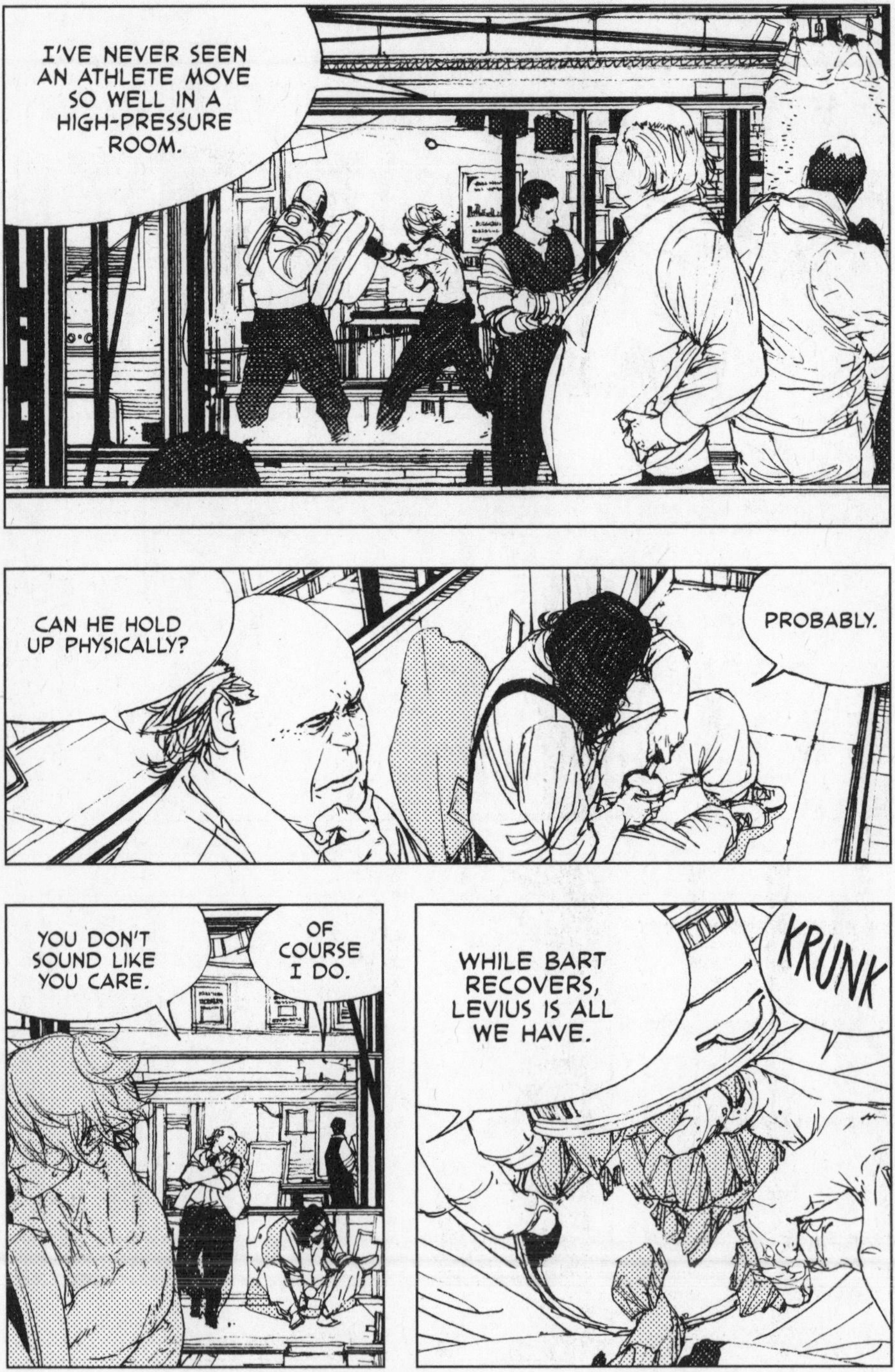
I'VE NEVER SEEN AN ATHLETE MOVE SO WELL IN A HIGH-PRESSURE ROOM.
CAN HE HOLD UP PHYSICALLY?
PROBABLY.
YOU DON'T SOUND LIKE YOU CARE.
OF COURSE I DO.
WHILE BART RECOVERS, LEVIUS IS ALL WE HAVE.
KRUNK

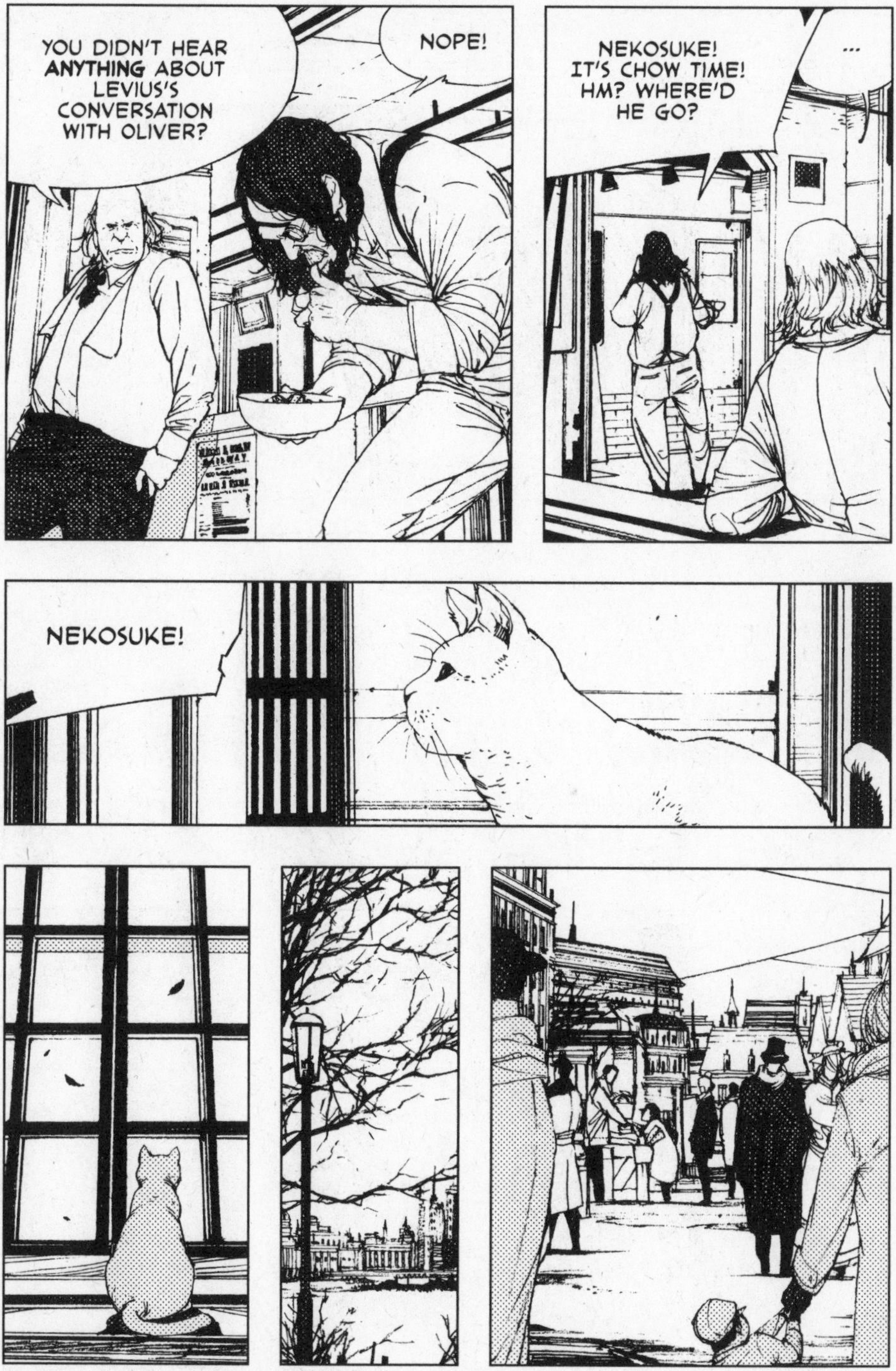
YOU DIDN'T HEAR **ANYTHING** ABOUT LEVIUS'S CONVERSATION WITH OLIVER?
NOPE!
NEKOSUKE! IT'S CHOW TIME! HM? WHERE'D HE GO?
...
NEKOSUKE!

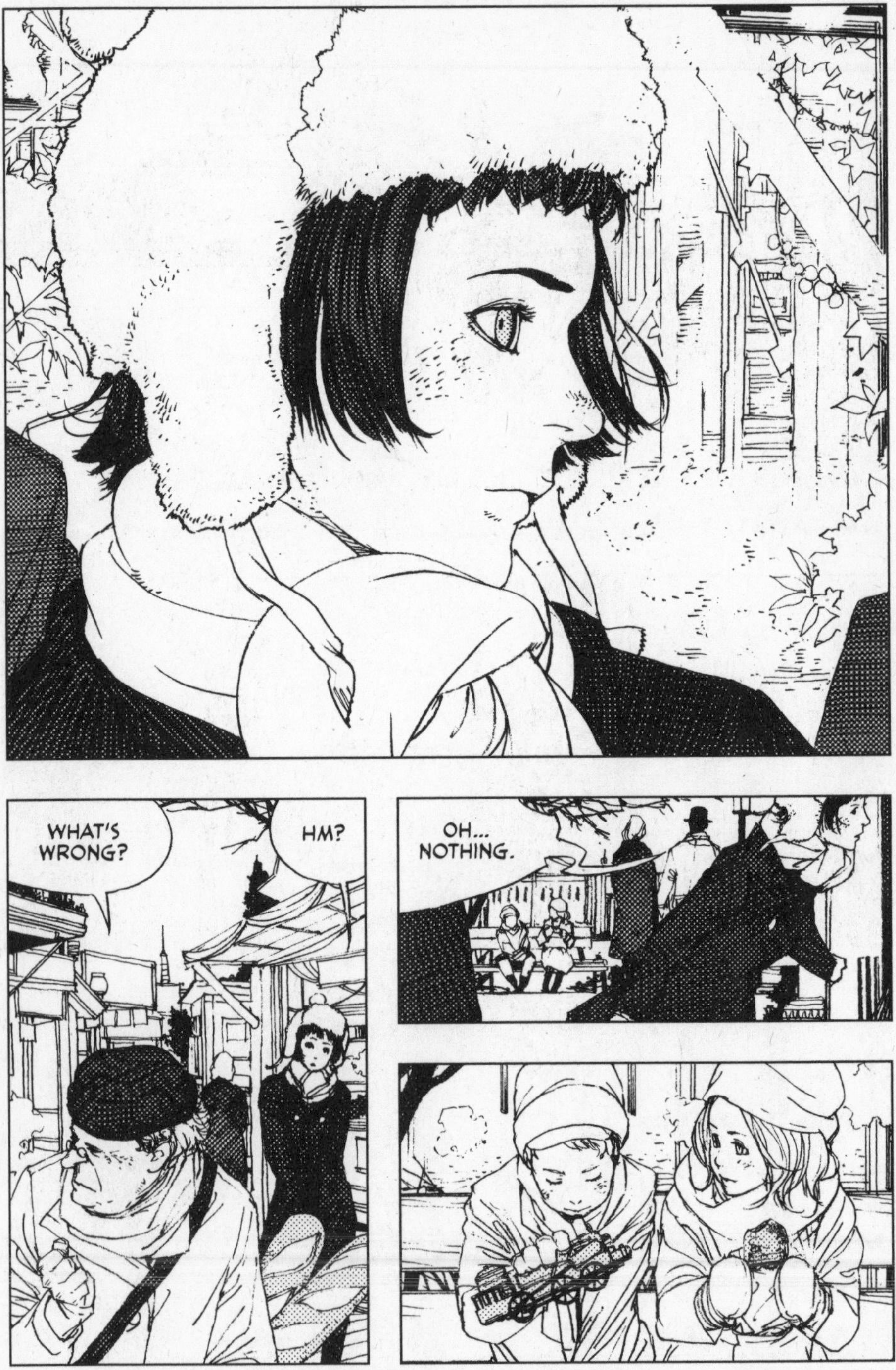
WHAT'S WRONG?
HM?
OH... NOTHING.

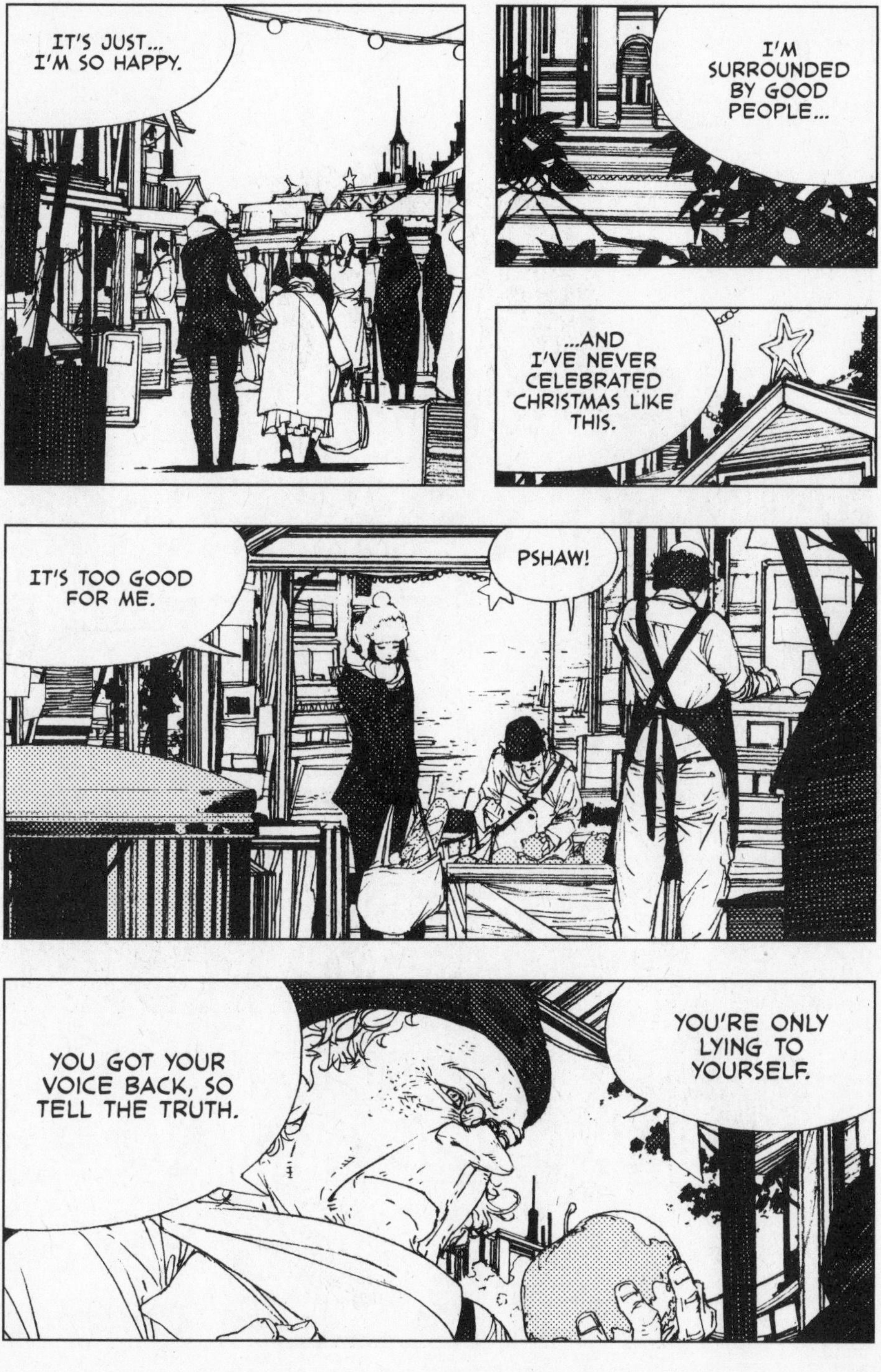
IT'S JUST... I'M SO HAPPY.
I'M SURROUNDED BY GOOD PEOPLE...
...AND I'VE NEVER CELEBRATED CHRISTMAS LIKE THIS.
IT'S TOO GOOD FOR ME.
PSHAW!
YOU GOT YOUR VOICE BACK, SO TELL THE TRUTH.
YOU'RE ONLY LYING TO YOURSELF.

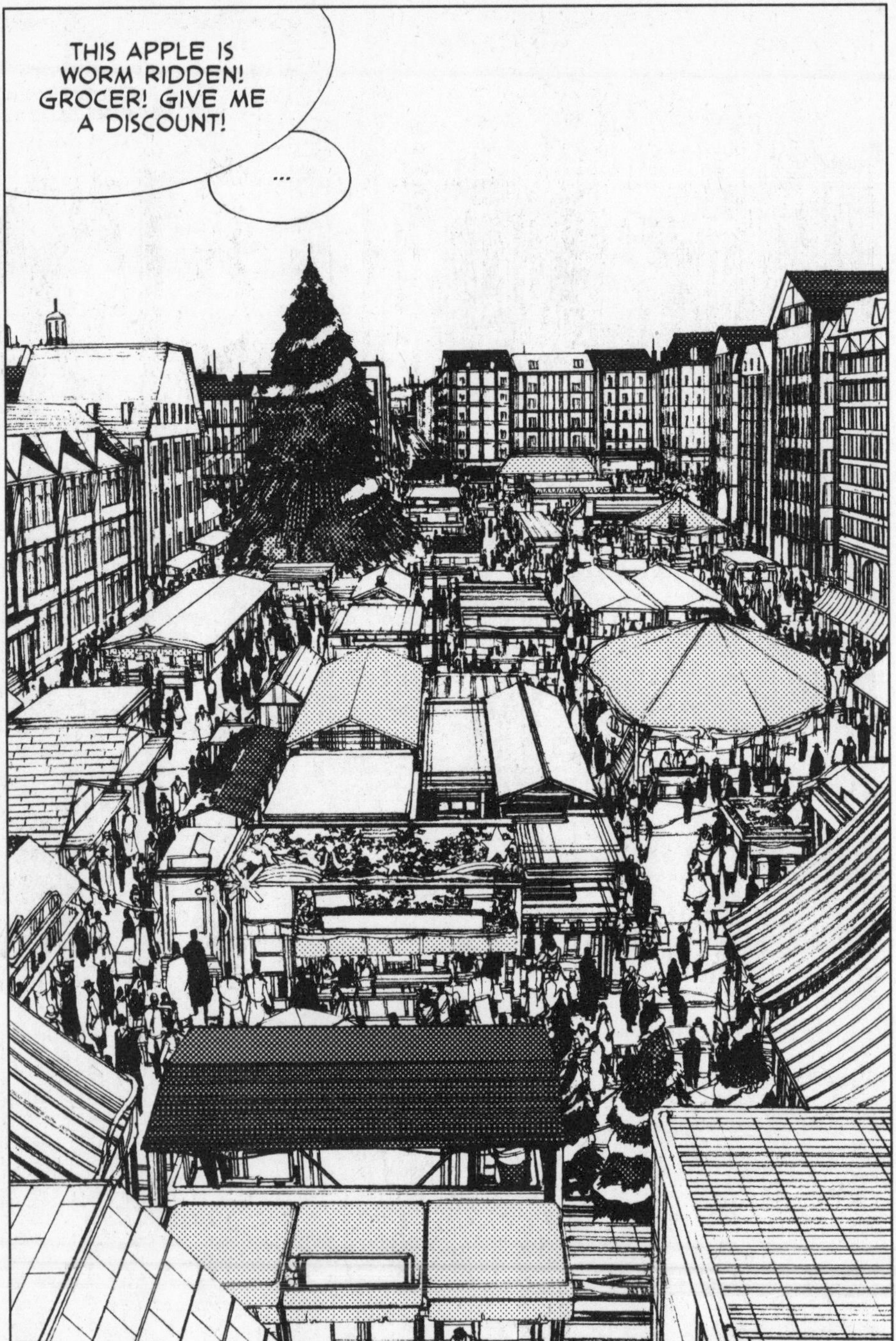
THIS APPLE IS WORM RIDDEN! GROCER! GIVE ME A DISCOUNT!
...

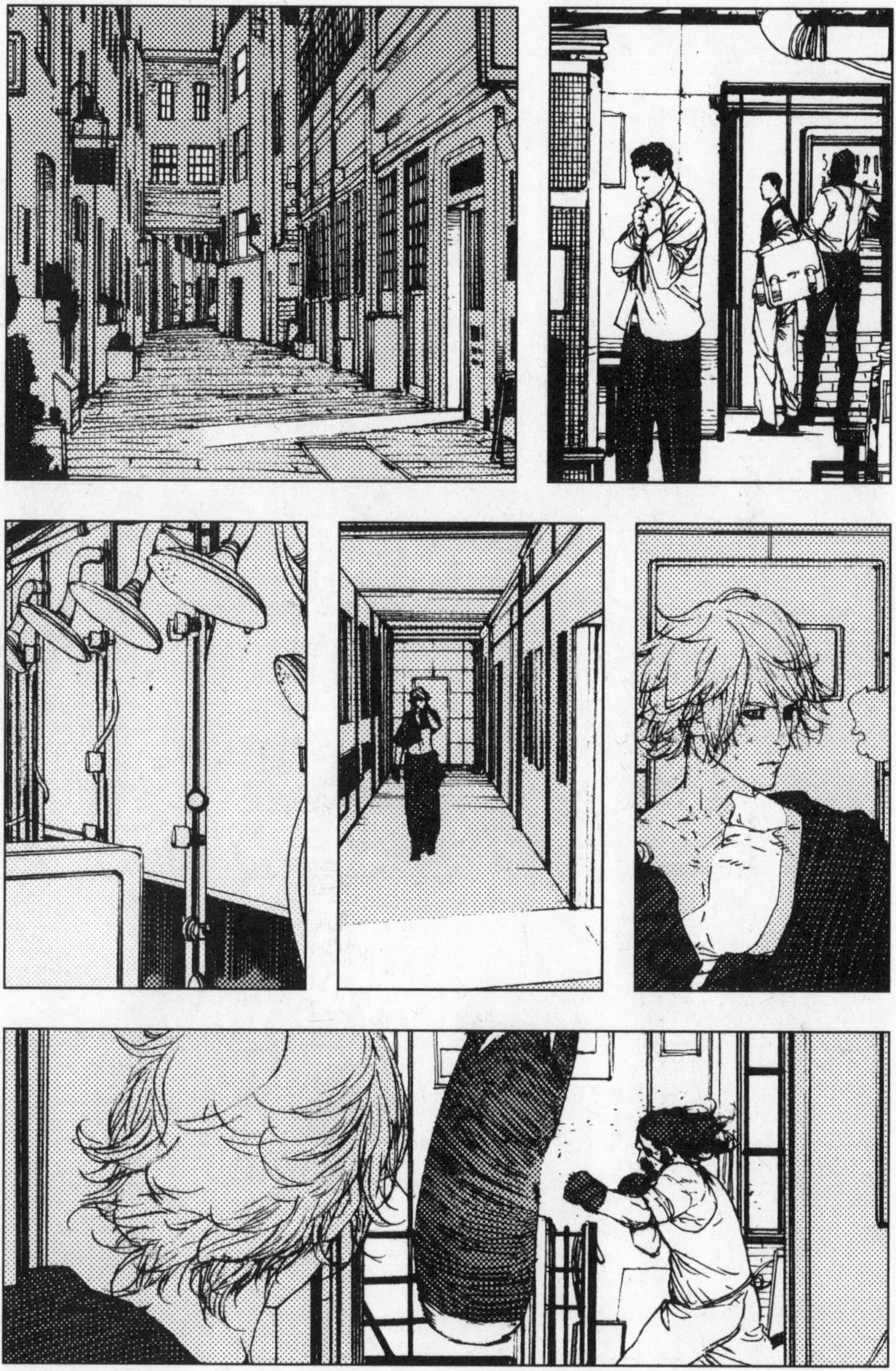

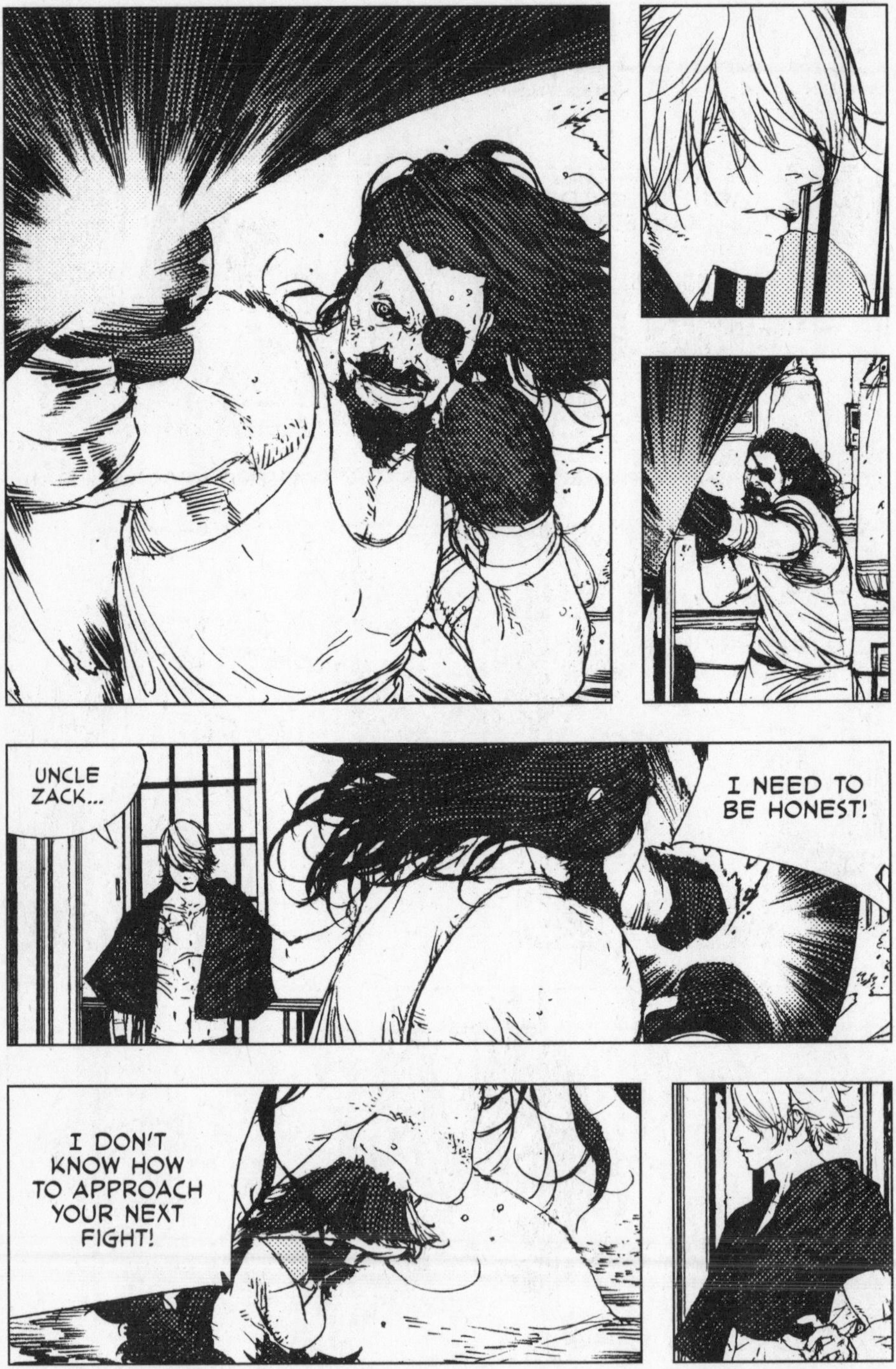
UNCLE ZACK...
I NEED TO BE HONEST!
I DON'T KNOW HOW TO APPROACH YOUR NEXT FIGHT!

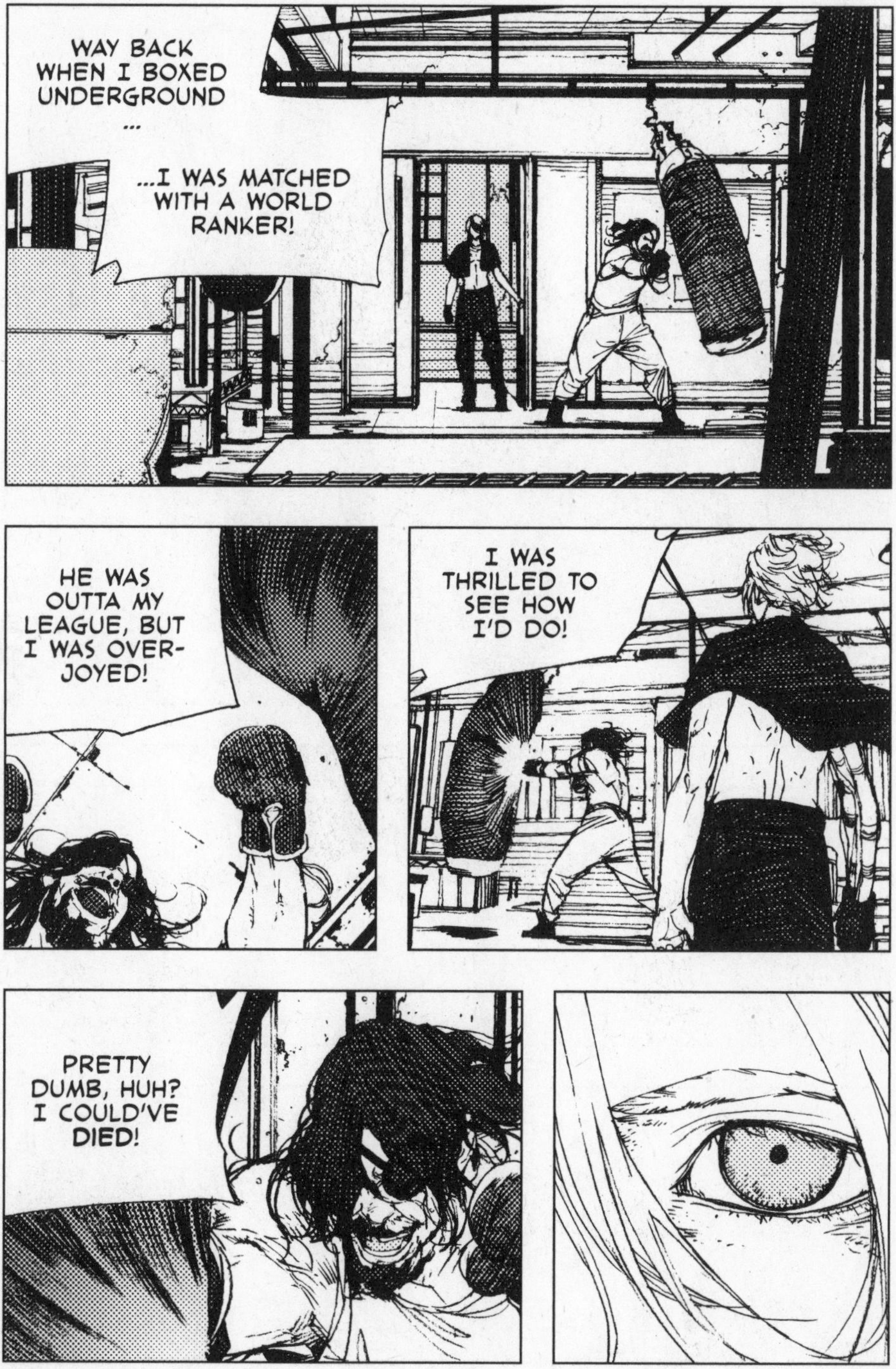

WAY BACK WHEN I BOXED UNDERGROUND ...
...I WAS MATCHED WITH A WORLD RANKER!
HE WAS OUTTA MY LEAGUE, BUT I WAS OVER-JOYED!
I WAS THRILLED TO SEE HOW I'D DO!
PRETTY DUMB, HUH? I COULD'VE DIED!

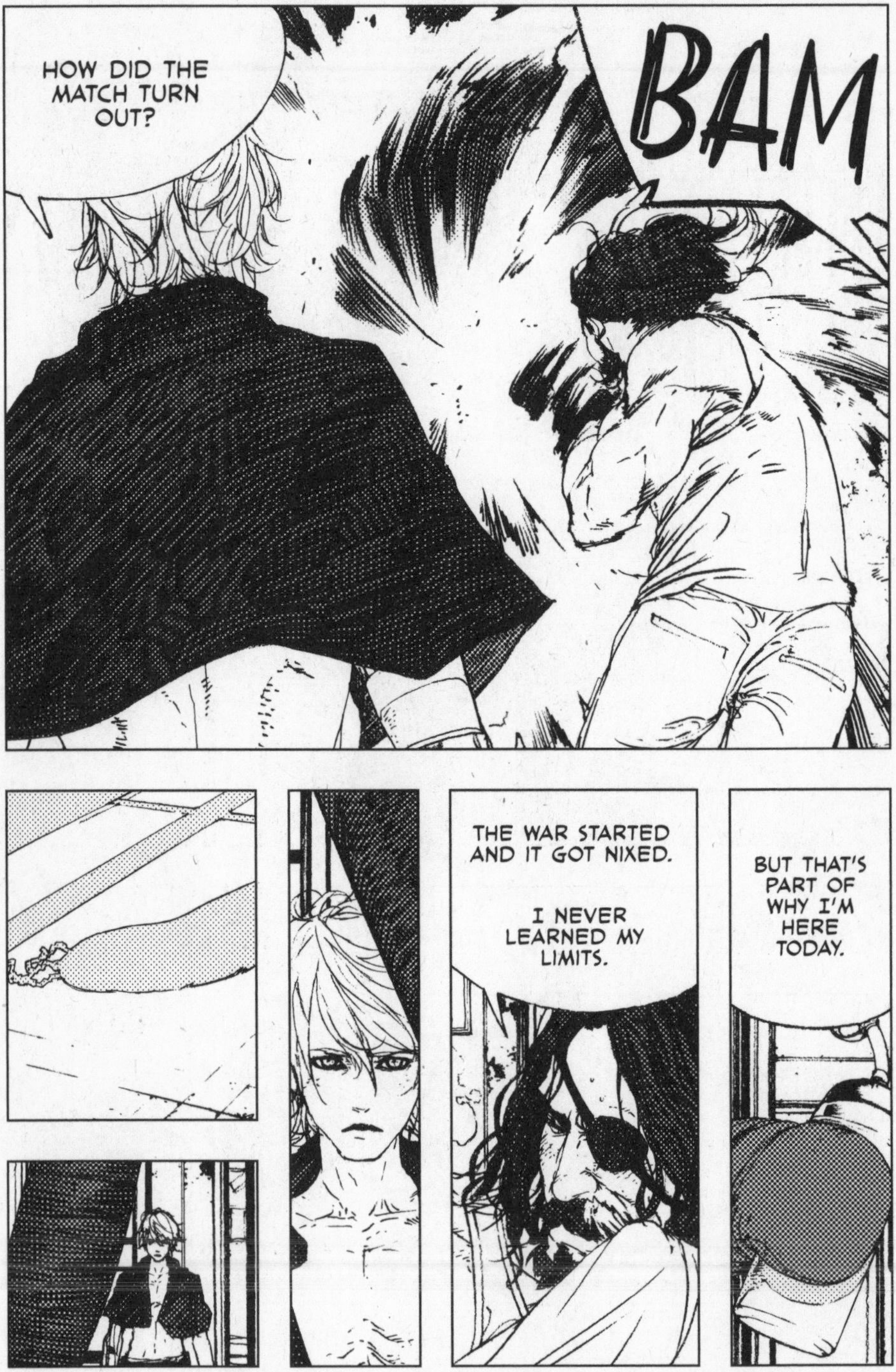
HOW DID THE MATCH TURN OUT?
BAM
THE WAR STARTED AND IT GOT NIXED.
I NEVER LEARNED MY LIMITS.
BUT THAT'S PART OF WHY I'M HERE TODAY.

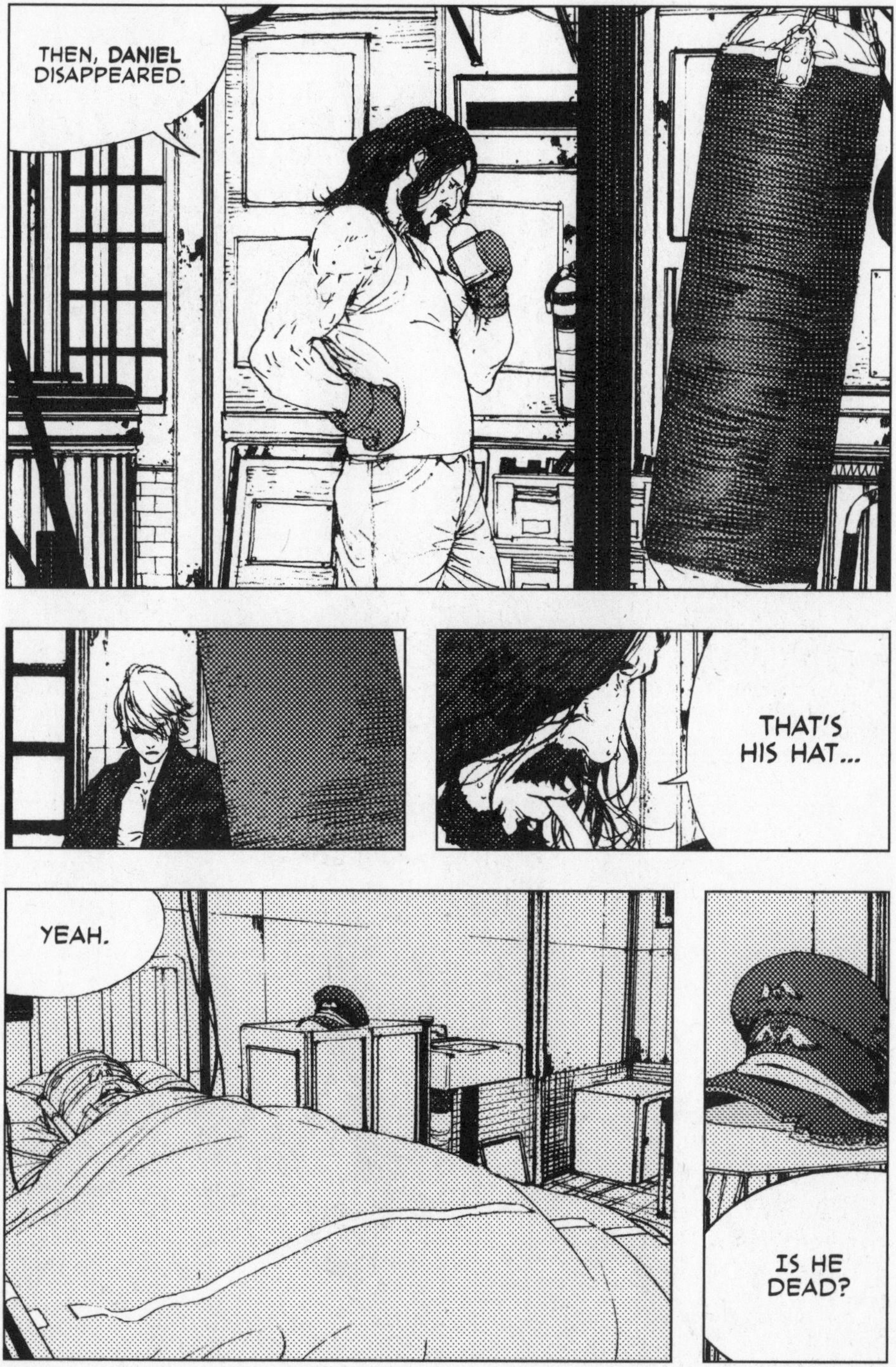
THEN, DANIEL DISAPPEARED.
THAT'S HIS HAT...
YEAH.
IS HE DEAD?

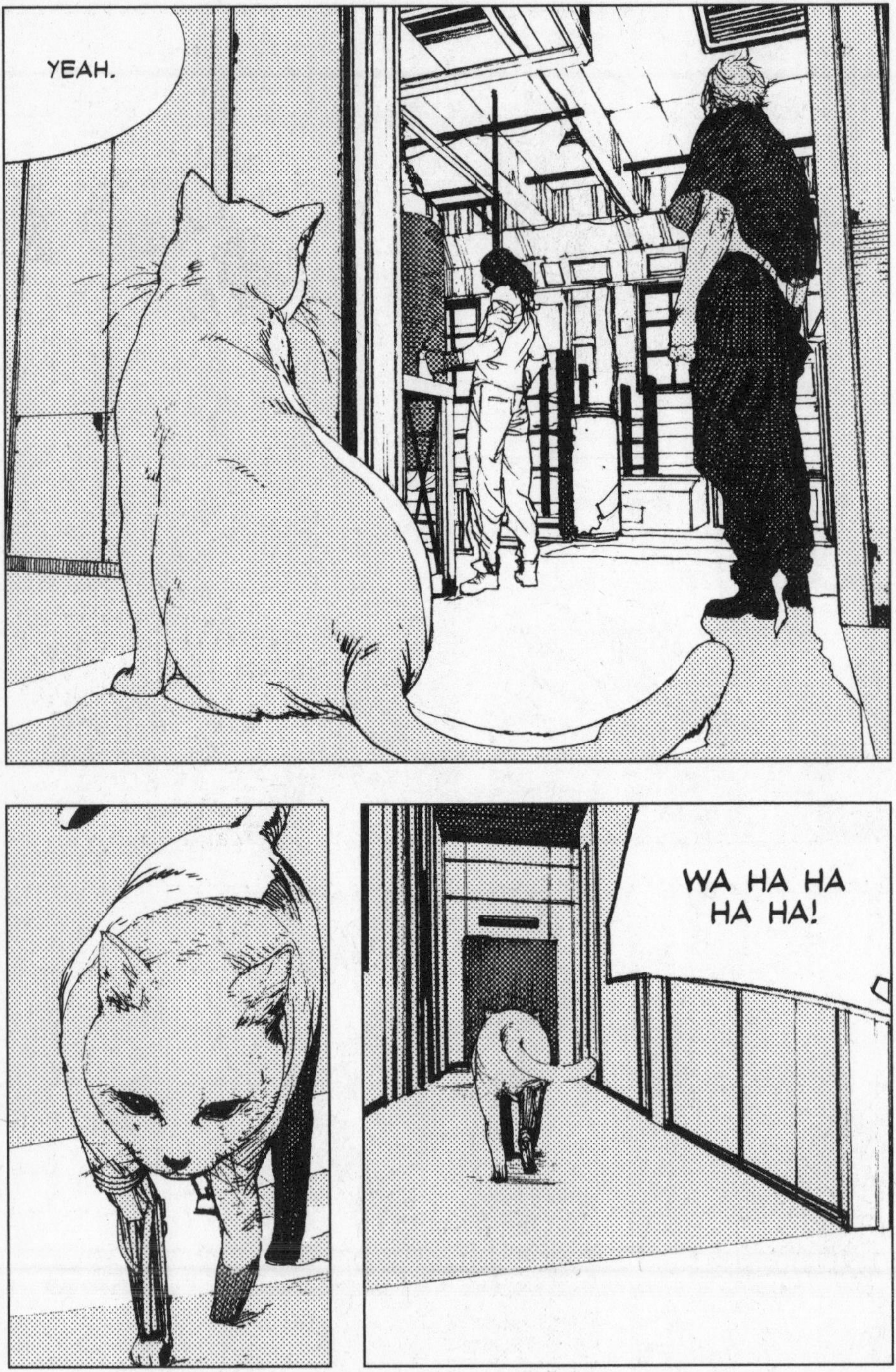
YEAH.
WA HA HA
HA HA!

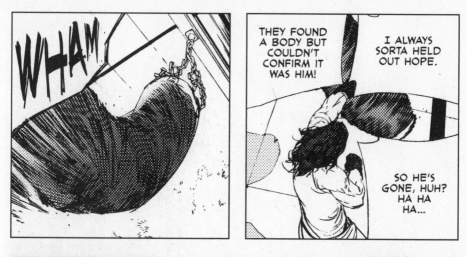

WHAM

THEY FOUND A BODY BUT COULDN'T CONFIRM IT WAS HIM!

I ALWAYS SORTA HELD OUT HOPE.

SO HE'S GONE, HUH? HA HA HA...

ARGHH!

HE WAS SURROUNDED BY GREENERY AND LOOKED PEACEFUL, LIKE HE'D FULFILLED HIS ROLE.

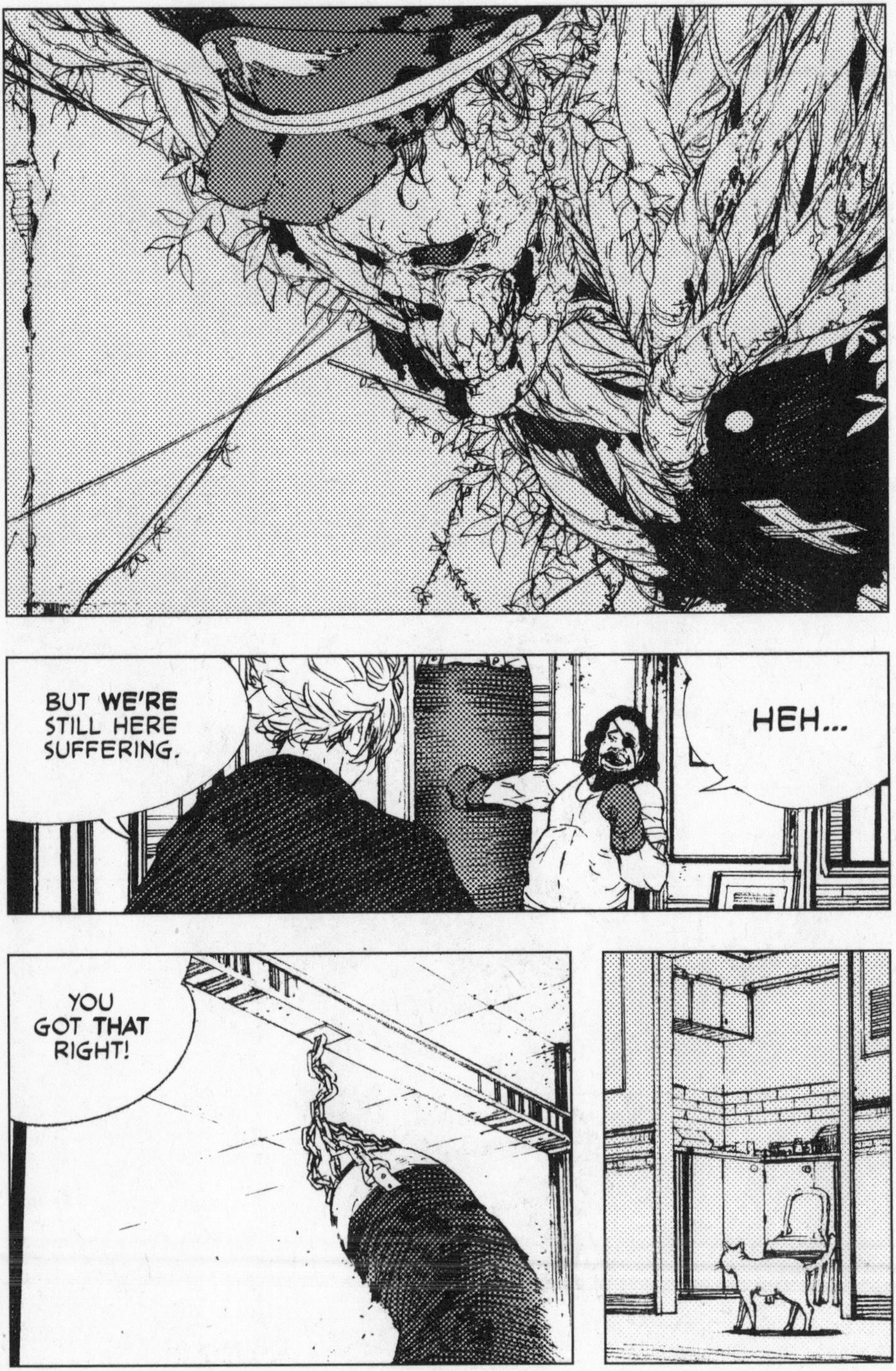
BUT WE'RE STILL HERE SUFFERING.
HEH...
YOU GOT THAT RIGHT!

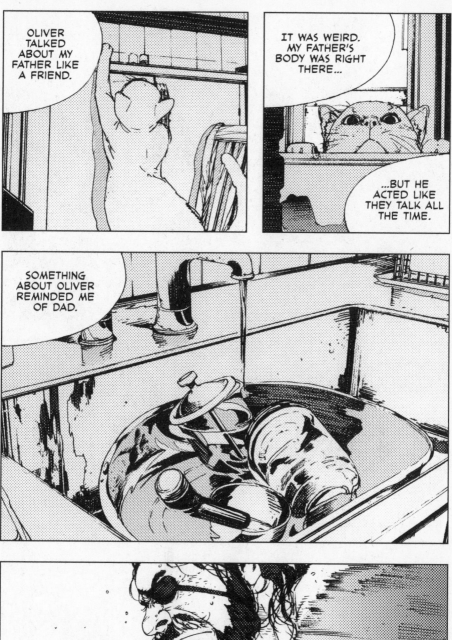

OLIVER TALKED ABOUT MY FATHER LIKE A FRIEND.

IT WAS WEIRD. MY FATHER'S BODY WAS RIGHT THERE...

...BUT HE ACTED LIKE THEY TALK ALL THE TIME.

SOMETHING ABOUT OLIVER REMINDED ME OF DAD.

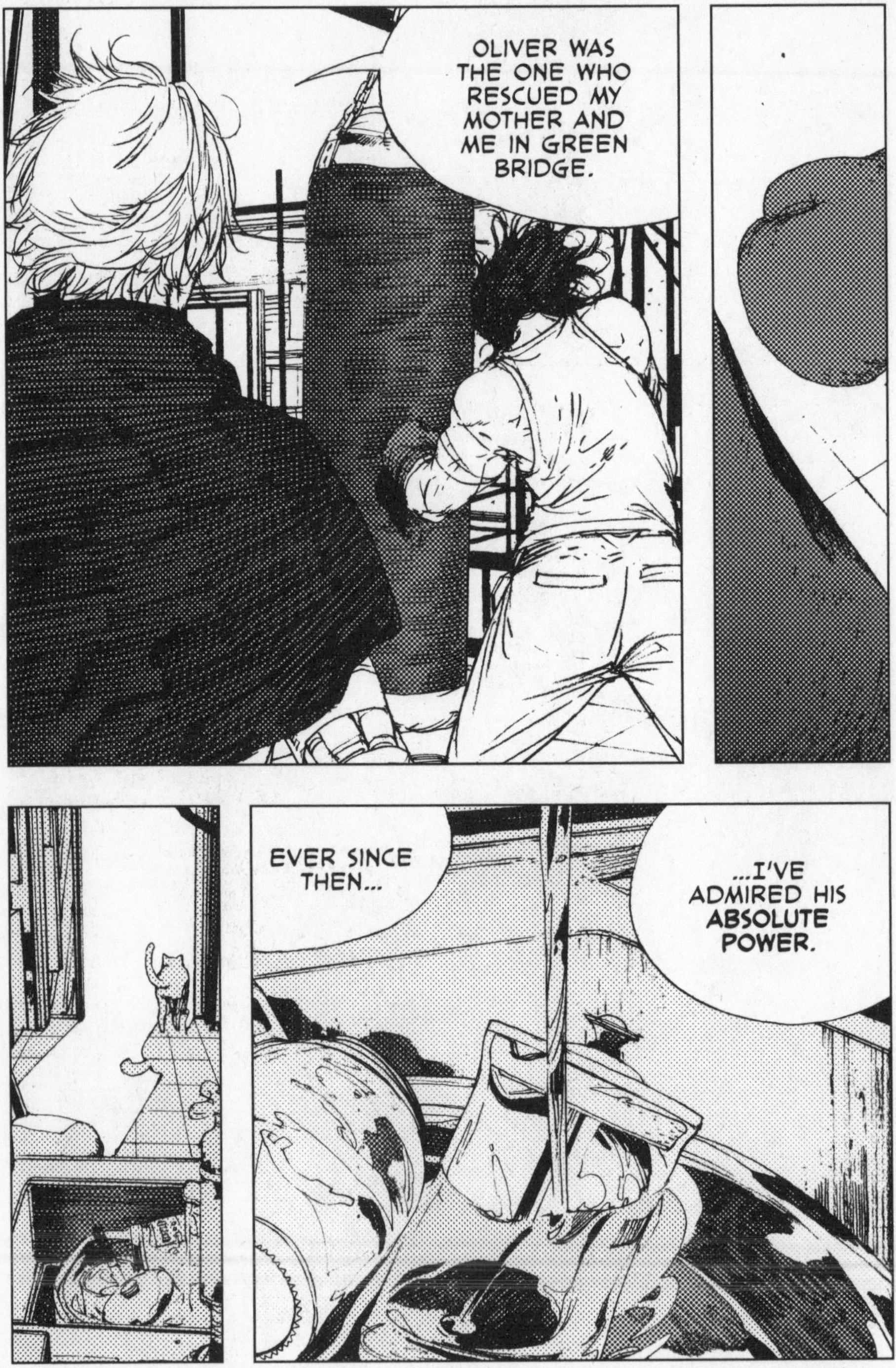
OLIVER WAS THE ONE WHO RESCUED MY MOTHER AND ME IN GREEN BRIDGE.
EVER SINCE THEN...
...I'VE ADMIRED HIS ABSOLUTE POWER.

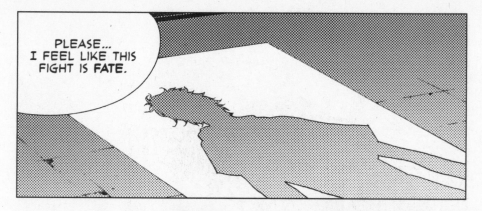

PLEASE...
I FEEL LIKE THIS
FIGHT IS **FATE.**

IF MY LIFE IS TO
CONTINUE...

...IT HAS TO BE
**THROUGH THIS
FIGHT.**

I HAVE TO BE
BETTER THAN
OLIVER.

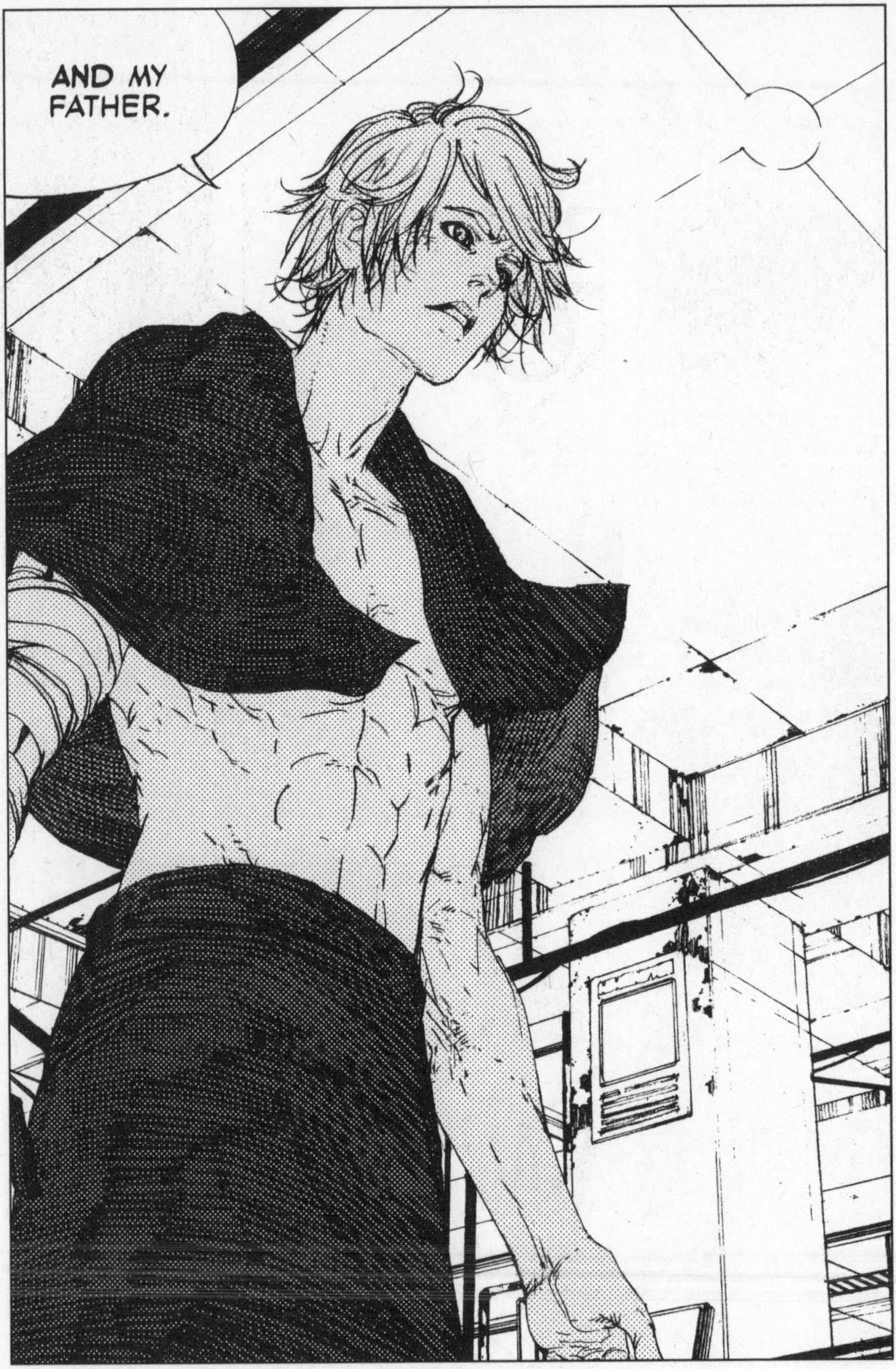
AND MY FATHER.

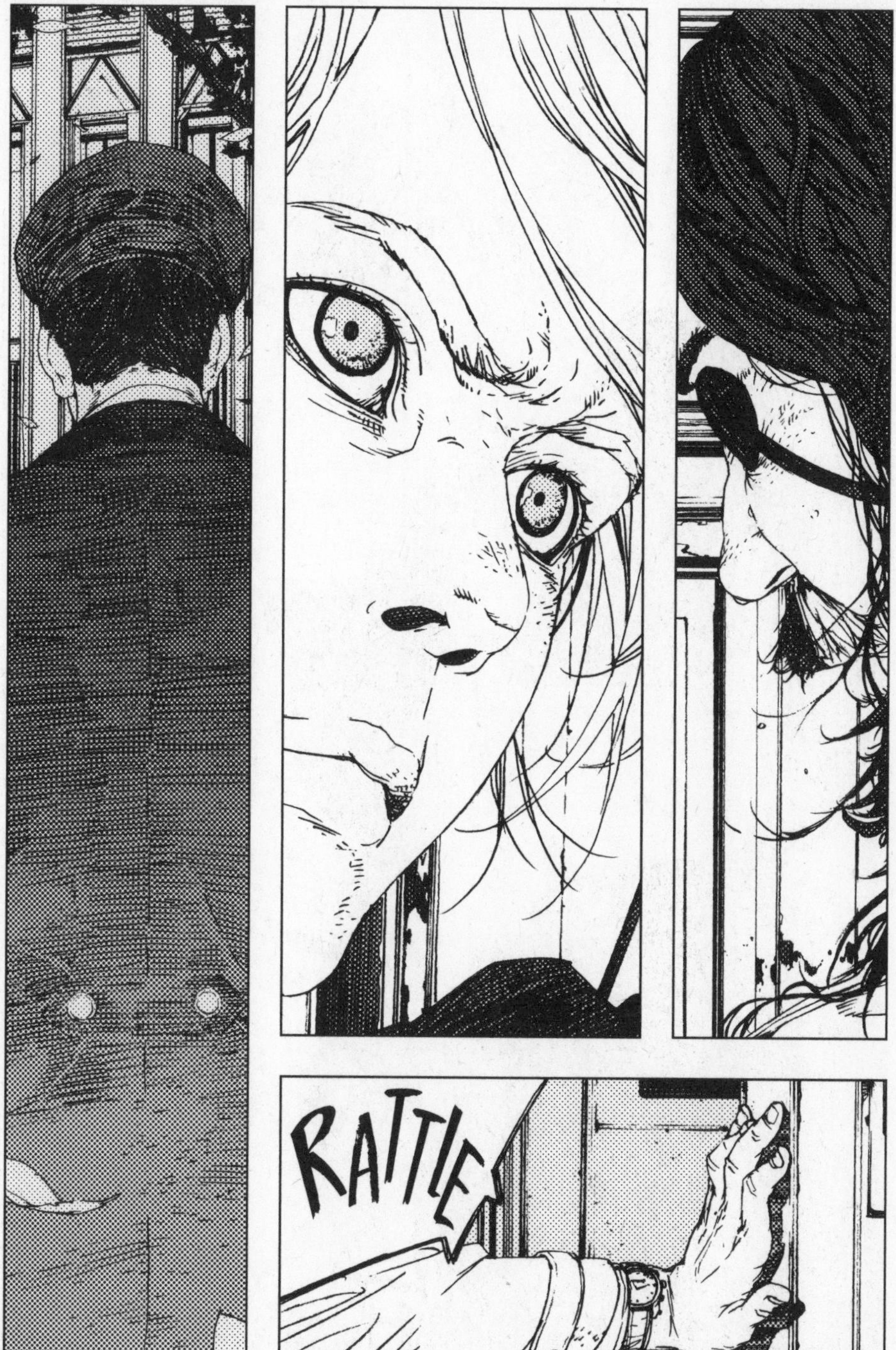
RATTLE

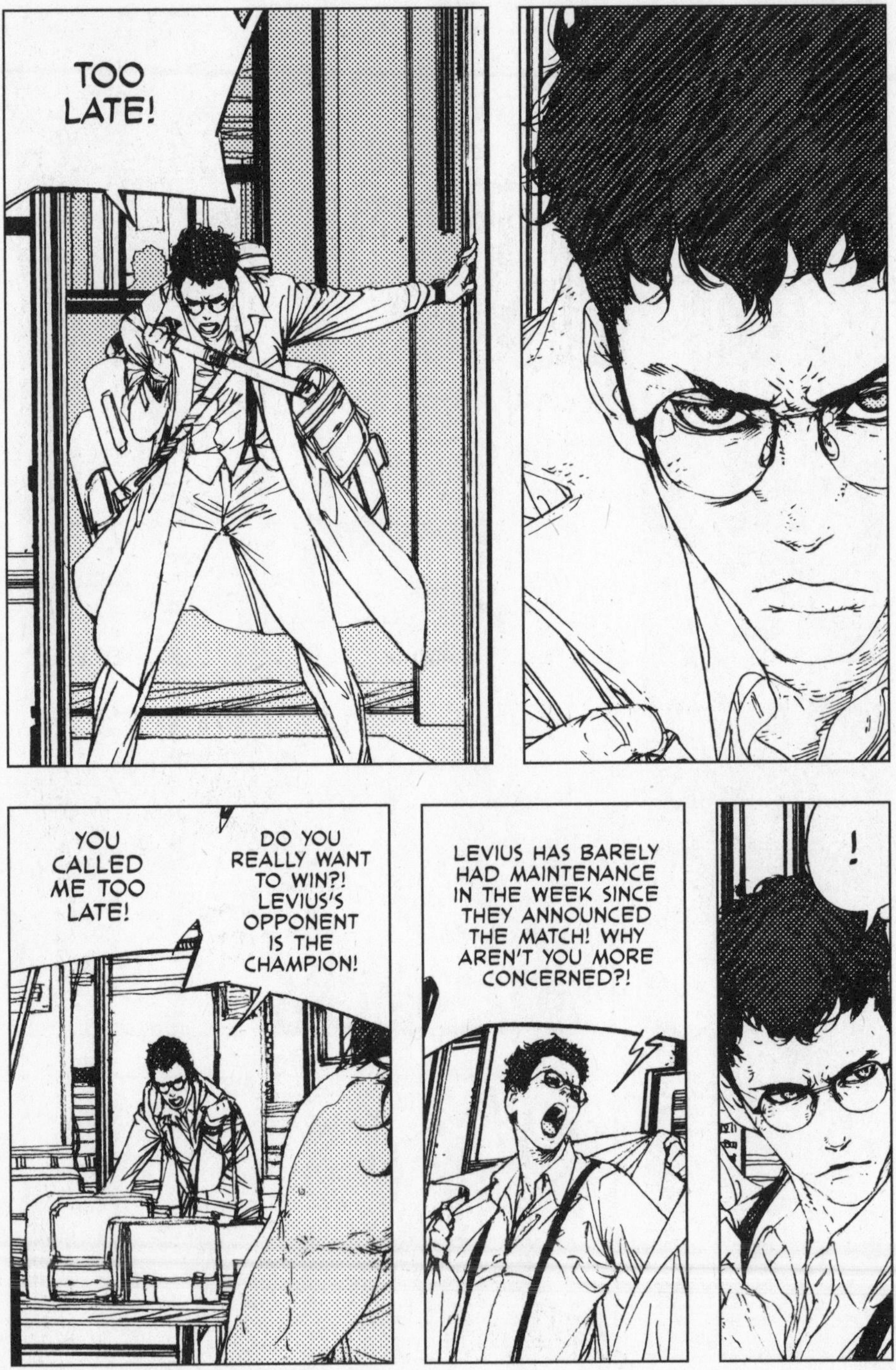
TOO LATE!
!
YOU CALLED ME TOO LATE!
DO YOU REALLY WANT TO WIN?! LEVIUS'S OPPONENT IS THE CHAMPION!
LEVIUS HAS BARELY HAD MAINTENANCE IN THE WEEK SINCE THEY ANNOUNCED THE MATCH! WHY AREN'T YOU MORE CONCERNED?!

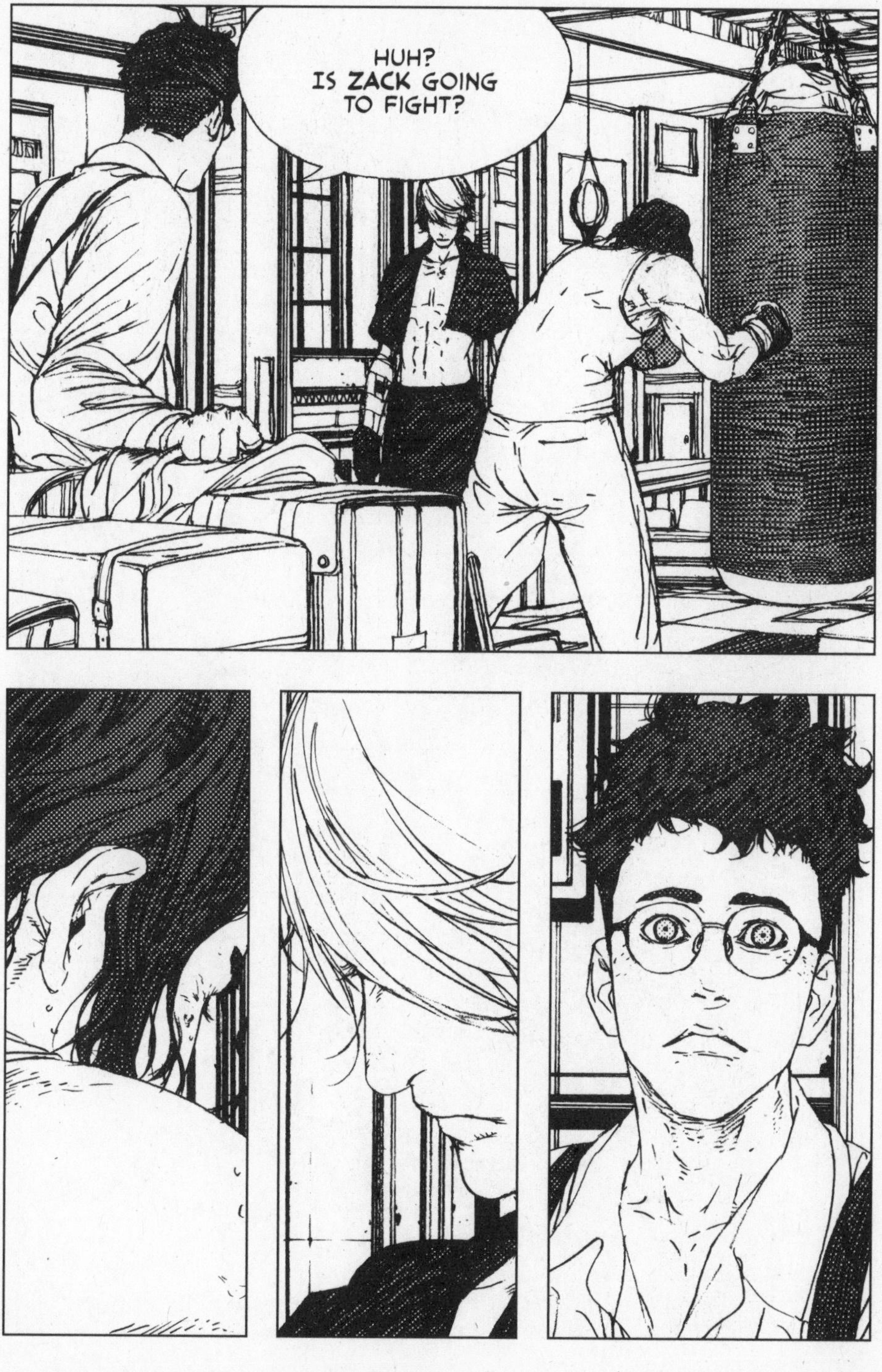
HUH?
IS ZACK GOING
TO FIGHT?

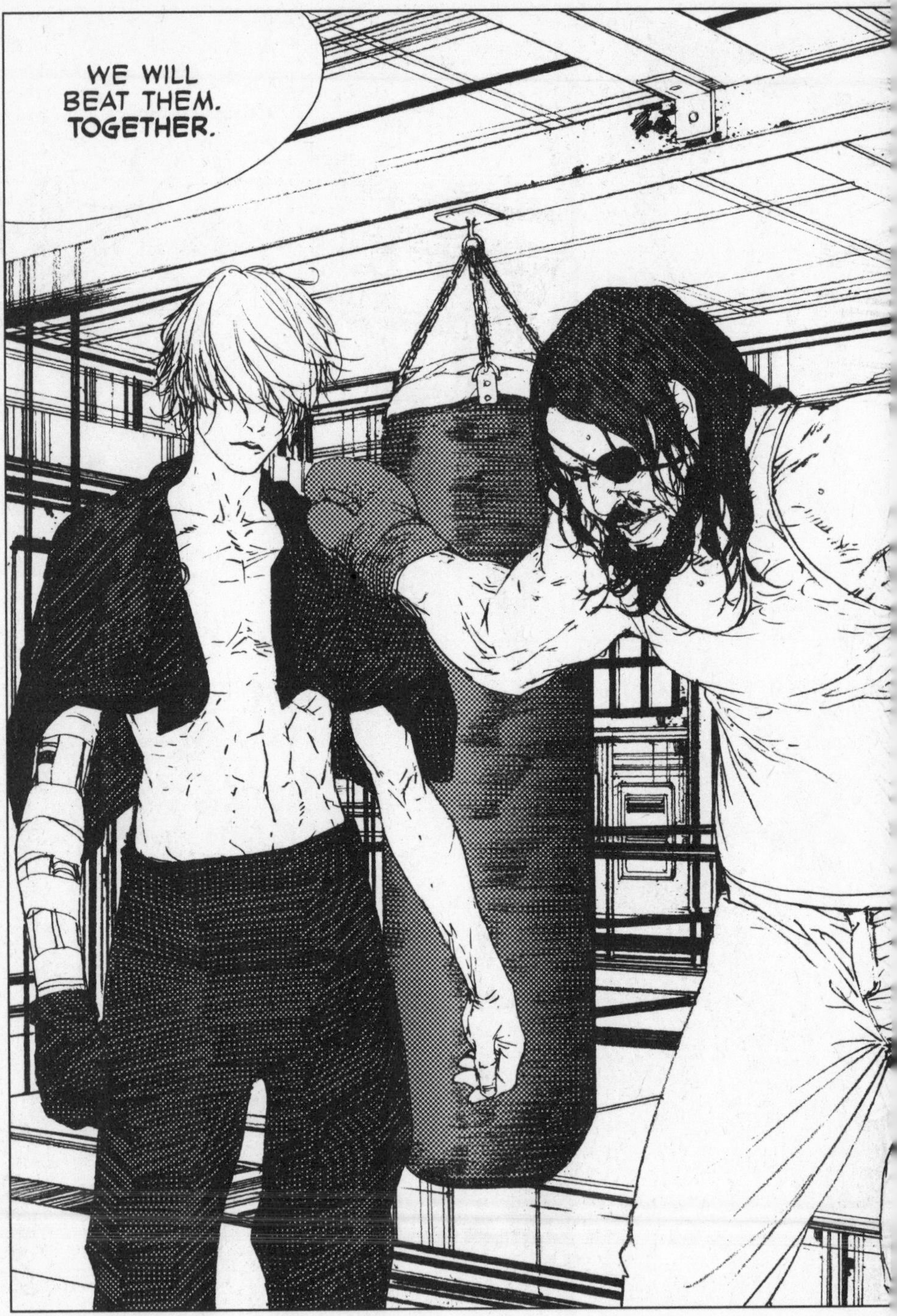
WE WILL
BEAT THEM.
TOGETHER.

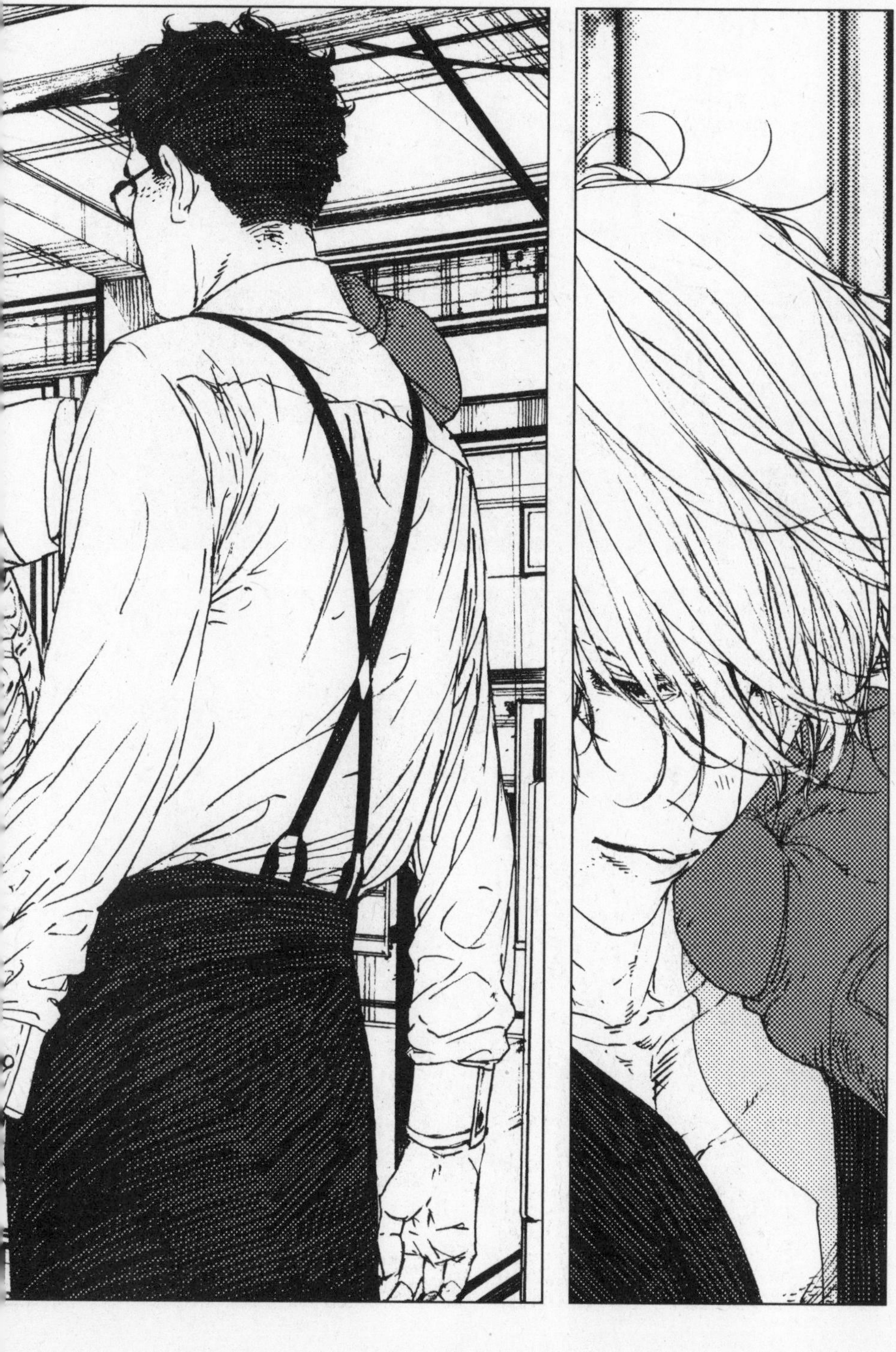

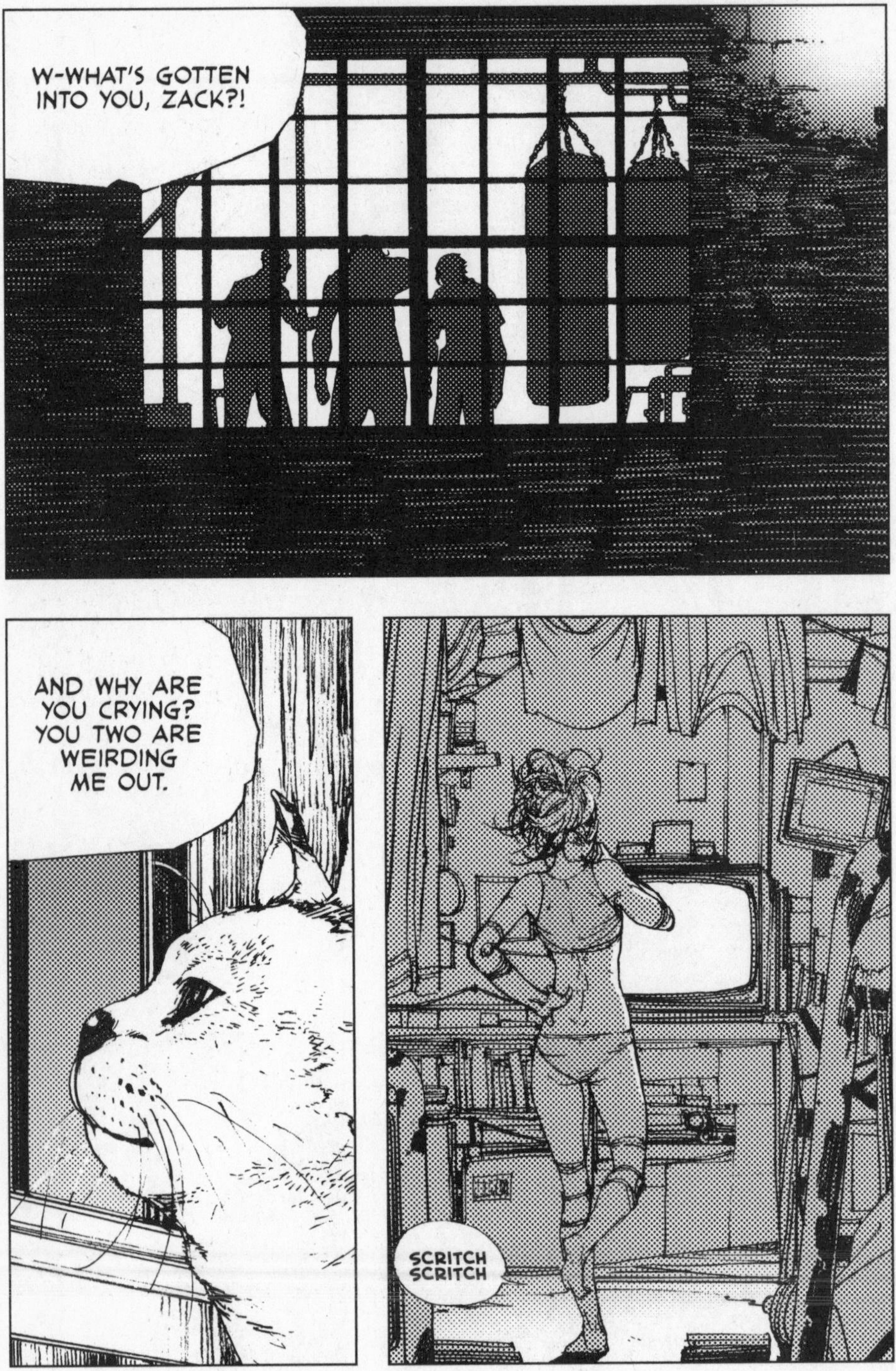
W-WHAT'S GOTTEN INTO YOU, ZACK?!
AND WHY ARE YOU CRYING? YOU TWO ARE WEIRDING ME OUT.
SCRITCH SCRITCH

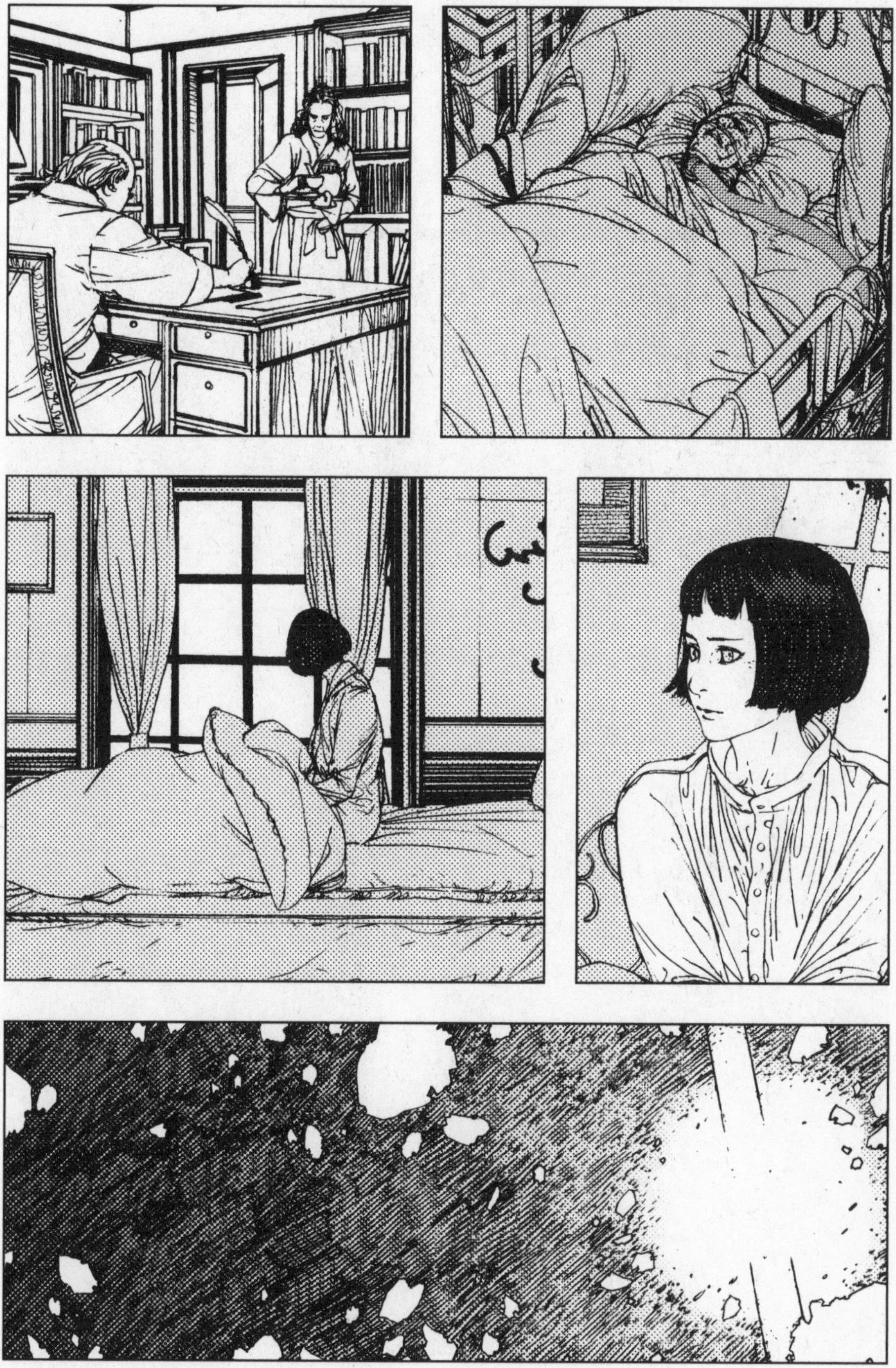

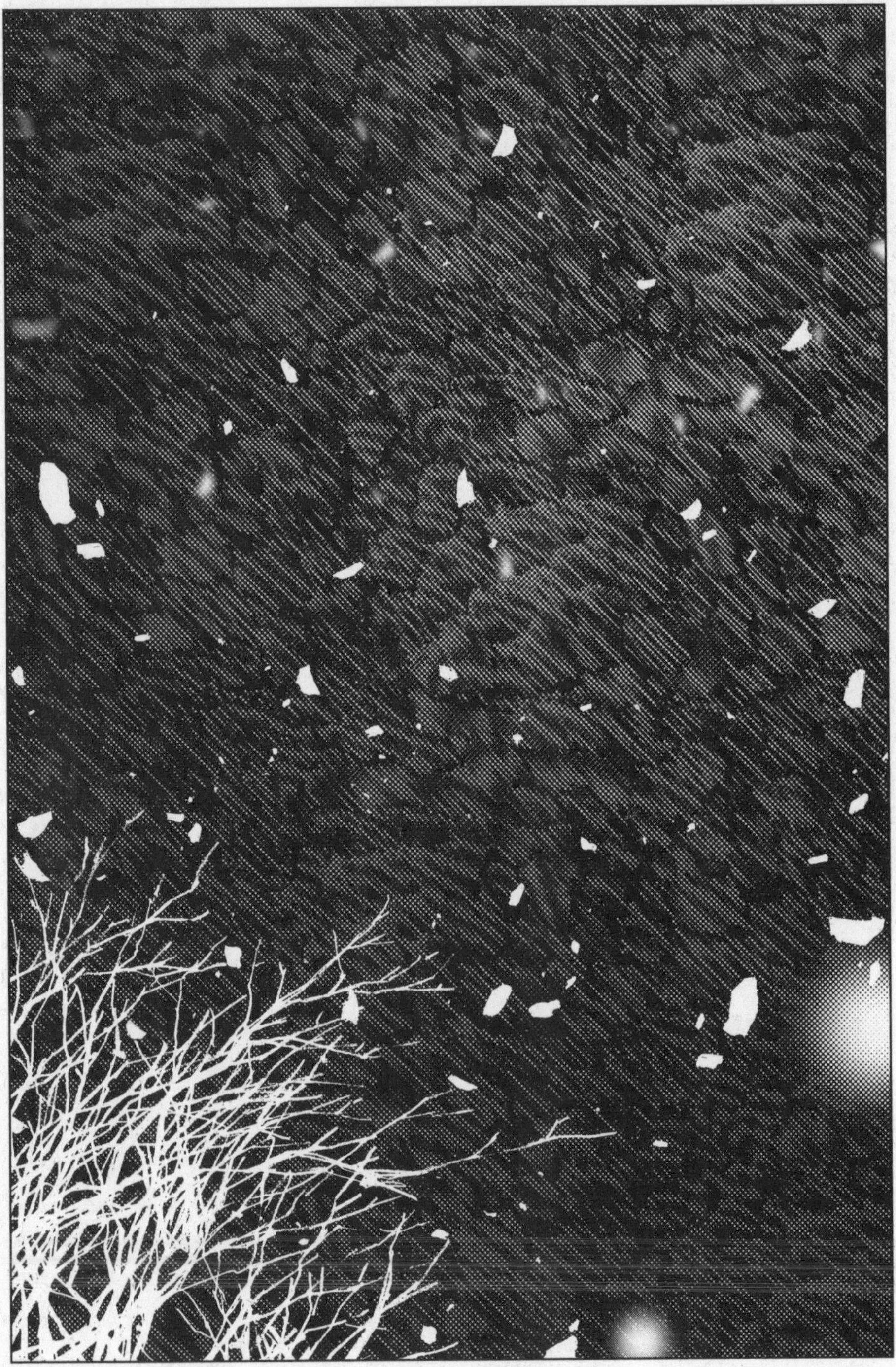

Levius/est
VOL. 3

Chapter 13

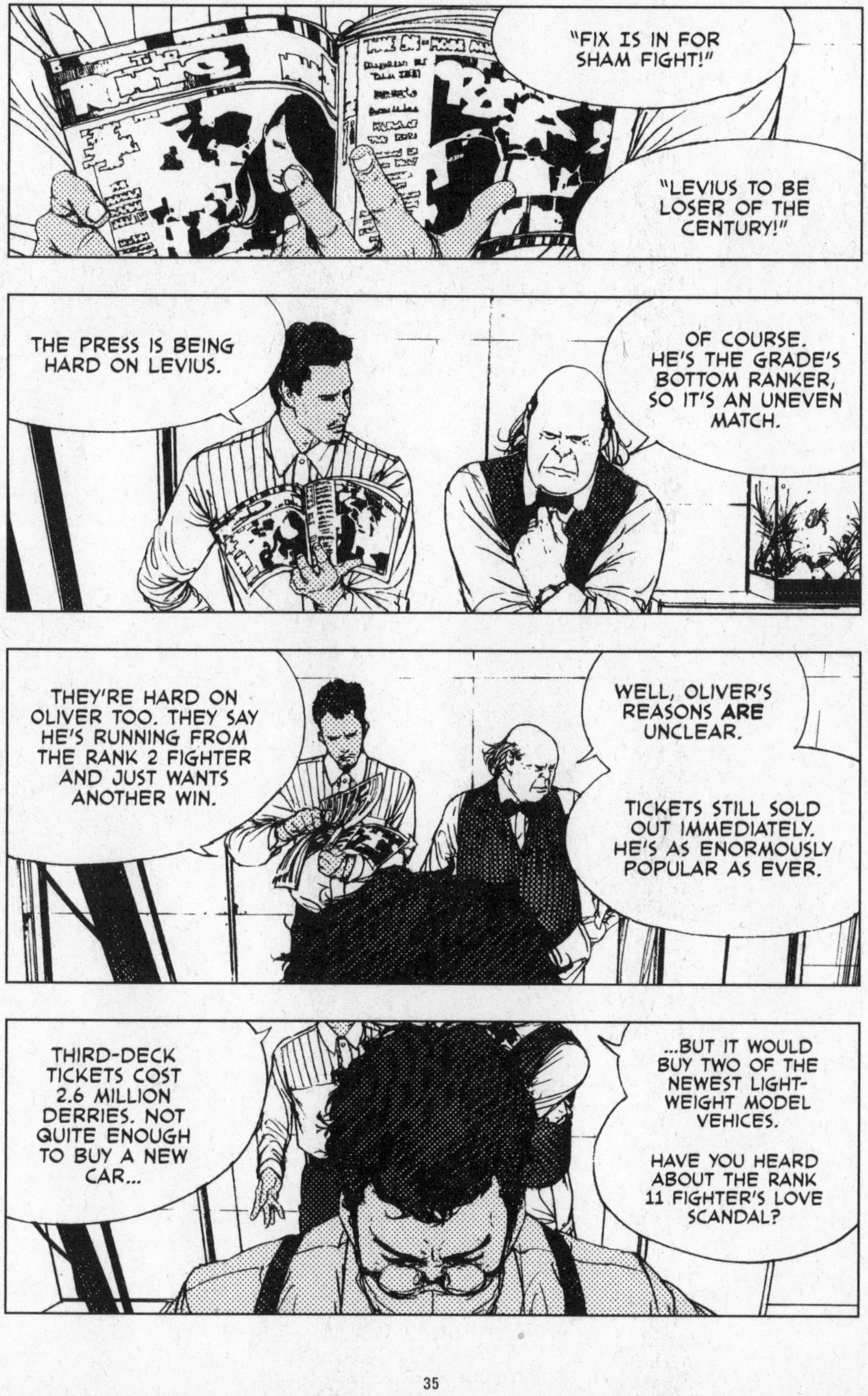
"FIX IS IN FOR SHAM FIGHT!"
"LEVIUS TO BE LOSER OF THE CENTURY!"
THE PRESS IS BEING HARD ON LEVIUS.
OF COURSE. HE'S THE GRADE'S BOTTOM RANKER, SO IT'S AN UNEVEN MATCH.
THEY'RE HARD ON OLIVER TOO. THEY SAY HE'S RUNNING FROM THE RANK 2 FIGHTER AND JUST WANTS ANOTHER WIN.
WELL, OLIVER'S REASONS **ARE** UNCLEAR.
TICKETS STILL SOLD OUT IMMEDIATELY. HE'S AS ENORMOUSLY POPULAR AS EVER.
THIRD-DECK TICKETS COST 2.6 MILLION DERRIES. NOT QUITE ENOUGH TO BUY A NEW CAR...
...BUT IT WOULD BUY TWO OF THE NEWEST LIGHT-WEIGHT MODEL VEHICES.
HAVE YOU HEARD ABOUT THE RANK 11 FIGHTER'S LOVE SCANDAL?

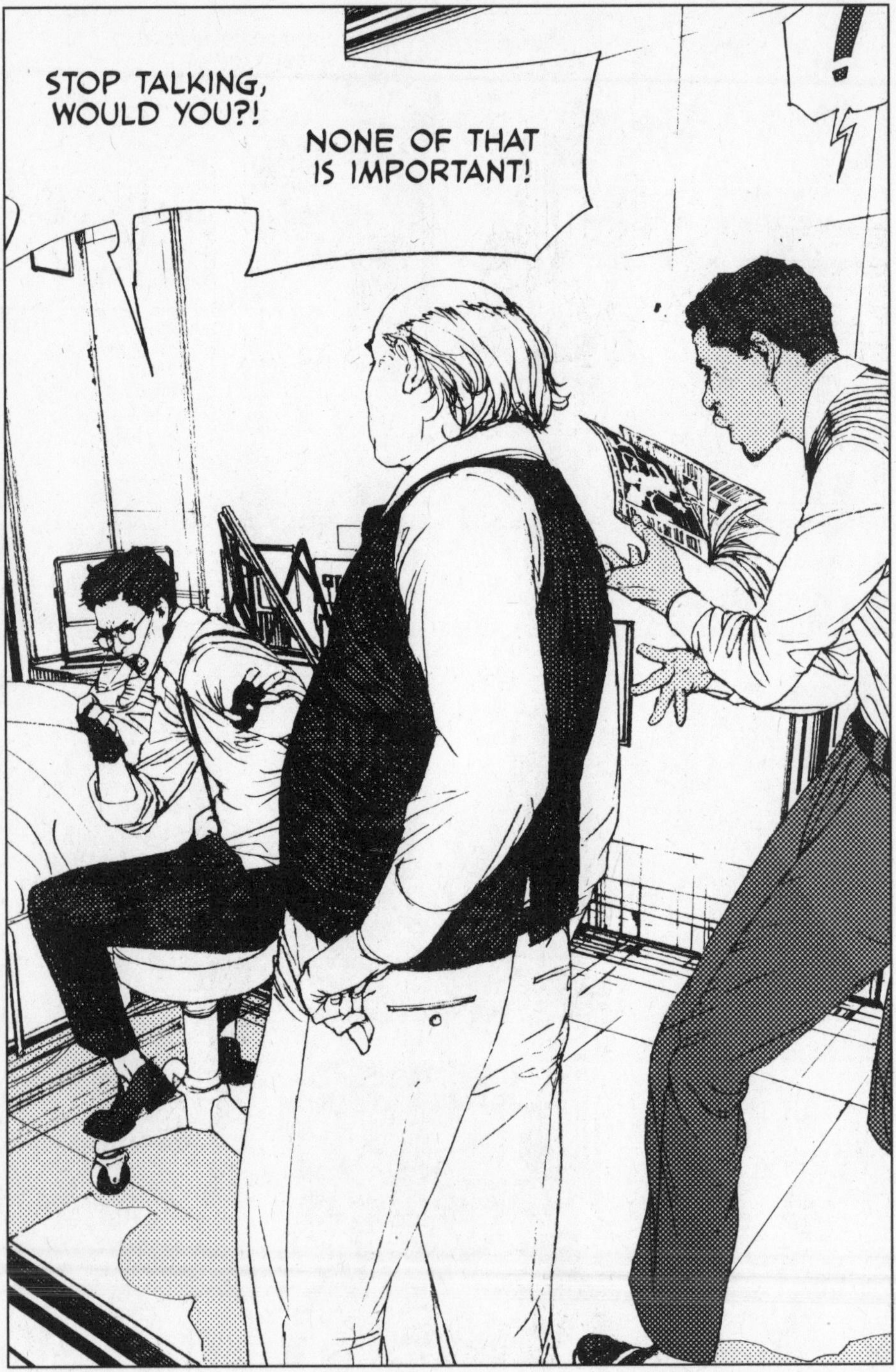
STOP TALKING, WOULD YOU?!
NONE OF THAT IS IMPORTANT!
!

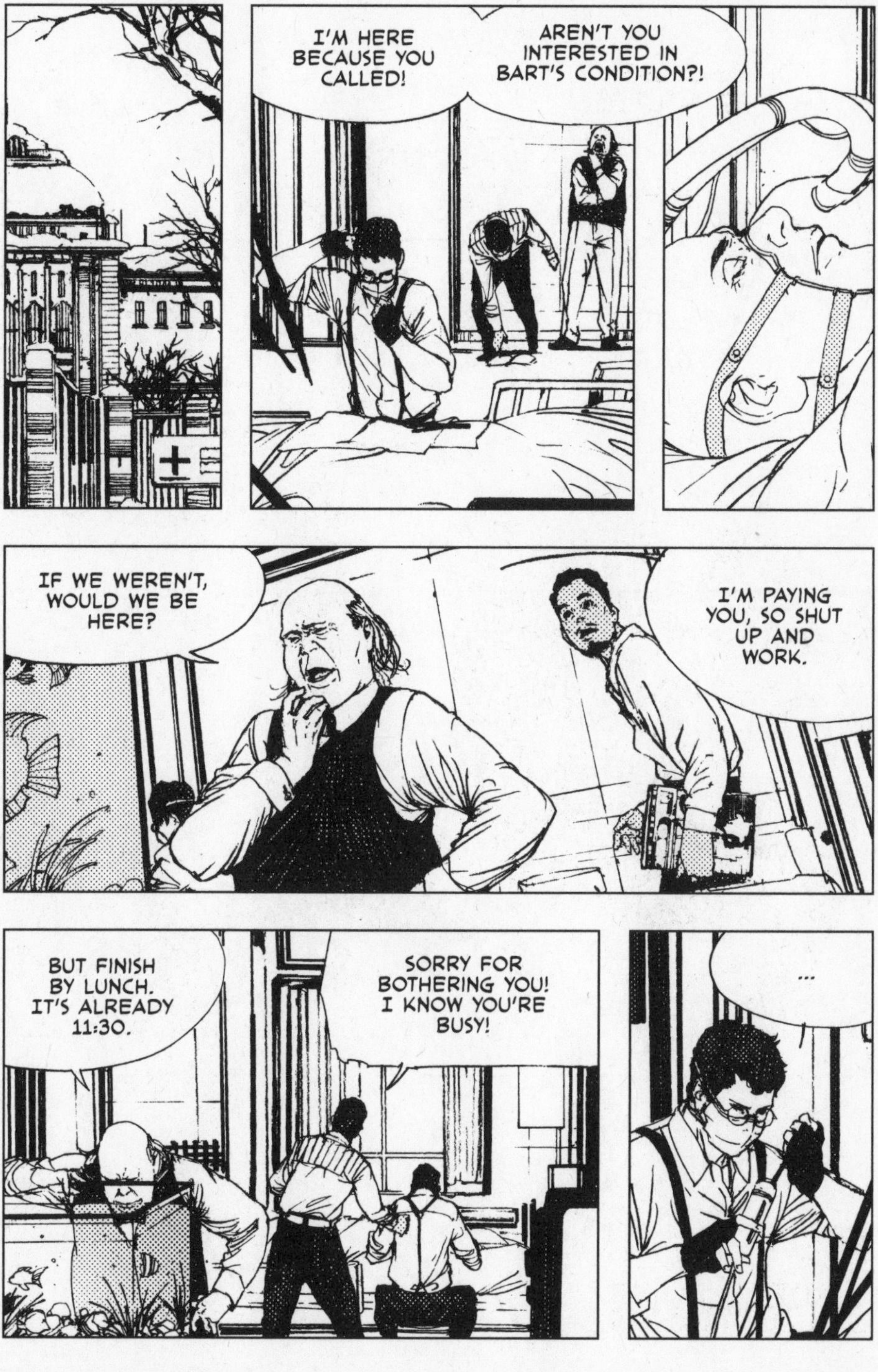
I'M HERE BECAUSE YOU CALLED!
AREN'T YOU INTERESTED IN BART'S CONDITION?!
IF WE WEREN'T, WOULD WE BE HERE?
I'M PAYING YOU, SO SHUT UP AND WORK.
BUT FINISH BY LUNCH. IT'S ALREADY 11:30.
SORRY FOR BOTHERING YOU! I KNOW YOU'RE BUSY!
...

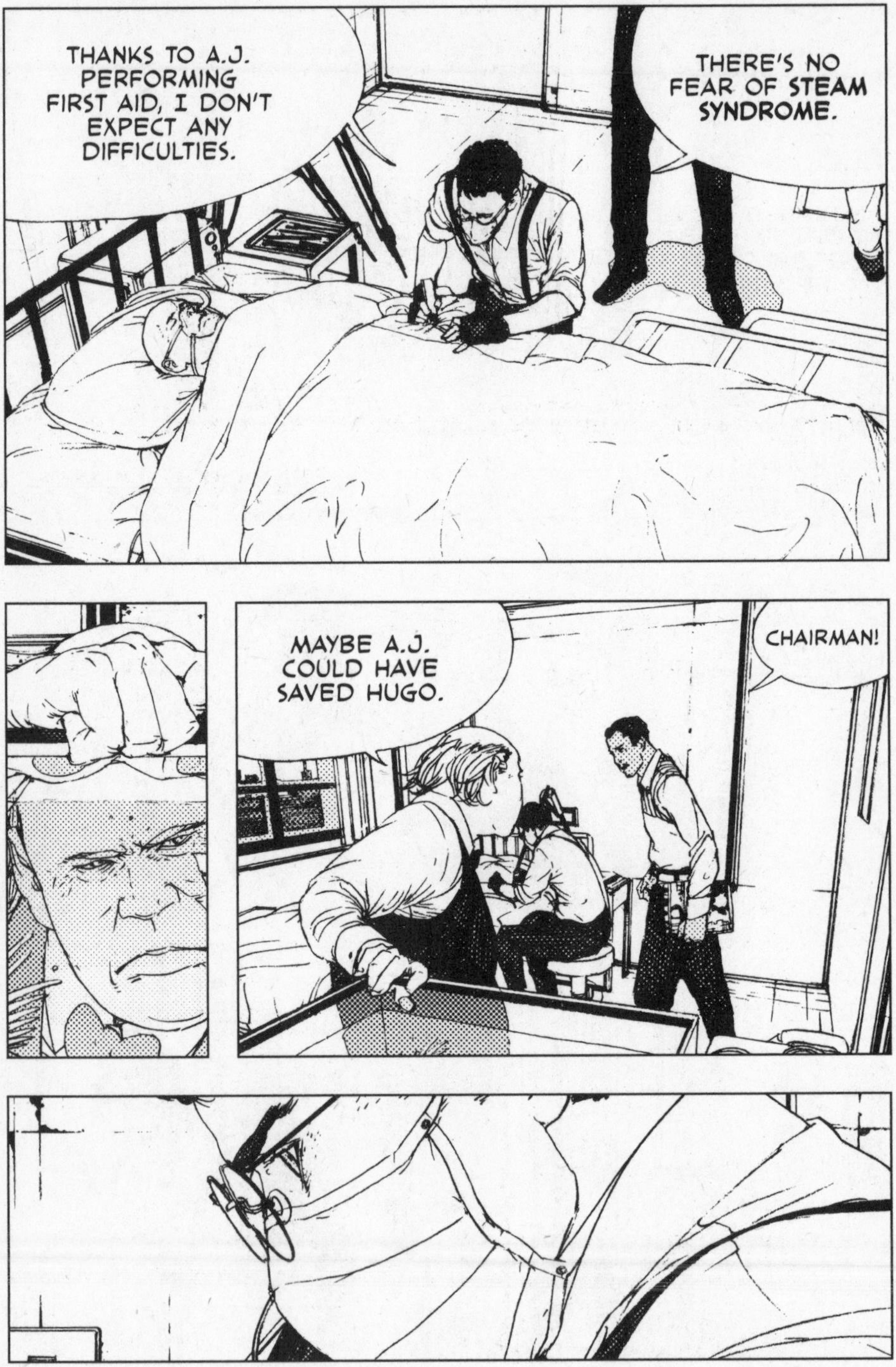
THANKS TO A.J. PERFORMING FIRST AID, I DON'T EXPECT ANY DIFFICULTIES.
THERE'S NO FEAR OF STEAM SYNDROME.
MAYBE A.J. COULD HAVE SAVED HUGO.
CHAIRMAN!

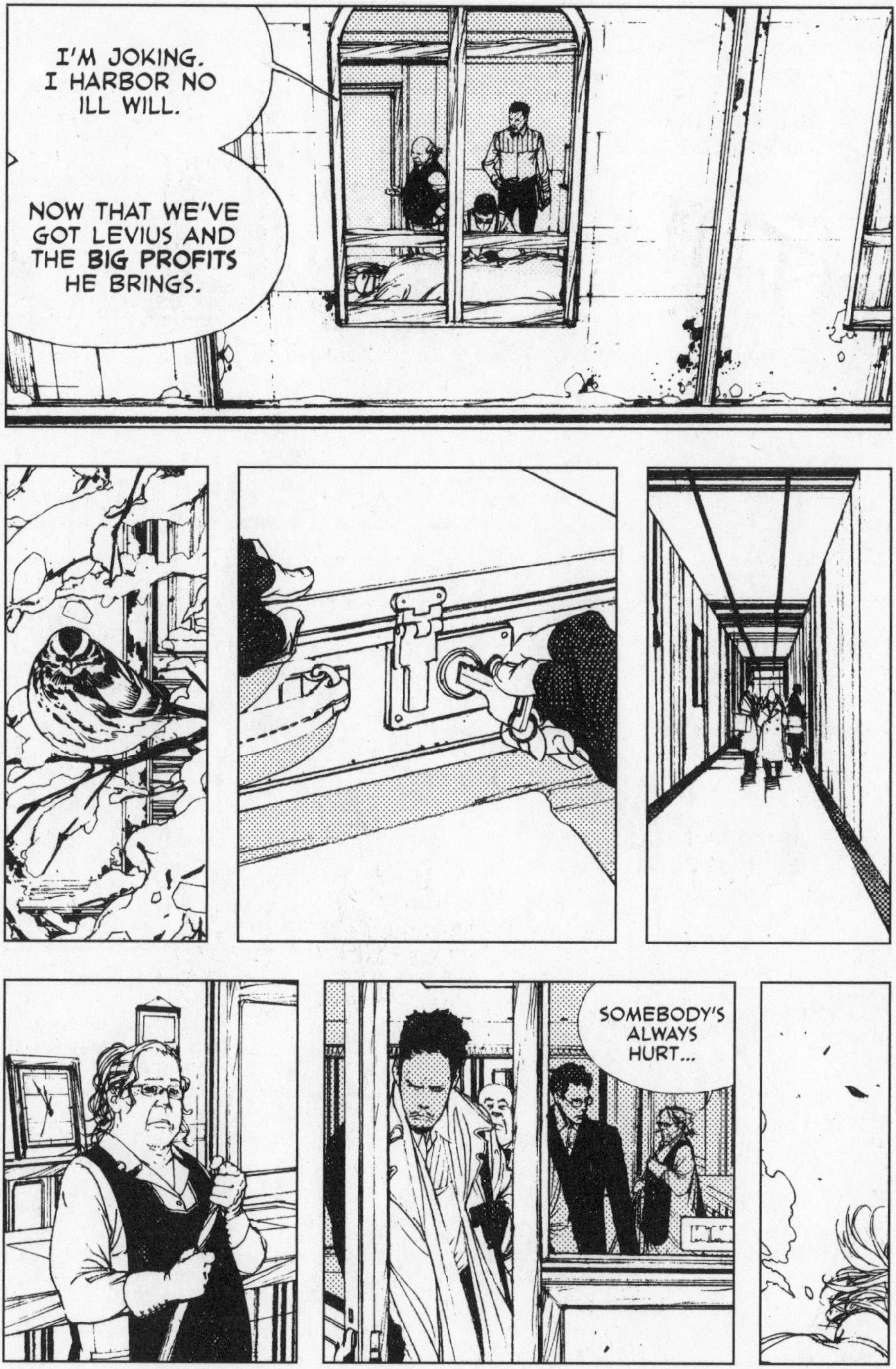
I'M JOKING. I HARBOR NO ILL WILL.
NOW THAT WE'VE GOT LEVIUS AND THE BIG PROFITS HE BRINGS.
SOMEBODY'S ALWAYS HURT...

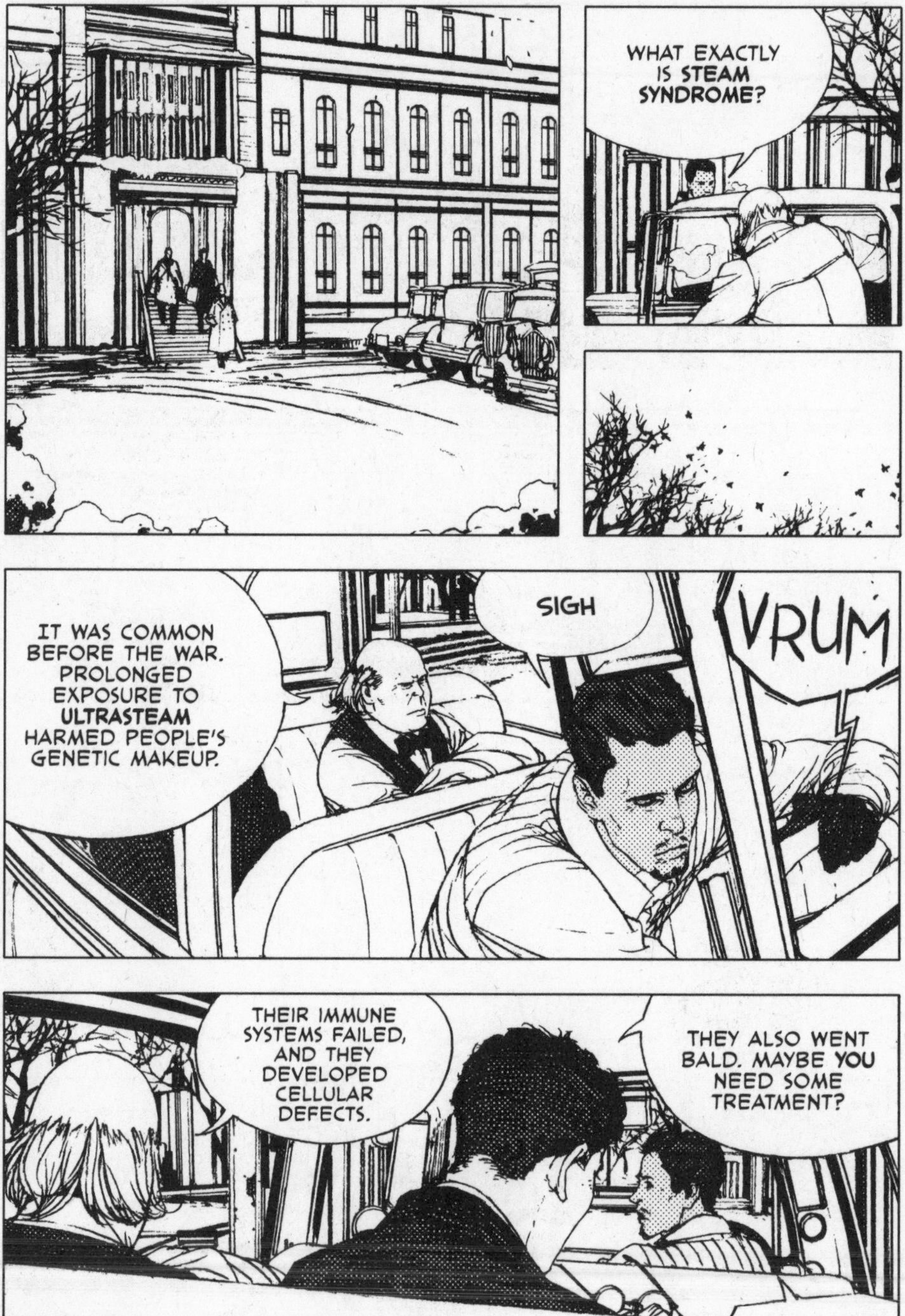
WHAT EXACTLY IS STEAM SYNDROME?
IT WAS COMMON BEFORE THE WAR. PROLONGED EXPOSURE TO ULTRASTEAM HARMED PEOPLE'S GENETIC MAKEUP.
SIGH
VRUM
THEIR IMMUNE SYSTEMS FAILED, AND THEY DEVELOPED CELLULAR DEFECTS.
THEY ALSO WENT BALD. MAYBE YOU NEED SOME TREATMENT?
BILL...

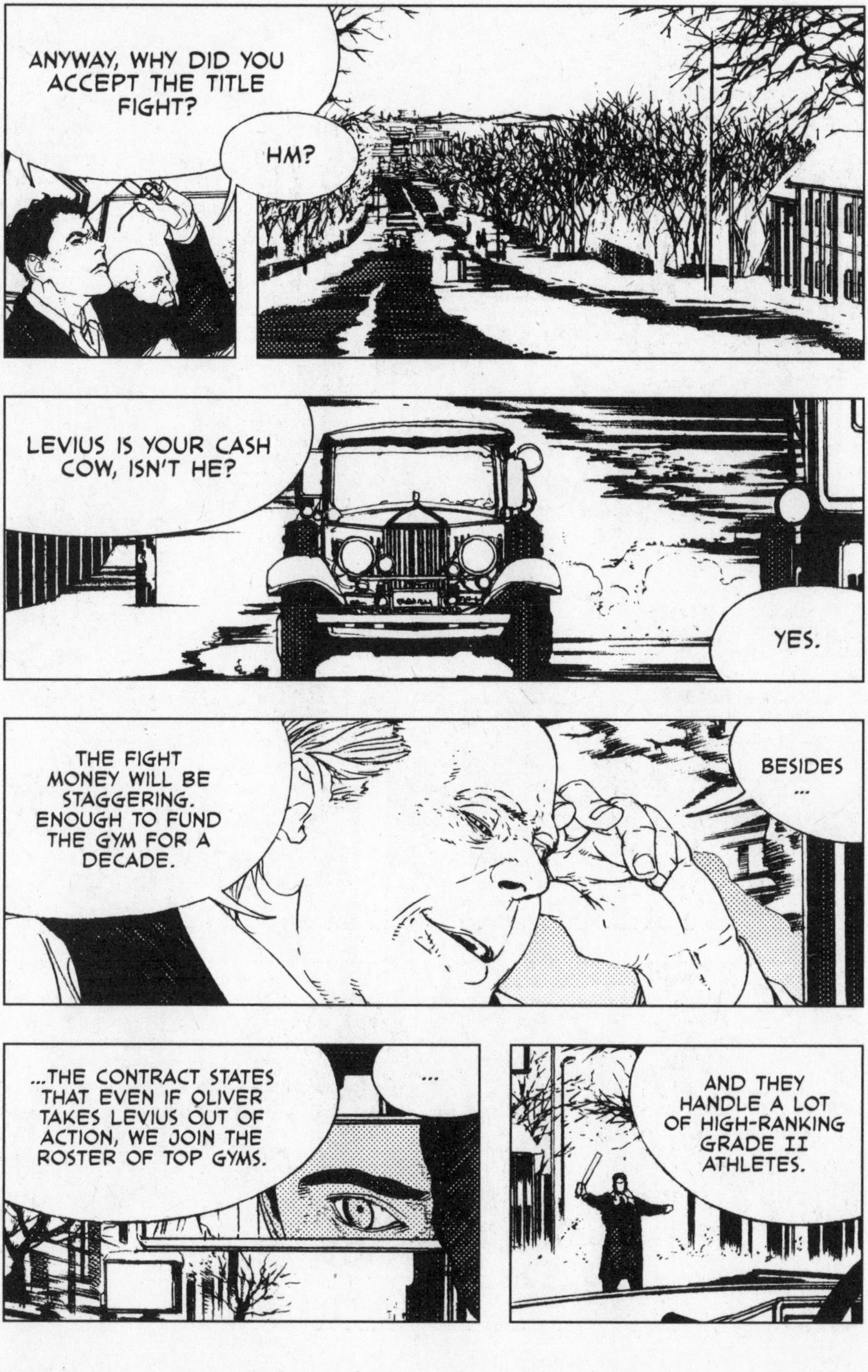
ANYWAY, WHY DID YOU ACCEPT THE TITLE FIGHT?
HM?
LEVIUS IS YOUR CASH COW, ISN'T HE?
YES.
THE FIGHT MONEY WILL BE STAGGERING. ENOUGH TO FUND THE GYM FOR A DECADE.
BESIDES ...
...THE CONTRACT STATES THAT EVEN IF OLIVER TAKES LEVIUS OUT OF ACTION, WE JOIN THE ROSTER OF TOP GYMS.
...
AND THEY HANDLE A LOT OF HIGH-RANKING GRADE II ATHLETES.

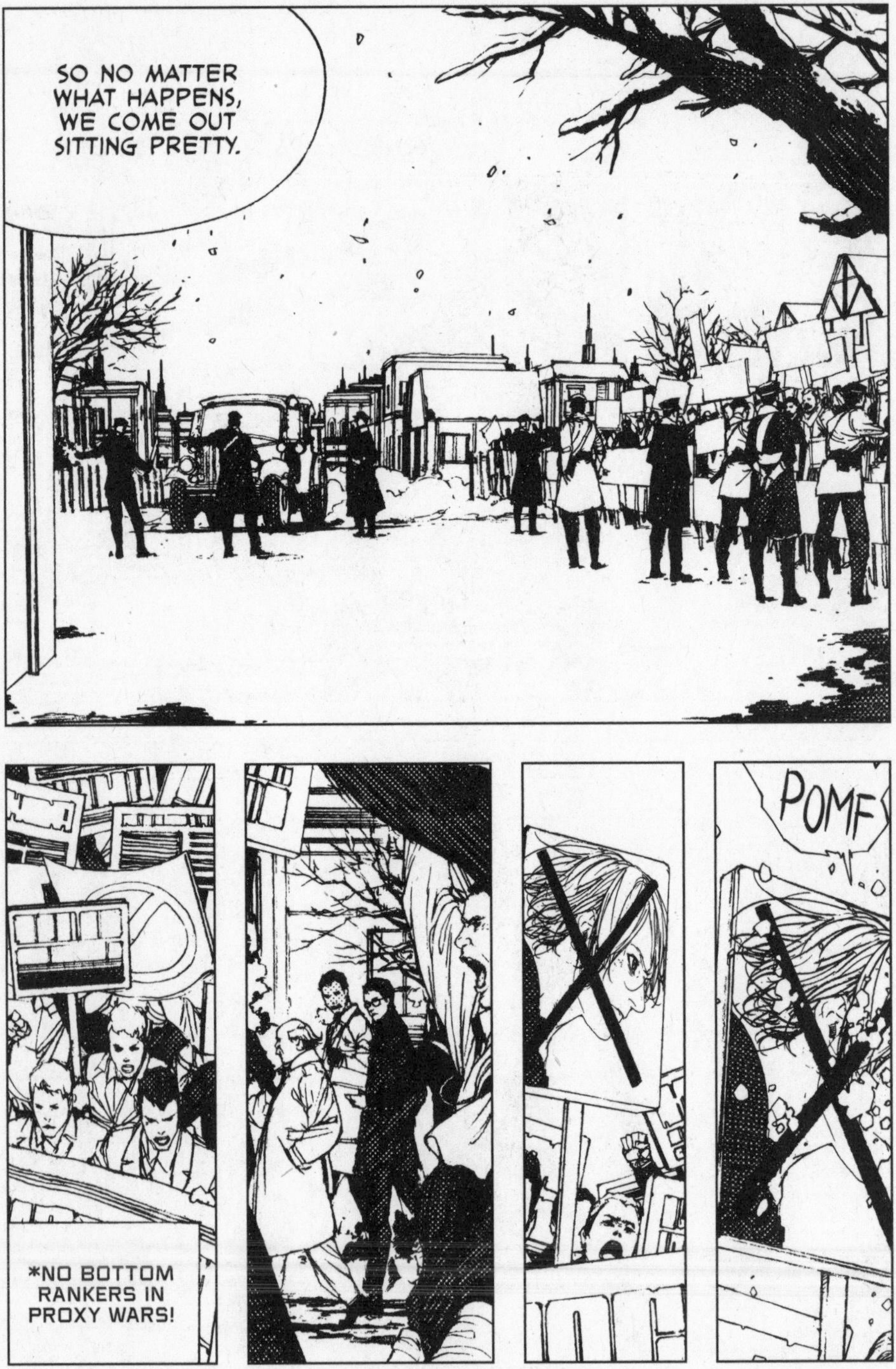
SO NO MATTER WHAT HAPPENS, WE COME OUT SITTING PRETTY.
*NO BOTTOM RANKERS IN PROXY WARS!
POMF

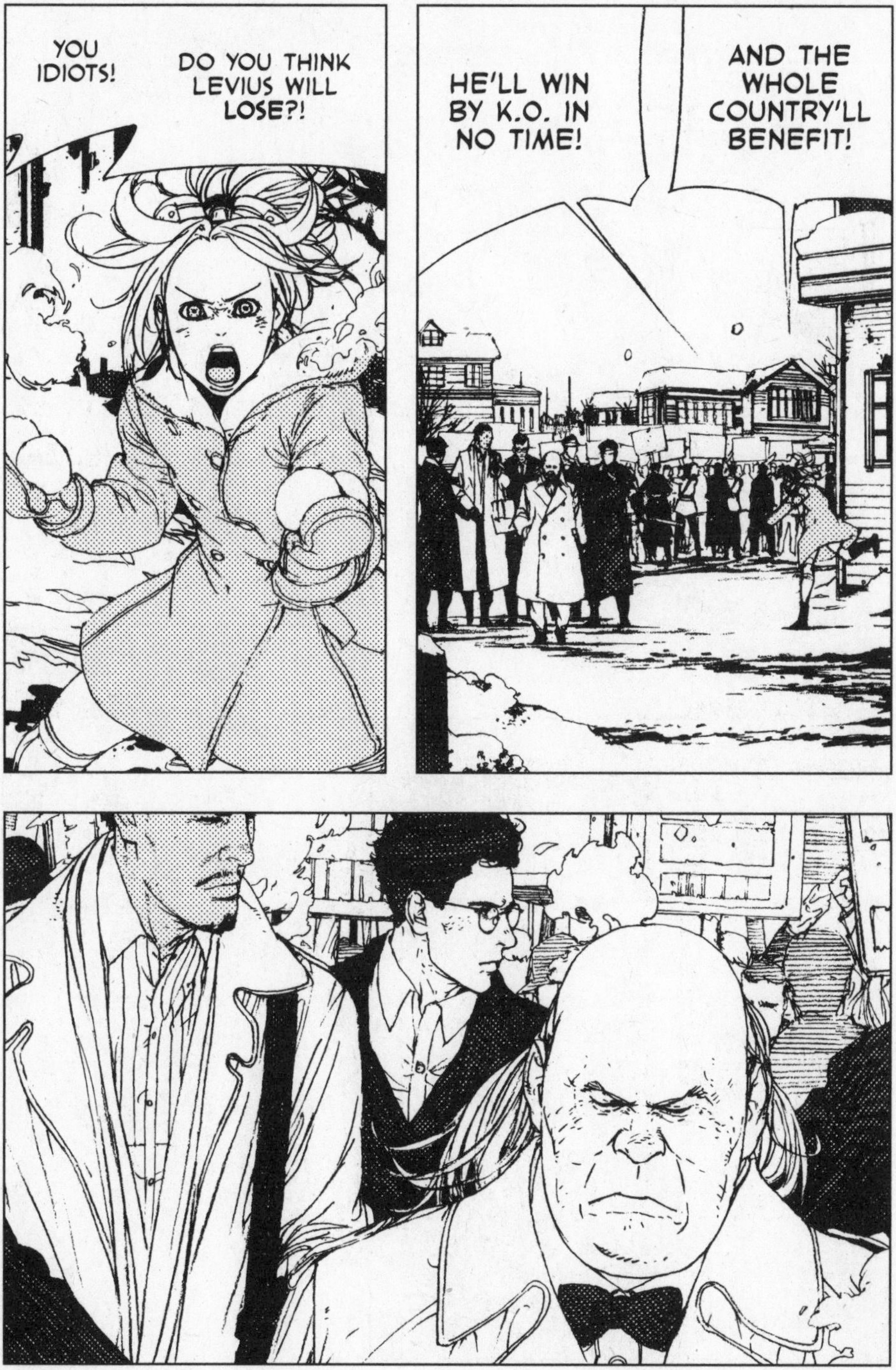
YOU IDIOTS!
DO YOU THINK LEVIUS WILL LOSE?!
HE'LL WIN BY K.O. IN NO TIME!
AND THE WHOLE COUNTRY'LL BENEFIT!

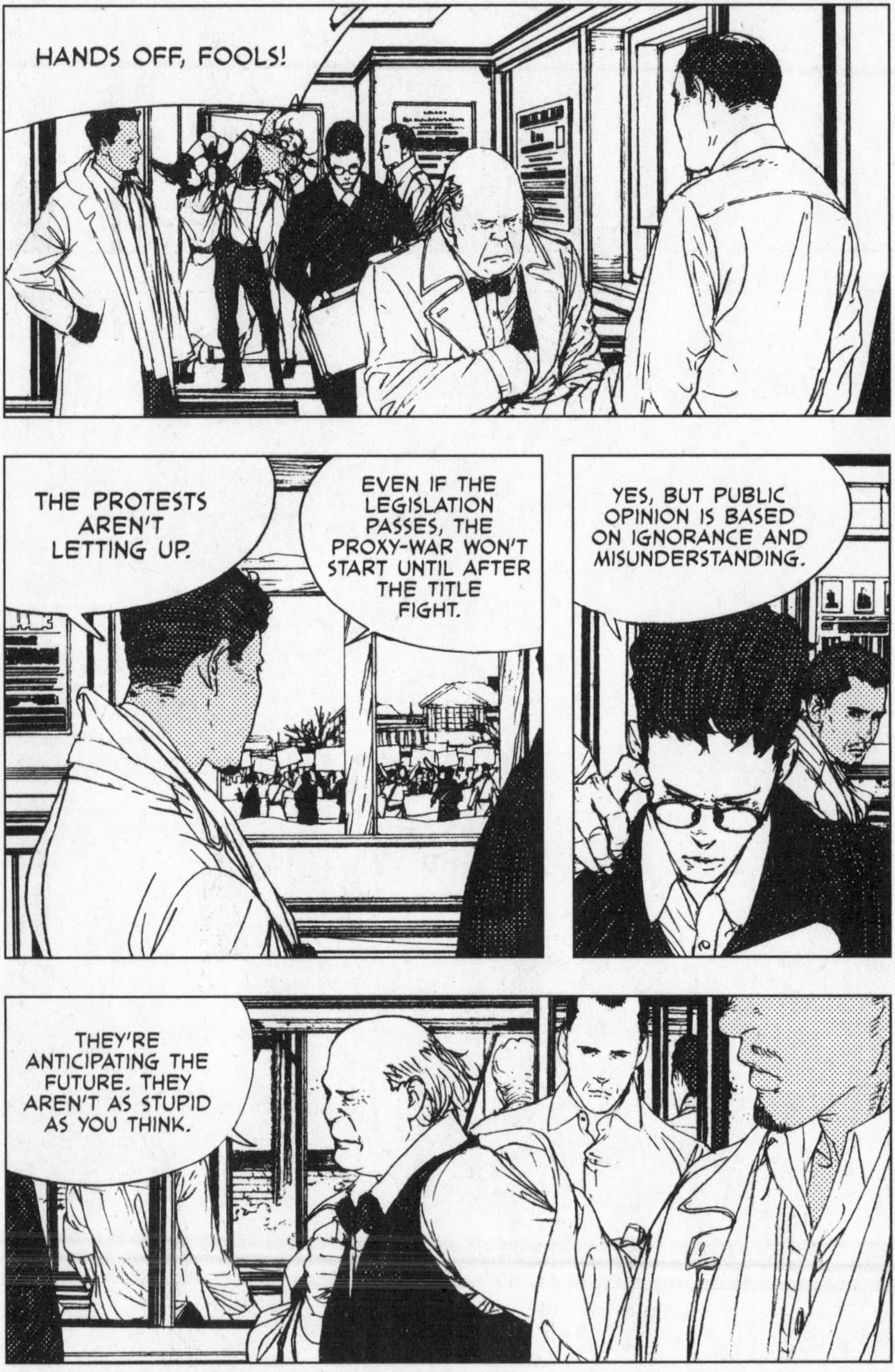
HANDS OFF, FOOLS!
THE PROTESTS AREN'T LETTING UP.
EVEN IF THE LEGISLATION PASSES, THE PROXY-WAR WON'T START UNTIL AFTER THE TITLE FIGHT.
YES, BUT PUBLIC OPINION IS BASED ON IGNORANCE AND MISUNDERSTANDING.
THEY'RE ANTICIPATING THE FUTURE. THEY AREN'T AS STUPID AS YOU THINK.

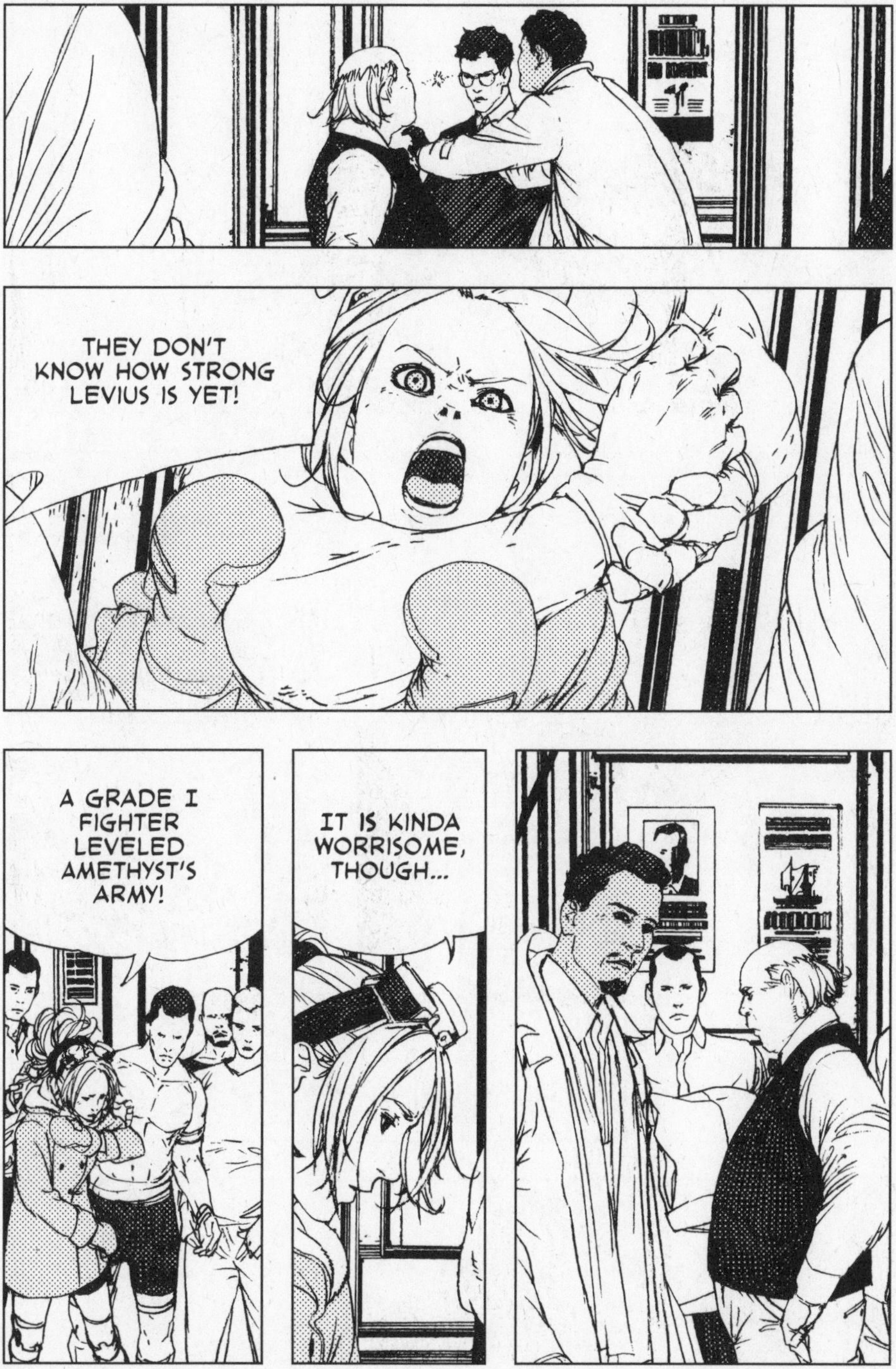
THEY DON'T KNOW HOW STRONG LEVIUS IS YET!
A GRADE I FIGHTER LEVELED AMETHYST'S ARMY!
IT IS KINDA WORRISOME, THOUGH...

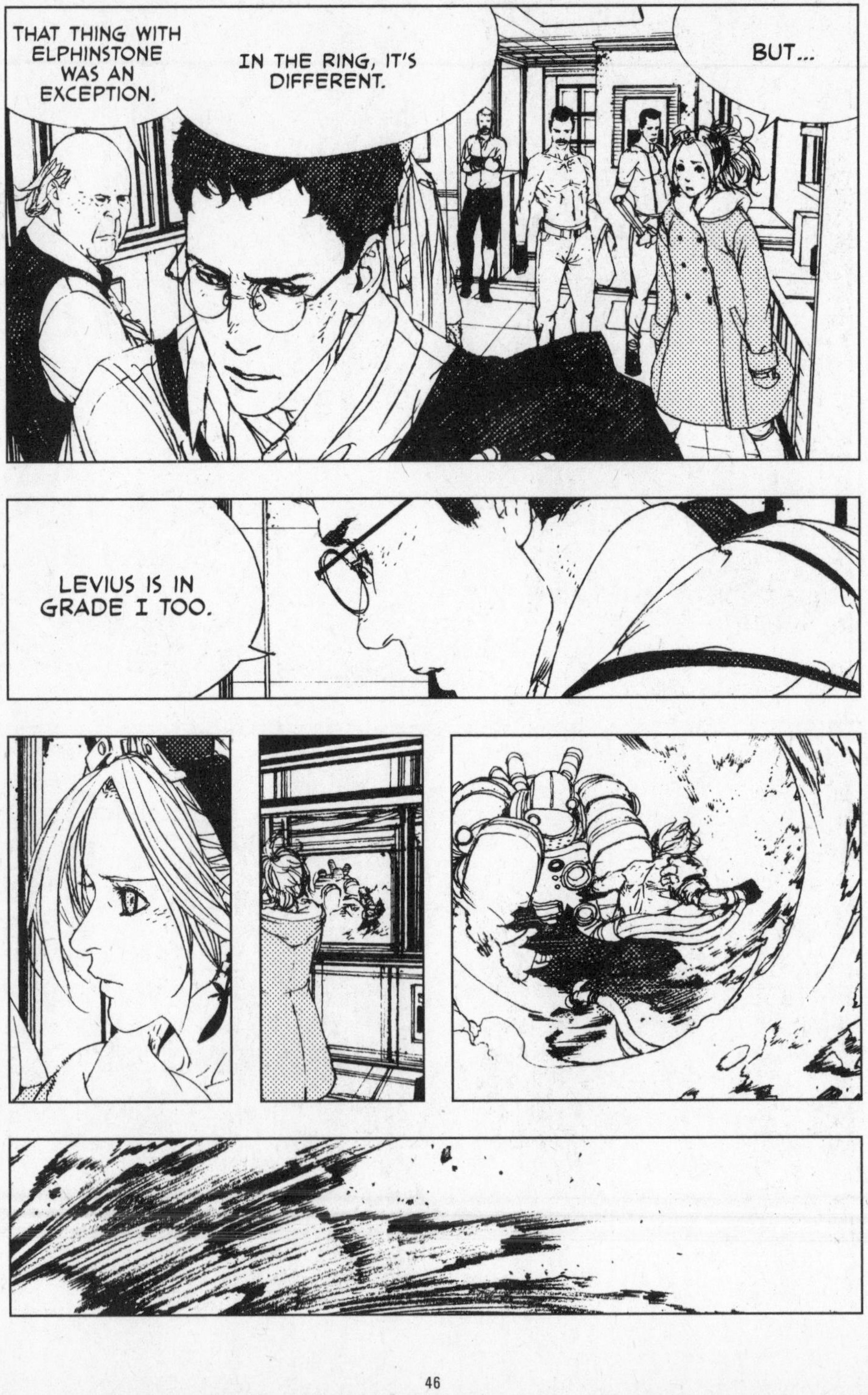
THAT THING WITH ELPHINSTONE WAS AN EXCEPTION.
IN THE RING, IT'S DIFFERENT.
BUT...
LEVIUS IS IN GRADE I TOO.

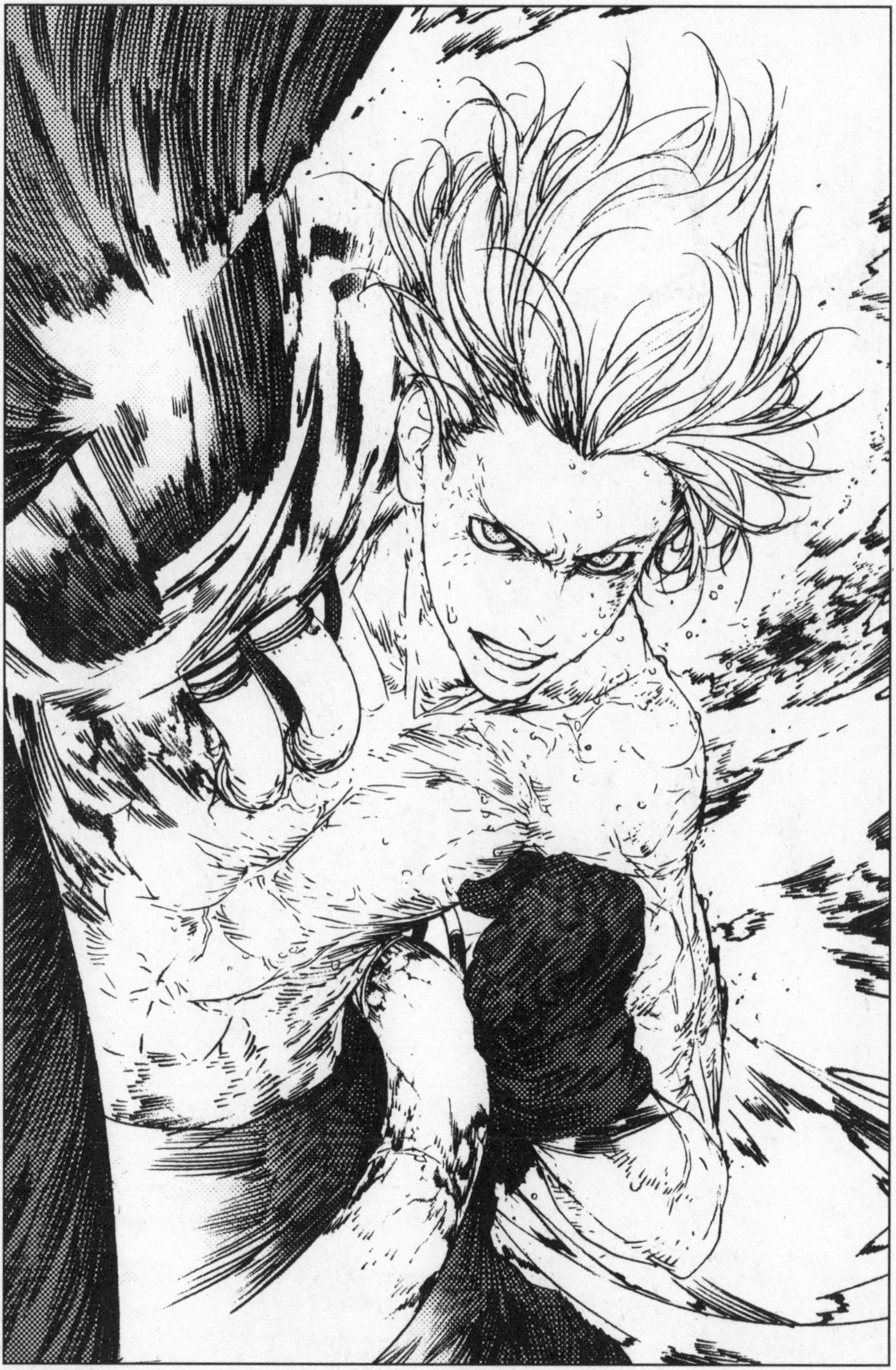

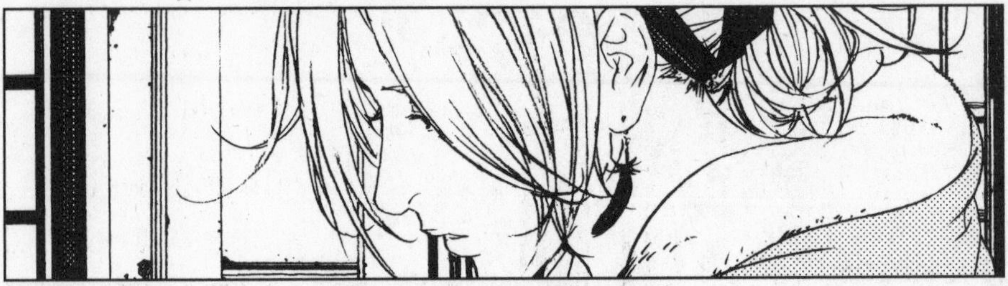

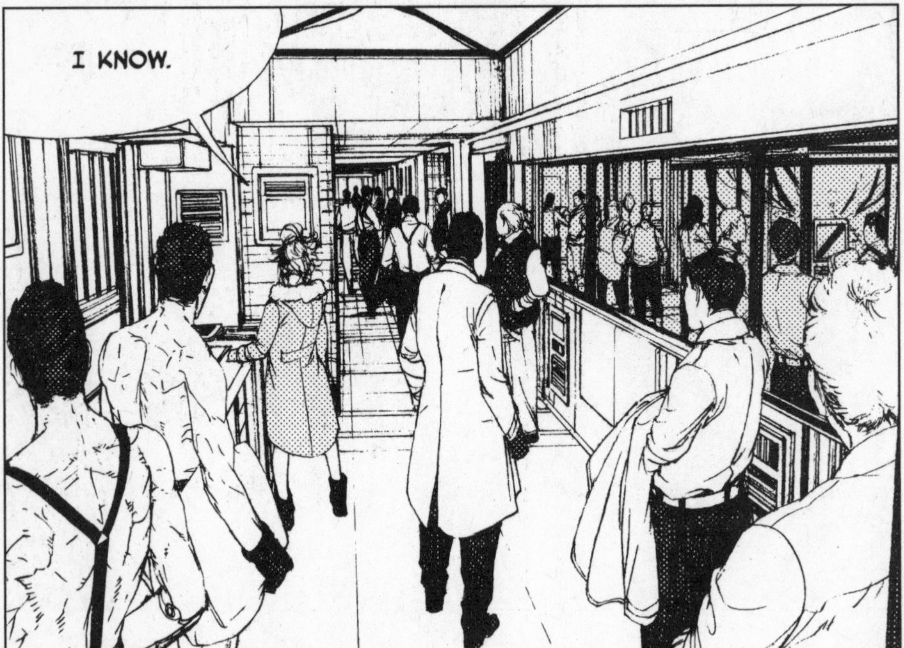
I KNOW.

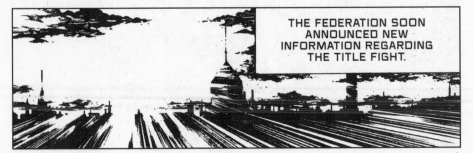

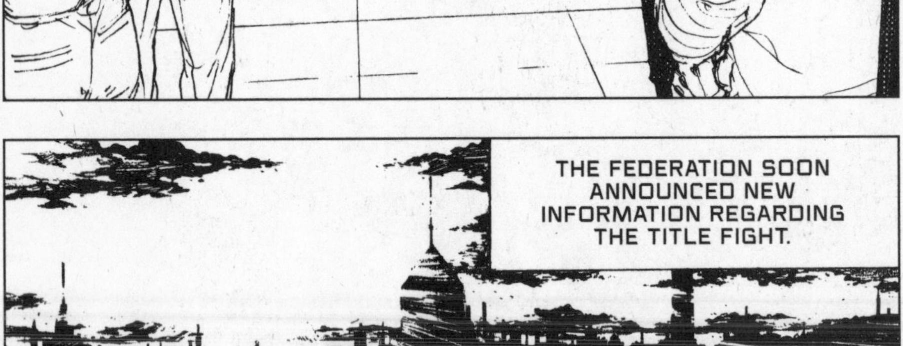
THE FEDERATION SOON ANNOUNCED NEW INFORMATION REGARDING THE TITLE FIGHT.

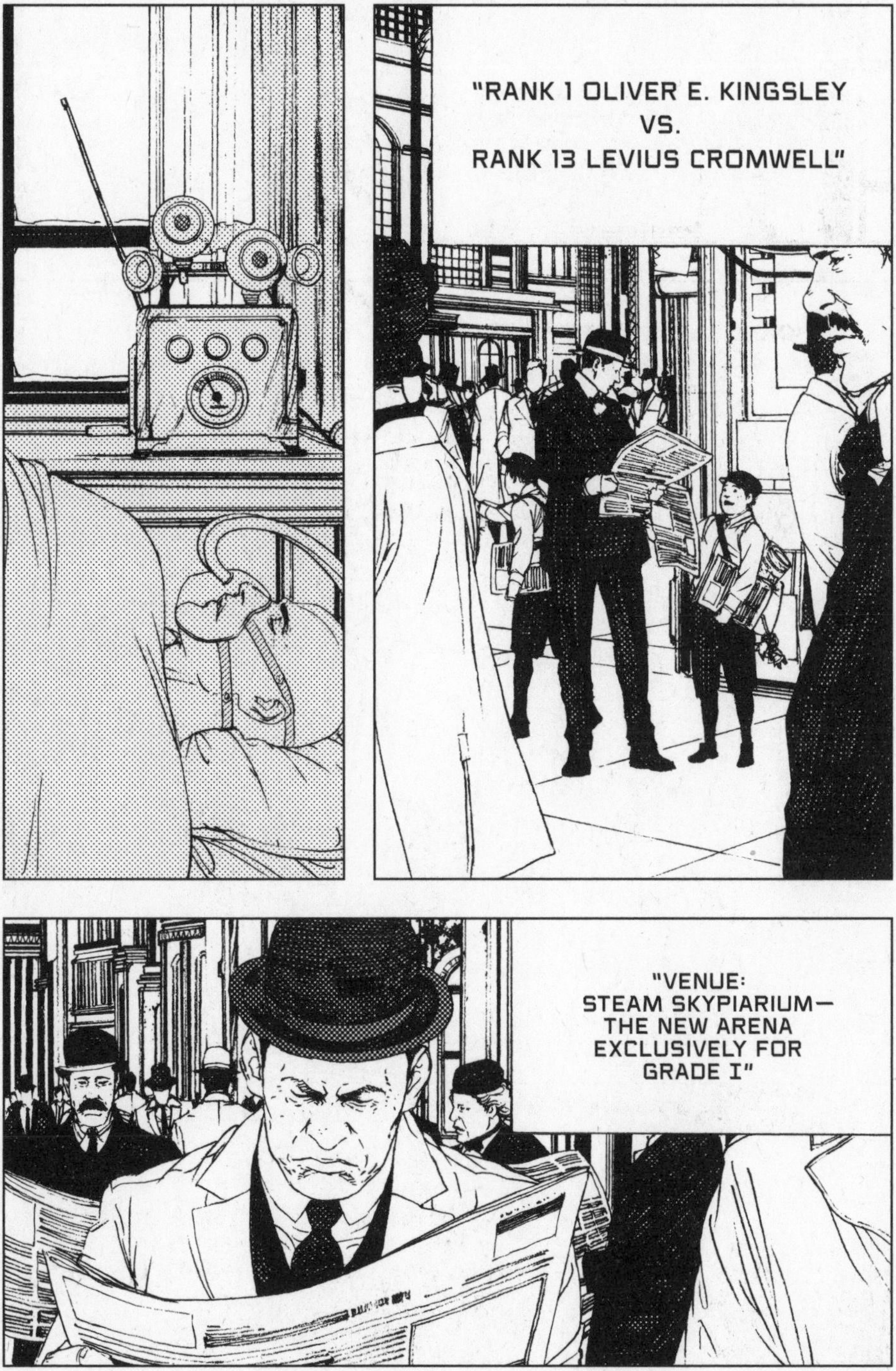
"RANK 1 OLIVER E. KINGSLEY
VS.
RANK 13 LEVIUS CROMWELL"
"VENUE:
STEAM SKYPIARIUM—
THE NEW ARENA
EXCLUSIVELY FOR
GRADE I"

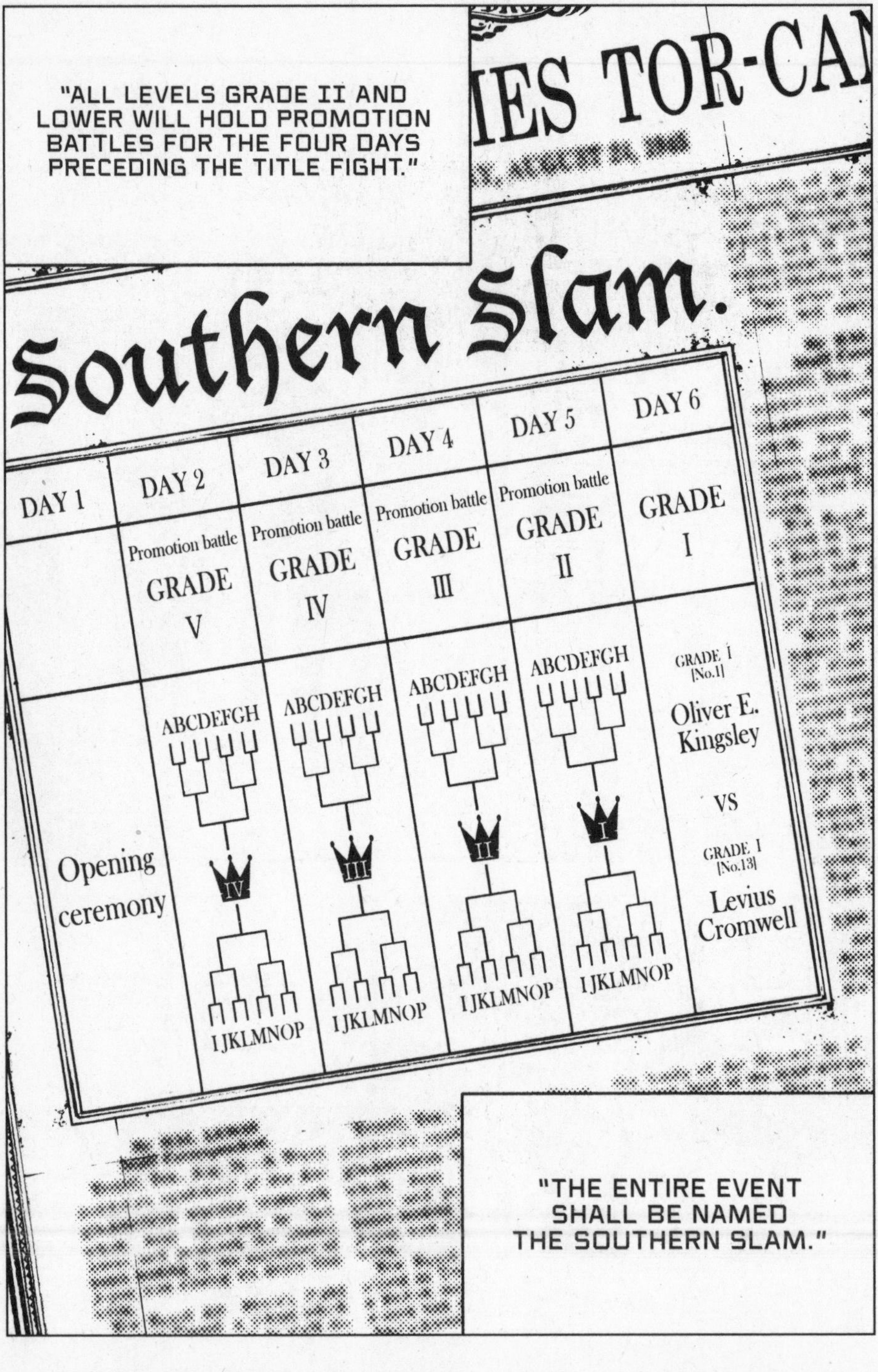
"ALL LEVELS GRADE II AND LOWER WILL HOLD PROMOTION BATTLES FOR THE FOUR DAYS PRECEDING THE TITLE FIGHT."
IES TOR-CA
Southern Slam.
DAY 1
DAY 2
DAY 3
DAY 4
DAY 5
DAY 6
Promotion battle GRADE V
Promotion battle GRADE IV
Promotion battle GRADE III
Promotion battle GRADE II
GRADE I
Opening ceremony
ABCDEFGH
IV
IJKLMNOP
ABCDEFGH
III
IJKLMNOP
ABCDEFGH
II
IJKLMNOP
ABCDEFGH
I
IJKLMNOP
GRADE I [No.1]
Oliver E. Kingsley
VS
GRADE I [No.13]
Levius Cromwell
"THE ENTIRE EVENT SHALL BE NAMED THE SOUTHERN SLAM."

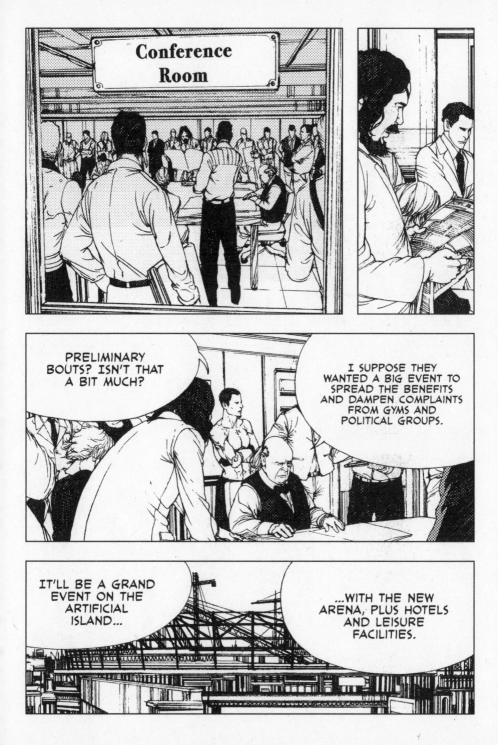

Conference Room

PRELIMINARY BOUTS? ISN'T THAT A BIT MUCH?

I SUPPOSE THEY WANTED A BIG EVENT TO SPREAD THE BENEFITS AND DAMPEN COMPLAINTS FROM GYMS AND POLITICAL GROUPS.

IT'LL BE A GRAND EVENT ON THE ARTIFICIAL ISLAND...

...WITH THE NEW ARENA, PLUS HOTELS AND LEISURE FACILITIES.

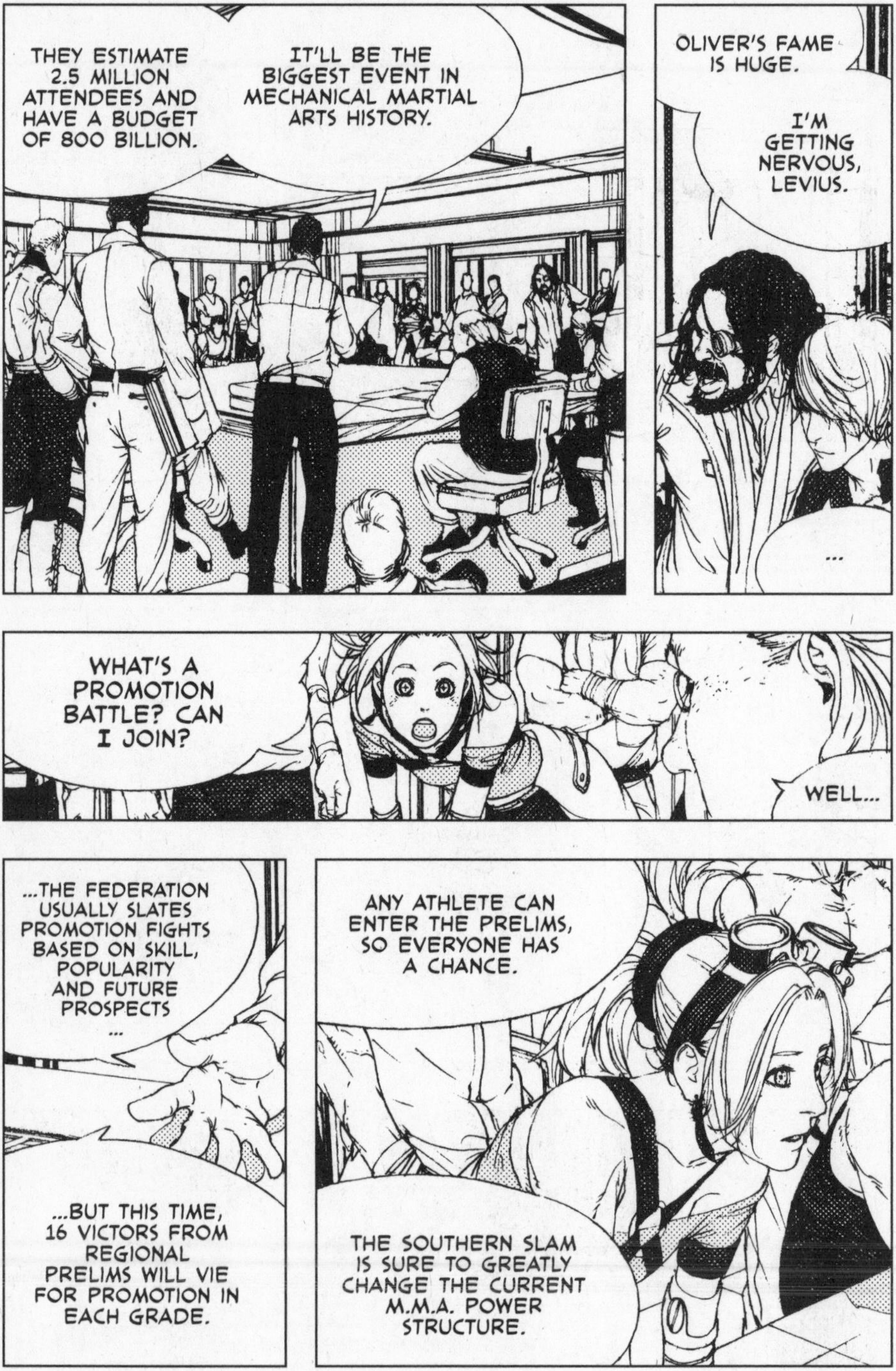
THEY ESTIMATE 2.5 MILLION ATTENDEES AND HAVE A BUDGET OF 800 BILLION.
IT'LL BE THE BIGGEST EVENT IN MECHANICAL MARTIAL ARTS HISTORY.
OLIVER'S FAME IS HUGE.
I'M GETTING NERVOUS, LEVIUS.
...
WHAT'S A PROMOTION BATTLE? CAN I JOIN?
WELL...
...THE FEDERATION USUALLY SLATES PROMOTION FIGHTS BASED ON SKILL, POPULARITY AND FUTURE PROSPECTS ...
...BUT THIS TIME, 16 VICTORS FROM REGIONAL PRELIMS WILL VIE FOR PROMOTION IN EACH GRADE.
ANY ATHLETE CAN ENTER THE PRELIMS, SO EVERYONE HAS A CHANCE.
THE SOUTHERN SLAM IS SURE TO GREATLY CHANGE THE CURRENT M.M.A. POWER STRUCTURE.

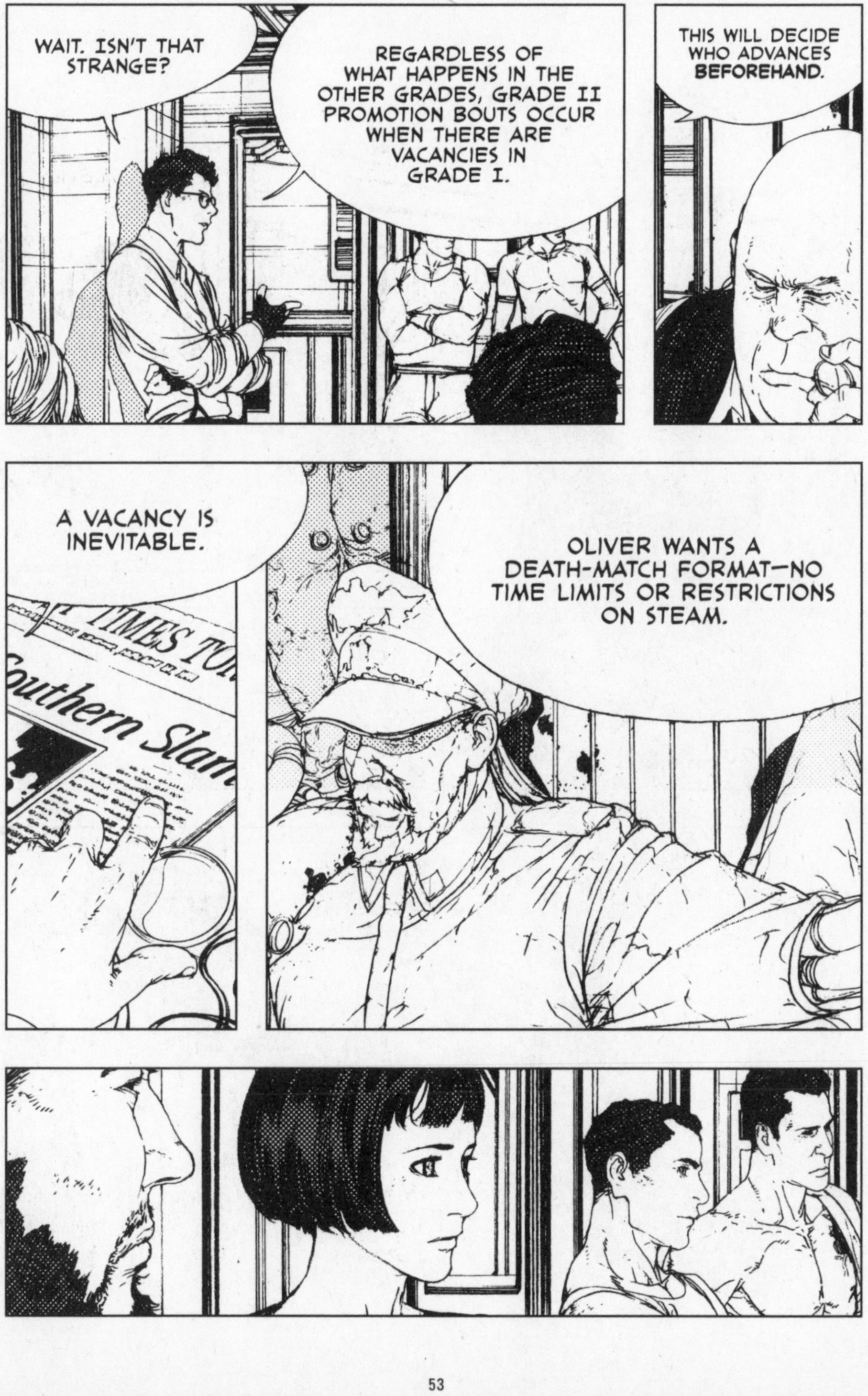
WAIT. ISN'T THAT STRANGE?
REGARDLESS OF WHAT HAPPENS IN THE OTHER GRADES, GRADE II PROMOTION BOUTS OCCUR WHEN THERE ARE VACANCIES IN GRADE I.
THIS WILL DECIDE WHO ADVANCES **BEFOREHAND.**
A VACANCY IS INEVITABLE.
OLIVER WANTS A DEATH-MATCH FORMAT—NO TIME LIMITS OR RESTRICTIONS ON STEAM.

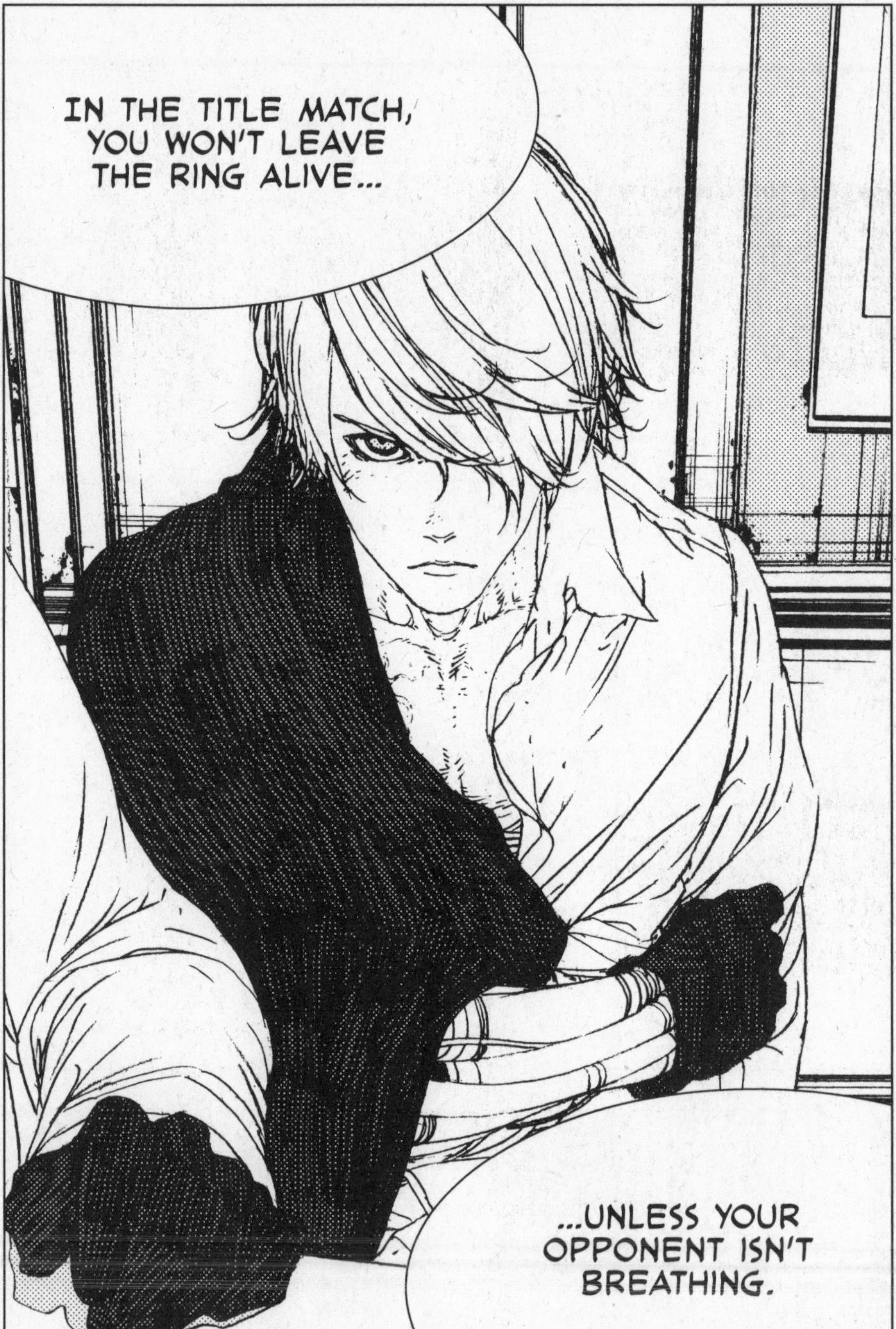
IN THE TITLE MATCH, YOU WON'T LEAVE THE RING ALIVE...
...UNLESS YOUR OPPONENT ISN'T BREATHING.

Levius/est
VOL. 3

Chapter 14

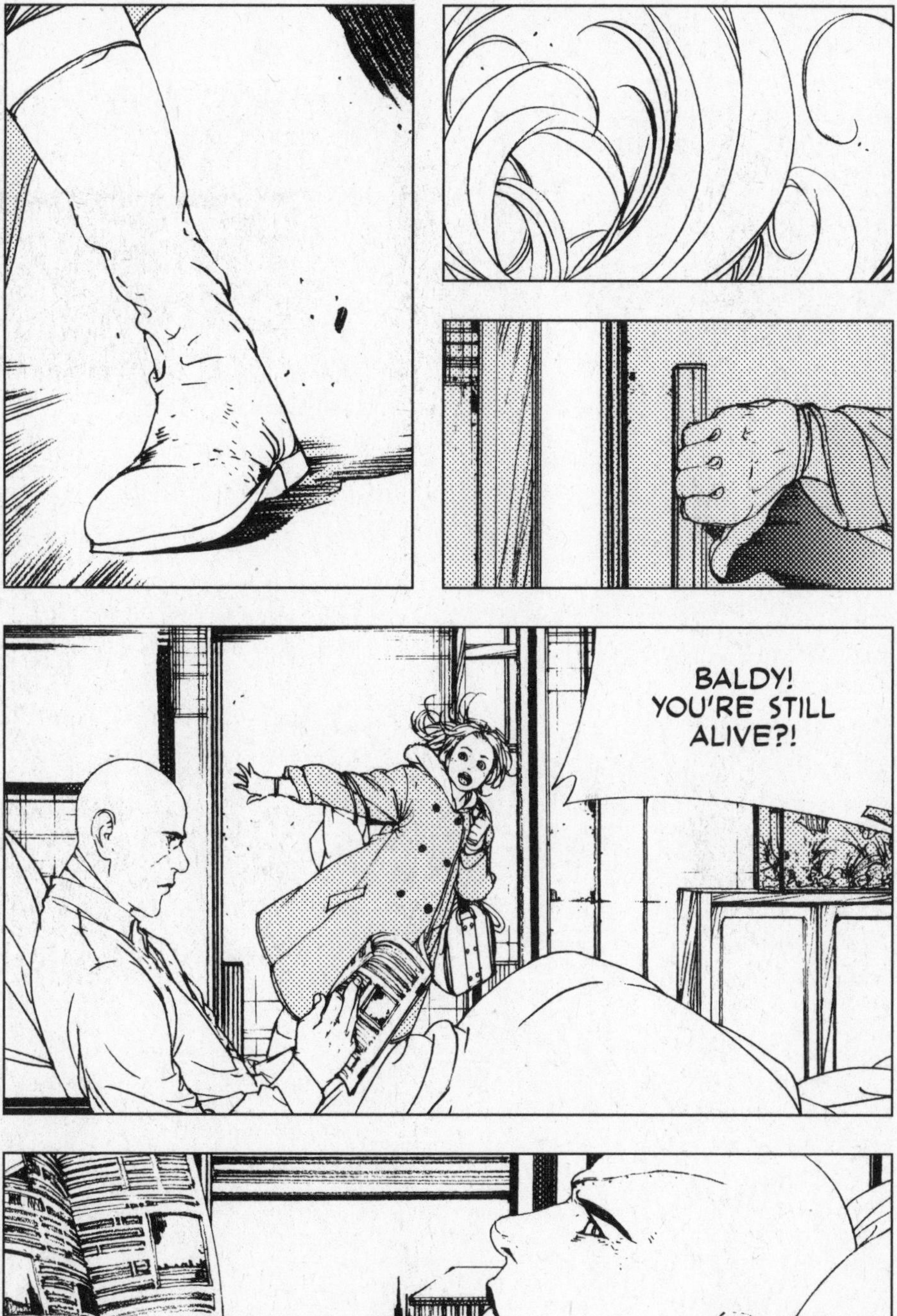
BALDY!
YOU'RE STILL
ALIVE?!

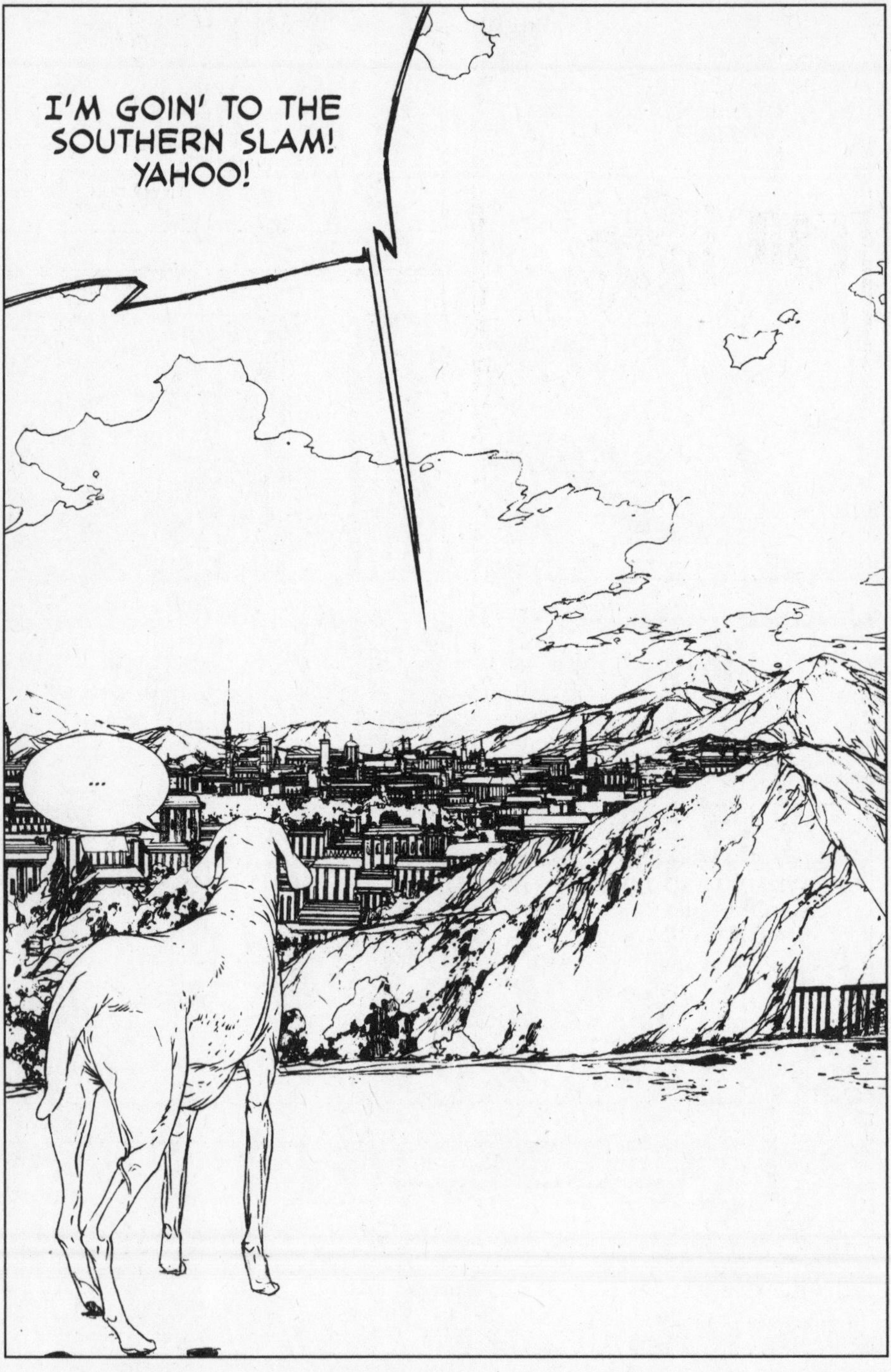
I'M GOIN' TO THE SOUTHERN SLAM! YAHOO!
...

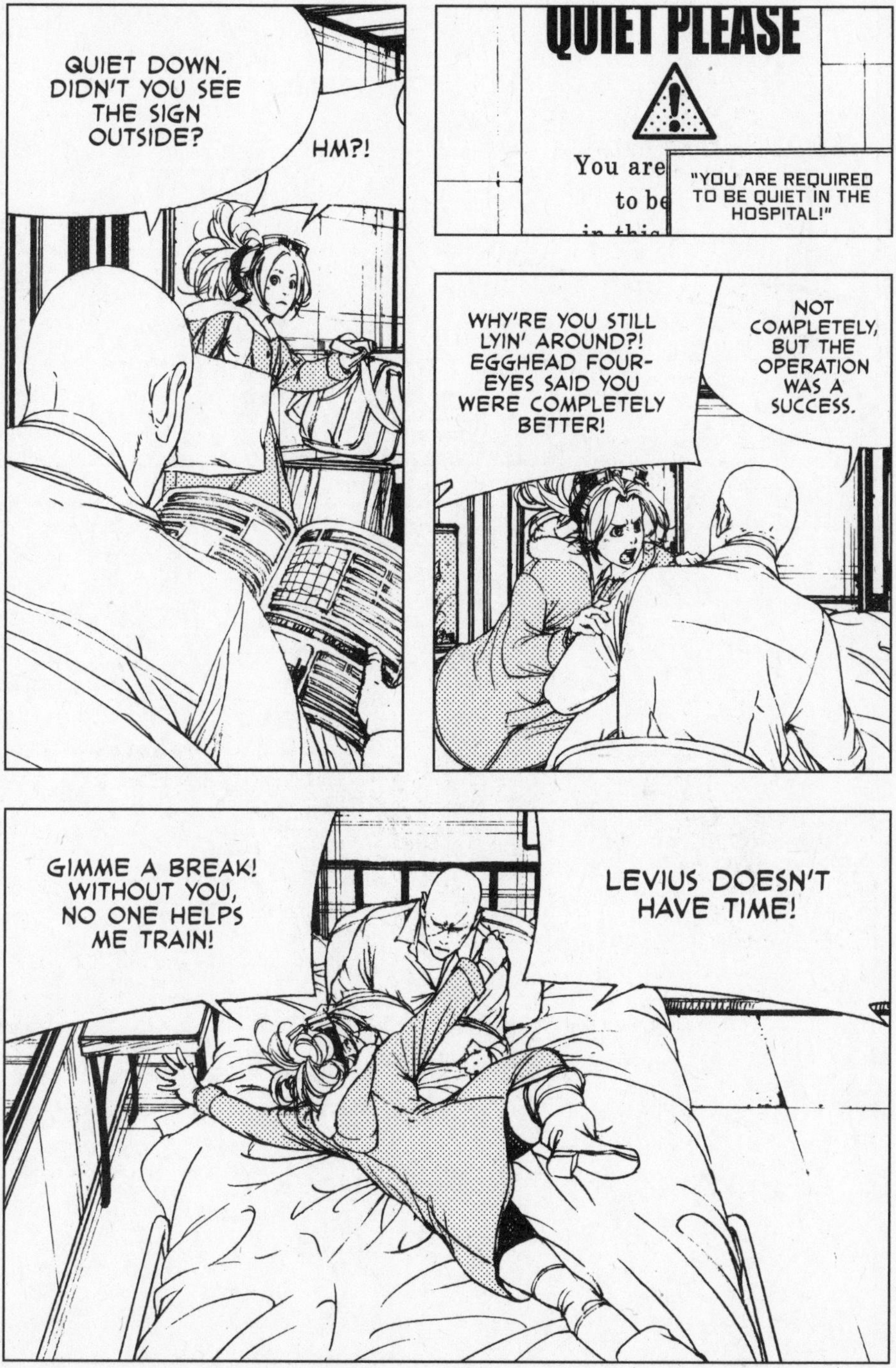
QUIET DOWN. DIDN'T YOU SEE THE SIGN OUTSIDE?
HM?!
QUIET PLEASE
You are to be in this
"YOU ARE REQUIRED TO BE QUIET IN THE HOSPITAL!"
WHY'RE YOU STILL LYIN' AROUND?! EGGHEAD FOUR-EYES SAID YOU WERE COMPLETELY BETTER!
NOT COMPLETELY, BUT THE OPERATION WAS A SUCCESS.
GIMME A BREAK! WITHOUT YOU, NO ONE HELPS ME TRAIN!
LEVIUS DOESN'T HAVE TIME!

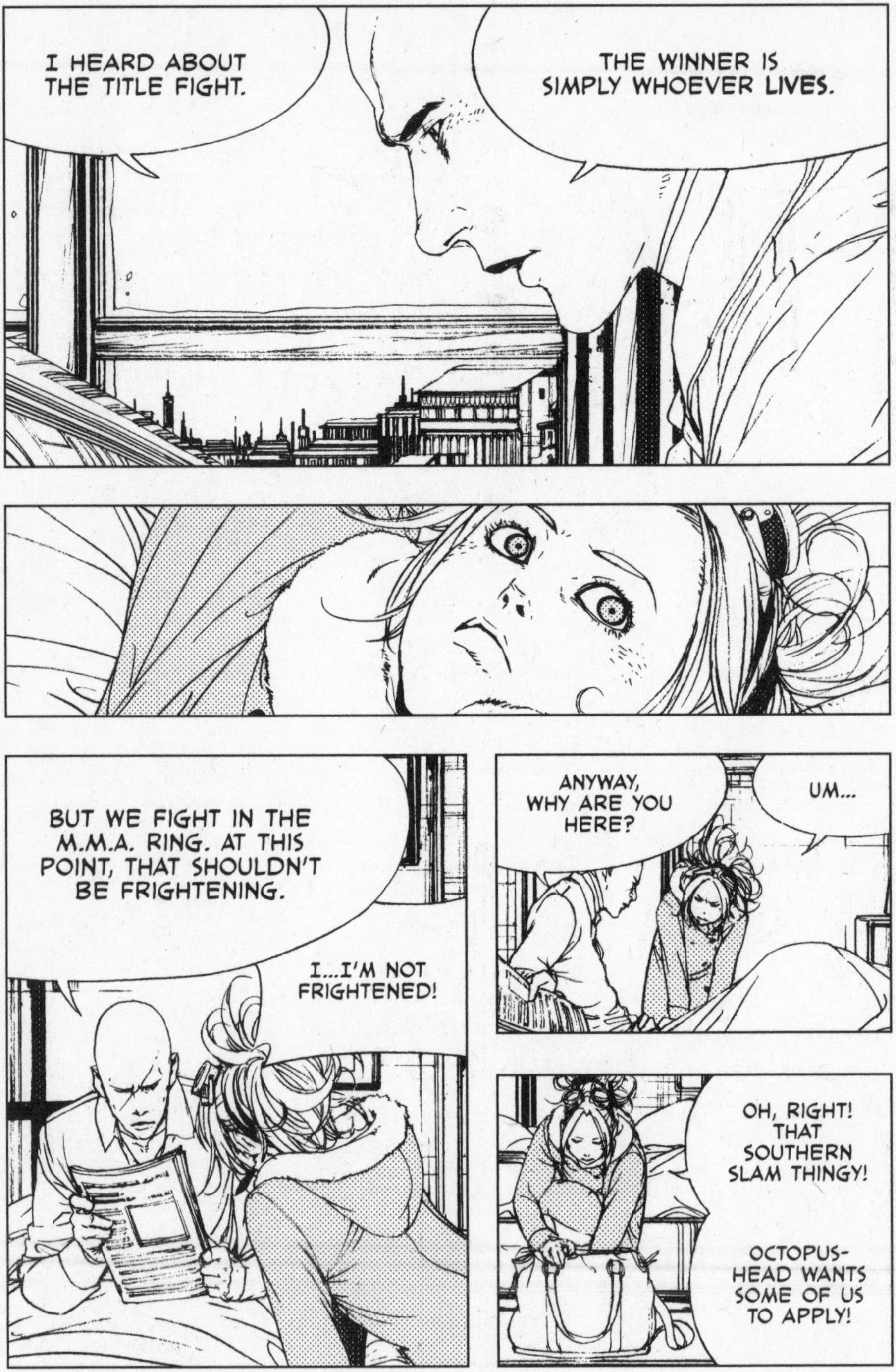
I HEARD ABOUT THE TITLE FIGHT.
THE WINNER IS SIMPLY WHOEVER LIVES.
BUT WE FIGHT IN THE M.M.A. RING. AT THIS POINT, THAT SHOULDN'T BE FRIGHTENING.
I...I'M NOT FRIGHTENED!
ANYWAY, WHY ARE YOU HERE?
UM...
OH, RIGHT! THAT SOUTHERN SLAM THINGY!
OCTOPUS-HEAD WANTS SOME OF US TO APPLY!

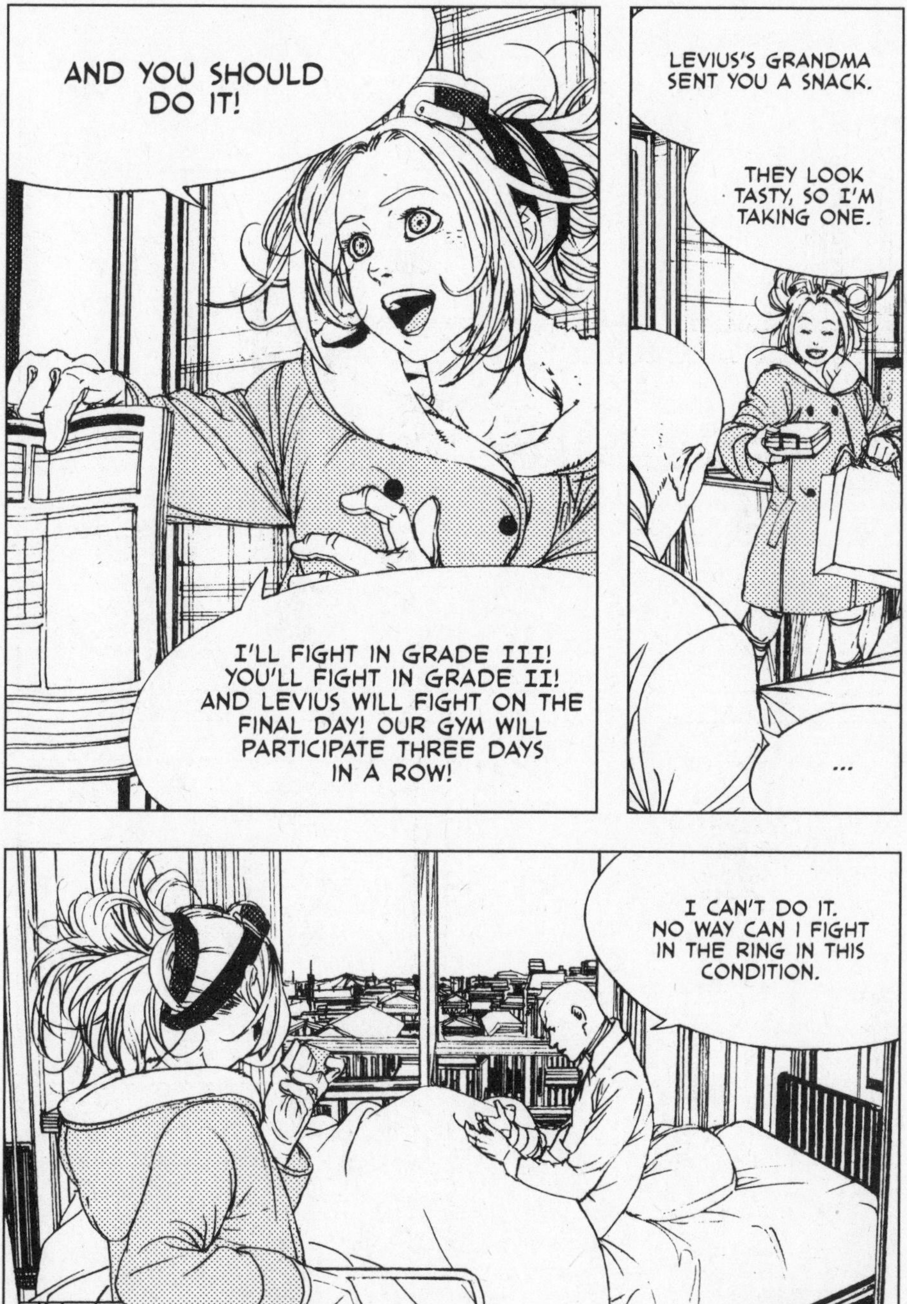
AND YOU SHOULD DO IT!
I'LL FIGHT IN GRADE III! YOU'LL FIGHT IN GRADE II! AND LEVIUS WILL FIGHT ON THE FINAL DAY! OUR GYM WILL PARTICIPATE THREE DAYS IN A ROW!
LEVIUS'S GRANDMA SENT YOU A SNACK.
THEY LOOK TASTY, SO I'M TAKING ONE.
...
I CAN'T DO IT. NO WAY CAN I FIGHT IN THE RING IN THIS CONDITION.

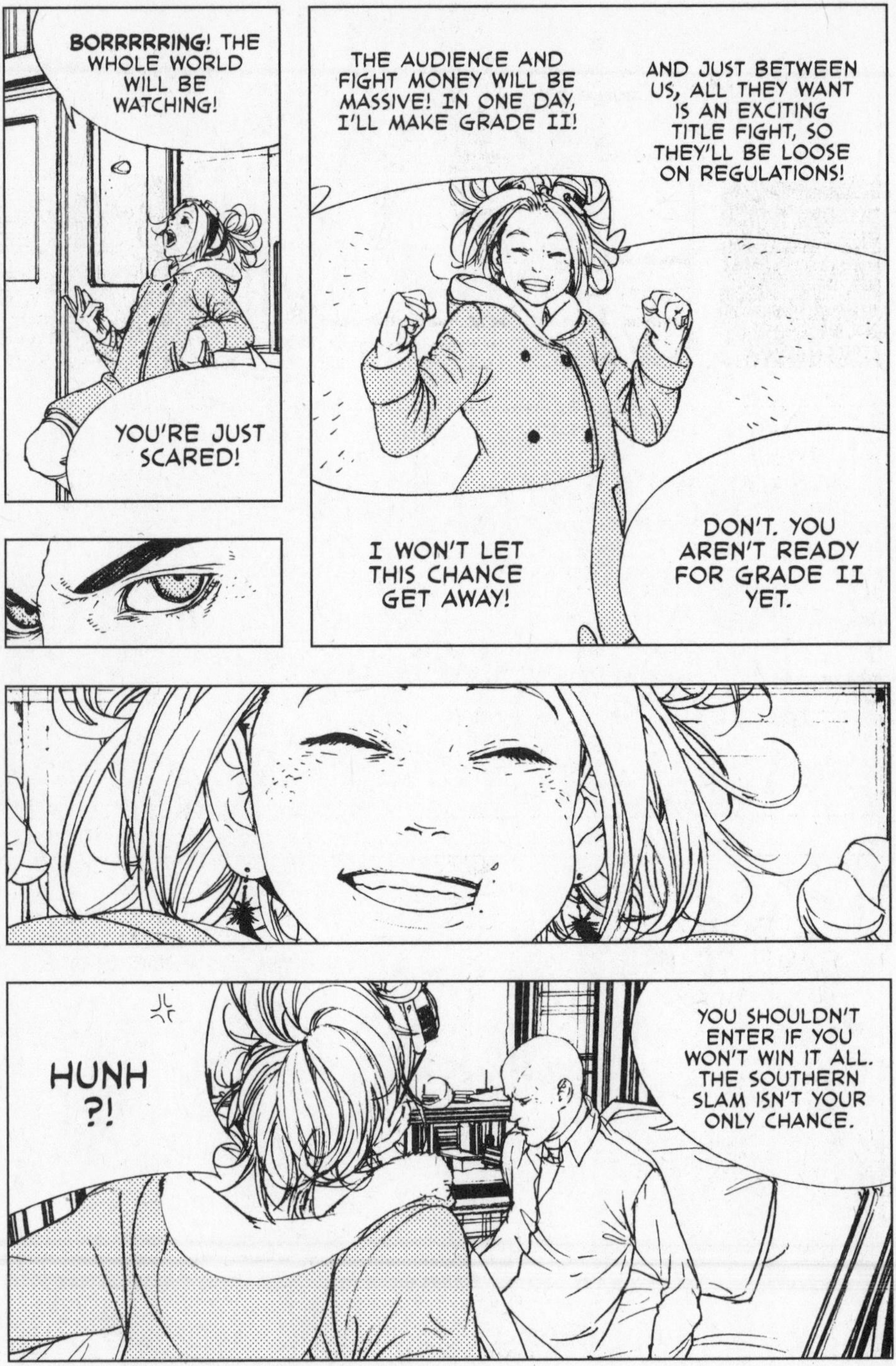
BORRRRRING! THE WHOLE WORLD WILL BE WATCHING!
YOU'RE JUST SCARED!
THE AUDIENCE AND FIGHT MONEY WILL BE MASSIVE! IN ONE DAY, I'LL MAKE GRADE II!
AND JUST BETWEEN US, ALL THEY WANT IS AN EXCITING TITLE FIGHT, SO THEY'LL BE LOOSE ON REGULATIONS!
I WON'T LET THIS CHANCE GET AWAY!
DON'T. YOU AREN'T READY FOR GRADE II YET.
HUNH ?!
YOU SHOULDN'T ENTER IF YOU WON'T WIN IT ALL. THE SOUTHERN SLAM ISN'T YOUR ONLY CHANCE.

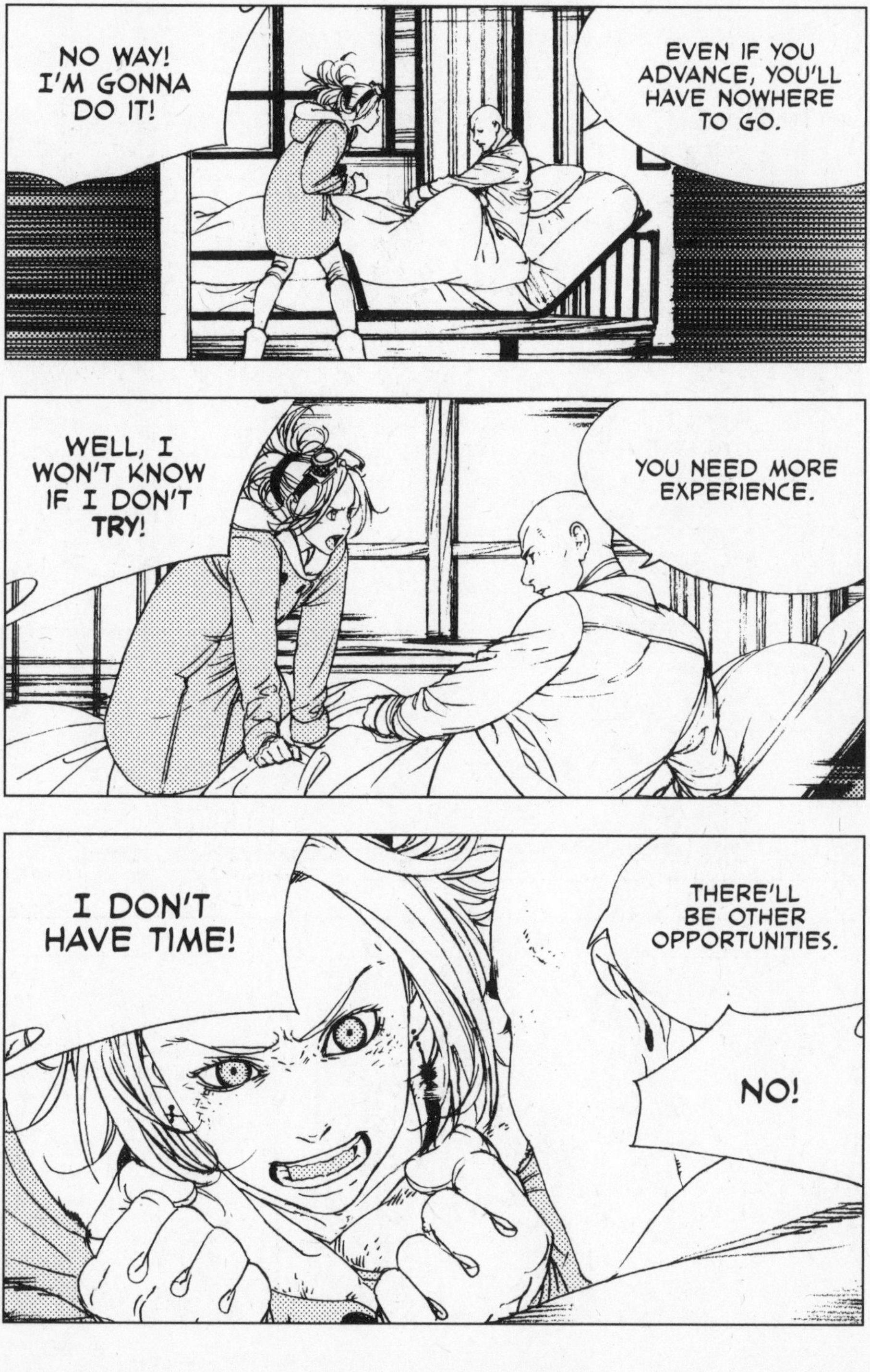
NO WAY! I'M GONNA DO IT!
EVEN IF YOU ADVANCE, YOU'LL HAVE NOWHERE TO GO.
WELL, I WON'T KNOW IF I DON'T **TRY**!
YOU NEED MORE EXPERIENCE.
I DON'T HAVE TIME!
THERE'LL BE OTHER OPPORTUNITIES.
NO!

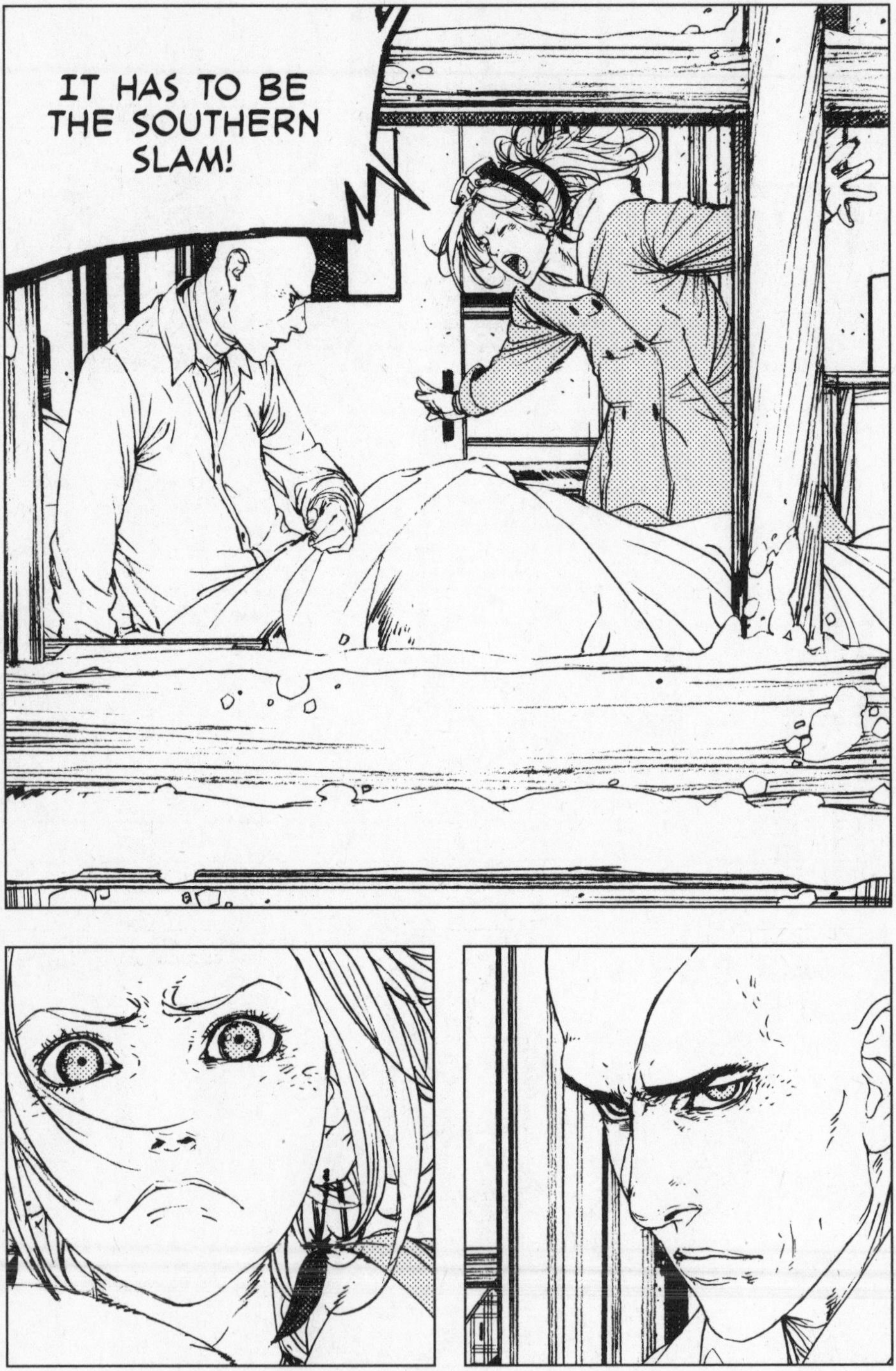
IT HAS TO BE THE SOUTHERN SLAM!

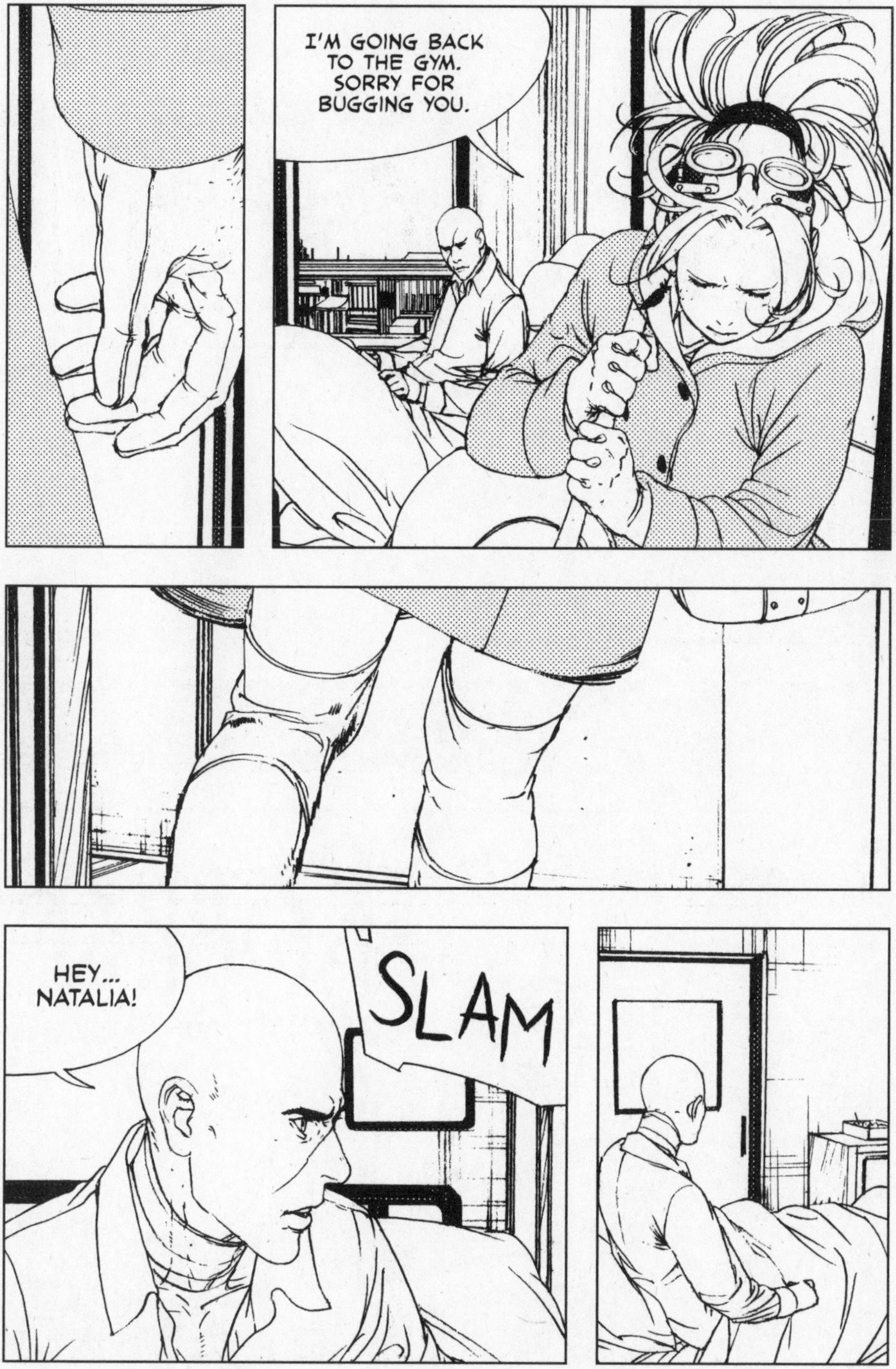
I'M GOING BACK TO THE GYM. SORRY FOR BUGGING YOU.
HEY... NATALIA!
SLAM

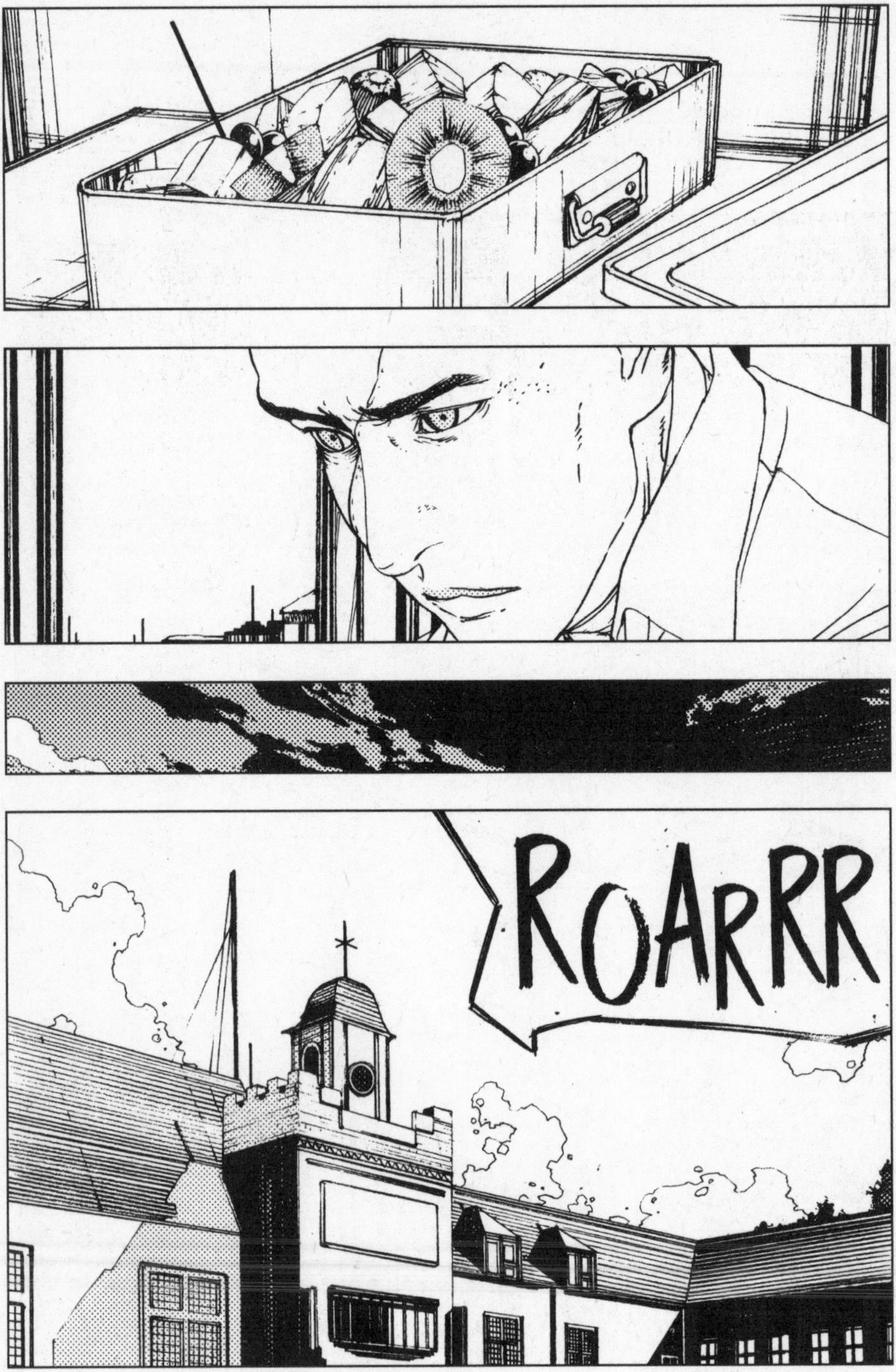
ROARRR

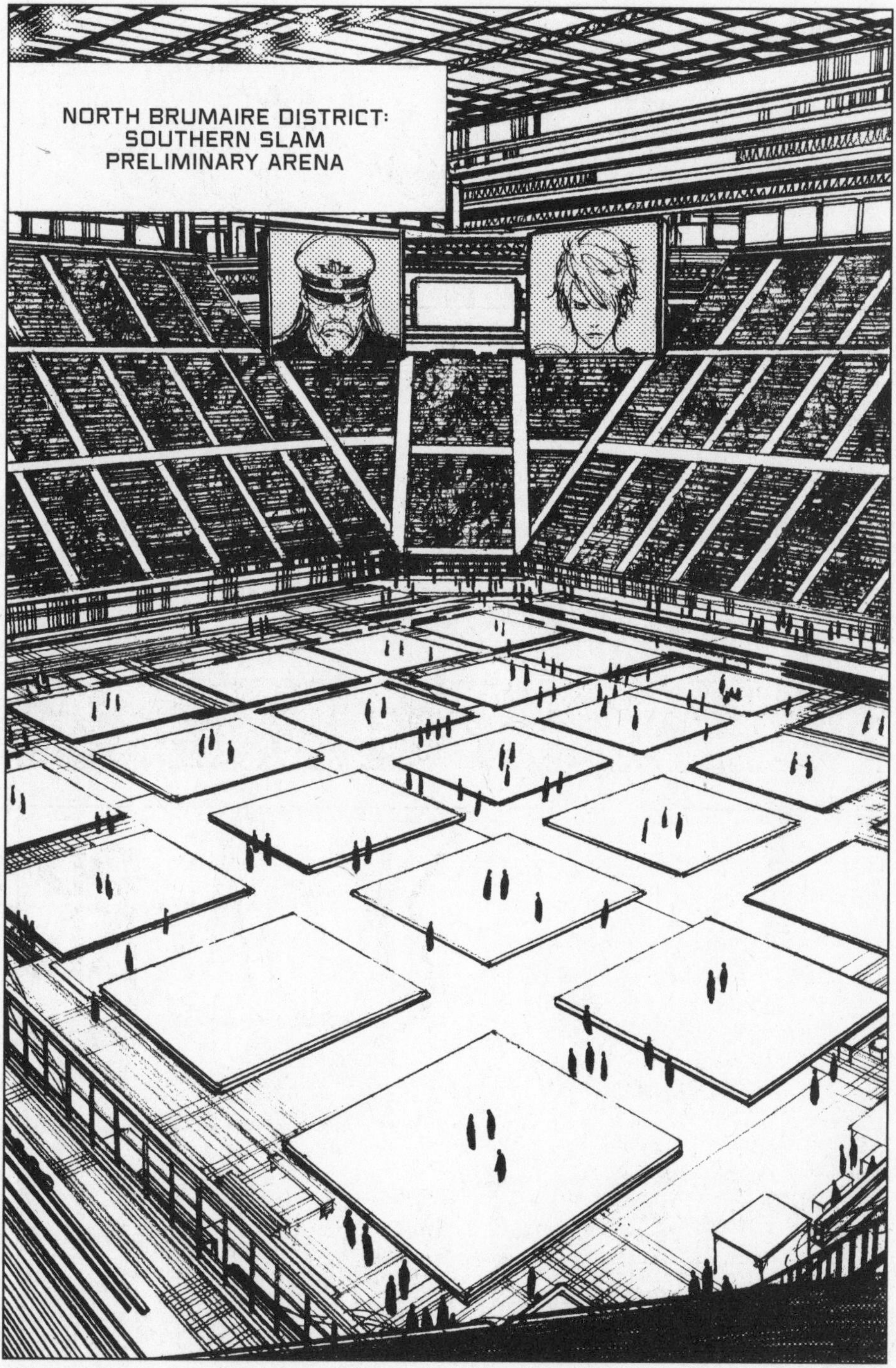
NORTH BRUMAIRE DISTRICT:
SOUTHERN SLAM
PRELIMINARY ARENA

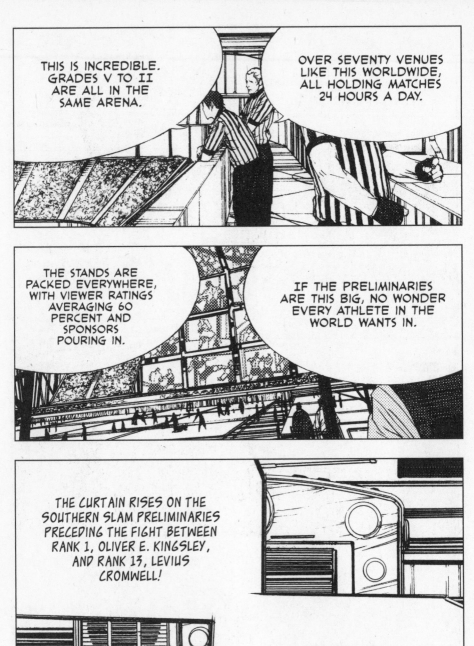

THIS IS INCREDIBLE. GRADES V TO II ARE ALL IN THE SAME ARENA.

OVER SEVENTY VENUES LIKE THIS WORLDWIDE, ALL HOLDING MATCHES 24 HOURS A DAY.

THE STANDS ARE PACKED EVERYWHERE, WITH VIEWER RATINGS AVERAGING 60 PERCENT AND SPONSORS POURING IN.

IF THE PRELIMINARIES ARE THIS BIG, NO WONDER EVERY ATHLETE IN THE WORLD WANTS IN.

THE CURTAIN RISES ON THE SOUTHERN SLAM PRELIMINARIES PRECEDING THE FIGHT BETWEEN RANK 1, OLIVER E. KINGSLEY, AND RANK 13, LEVIUS CROMWELL!

SO LET'S REVIEW THE TOURNAMENT FORMAT!

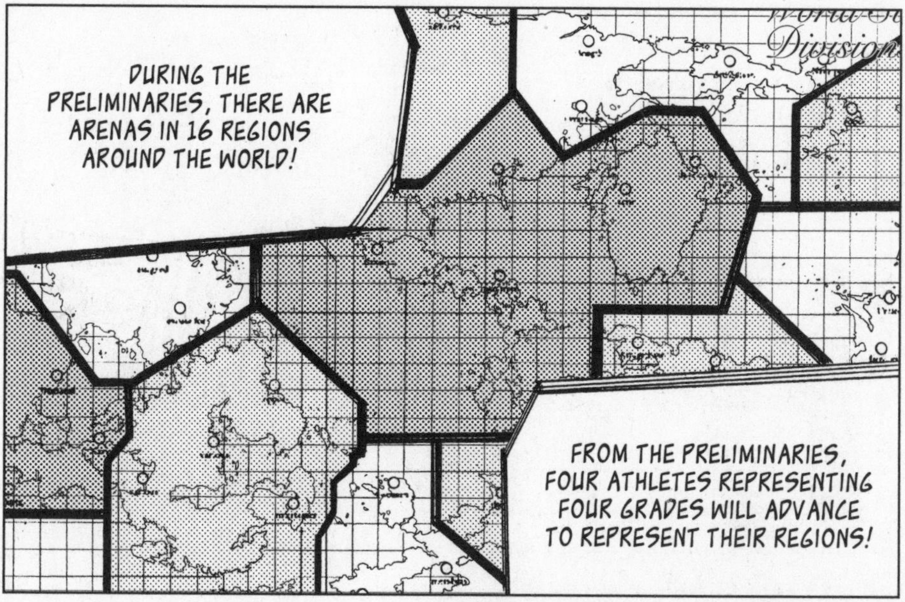
DURING THE PRELIMINARIES, THERE ARE ARENAS IN 16 REGIONS AROUND THE WORLD!
FROM THE PRELIMINARIES, FOUR ATHLETES REPRESENTING FOUR GRADES WILL ADVANCE TO REPRESENT THEIR REGIONS!
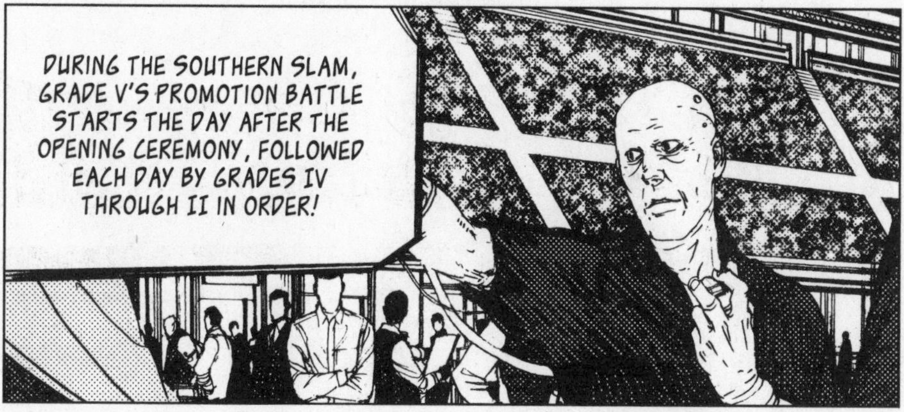
DURING THE SOUTHERN SLAM, GRADE V'S PROMOTION BATTLE STARTS THE DAY AFTER THE OPENING CEREMONY, FOLLOWED EACH DAY BY GRADES IV THROUGH II IN ORDER!
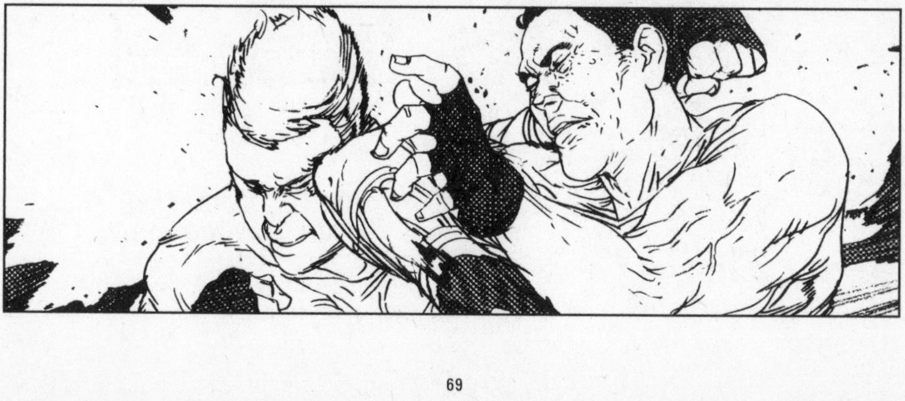

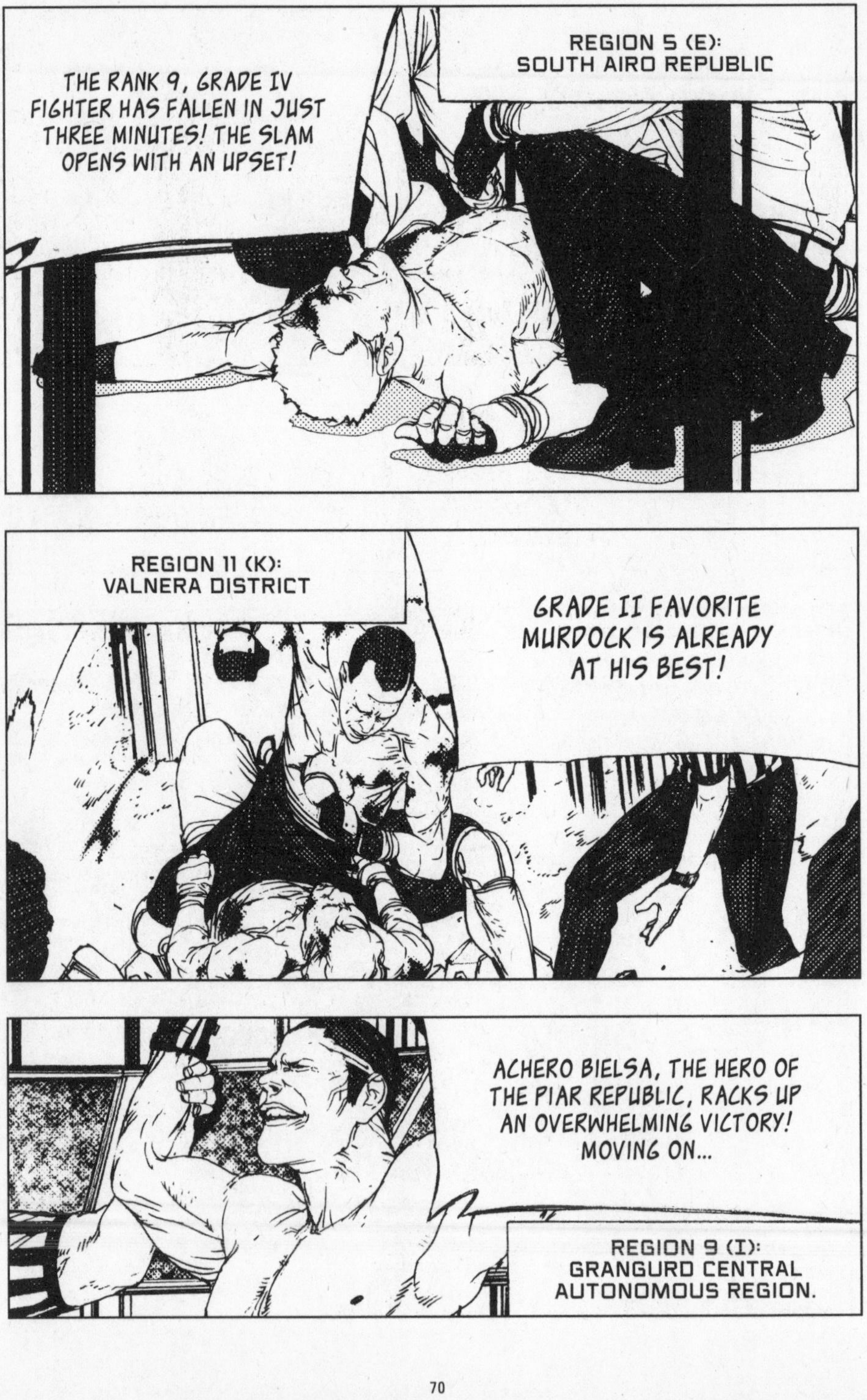
REGION 5 (E):
SOUTH AIRO REPUBLIC
THE RANK 9, GRADE IV FIGHTER HAS FALLEN IN JUST THREE MINUTES! THE SLAM OPENS WITH AN UPSET!
REGION 11 (K):
VALNERA DISTRICT
GRADE II FAVORITE MURDOCK IS ALREADY AT HIS BEST!
ACHERO BIELSA, THE HERO OF THE PIAR REPUBLIC, RACKS UP AN OVERWHELMING VICTORY! MOVING ON...
REGION 9 (I):
GRANGURD CENTRAL AUTONOMOUS REGION.

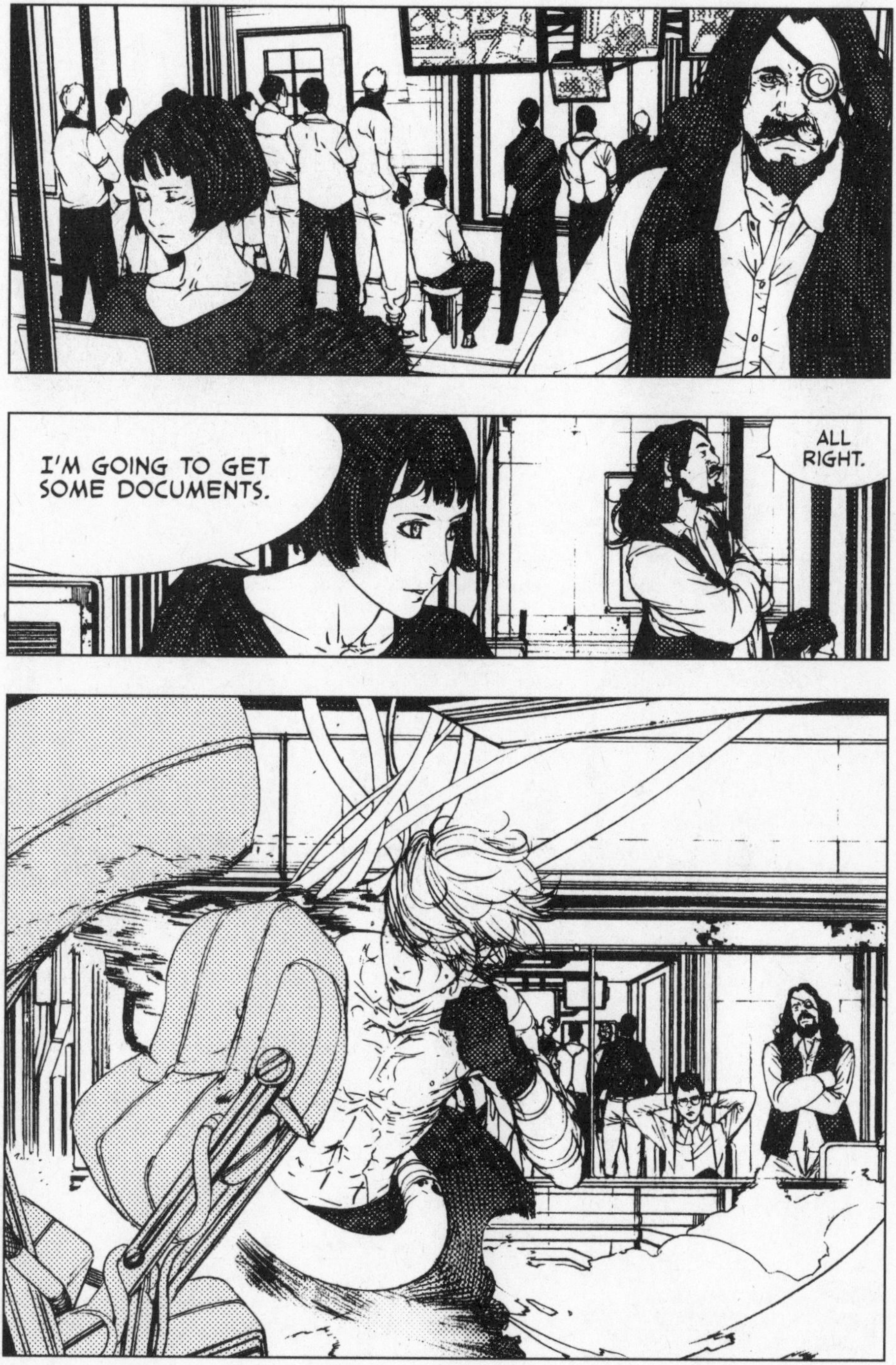
I'M GOING TO GET SOME DOCUMENTS.
ALL RIGHT.

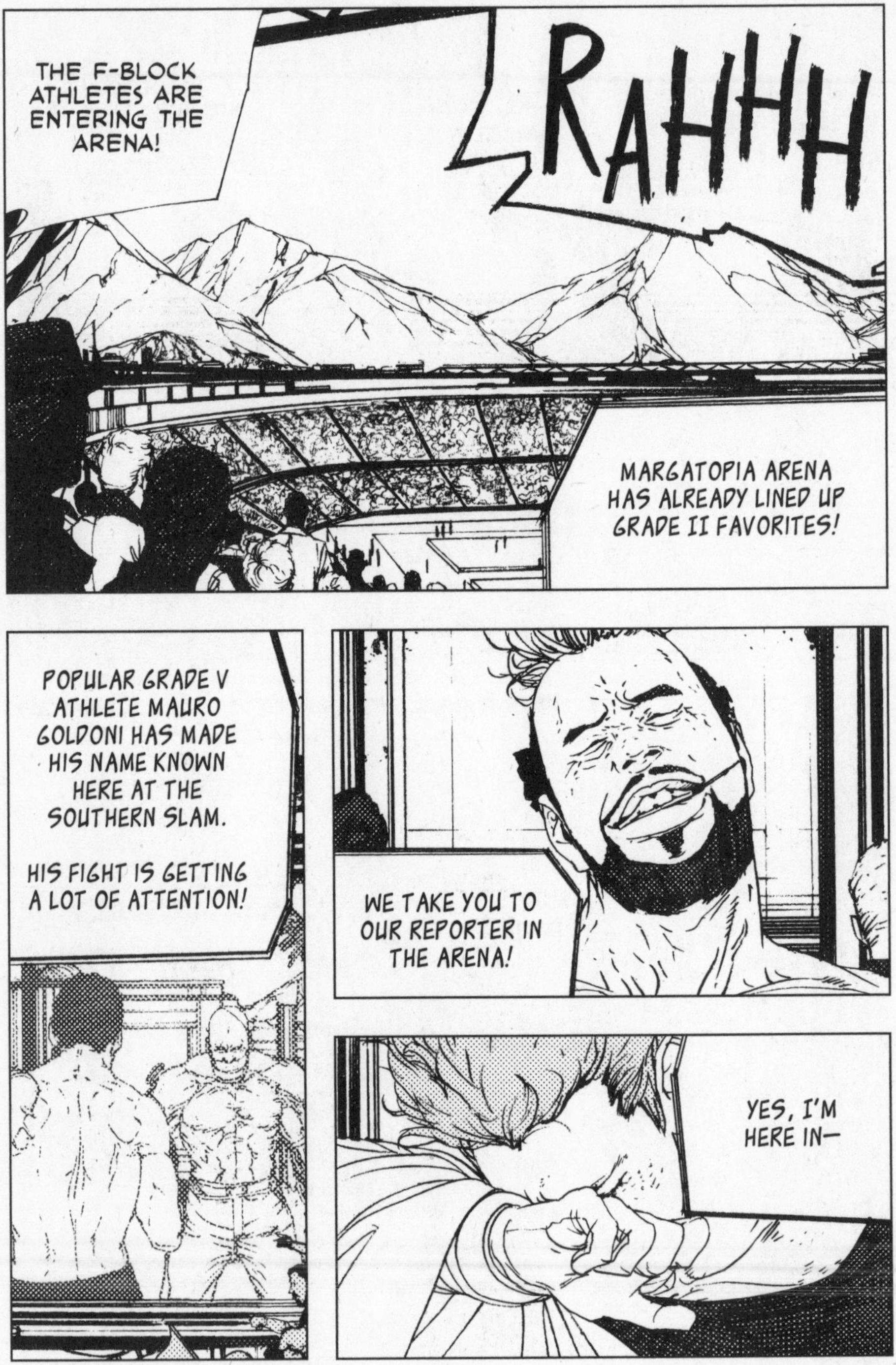
THE F-BLOCK ATHLETES ARE ENTERING THE ARENA!
RAHHH
MARGATOPIA ARENA HAS ALREADY LINED UP GRADE II FAVORITES!
POPULAR GRADE V ATHLETE MAURO GOLDONI HAS MADE HIS NAME KNOWN HERE AT THE SOUTHERN SLAM.
HIS FIGHT IS GETTING A LOT OF ATTENTION!
WE TAKE YOU TO OUR REPORTER IN THE ARENA!
YES, I'M HERE IN—

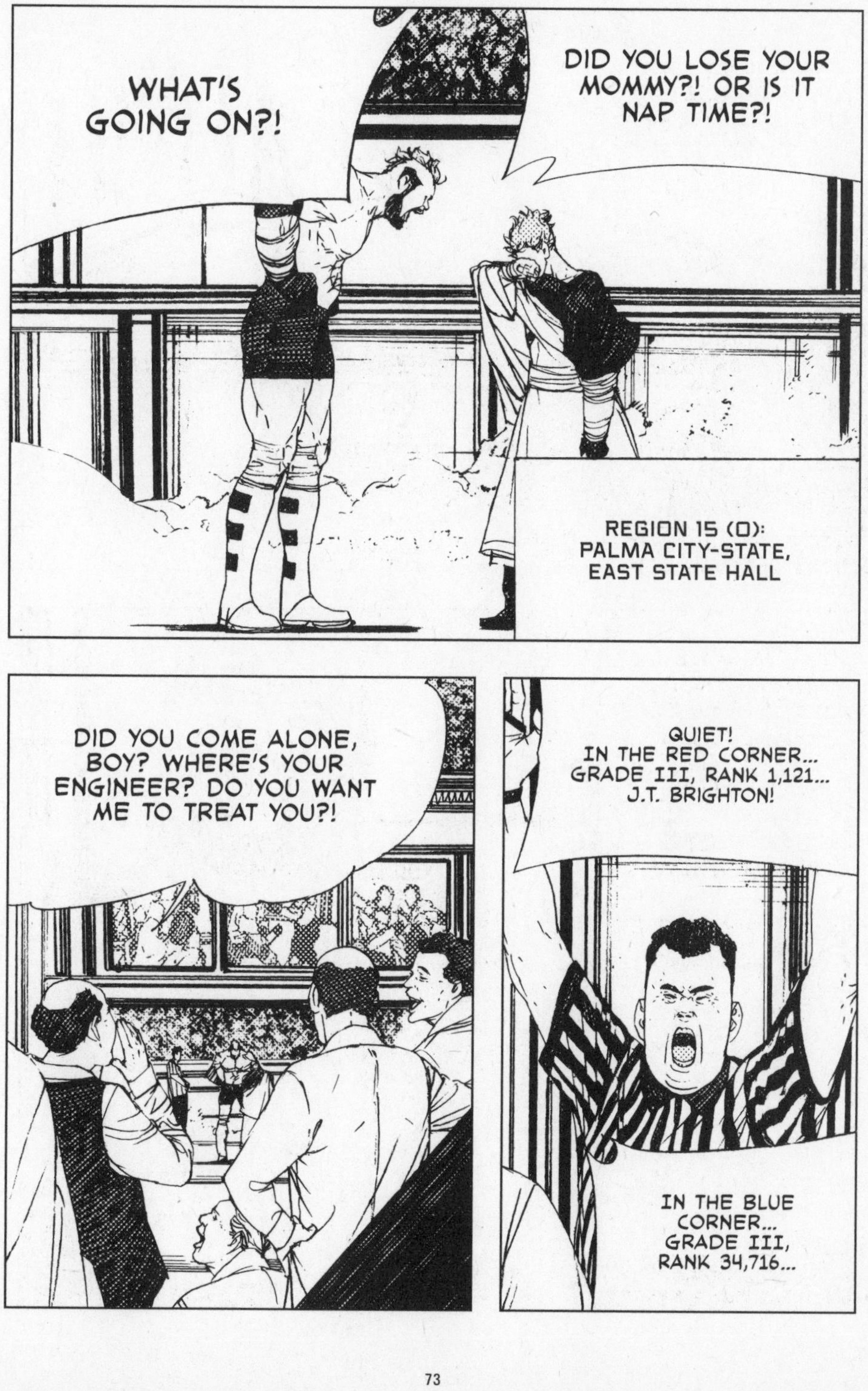
WHAT'S GOING ON?!
DID YOU LOSE YOUR MOMMY?! OR IS IT NAP TIME?!
REGION 15 (0): PALMA CITY-STATE, EAST STATE HALL
DID YOU COME ALONE, BOY? WHERE'S YOUR ENGINEER? DO YOU WANT ME TO TREAT YOU?!
QUIET! IN THE RED CORNER... GRADE III, RANK 1,121... J.T. BRIGHTON!
IN THE BLUE CORNER... GRADE III, RANK 34,716...

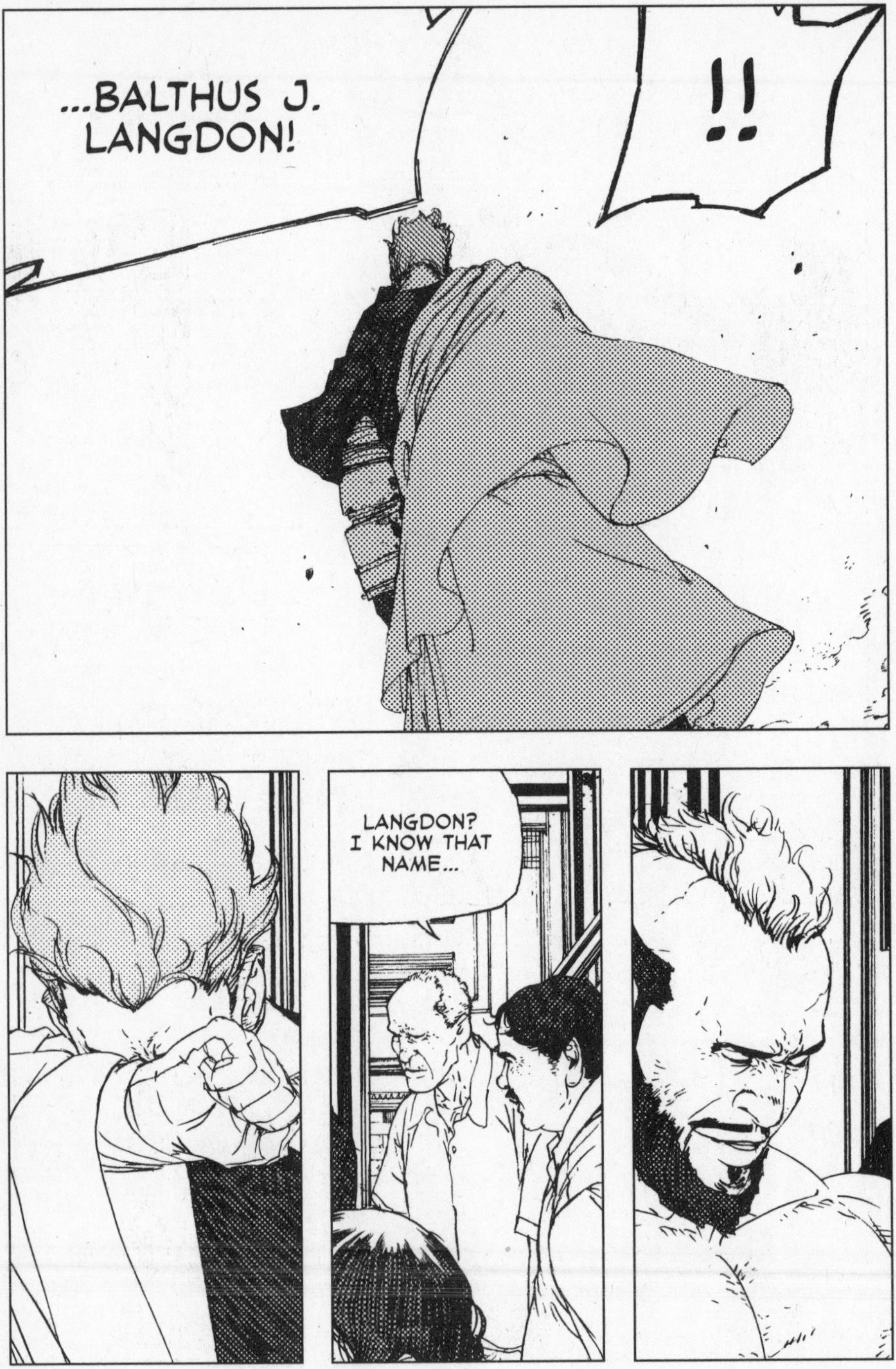

...BALTHUS J. LANGDON!
!!
LANGDON? I KNOW THAT NAME...

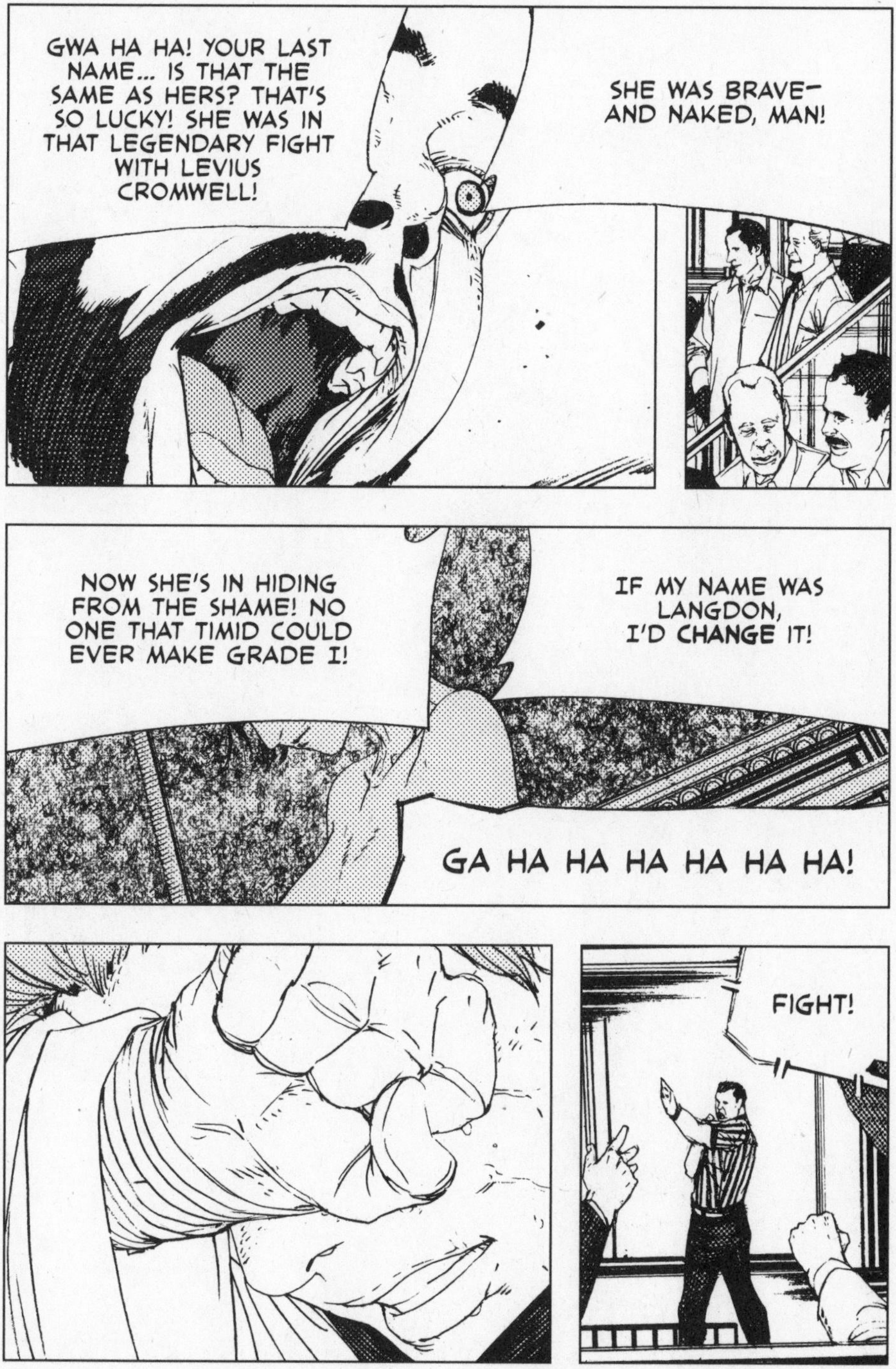
GWA HA HA! YOUR LAST NAME... IS THAT THE SAME AS HERS? THAT'S SO LUCKY! SHE WAS IN THAT LEGENDARY FIGHT WITH LEVIUS CROMWELL!
SHE WAS BRAVE-AND NAKED, MAN!
NOW SHE'S IN HIDING FROM THE SHAME! NO ONE THAT TIMID COULD EVER MAKE GRADE I!
IF MY NAME WAS LANGDON, I'D CHANGE IT!
GA HA HA HA HA HA HA!
FIGHT!

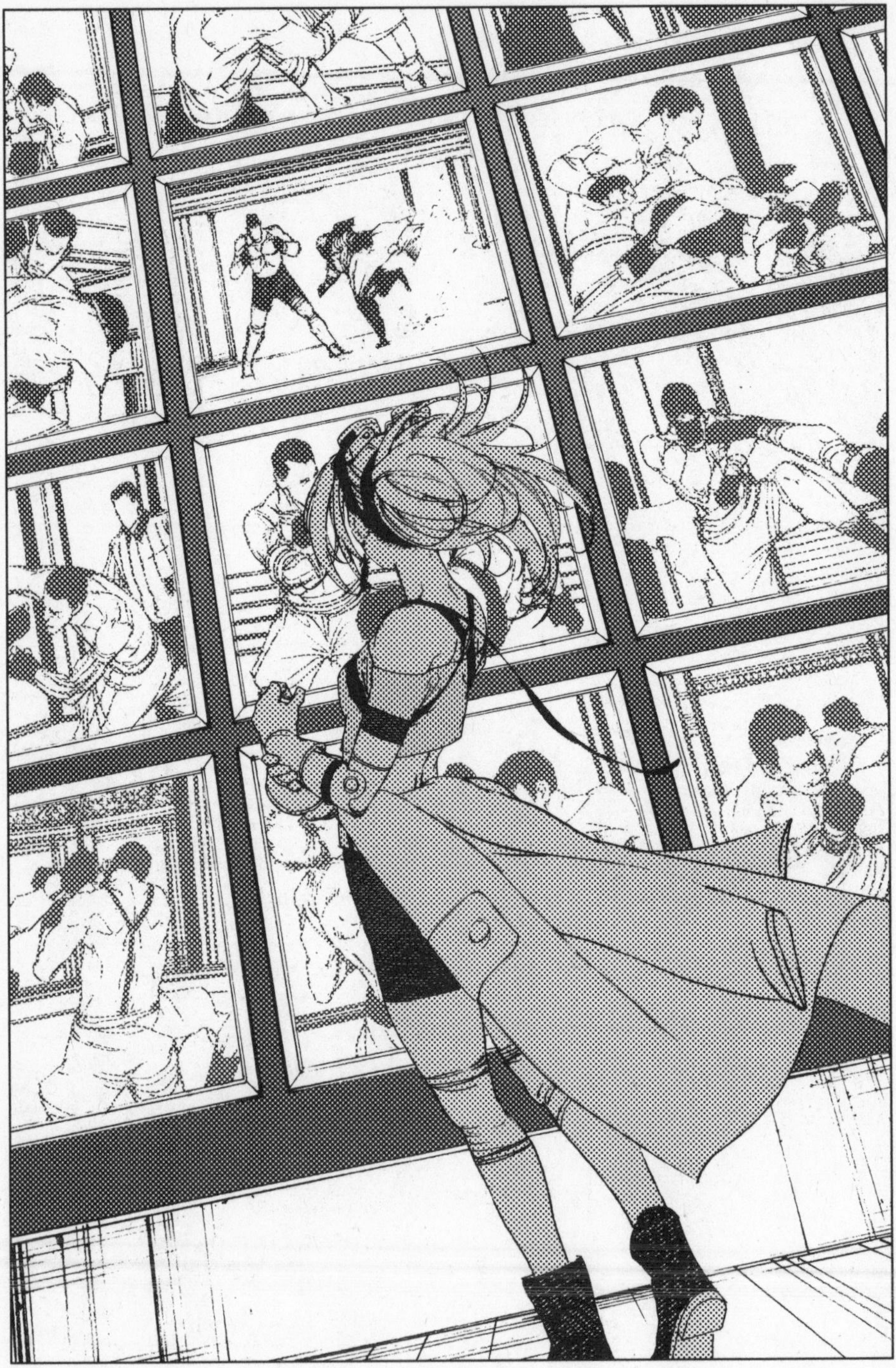

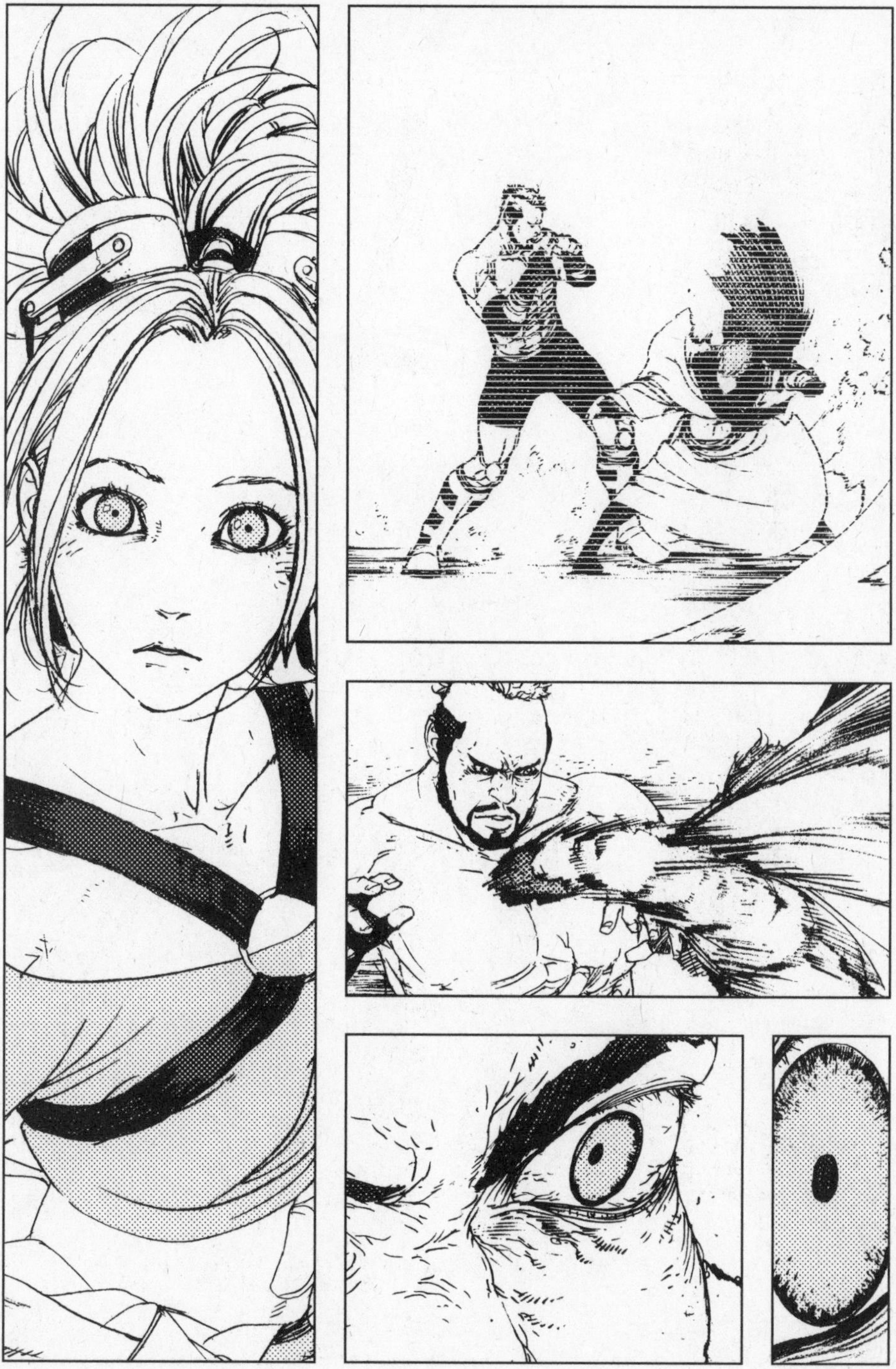

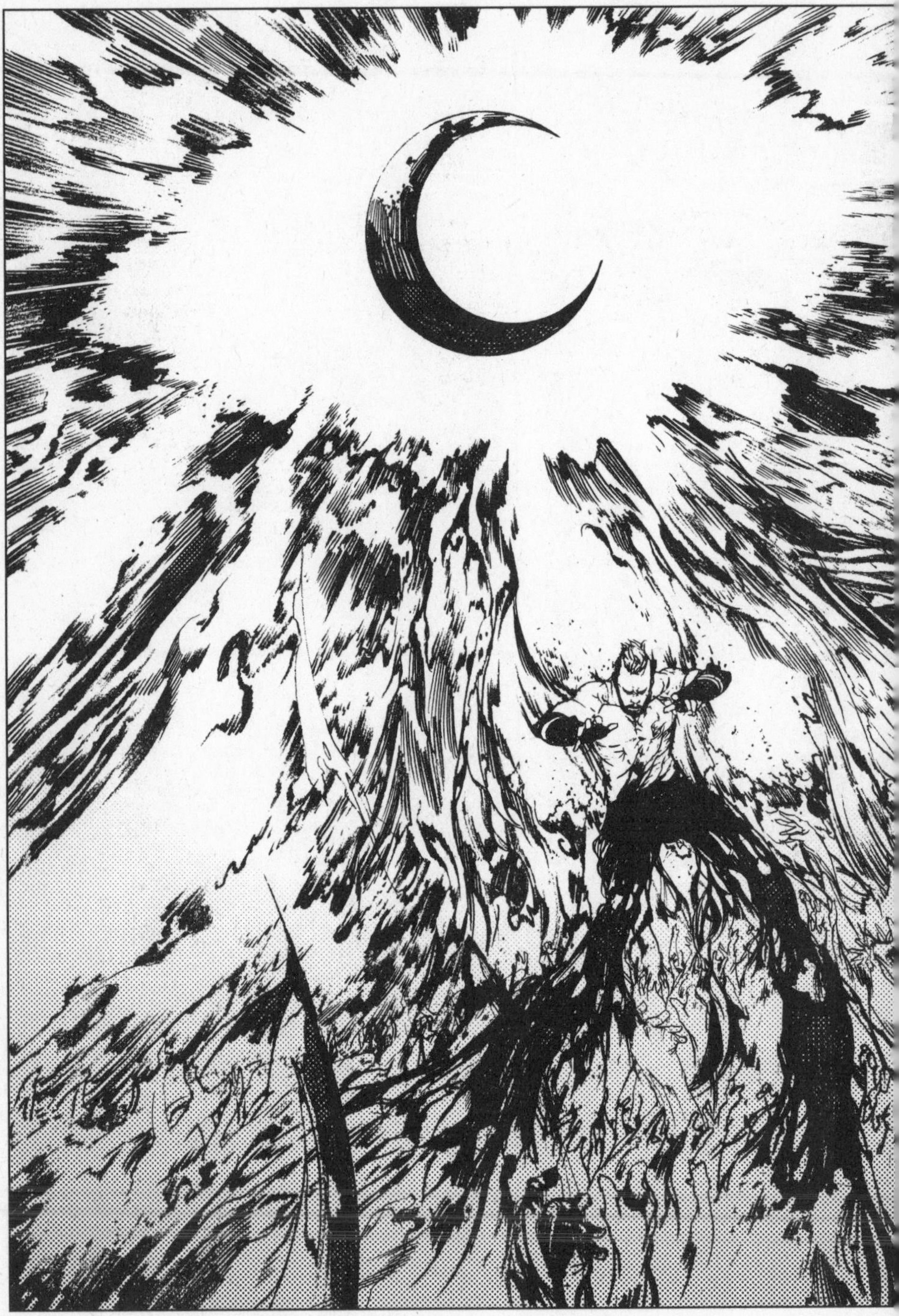

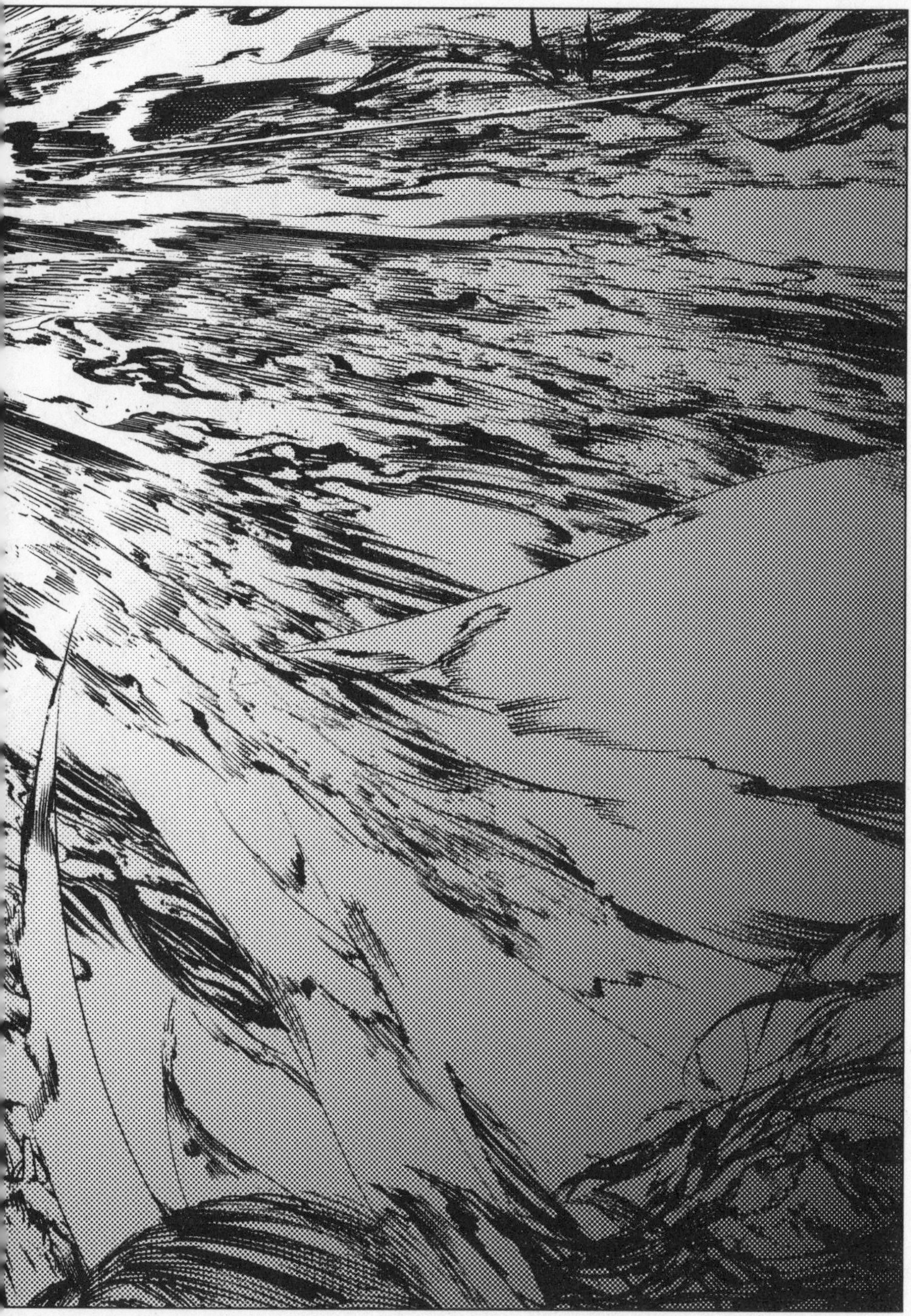

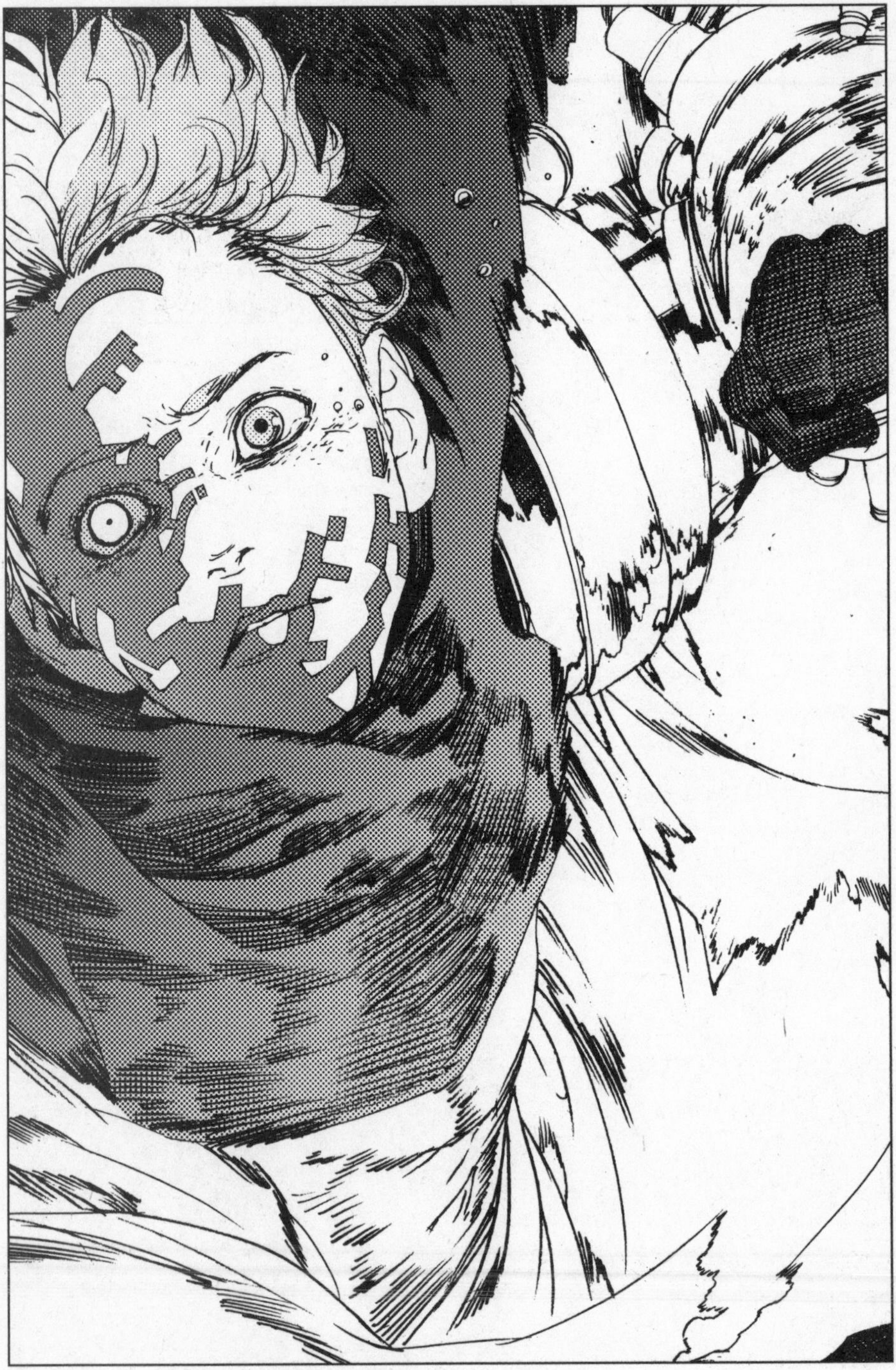

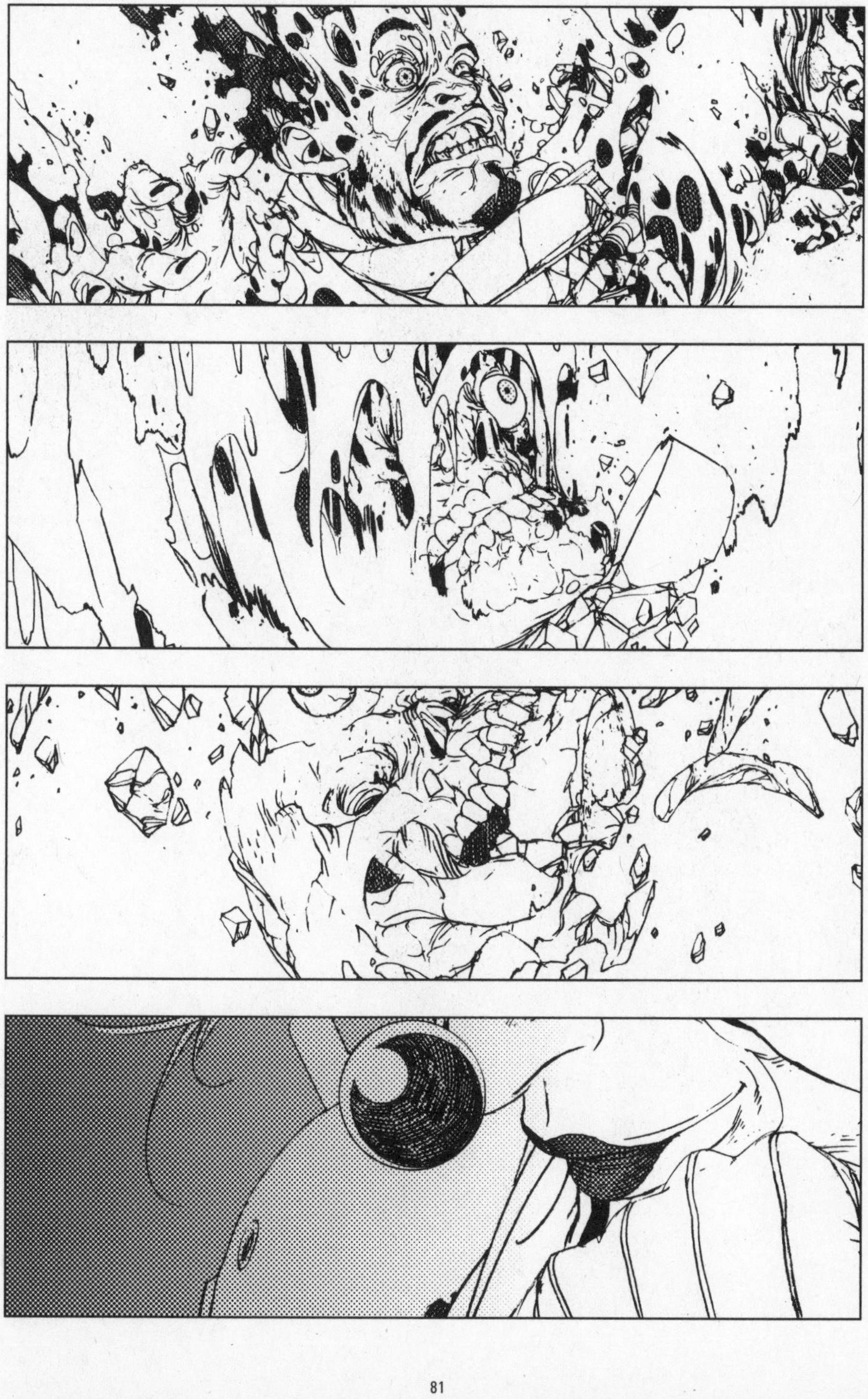

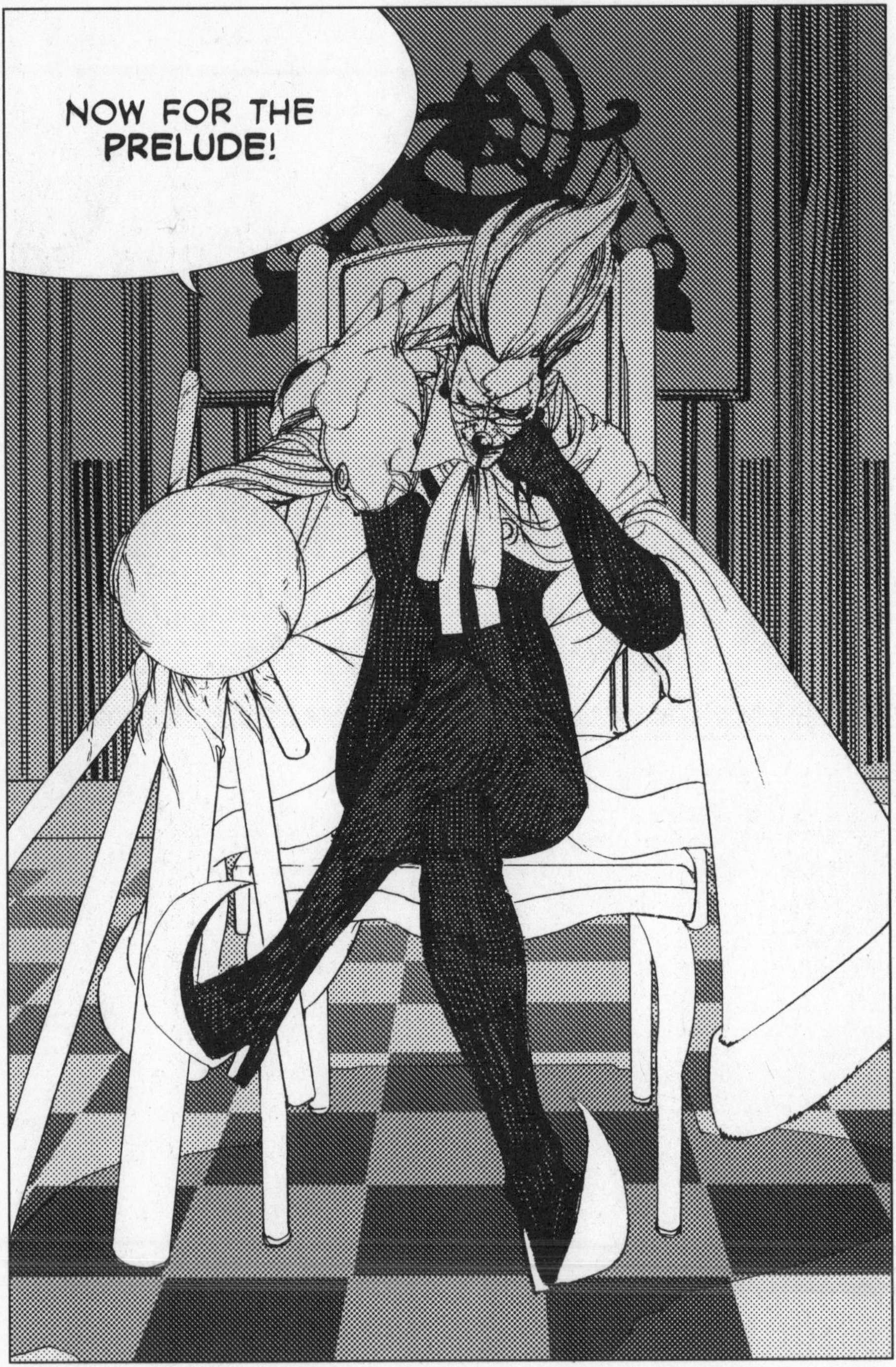
NOW FOR THE PRELUDE!

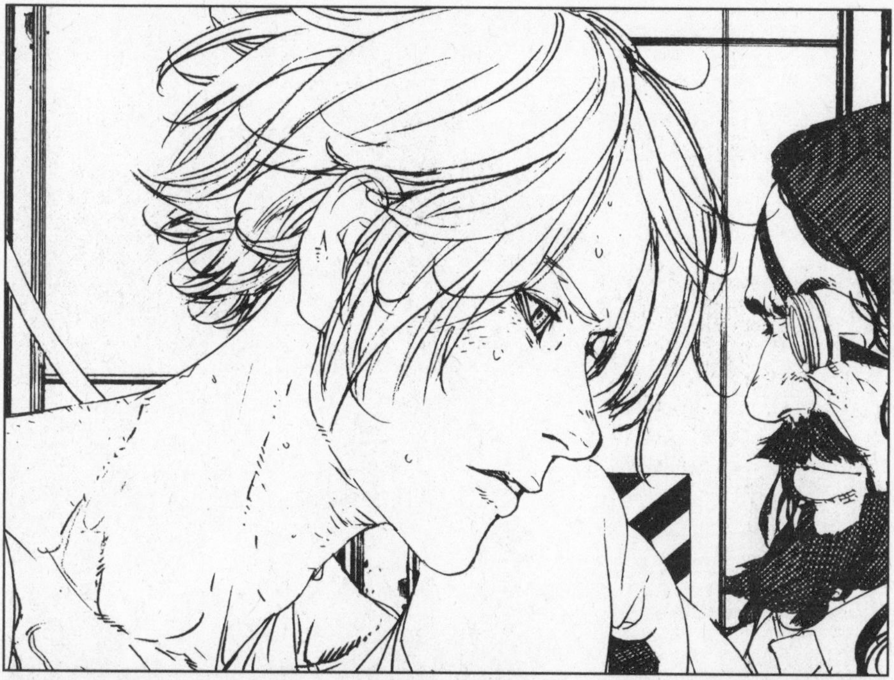

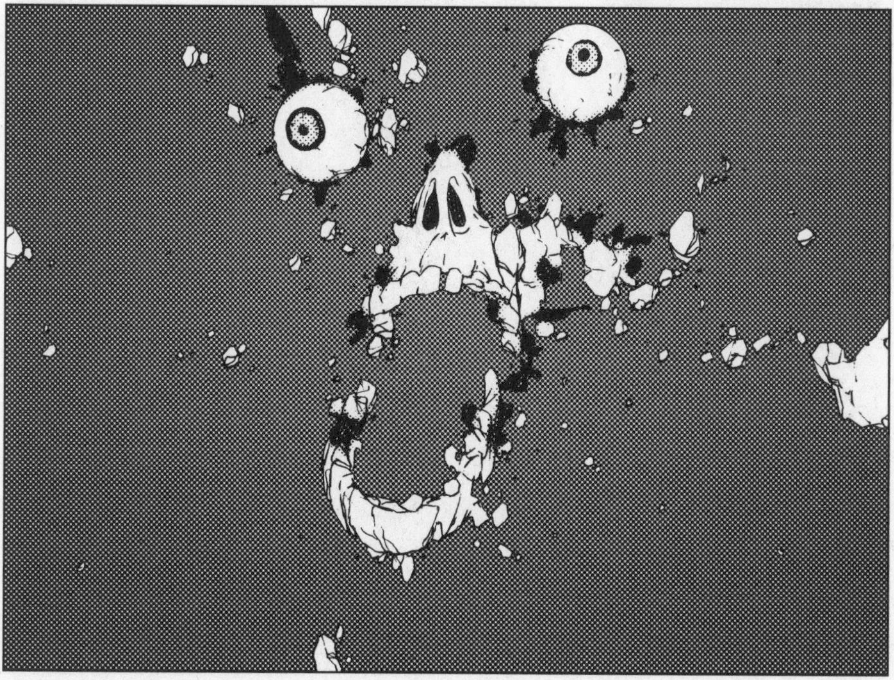

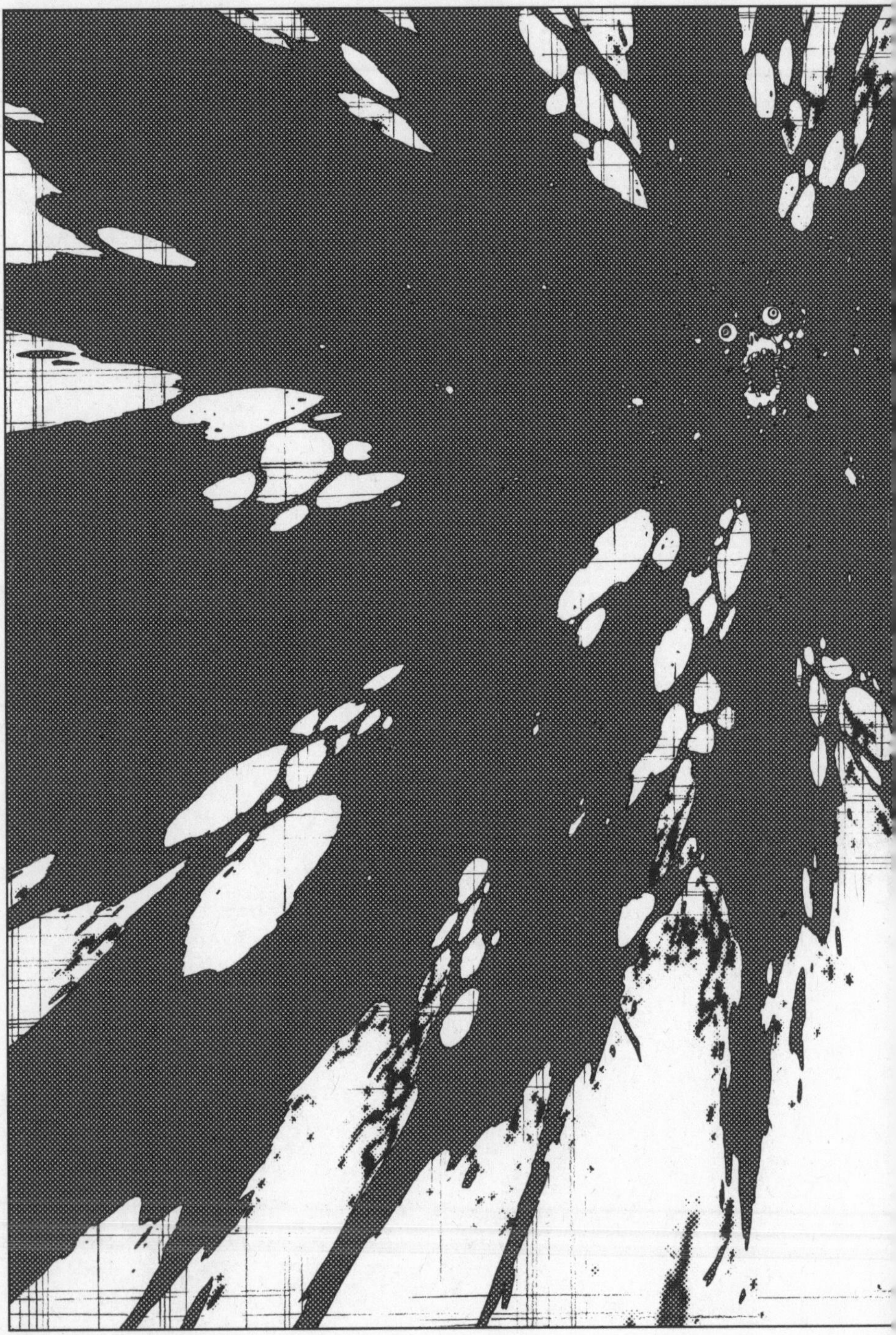

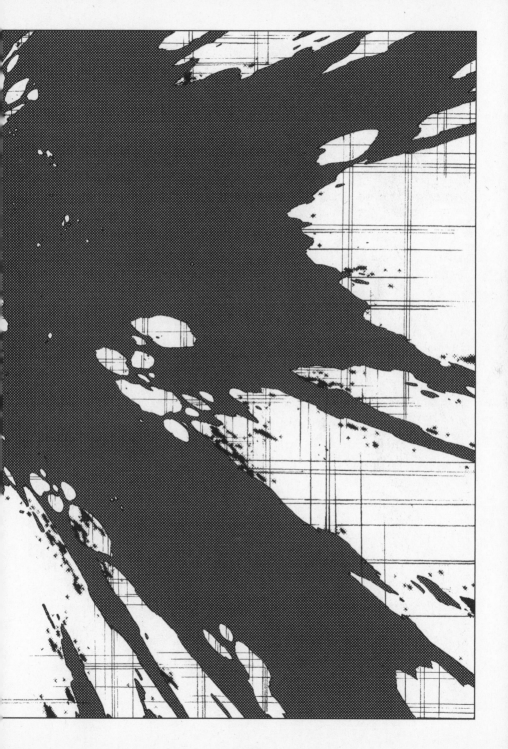

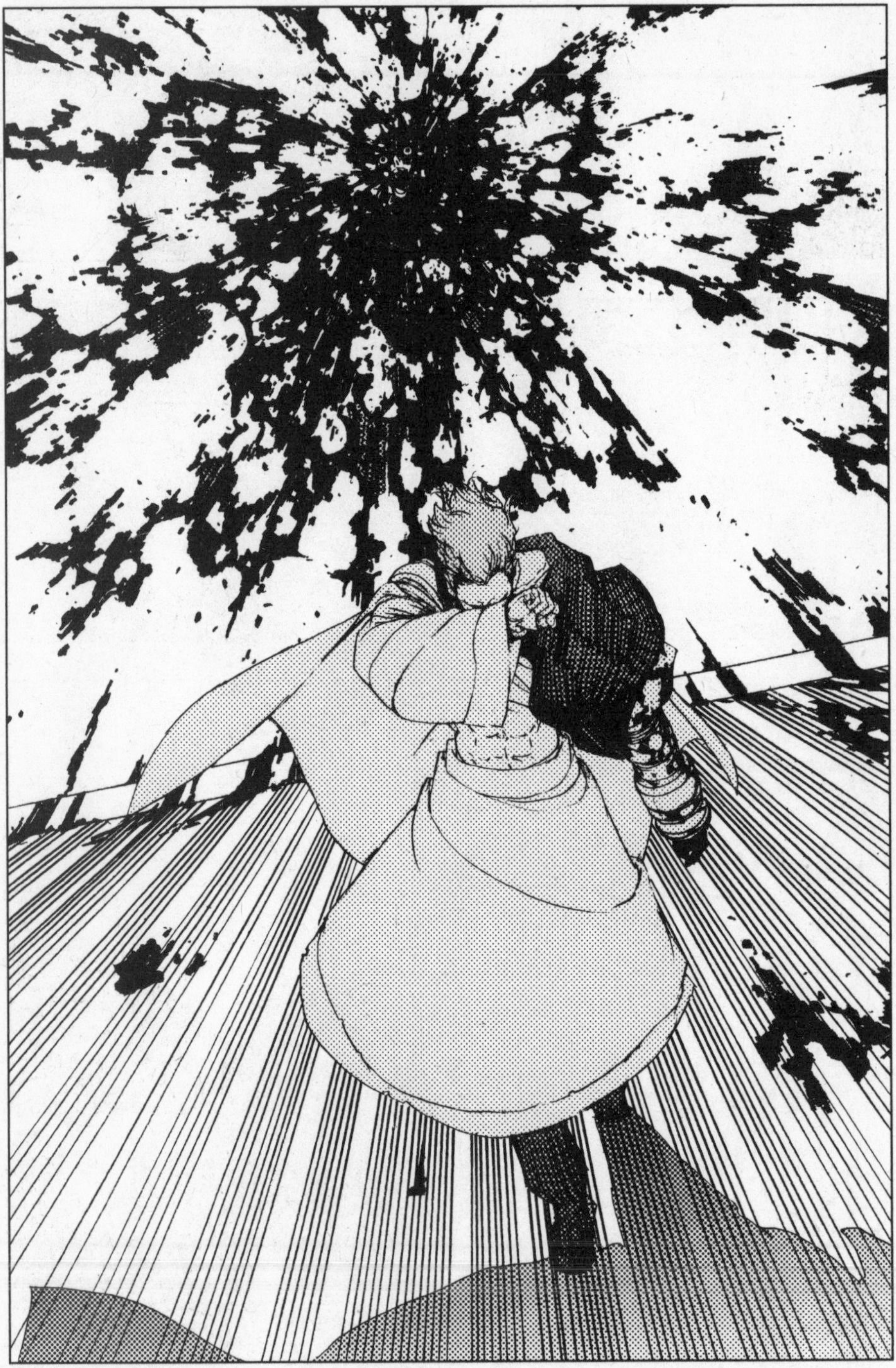

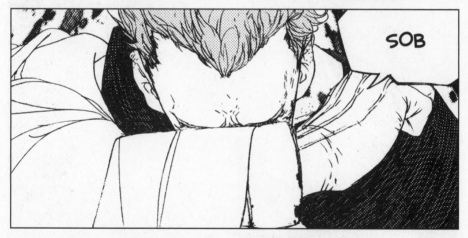

SOB

BAM

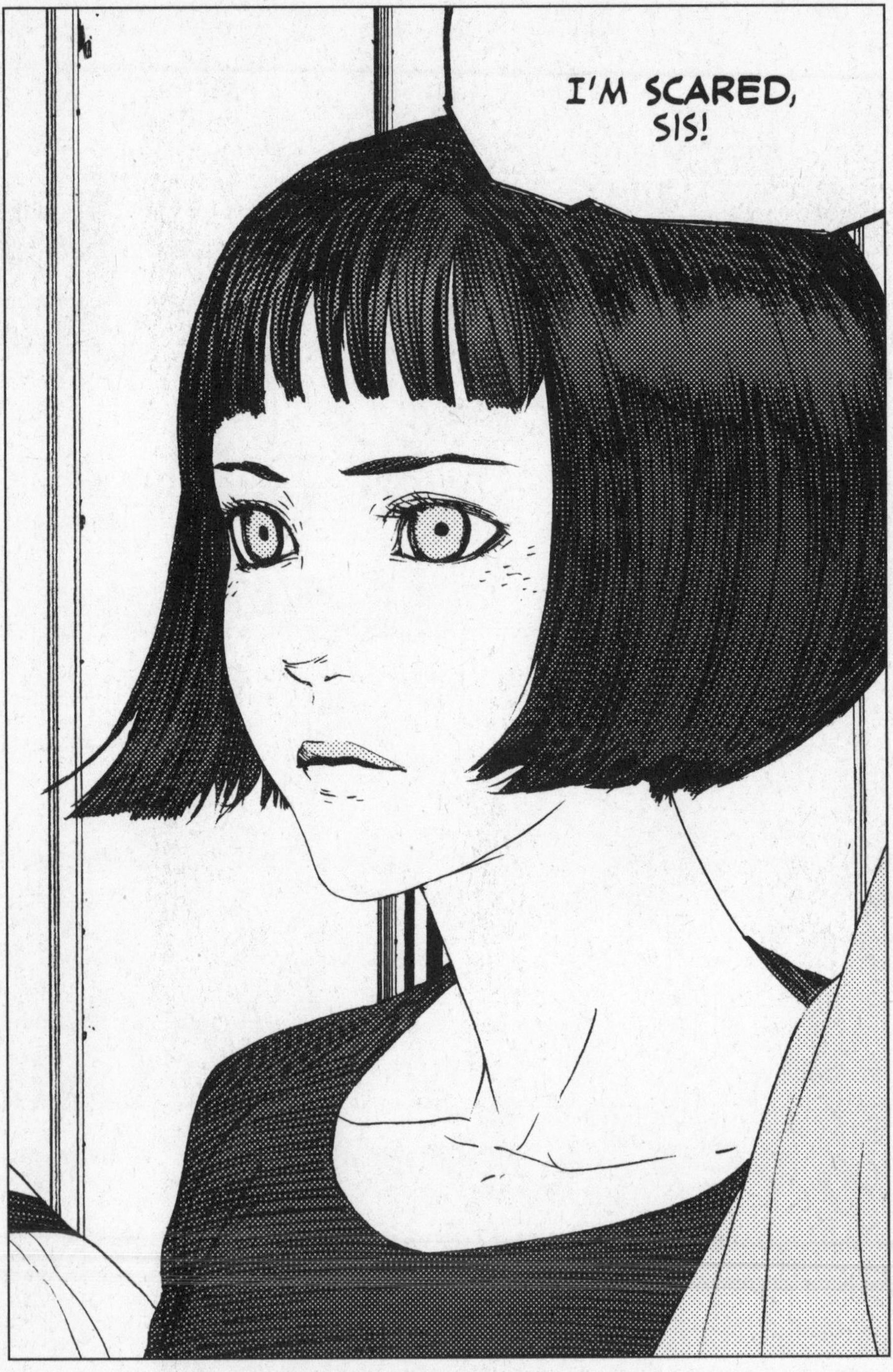
I'M SCARED, SIS!

Levius/est
VOL. 3

Chapter 15

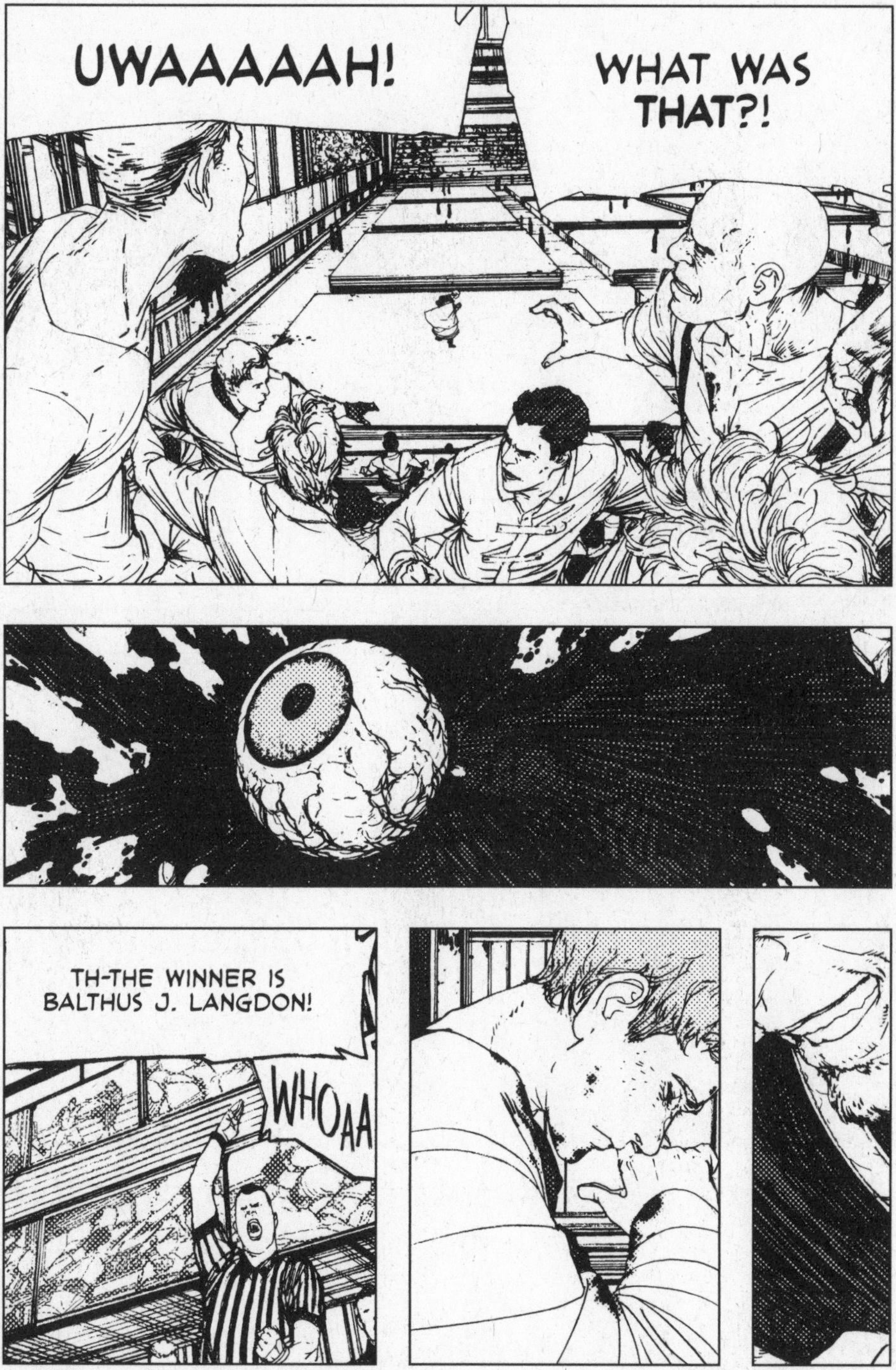
UWAAAAAH!
WHAT WAS THAT?!
TH-THE WINNER IS BALTHUS J. LANGDON!
WHOAA

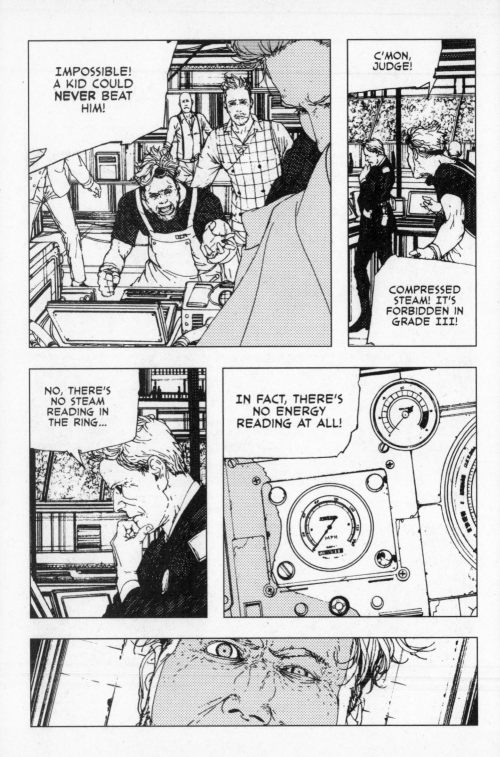

IMPOSSIBLE! A KID COULD **NEVER** BEAT HIM!

C'MON, JUDGE!

COMPRESSED STEAM! IT'S FORBIDDEN IN GRADE III!

NO, THERE'S NO STEAM READING IN THE RING...

IN FACT, THERE'S NO ENERGY READING AT ALL!

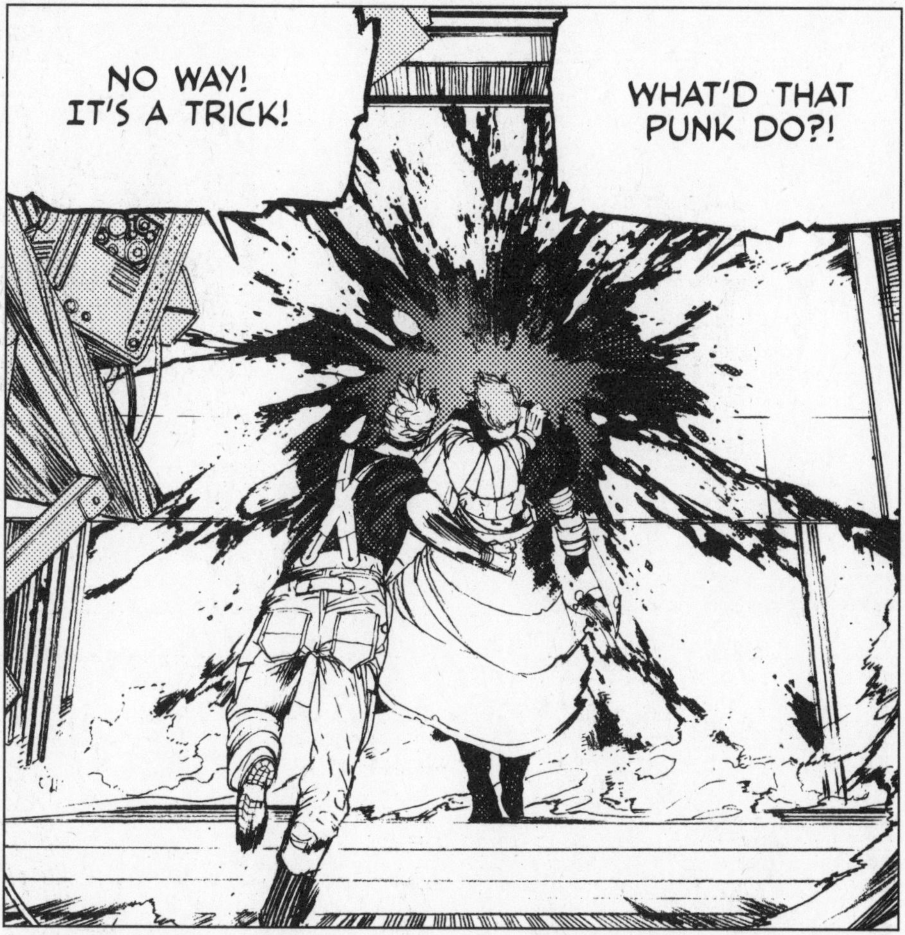
NO WAY! IT'S A TRICK!
WHAT'D THAT PUNK DO?!

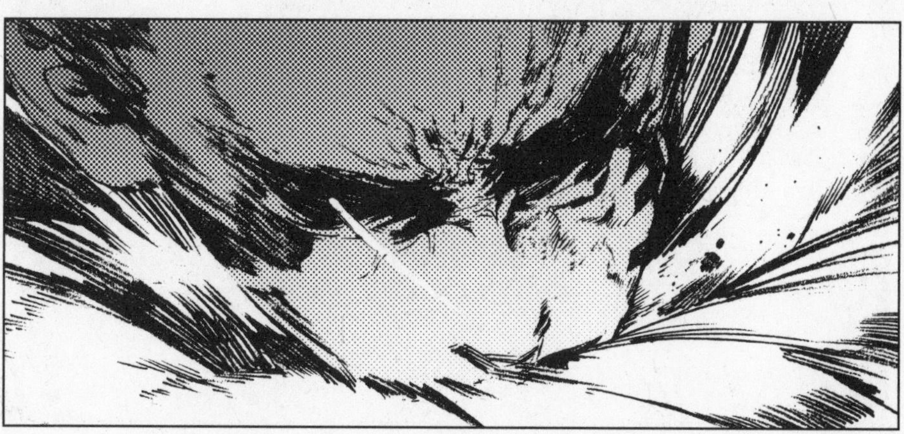

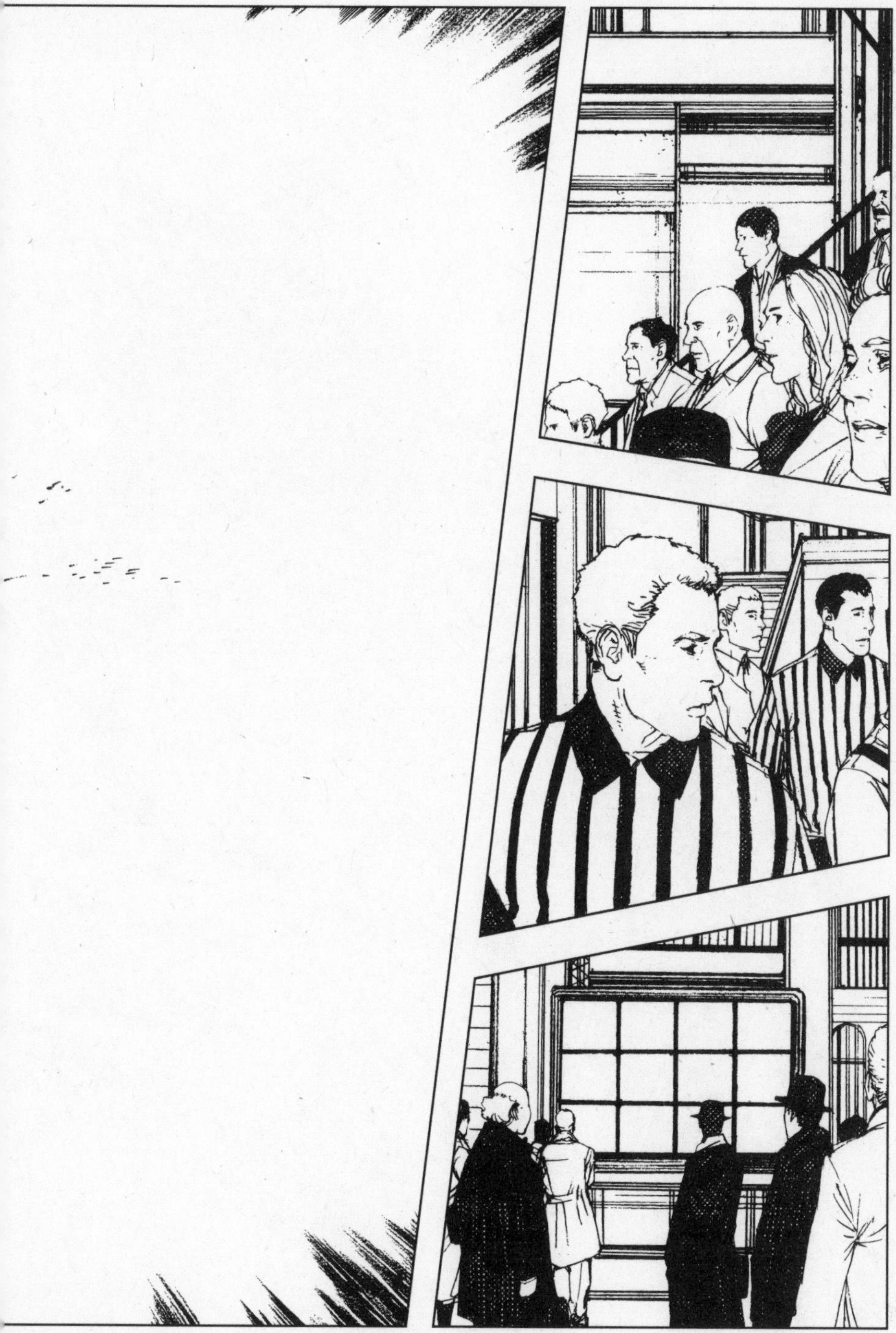

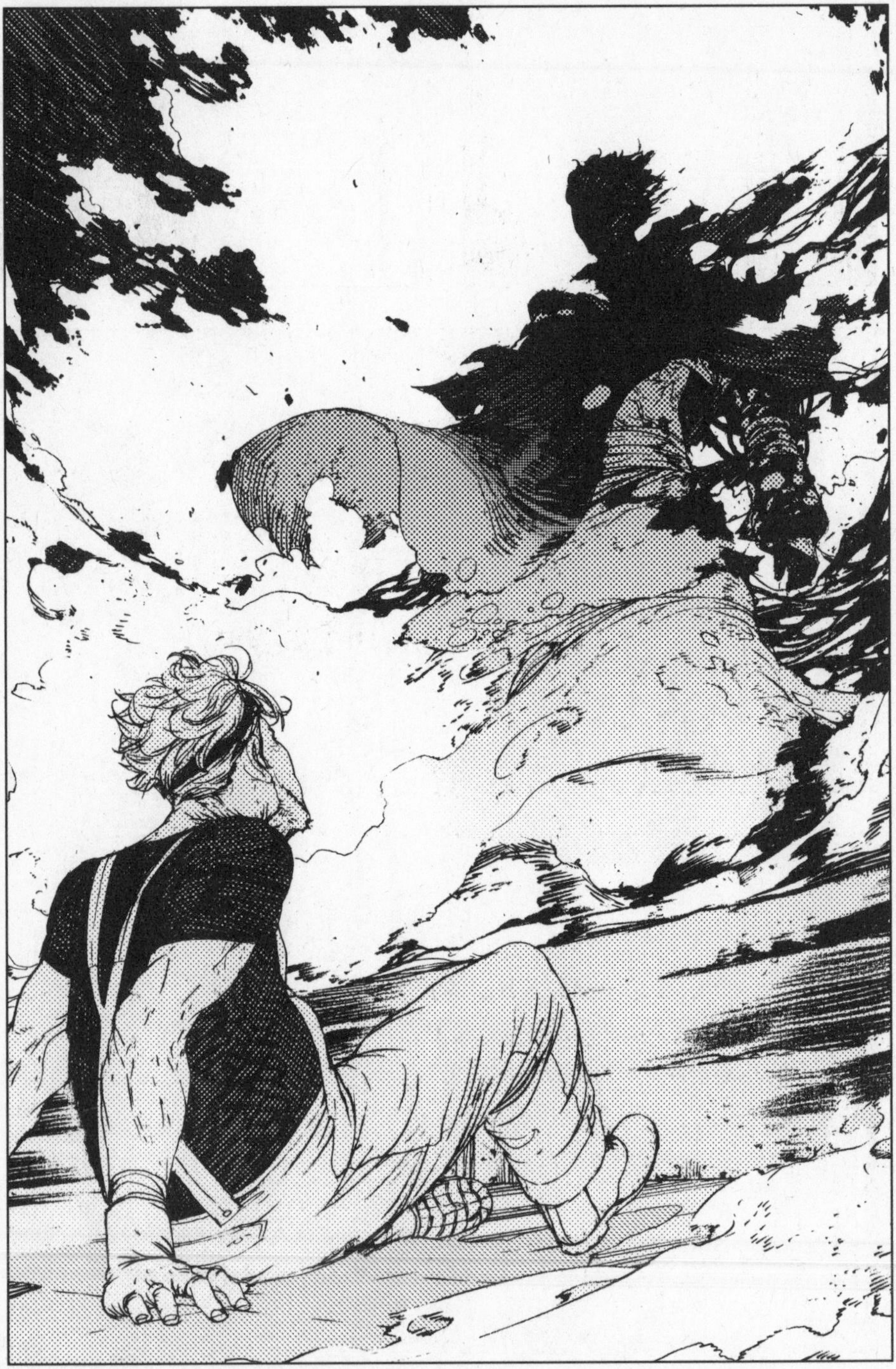

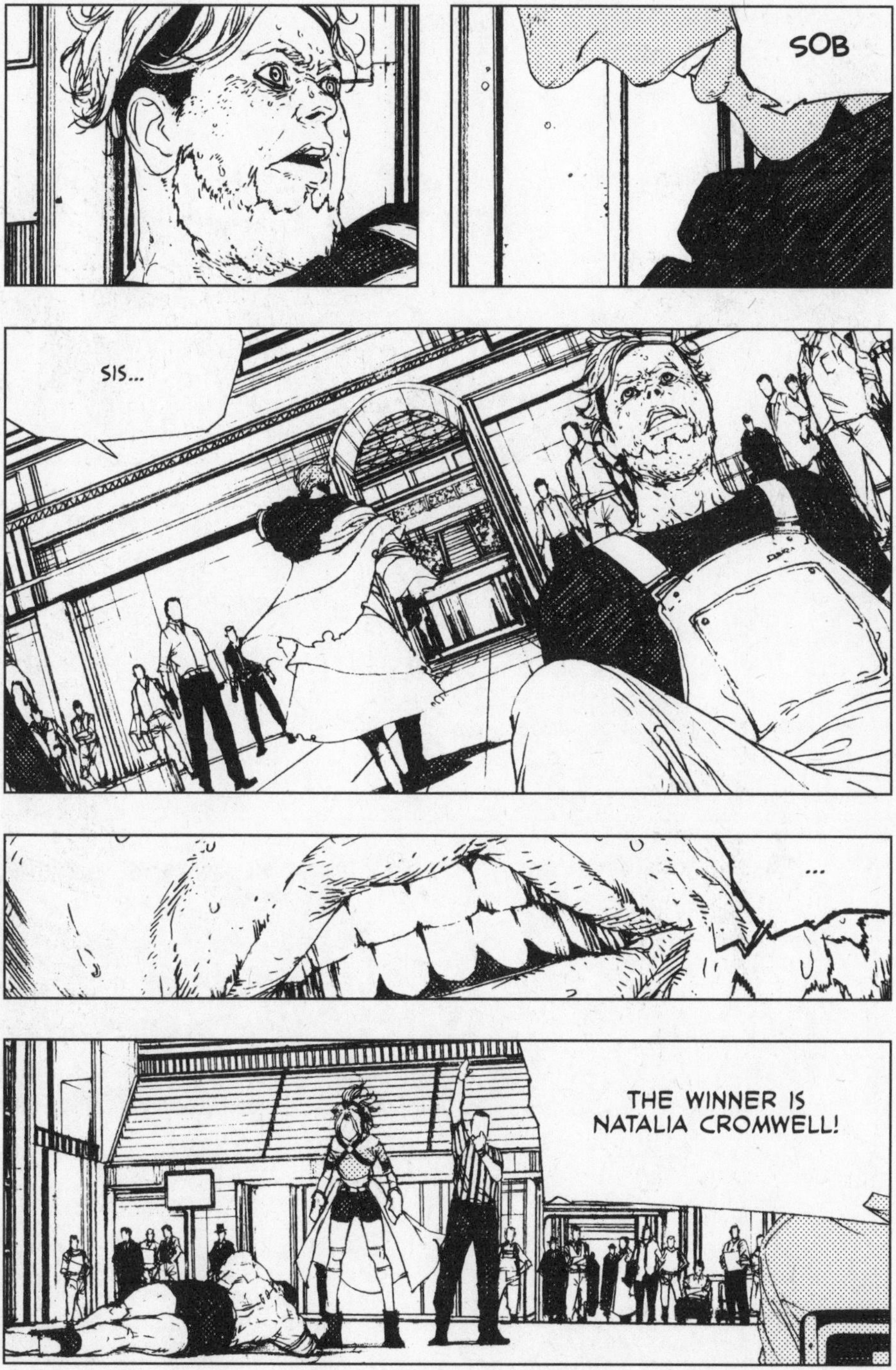
SOB
SIS...
...
THE WINNER IS NATALIA CROMWELL!

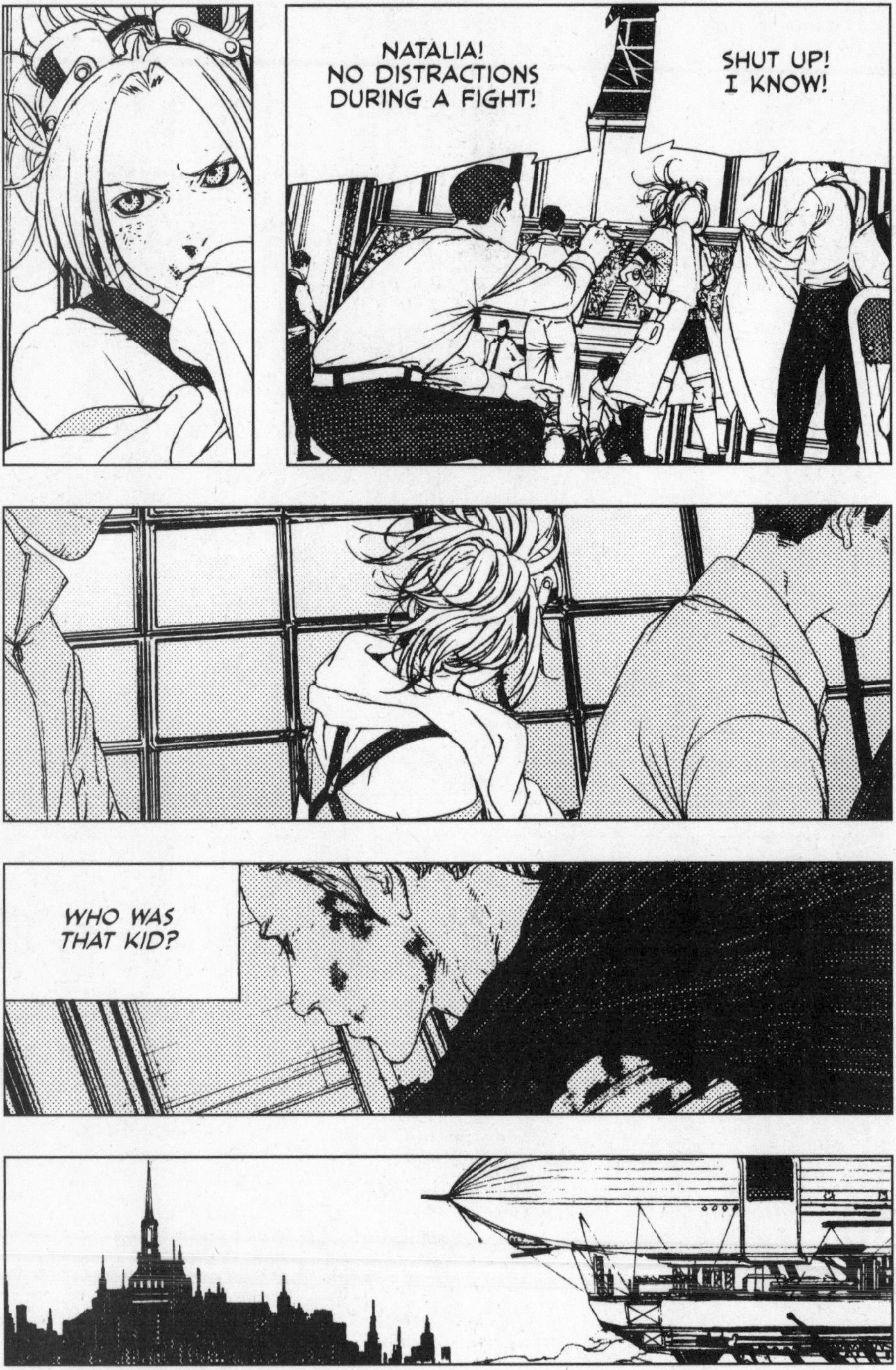
NATALIA! NO DISTRACTIONS DURING A FIGHT!
SHUT UP! I KNOW!
WHO WAS THAT KID?

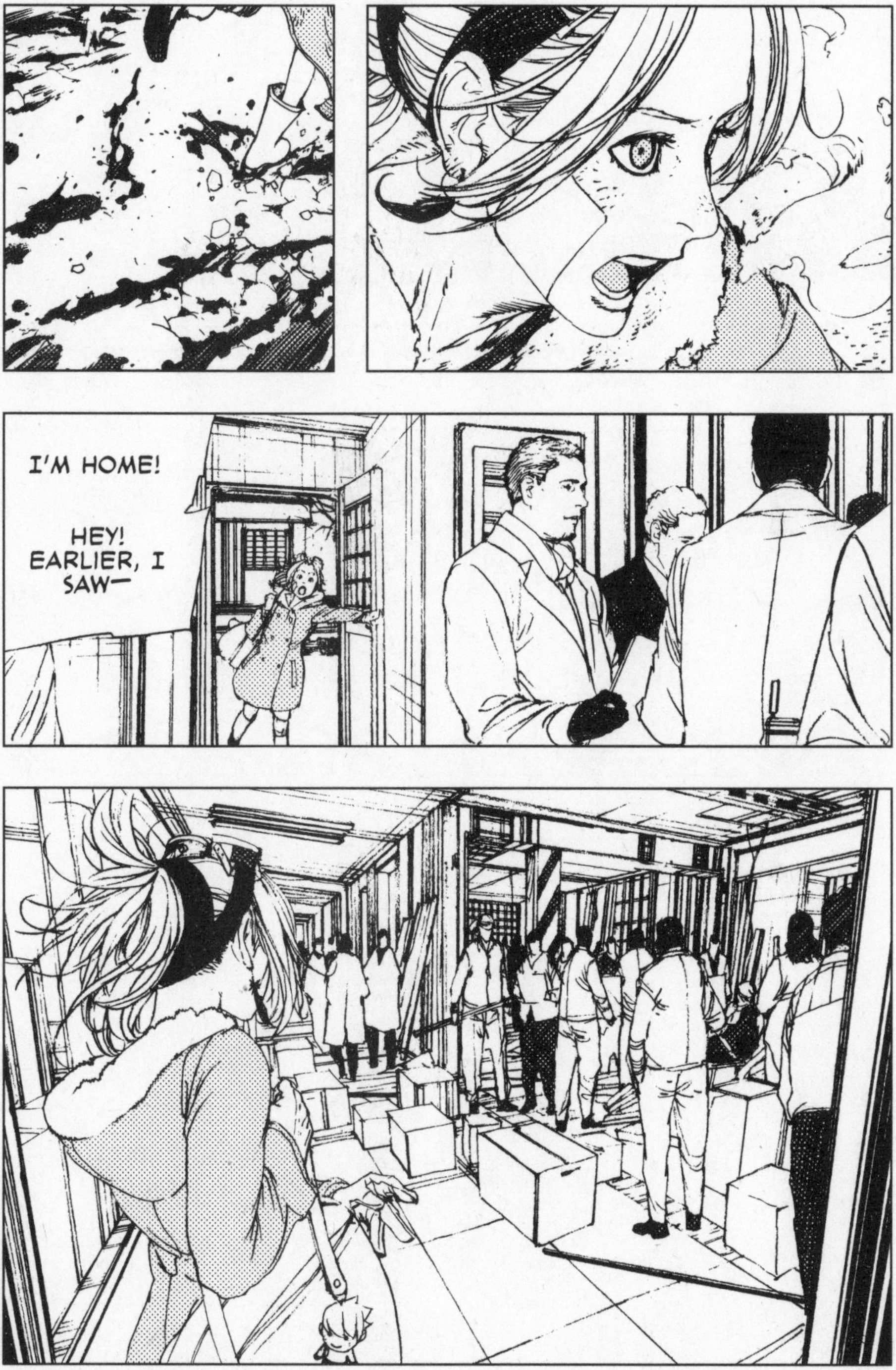
I'M HOME!
HEY! EARLIER, I SAW—

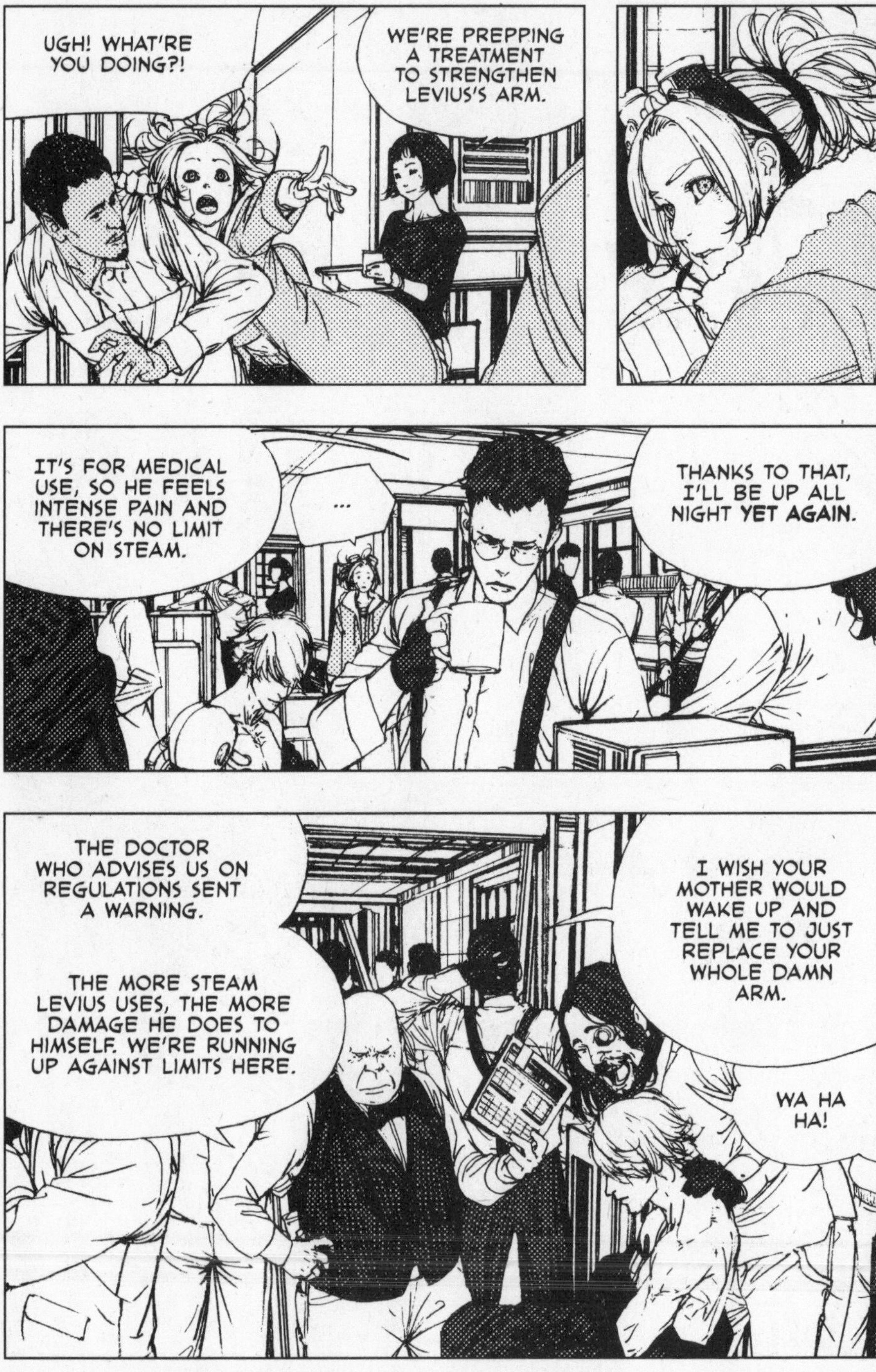
UGH! WHAT'RE YOU DOING?!
WE'RE PREPPING A TREATMENT TO STRENGTHEN LEVIUS'S ARM.
IT'S FOR MEDICAL USE, SO HE FEELS INTENSE PAIN AND THERE'S NO LIMIT ON STEAM.
...
THANKS TO THAT, I'LL BE UP ALL NIGHT **YET AGAIN**.
THE DOCTOR WHO ADVISES US ON REGULATIONS SENT A WARNING.
THE MORE STEAM LEVIUS USES, THE MORE DAMAGE HE DOES TO HIMSELF. WE'RE RUNNING UP AGAINST LIMITS HERE.
I WISH YOUR MOTHER WOULD WAKE UP AND TELL ME TO JUST REPLACE YOUR WHOLE DAMN ARM.
WA HA HA!

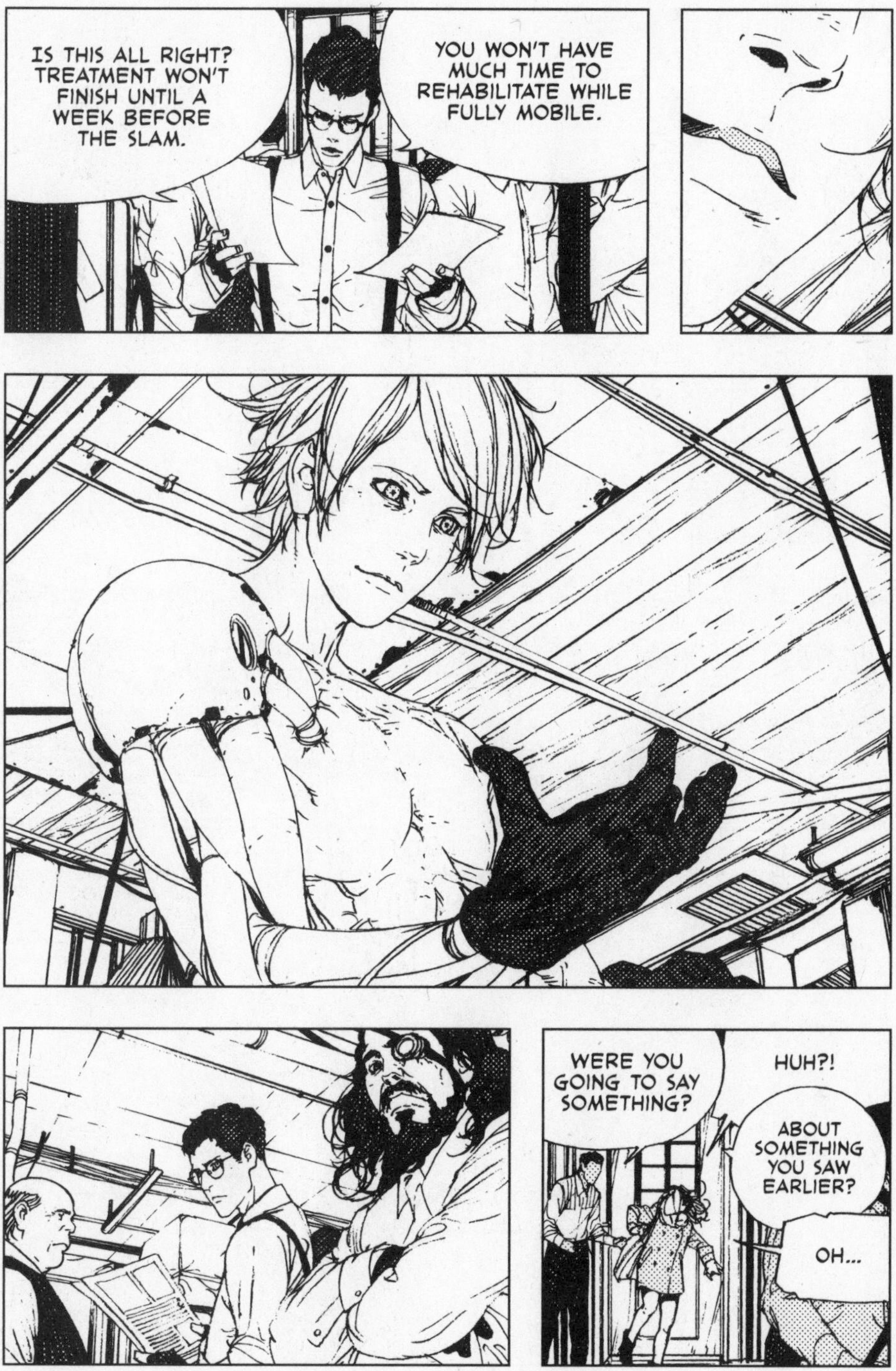
IS THIS ALL RIGHT? TREATMENT WON'T FINISH UNTIL A WEEK BEFORE THE SLAM.
YOU WON'T HAVE MUCH TIME TO REHABILITATE WHILE FULLY MOBILE.
WERE YOU GOING TO SAY SOMETHING?
HUH?!
ABOUT SOMETHING YOU SAW EARLIER?
OH...

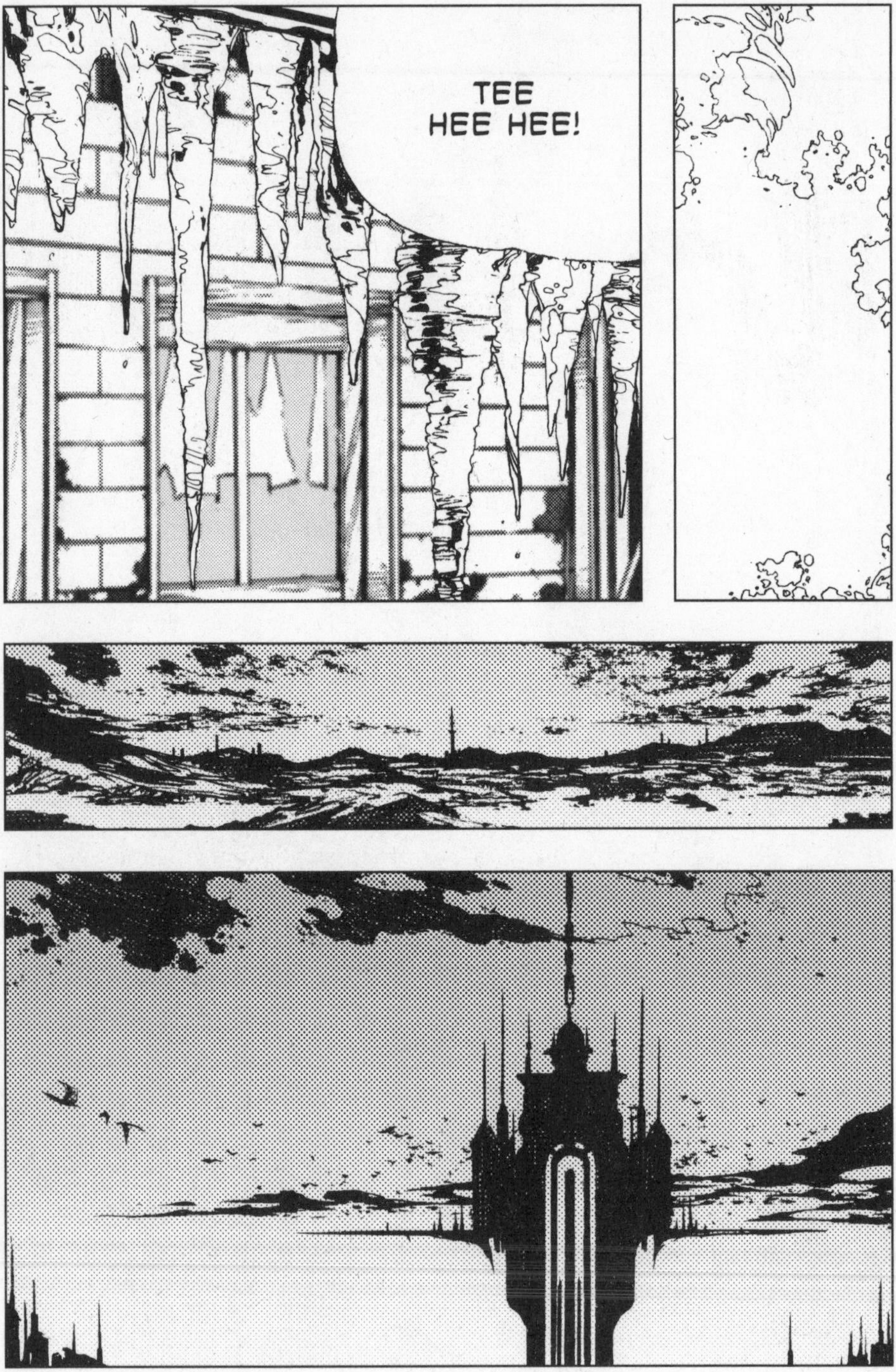
TEE HEE HEE!

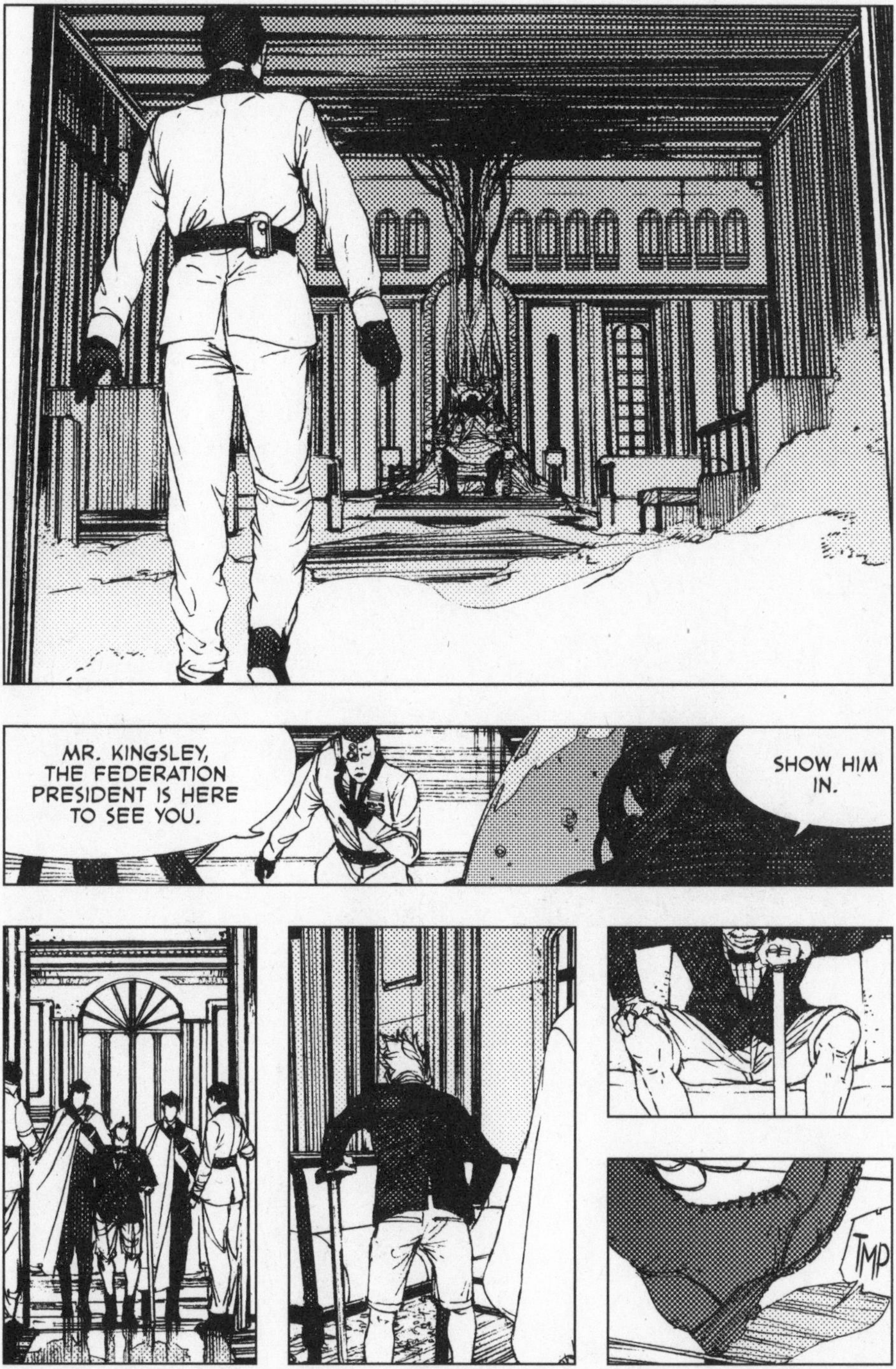
MR. KINGSLEY, THE FEDERATION PRESIDENT IS HERE TO SEE YOU.
SHOW HIM IN.
TMP

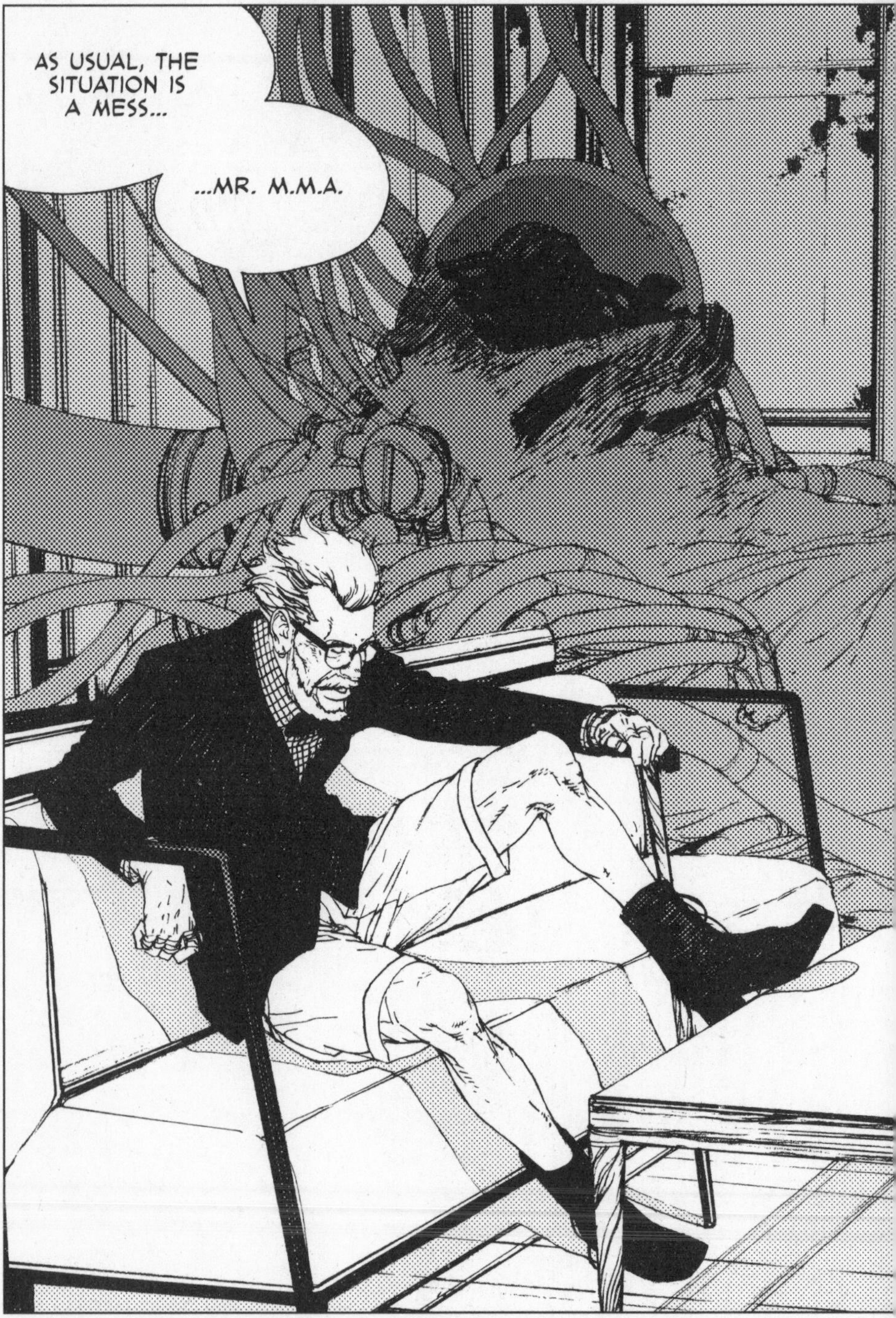
AS USUAL, THE SITUATION IS A MESS...
...MR. M.M.A.

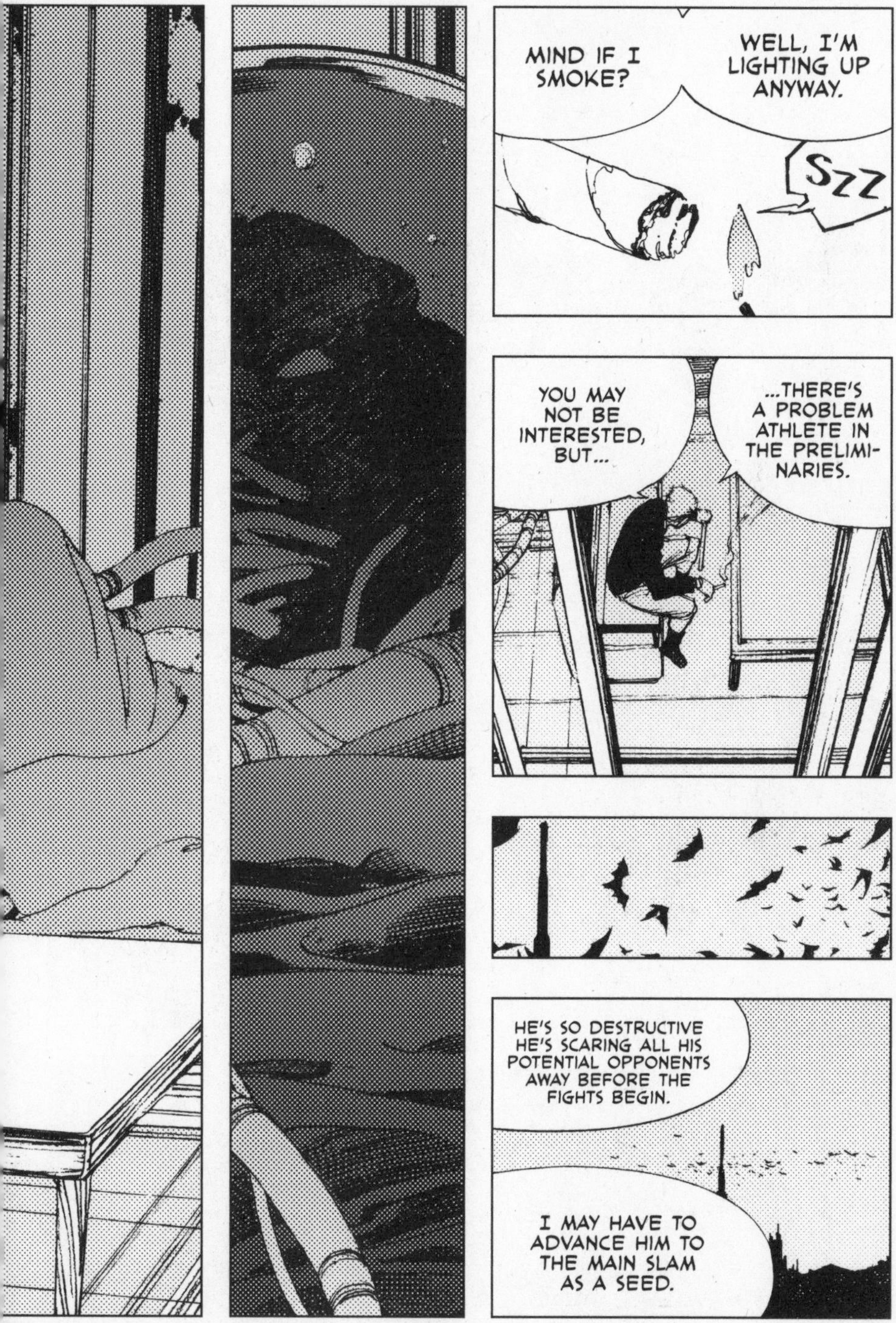
MIND IF I SMOKE?
WELL, I'M LIGHTING UP ANYWAY.
SZZ
YOU MAY NOT BE INTERESTED, BUT...
...THERE'S A PROBLEM ATHLETE IN THE PRELIMI-NARIES.
HE'S SO DESTRUCTIVE HE'S SCARING ALL HIS POTENTIAL OPPONENTS AWAY BEFORE THE FIGHTS BEGIN.
I MAY HAVE TO ADVANCE HIM TO THE MAIN SLAM AS A SEED.

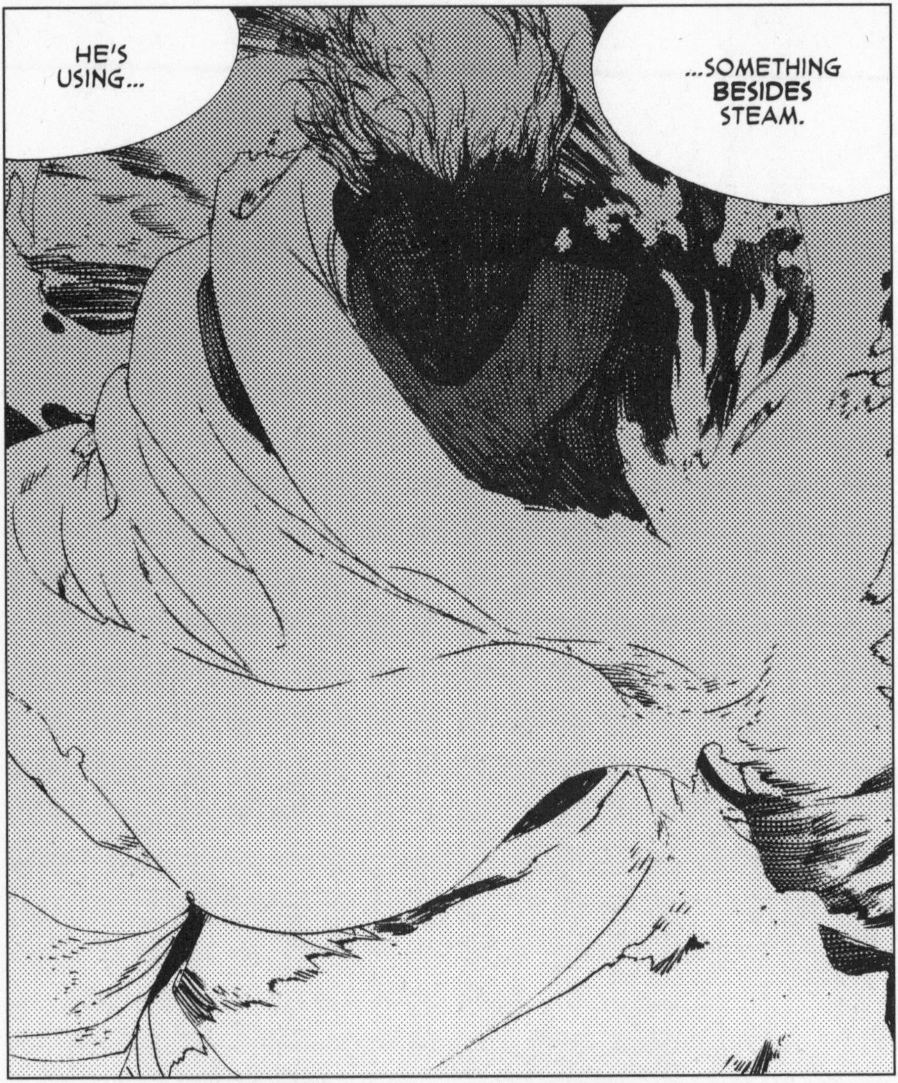
HE'S USING...
...SOMETHING BESIDES STEAM.
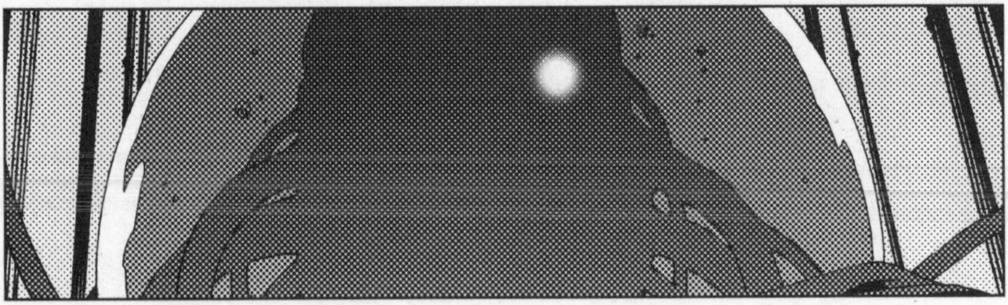

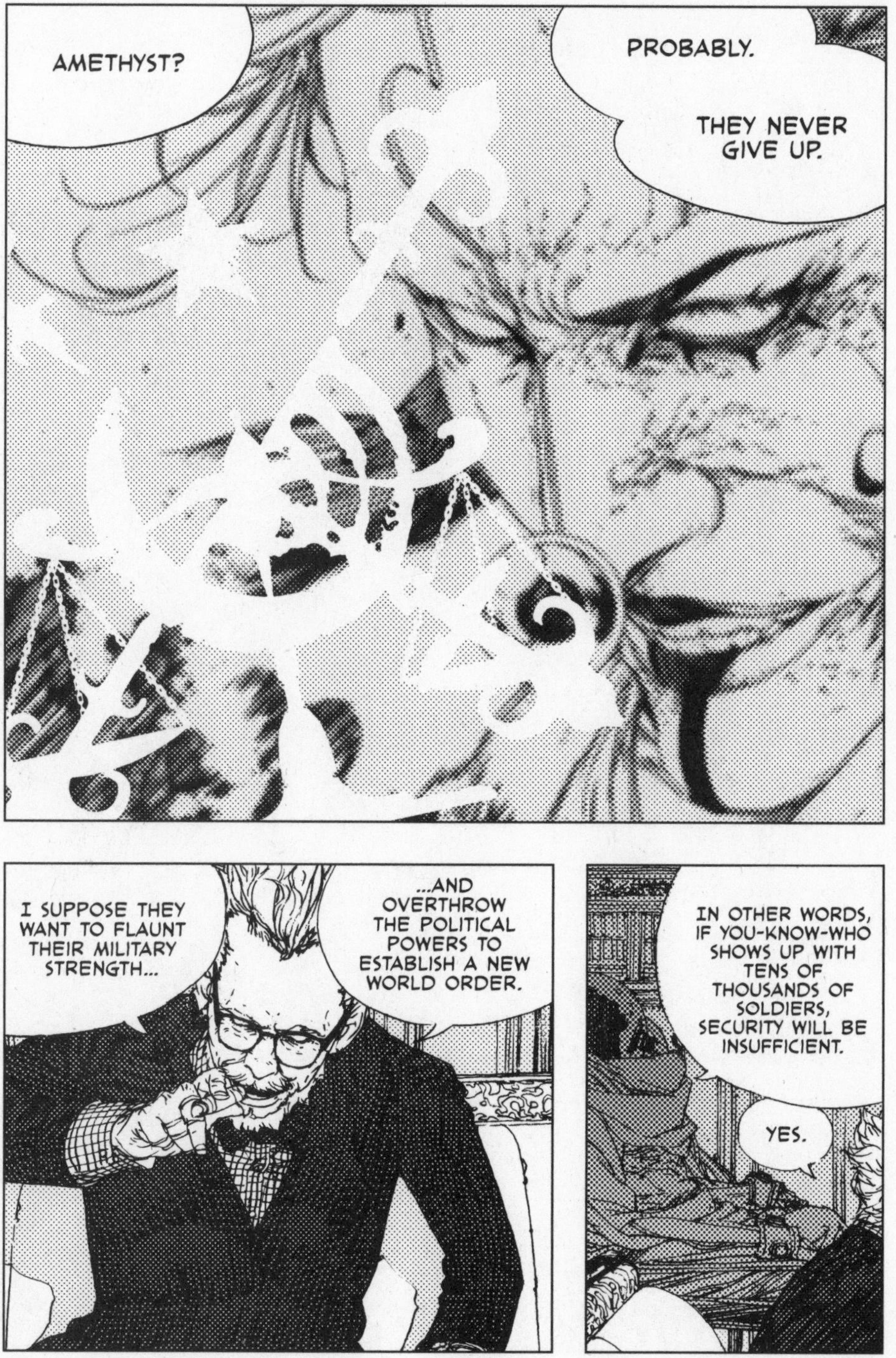
AMETHYST?
PROBABLY.
THEY NEVER GIVE UP.
I SUPPOSE THEY WANT TO FLAUNT THEIR MILITARY STRENGTH...
...AND OVERTHROW THE POLITICAL POWERS TO ESTABLISH A NEW WORLD ORDER.
IN OTHER WORDS, IF YOU-KNOW-WHO SHOWS UP WITH TENS OF THOUSANDS OF SOLDIERS, SECURITY WILL BE INSUFFICIENT.
YES.

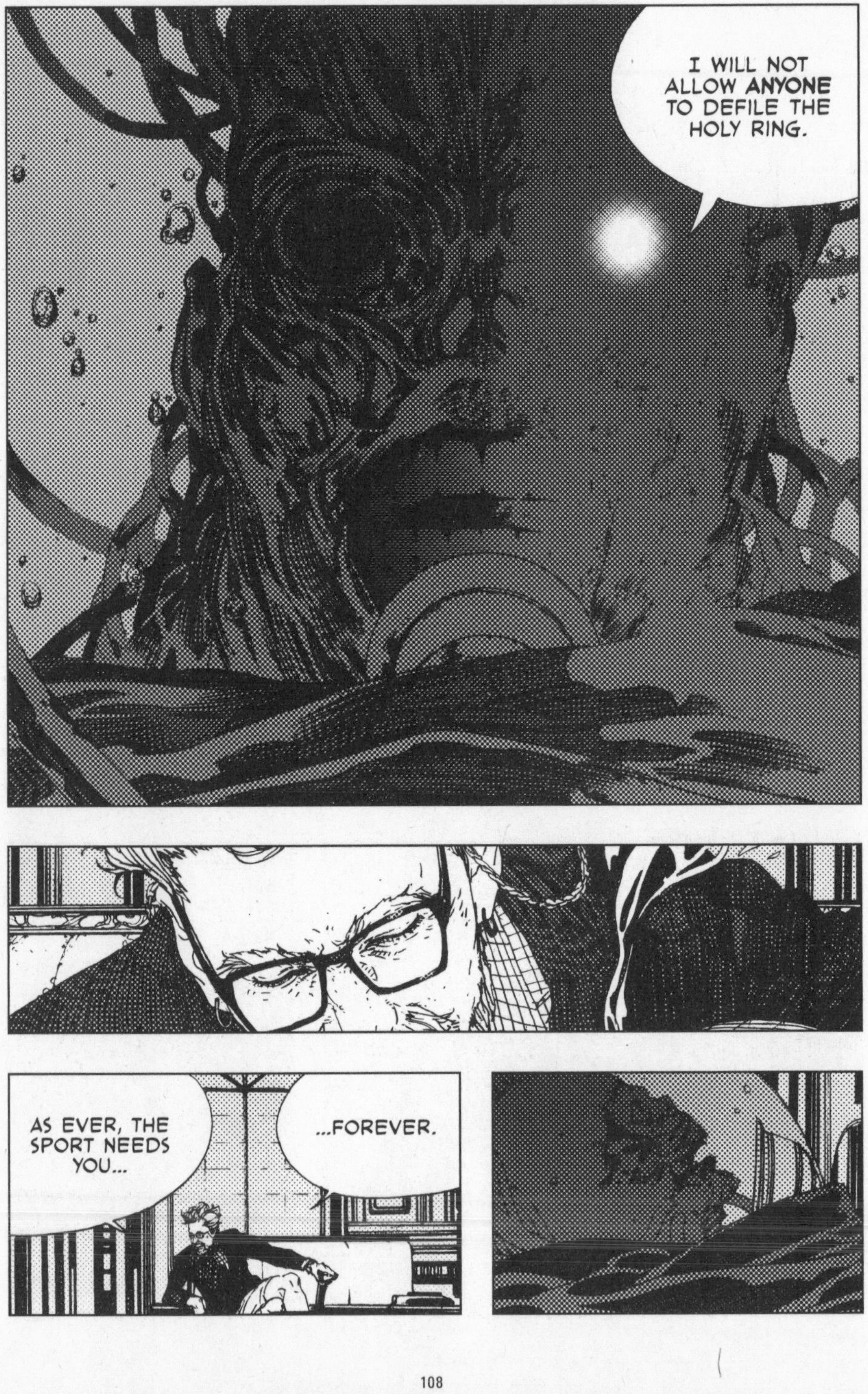
I WILL NOT ALLOW **ANYONE** TO DEFILE THE HOLY RING.
AS EVER, THE SPORT NEEDS YOU...
...FOREVER.

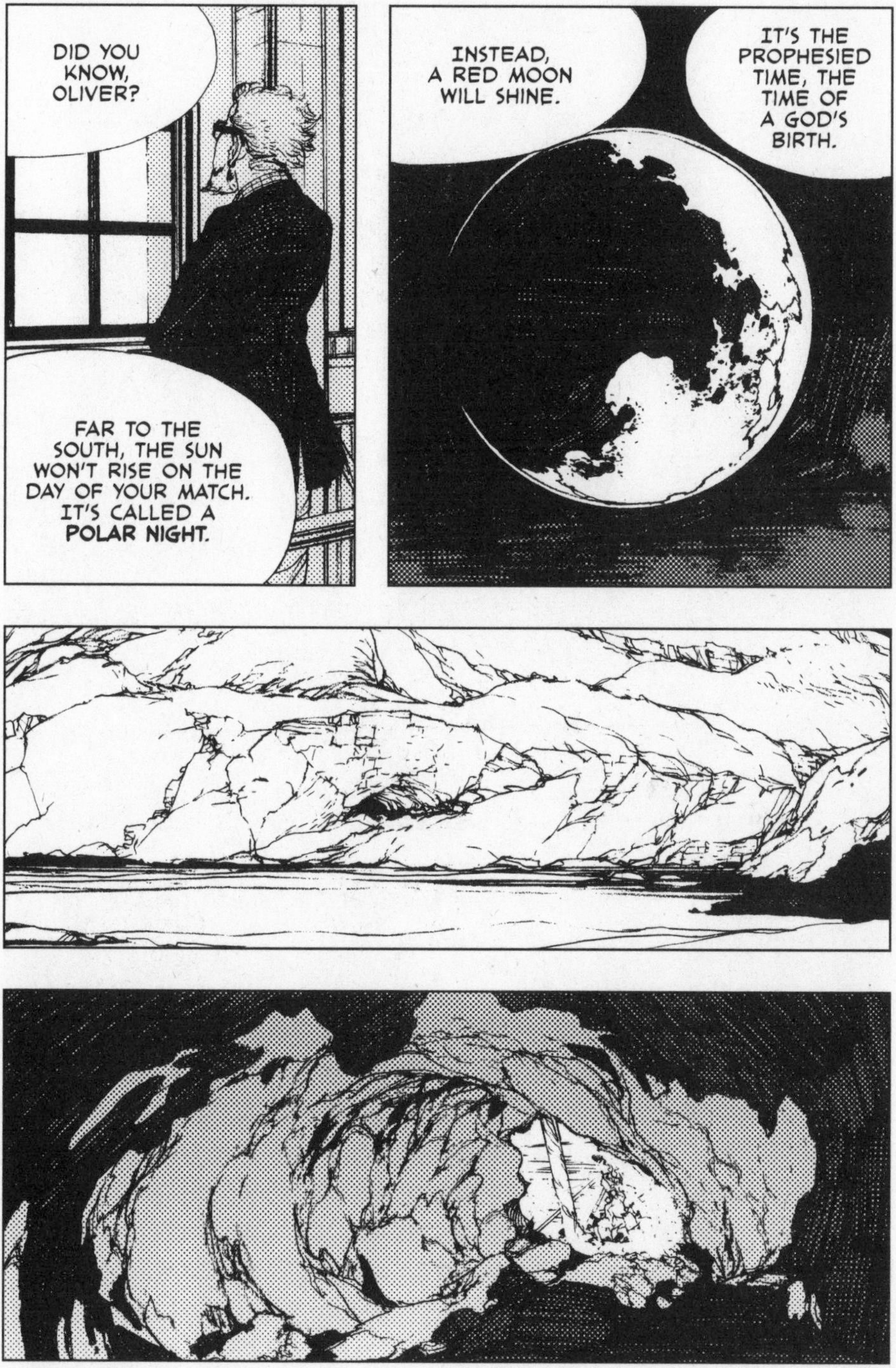
DID YOU KNOW, OLIVER?
FAR TO THE SOUTH, THE SUN WON'T RISE ON THE DAY OF YOUR MATCH. IT'S CALLED A **POLAR NIGHT.**
INSTEAD, A RED MOON WILL SHINE.
IT'S THE PROPHESIED TIME, THE TIME OF A GOD'S BIRTH.

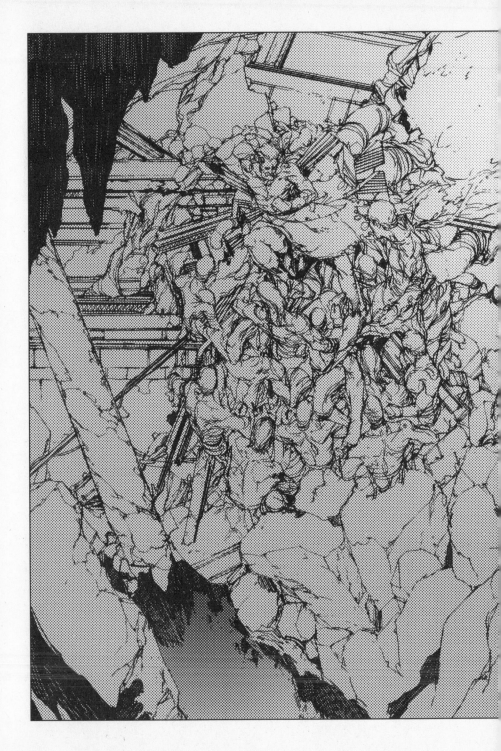

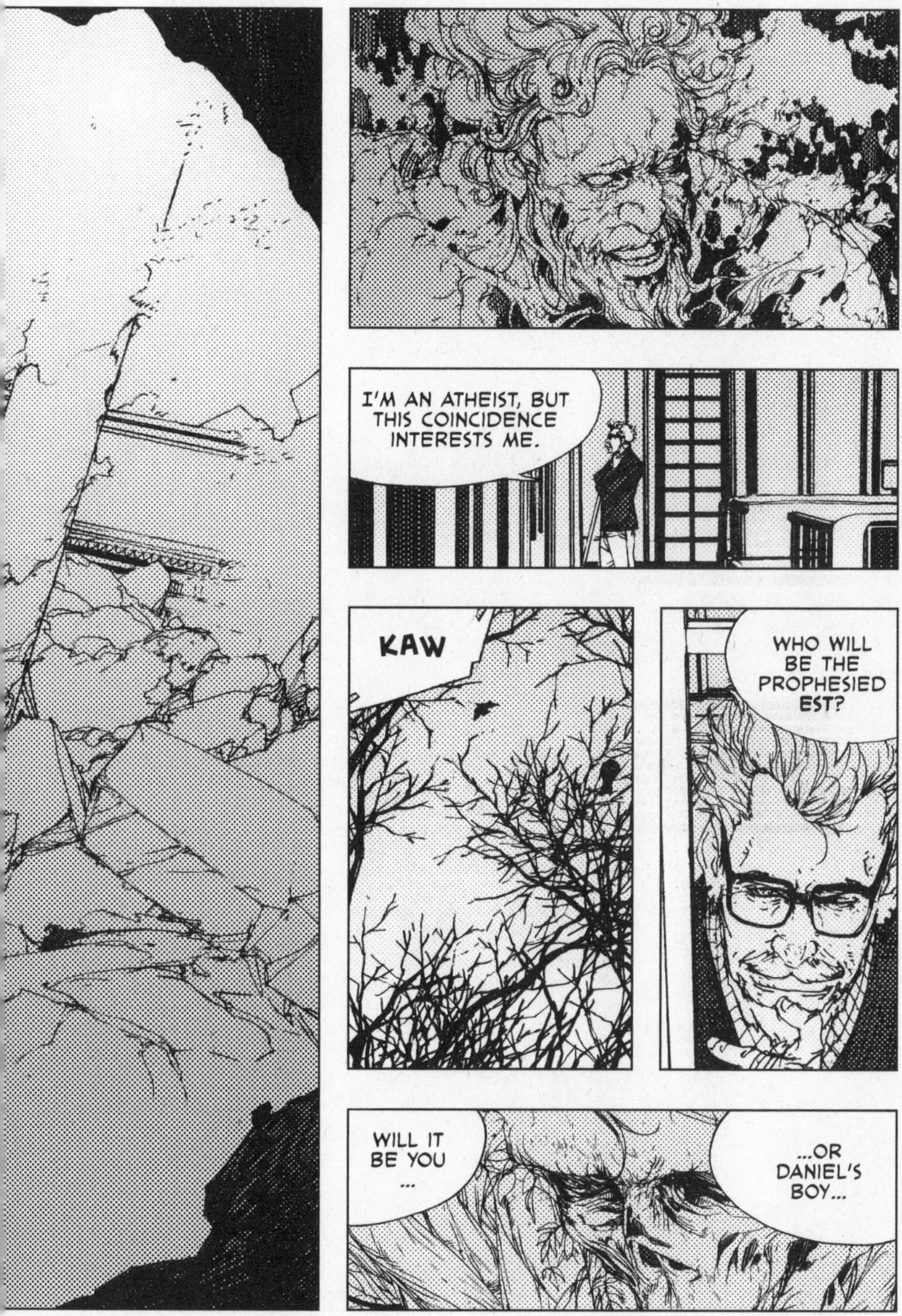
I'M AN ATHEIST, BUT THIS COINCIDENCE INTERESTS ME.
KAW
WHO WILL BE THE PROPHESIED EST?
WILL IT BE YOU ...
...OR DANIEL'S BOY...

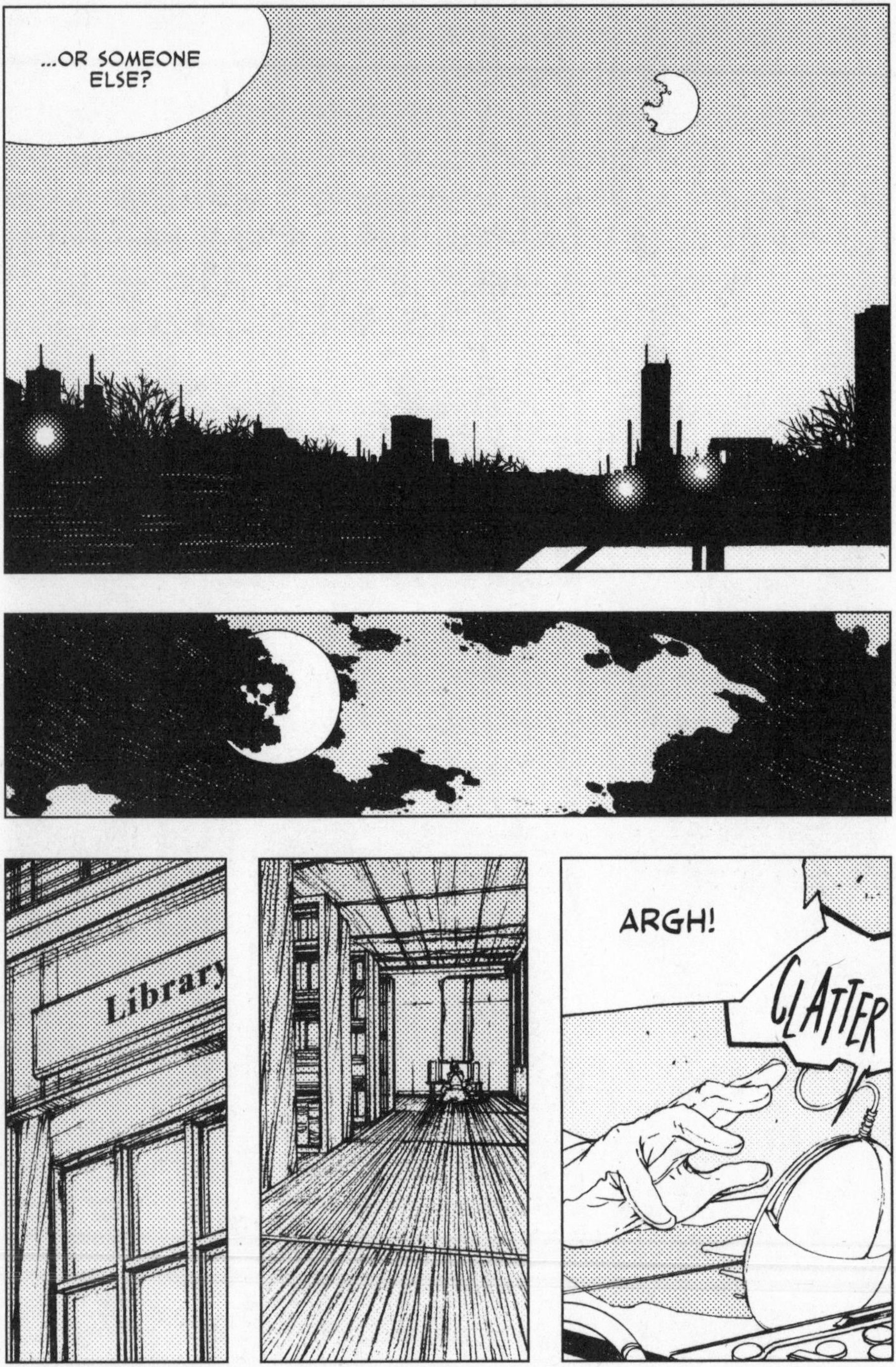
...OR SOMEONE ELSE?
Library
ARGH!
CLATTER

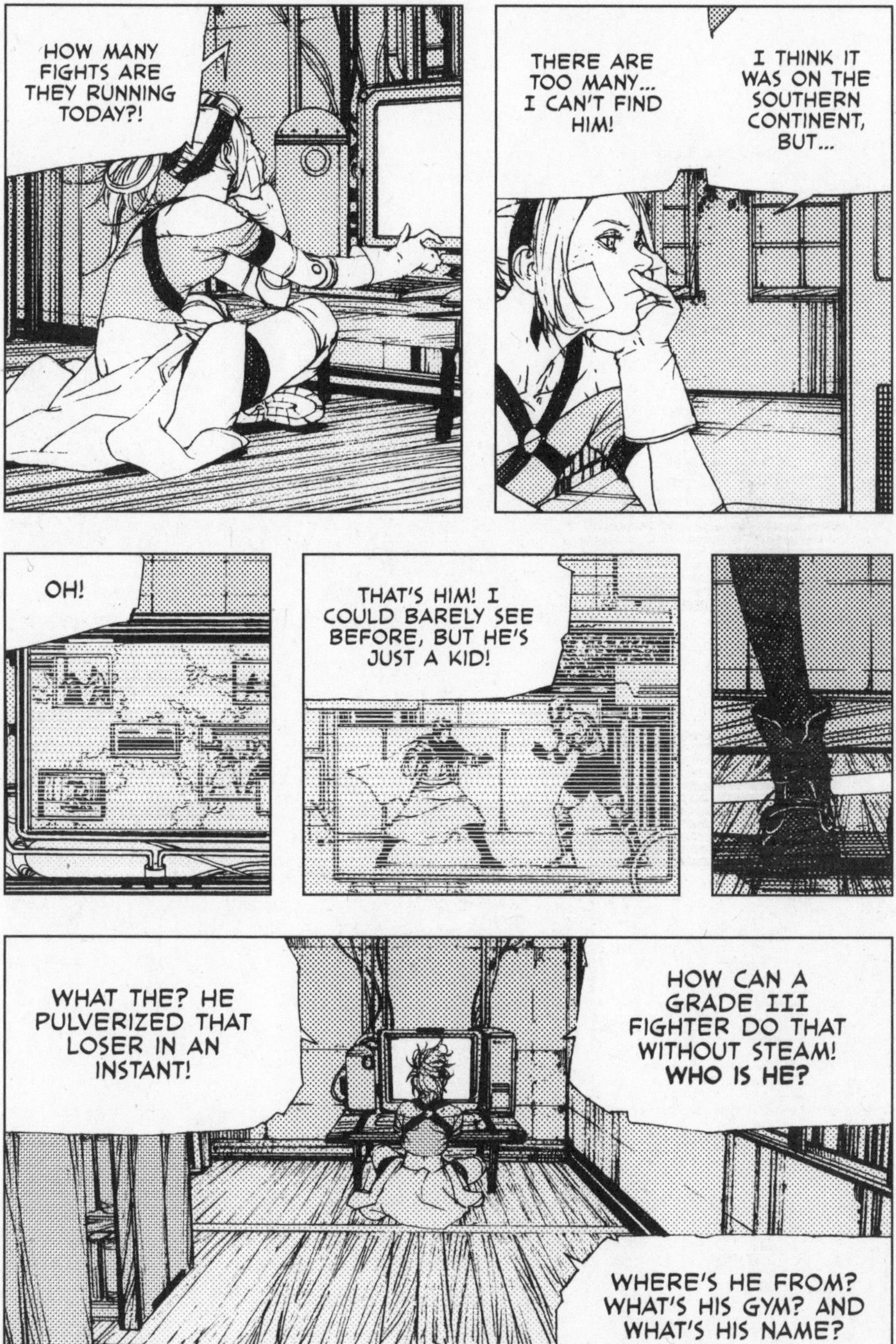
HOW MANY FIGHTS ARE THEY RUNNING TODAY?!
THERE ARE TOO MANY... I CAN'T FIND HIM!
I THINK IT WAS ON THE SOUTHERN CONTINENT, BUT...
OH!
THAT'S HIM! I COULD BARELY SEE BEFORE, BUT HE'S JUST A KID!
WHAT THE? HE PULVERIZED THAT LOSER IN AN INSTANT!
HOW CAN A GRADE III FIGHTER DO THAT WITHOUT STEAM! WHO IS HE?
WHERE'S HE FROM? WHAT'S HIS GYM? AND WHAT'S HIS NAME?

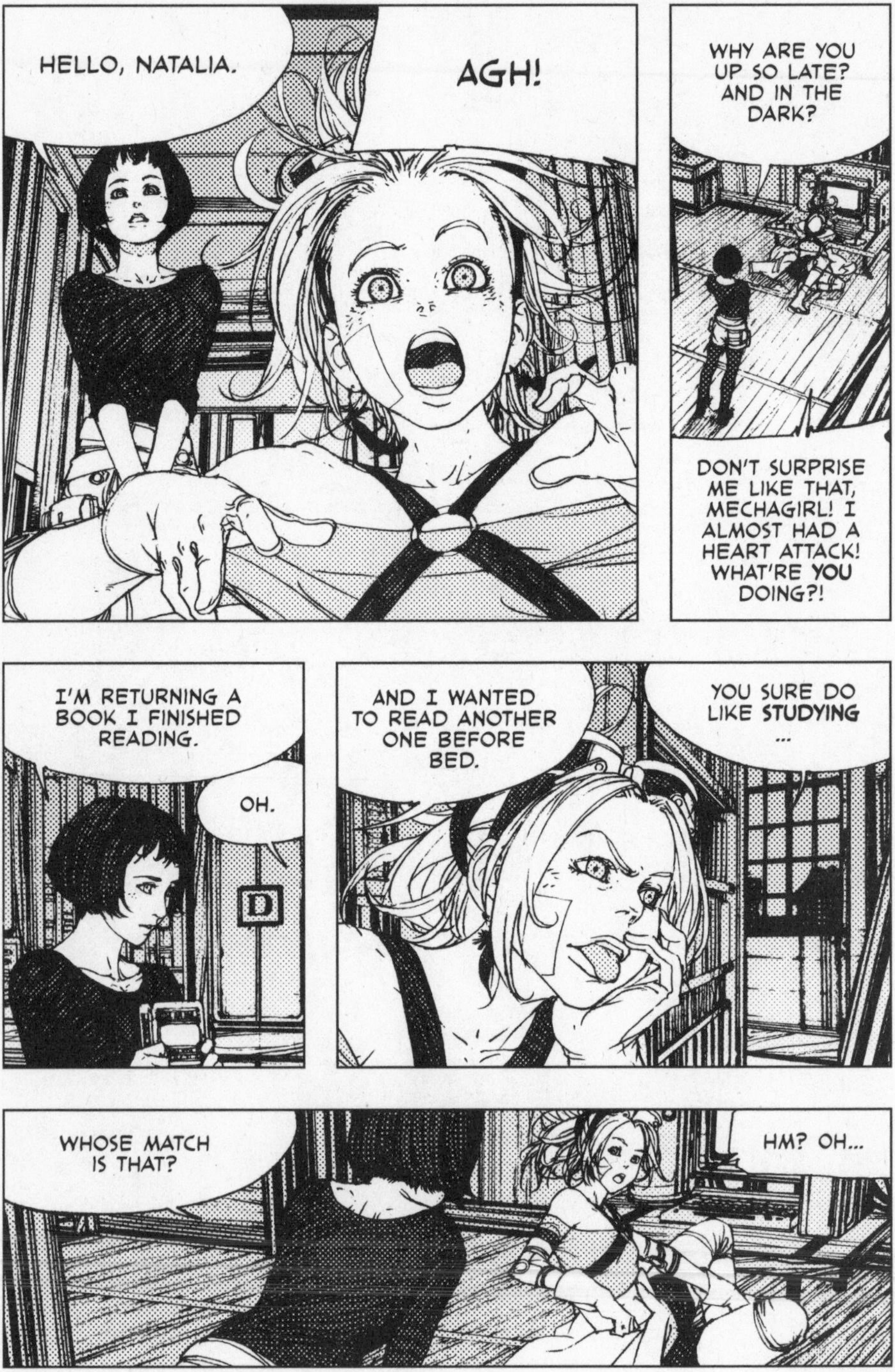
HELLO, NATALIA.
AGH!
WHY ARE YOU UP SO LATE? AND IN THE DARK?
DON'T SURPRISE ME LIKE THAT, MECHAGIRL! I ALMOST HAD A HEART ATTACK! WHAT'RE **YOU** DOING?!
I'M RETURNING A BOOK I FINISHED READING.
OH.
AND I WANTED TO READ ANOTHER ONE BEFORE BED.
YOU SURE DO LIKE **STUDYING** ...
WHOSE MATCH IS THAT?
HM? OH...

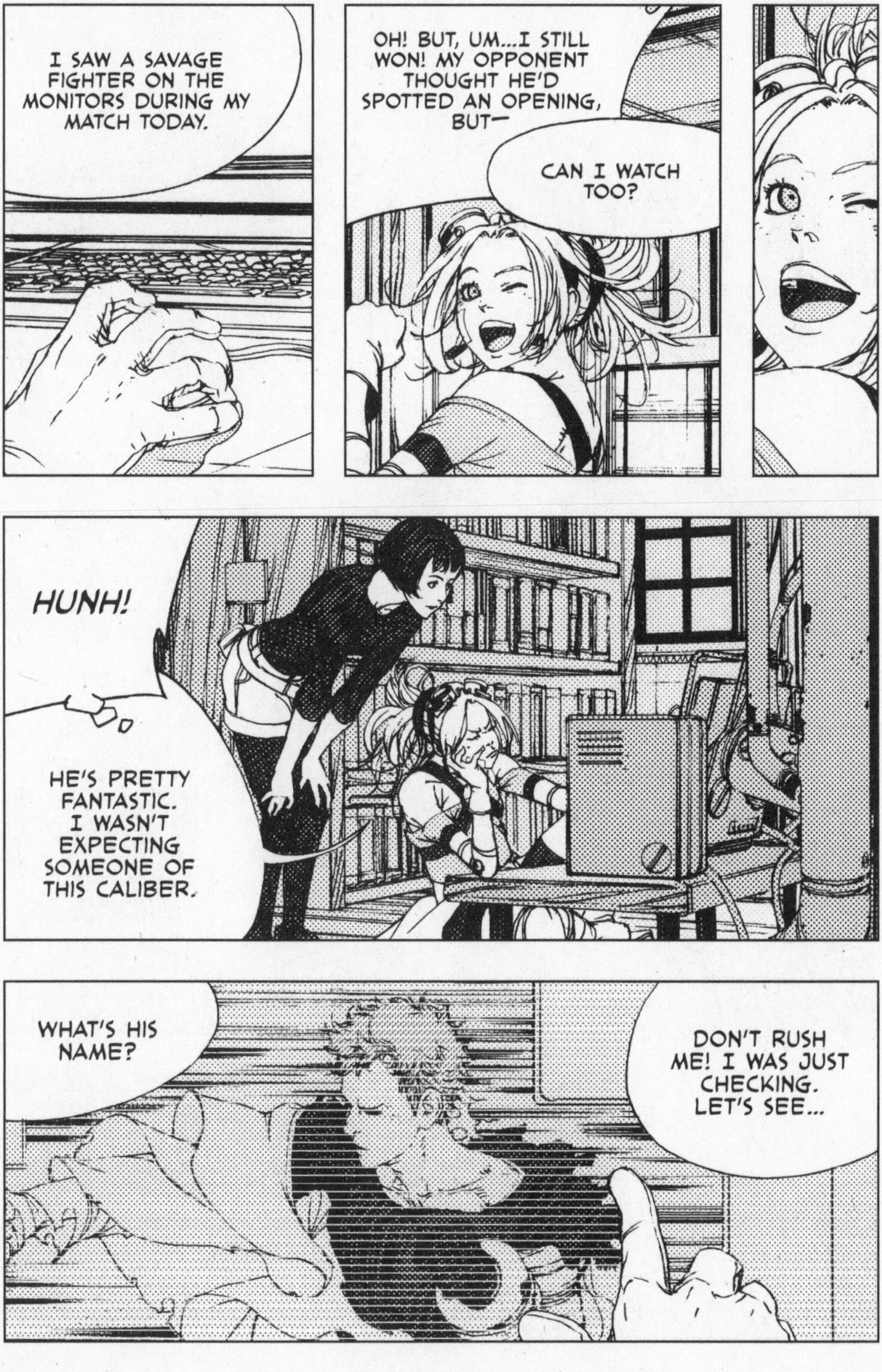
I SAW A SAVAGE FIGHTER ON THE MONITORS DURING MY MATCH TODAY.
OH! BUT, UM...I STILL WON! MY OPPONENT THOUGHT HE'D SPOTTED AN OPENING, BUT—
CAN I WATCH TOO?
HUNH!
HE'S PRETTY FANTASTIC. I WASN'T EXPECTING SOMEONE OF THIS CALIBER.
WHAT'S HIS NAME?
DON'T RUSH ME! I WAS JUST CHECKING. LET'S SEE...

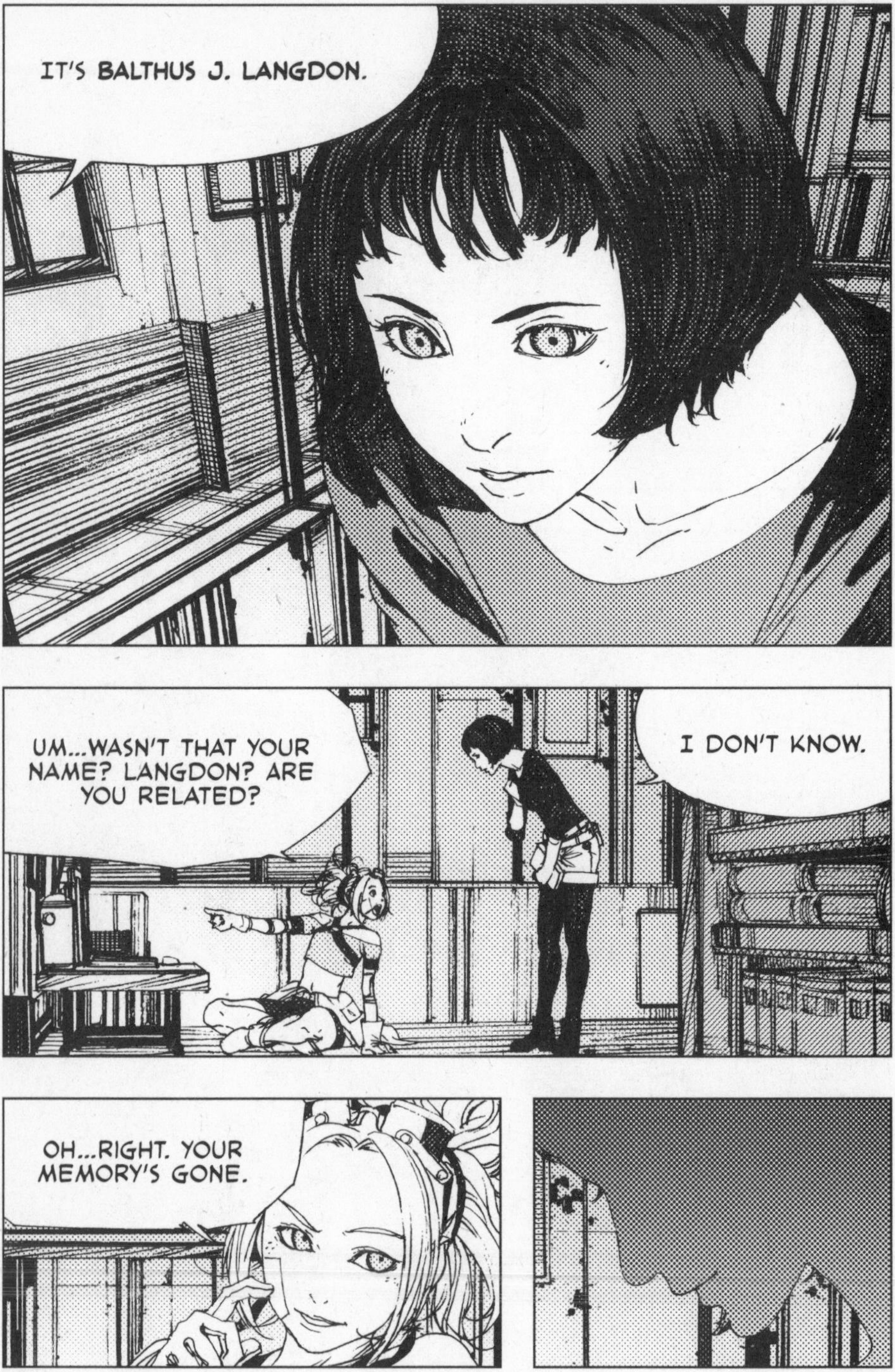
IT'S BALTHUS J. LANGDON.
UM...WASN'T THAT YOUR NAME? LANGDON? ARE YOU RELATED?
I DON'T KNOW.
OH...RIGHT. YOUR MEMORY'S GONE.

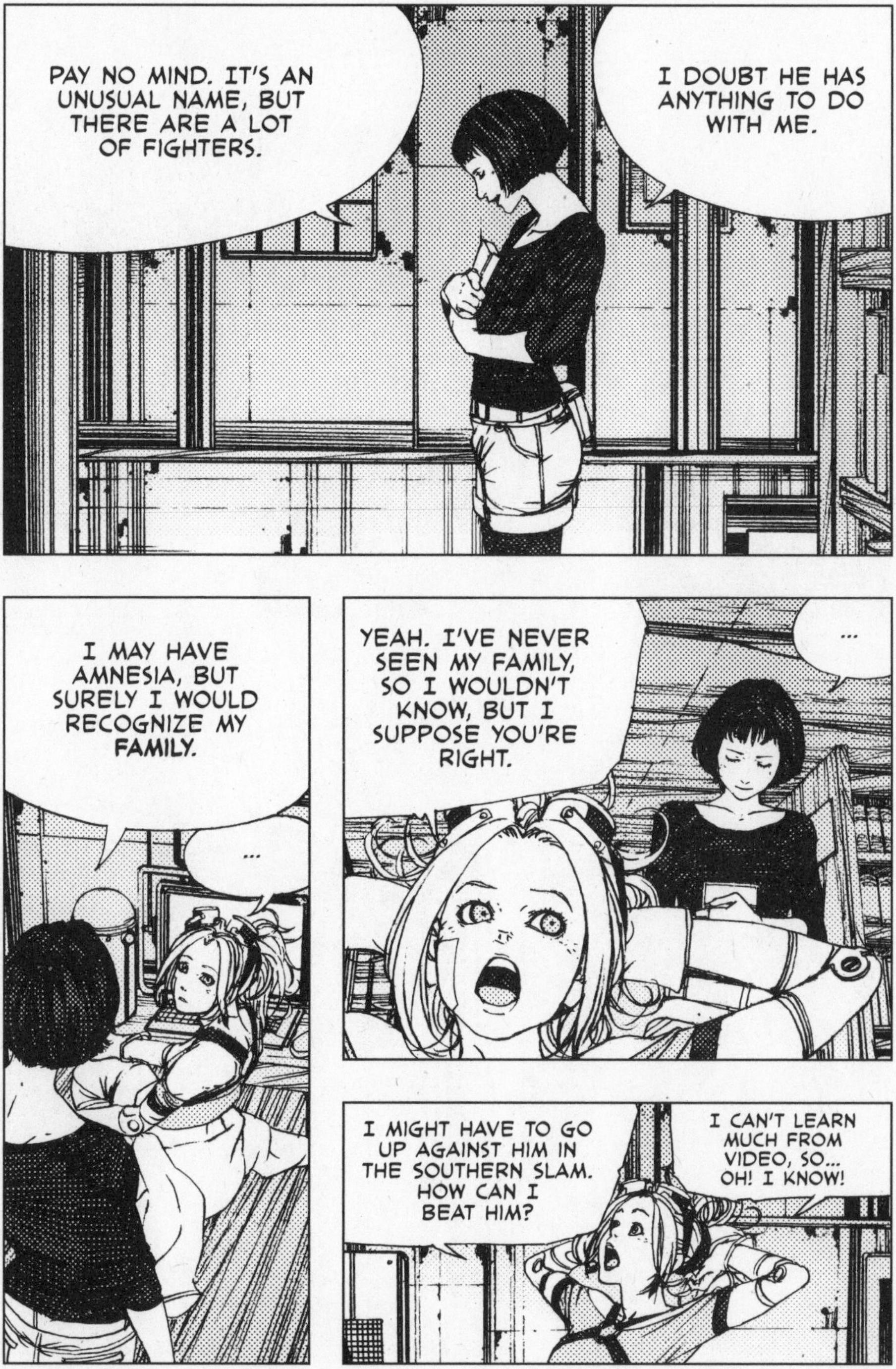
PAY NO MIND. IT'S AN UNUSUAL NAME, BUT THERE ARE A LOT OF FIGHTERS.
I DOUBT HE HAS ANYTHING TO DO WITH ME.
I MAY HAVE AMNESIA, BUT SURELY I WOULD RECOGNIZE MY FAMILY.
...
YEAH. I'VE NEVER SEEN MY FAMILY, SO I WOULDN'T KNOW, BUT I SUPPOSE YOU'RE RIGHT.
...
I MIGHT HAVE TO GO UP AGAINST HIM IN THE SOUTHERN SLAM. HOW CAN I BEAT HIM?
I CAN'T LEARN MUCH FROM VIDEO, SO... OH! I KNOW!

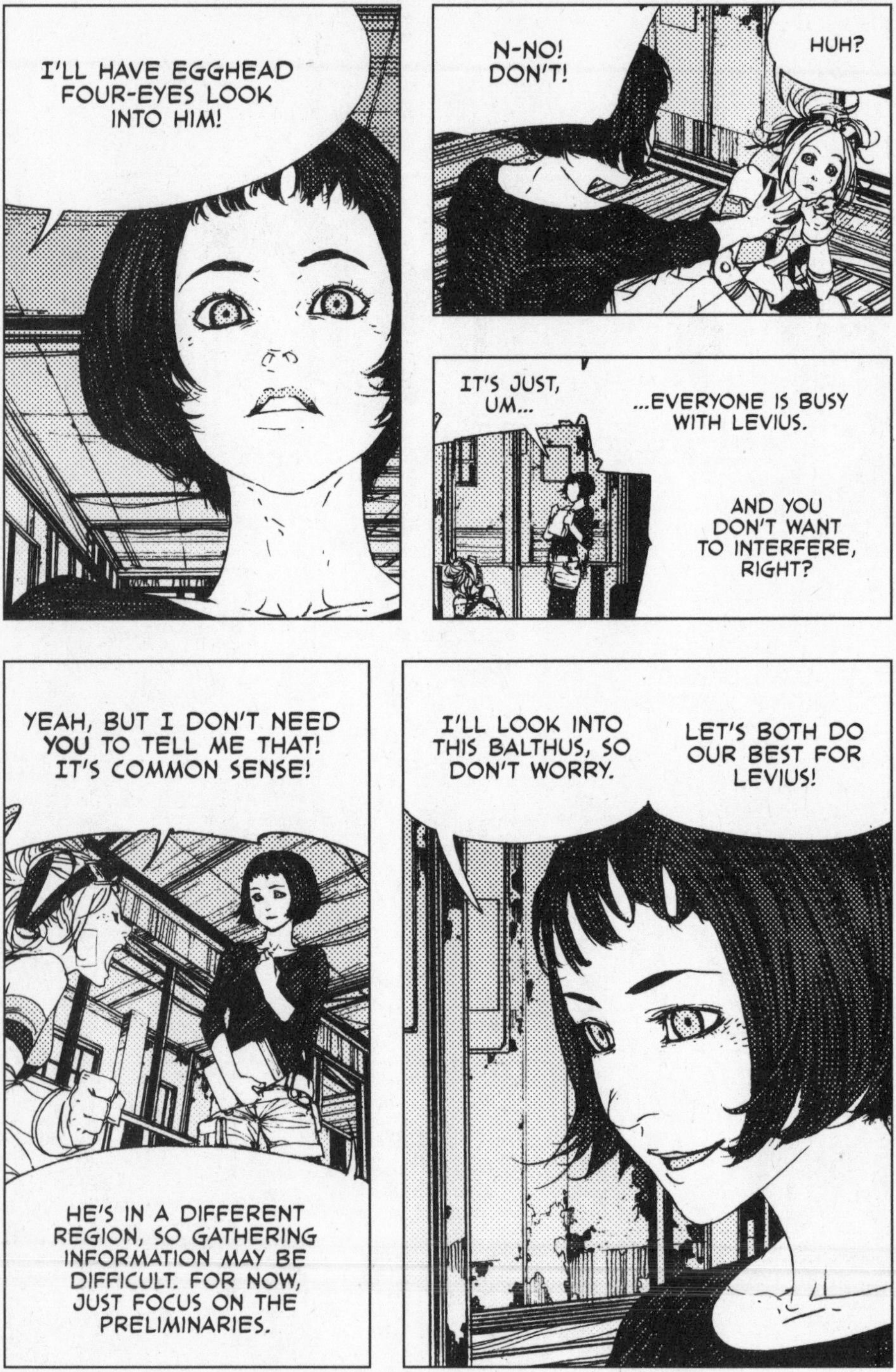
I'LL HAVE EGGHEAD FOUR-EYES LOOK INTO HIM!
N-NO! DON'T!
HUH?
IT'S JUST, UM...
...EVERYONE IS BUSY WITH LEVIUS.
AND YOU DON'T WANT TO INTERFERE, RIGHT?
YEAH, BUT I DON'T NEED YOU TO TELL ME THAT! IT'S COMMON SENSE!
HE'S IN A DIFFERENT REGION, SO GATHERING INFORMATION MAY BE DIFFICULT. FOR NOW, JUST FOCUS ON THE PRELIMINARIES.
I'LL LOOK INTO THIS BALTHUS, SO DON'T WORRY.
LET'S BOTH DO OUR BEST FOR LEVIUS!

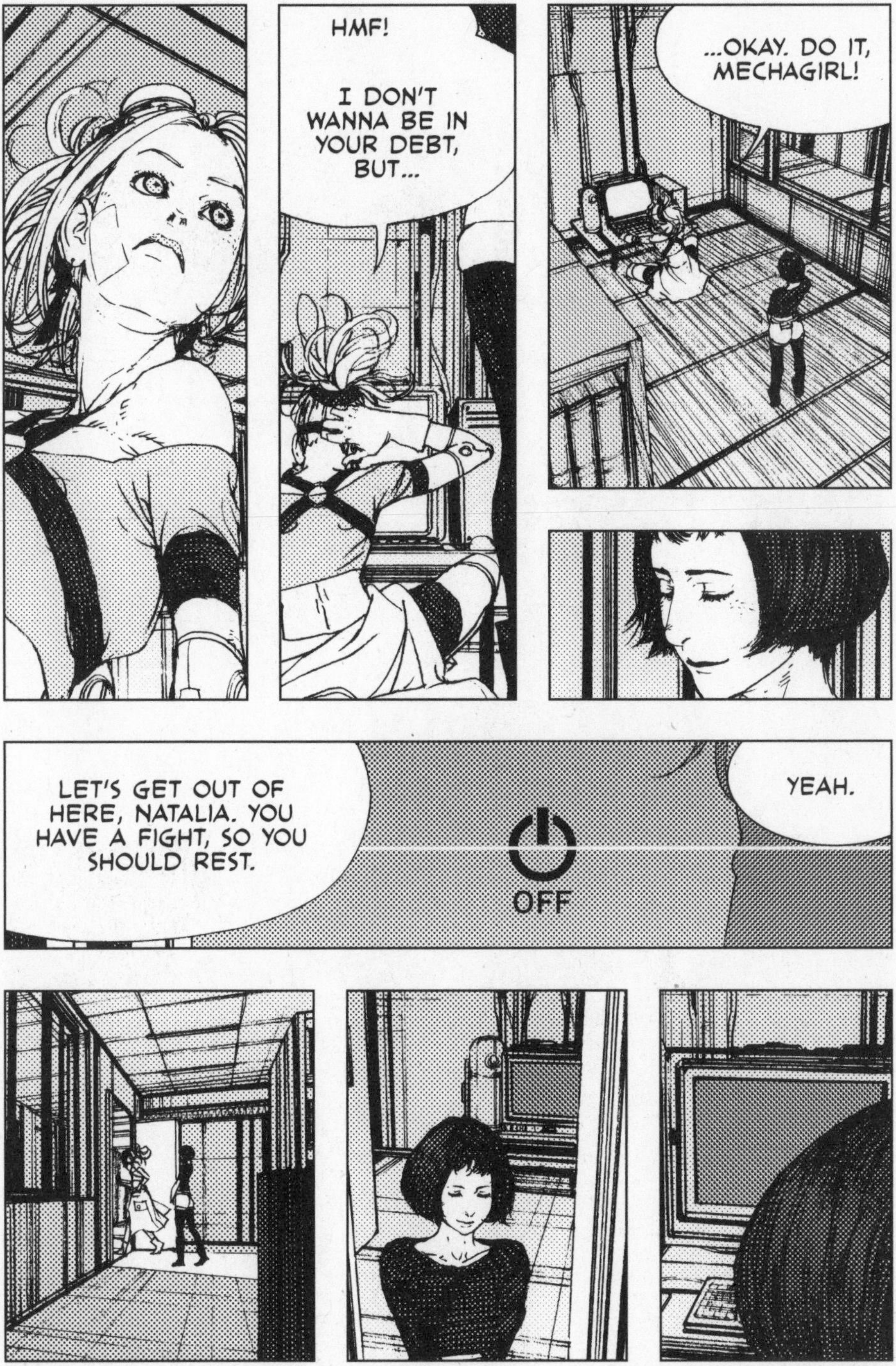
HMF!
I DON'T WANNA BE IN YOUR DEBT, BUT...
...OKAY. DO IT, MECHAGIRL!
LET'S GET OUT OF HERE, NATALIA. YOU HAVE A FIGHT, SO YOU SHOULD REST.
OFF
YEAH.

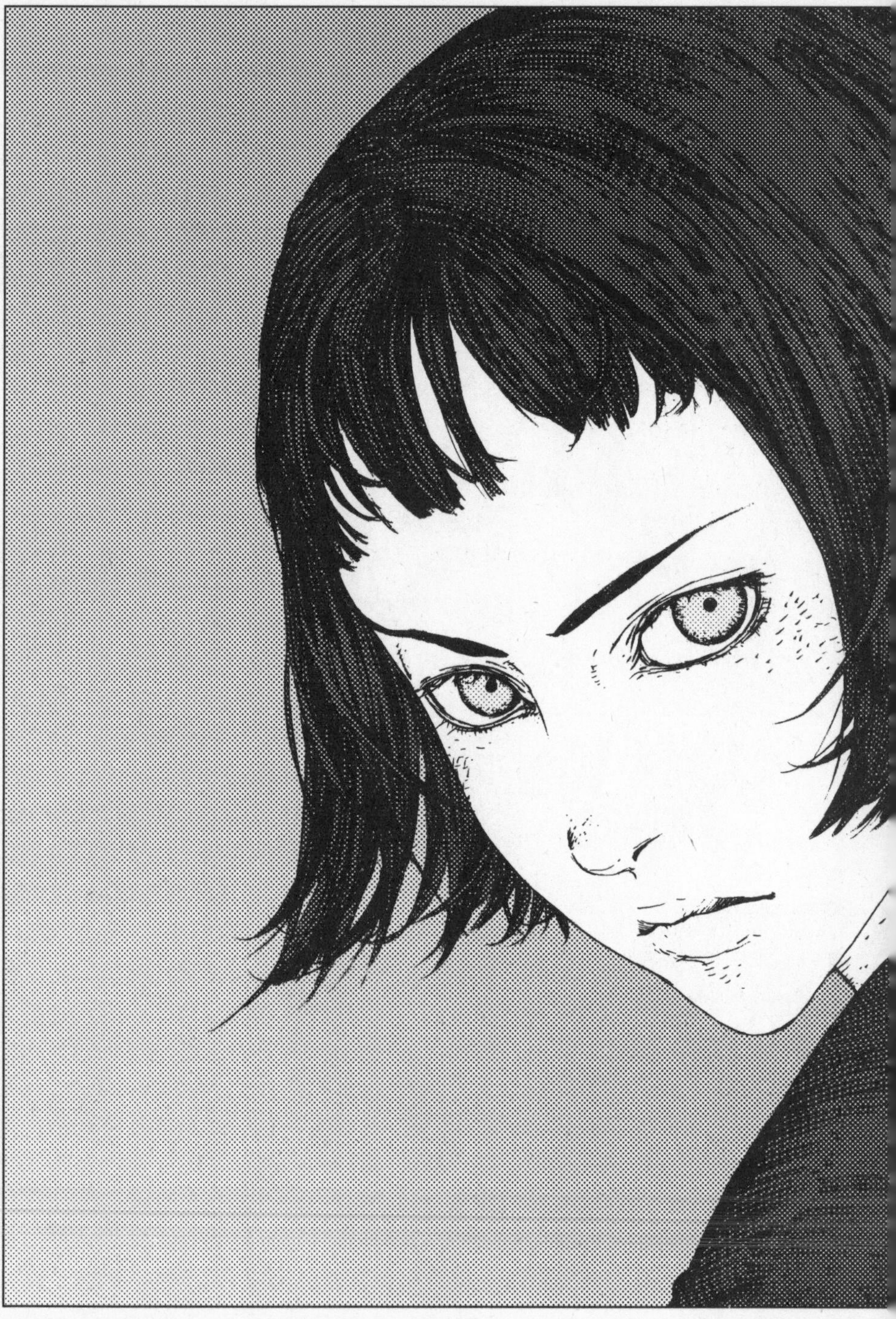

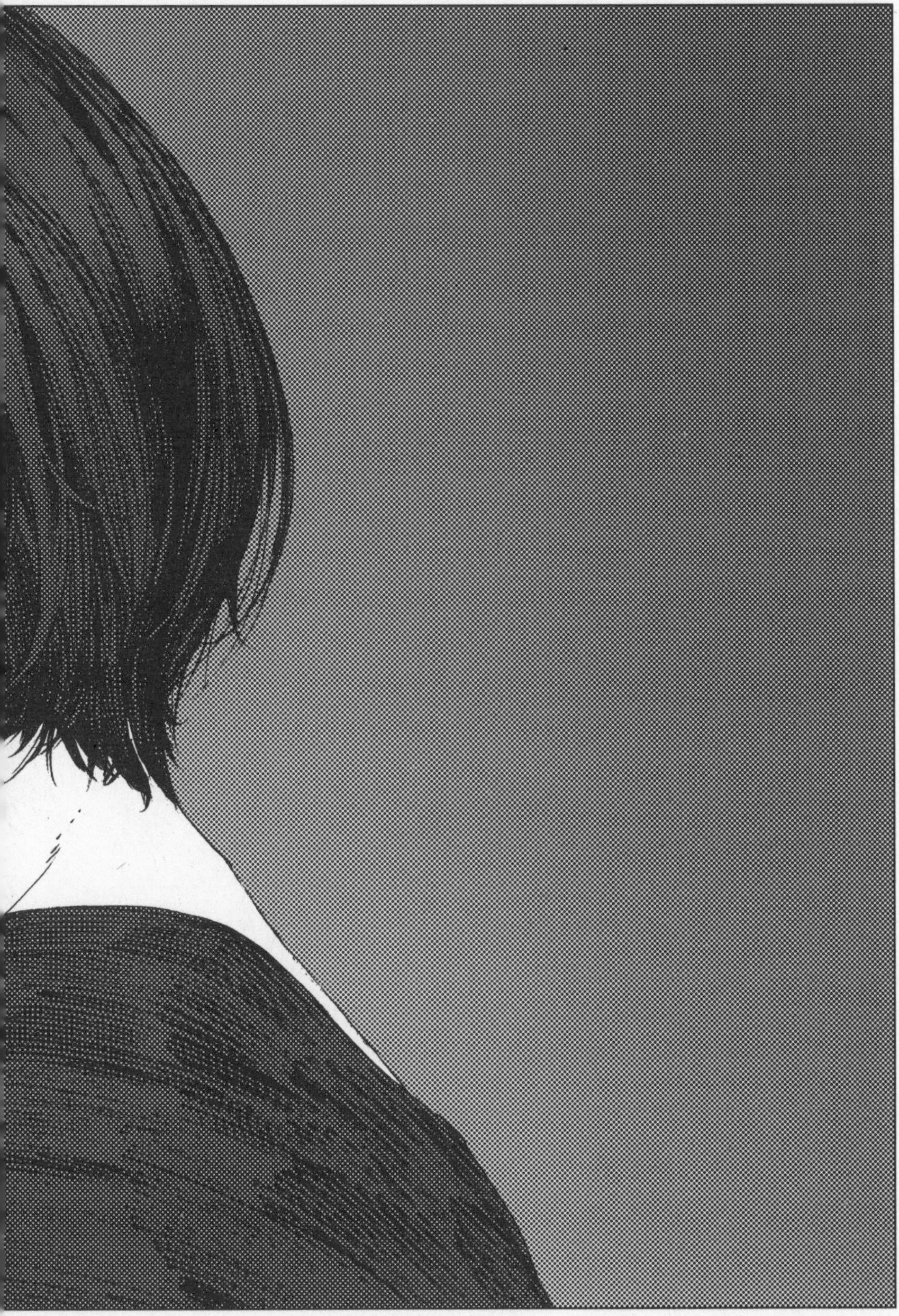

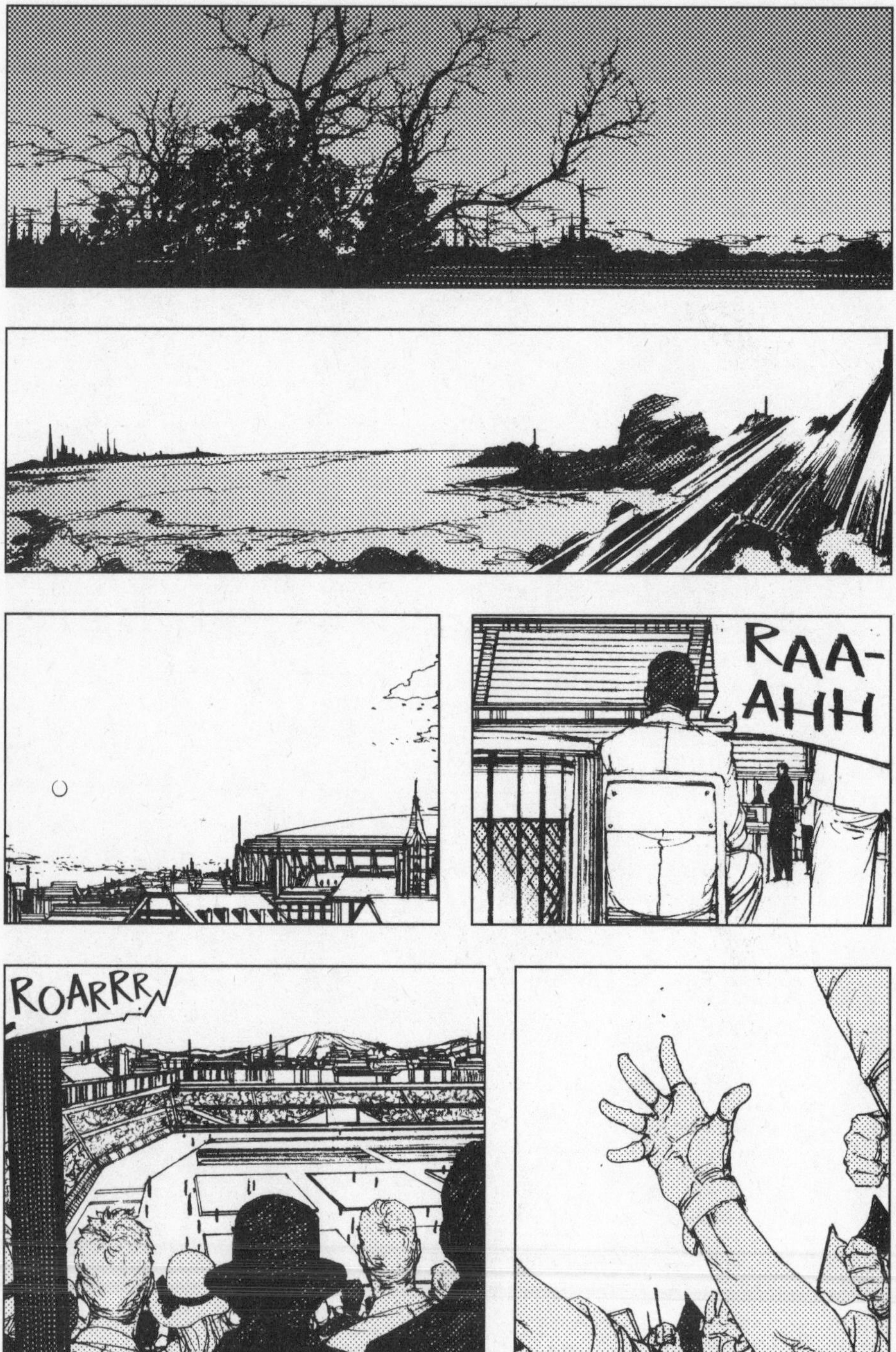
RAA-
AHH
ROARRR

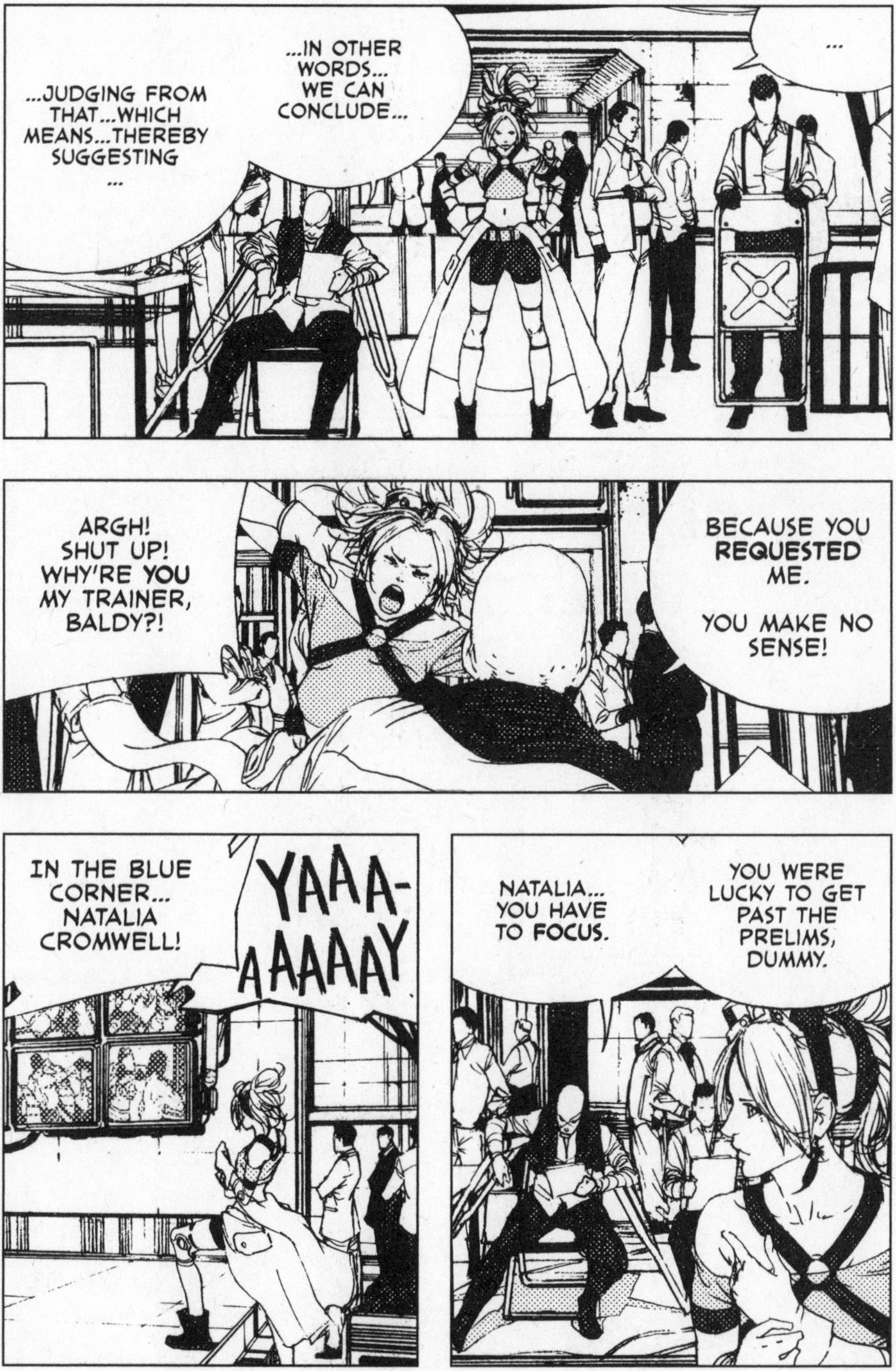
...JUDGING FROM THAT...WHICH MEANS...THEREBY SUGGESTING ...
...IN OTHER WORDS... WE CAN CONCLUDE...
...
ARGH! SHUT UP! WHY'RE YOU MY TRAINER, BALDY?!
BECAUSE YOU REQUESTED ME.
YOU MAKE NO SENSE!
IN THE BLUE CORNER... NATALIA CROMWELL!
YAAA-AAAAAY
NATALIA... YOU HAVE TO FOCUS.
YOU WERE LUCKY TO GET PAST THE PRELIMS, DUMMY.

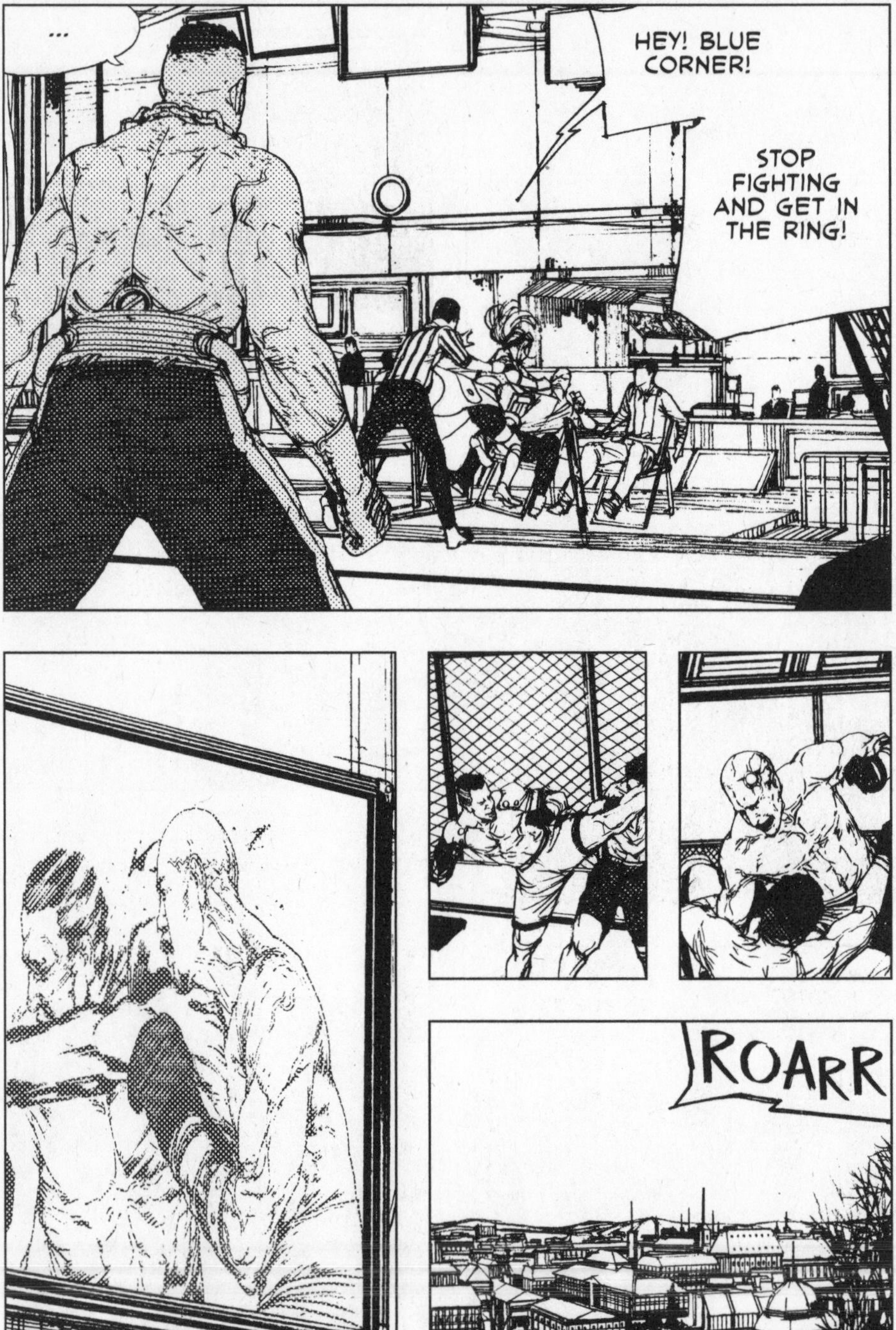
...
HEY! BLUE CORNER!
STOP FIGHTING AND GET IN THE RING!
ROARR

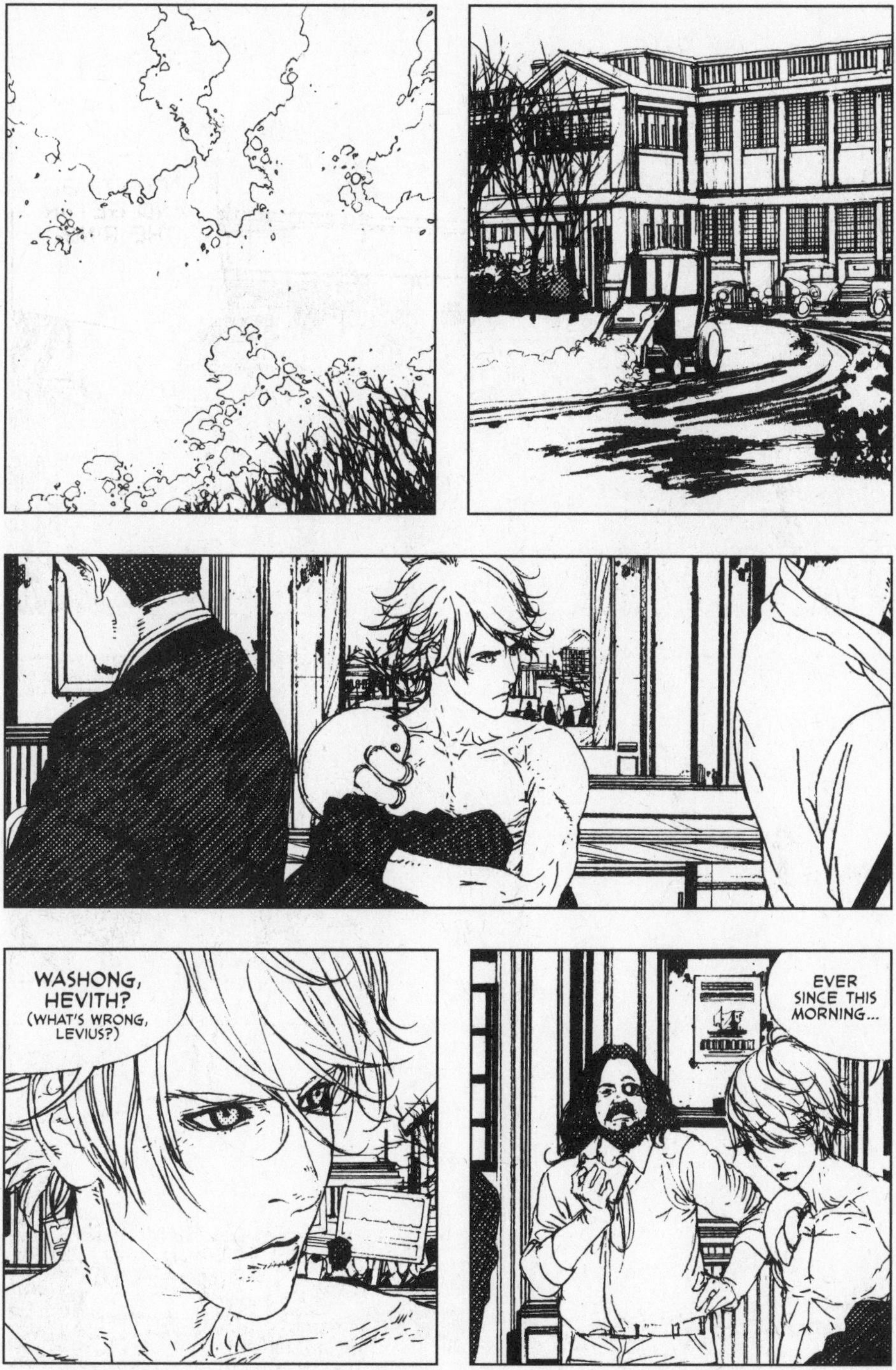
WASHONG, HEVITH?
(WHAT'S WRONG, LEVIUS?)
EVER SINCE THIS MORNING...

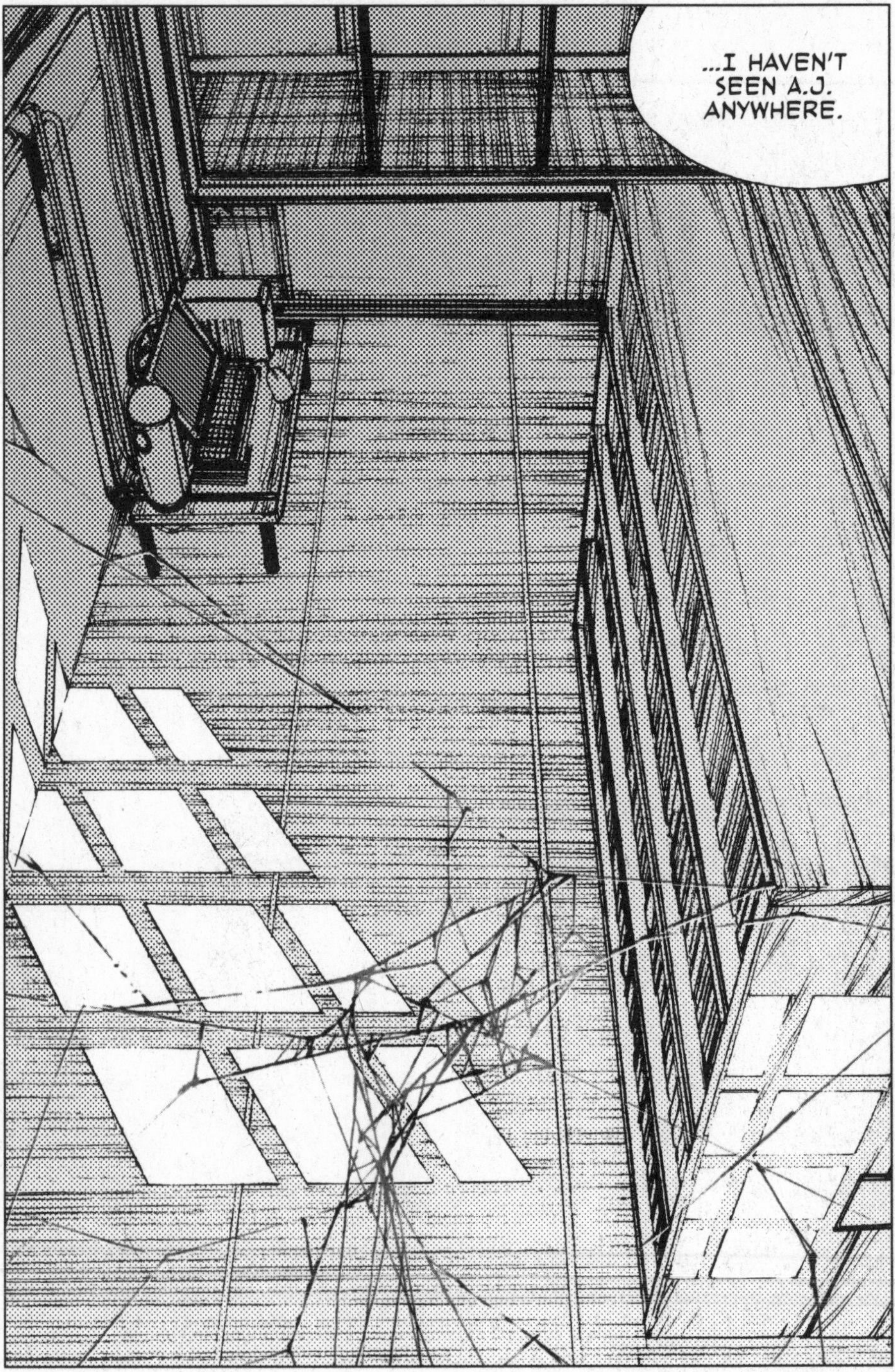
...I HAVEN'T SEEN A.J. ANYWHERE.

Levius/est
VOL. 3

Chapter 16

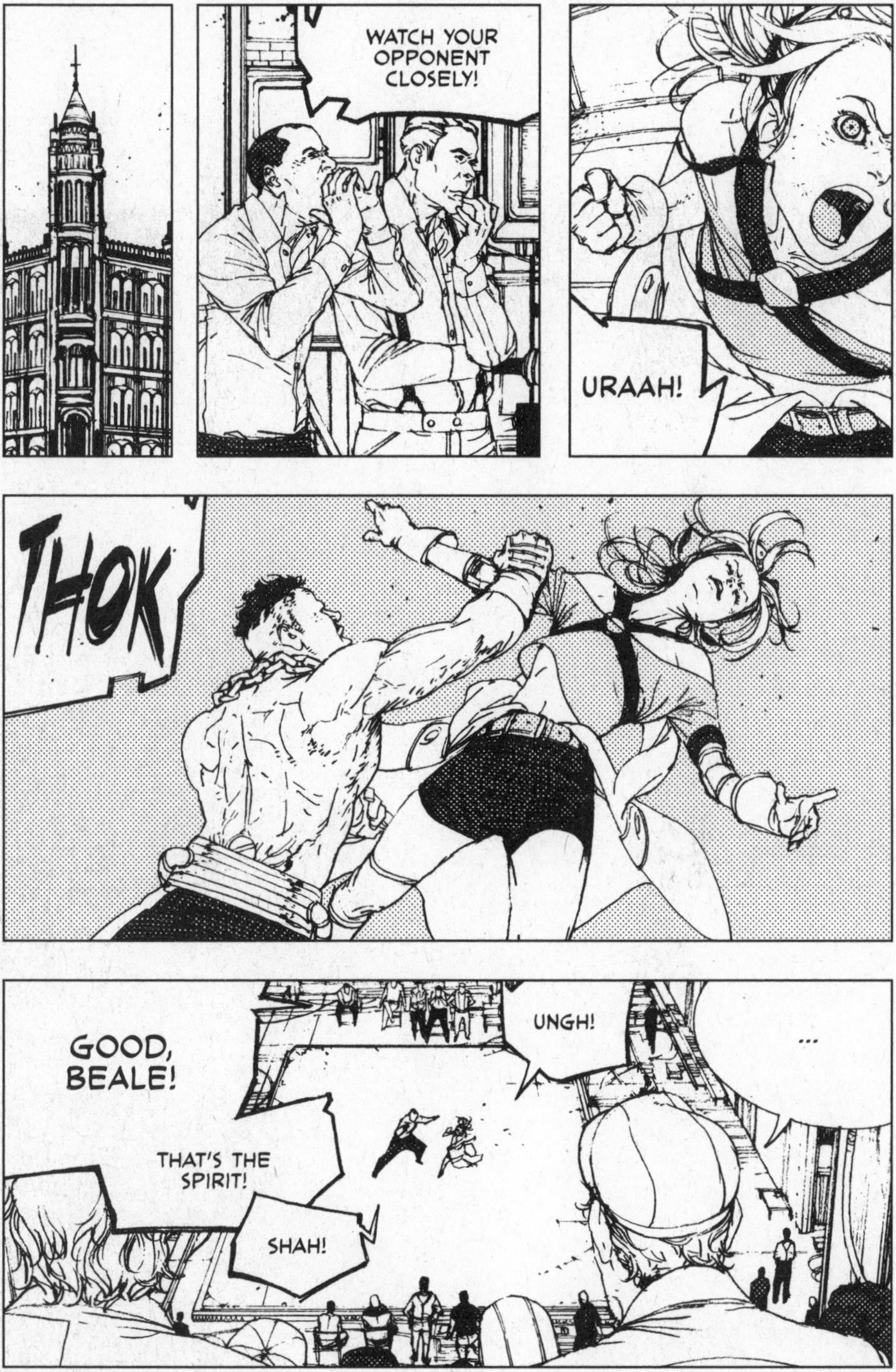
WATCH YOUR OPPONENT CLOSELY!
URAAH!
THOK
GOOD, BEALE!
THAT'S THE SPIRIT!
SHAH!
UNGH!
...

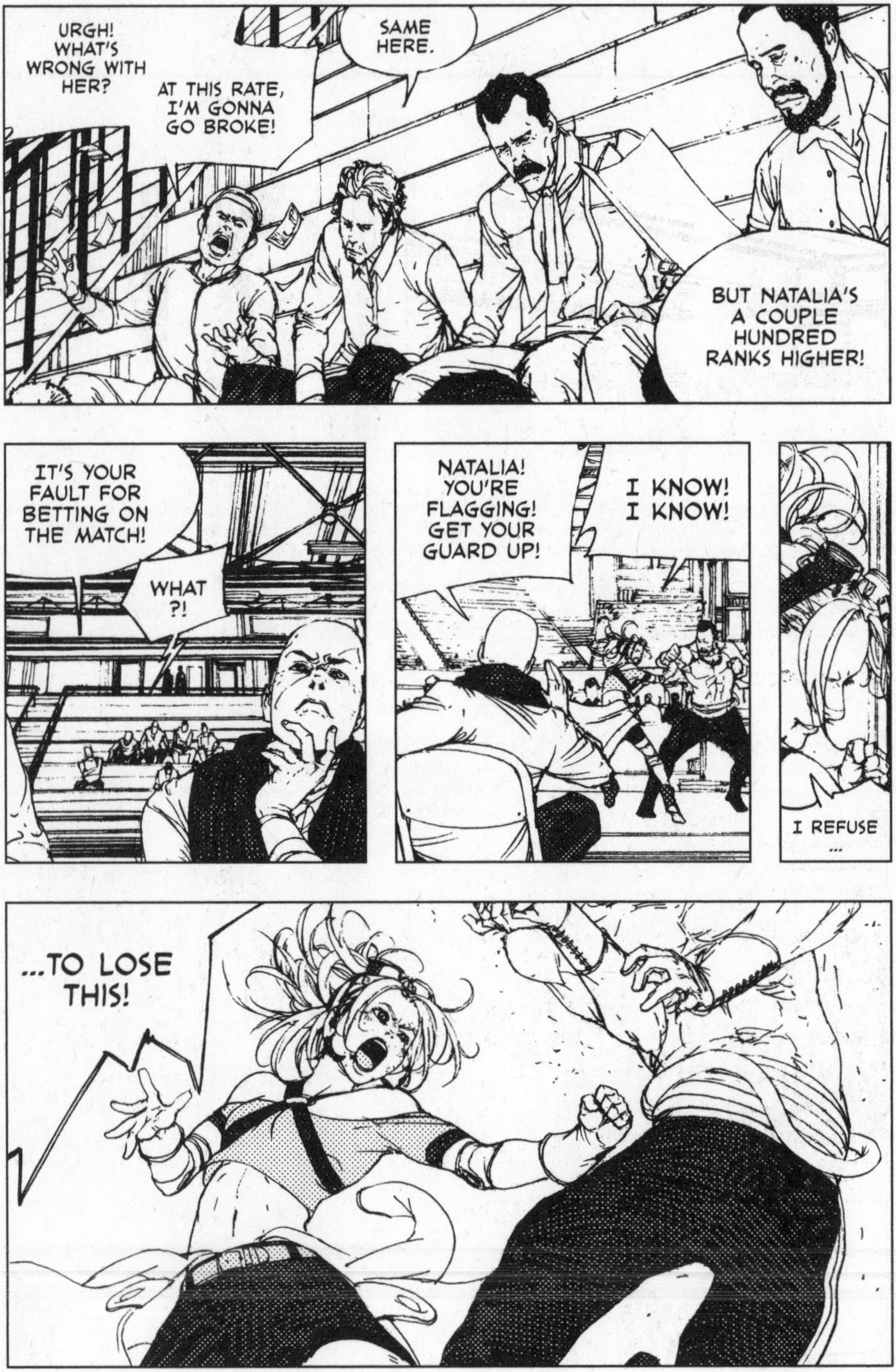
URGH! WHAT'S WRONG WITH HER?
AT THIS RATE, I'M GONNA GO BROKE!
SAME HERE.
BUT NATALIA'S A COUPLE HUNDRED RANKS HIGHER!
IT'S YOUR FAULT FOR BETTING ON THE MATCH!
WHAT ?!
NATALIA! YOU'RE FLAGGING! GET YOUR GUARD UP!
I KNOW! I KNOW!
I REFUSE ...
...TO LOSE THIS!

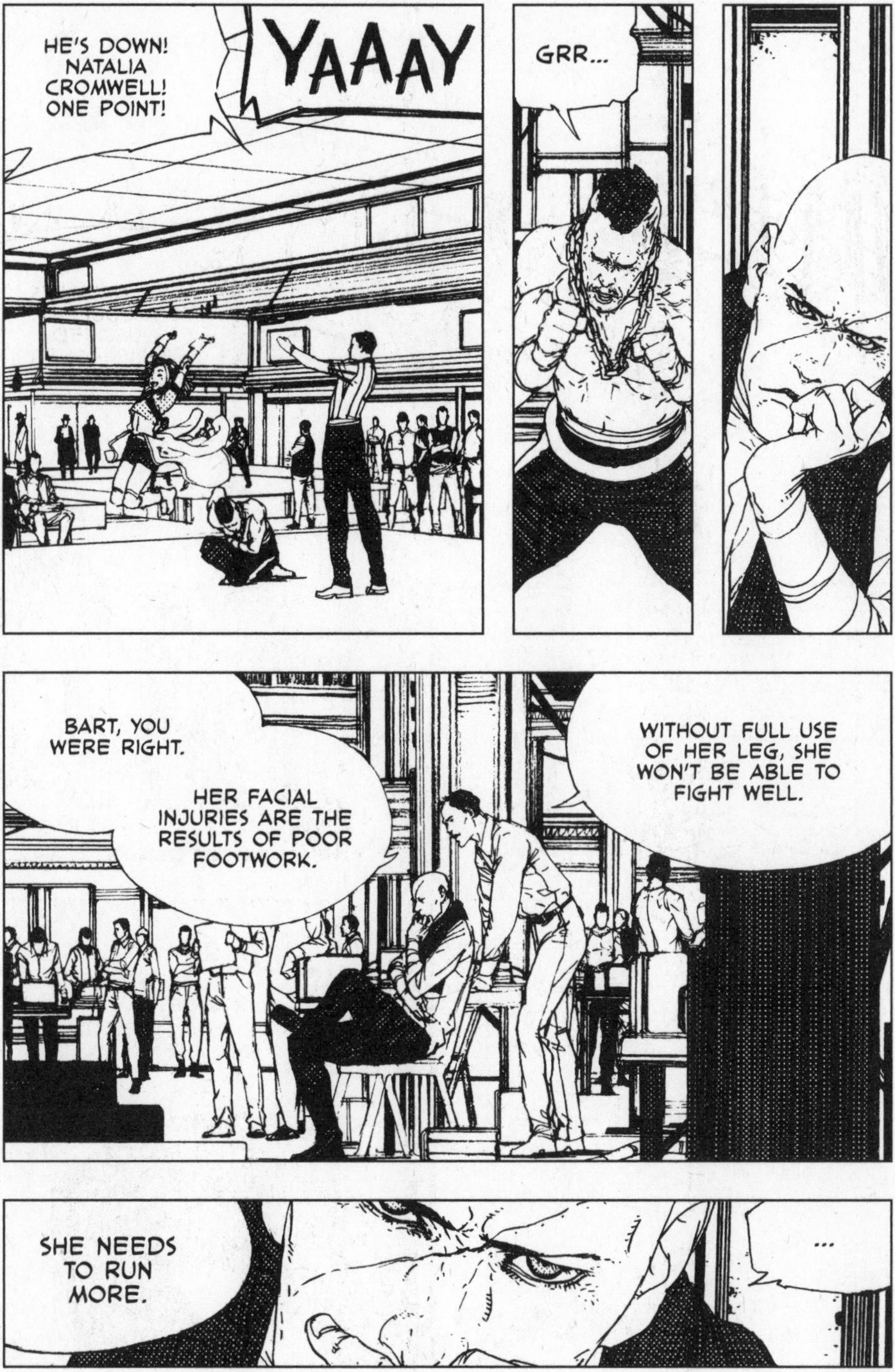
HE'S DOWN! NATALIA CROMWELL! ONE POINT!
YAAAY
GRR...
BART, YOU WERE RIGHT.
HER FACIAL INJURIES ARE THE RESULTS OF POOR FOOTWORK.
WITHOUT FULL USE OF HER LEG, SHE WON'T BE ABLE TO FIGHT WELL.
SHE NEEDS TO RUN MORE.
...

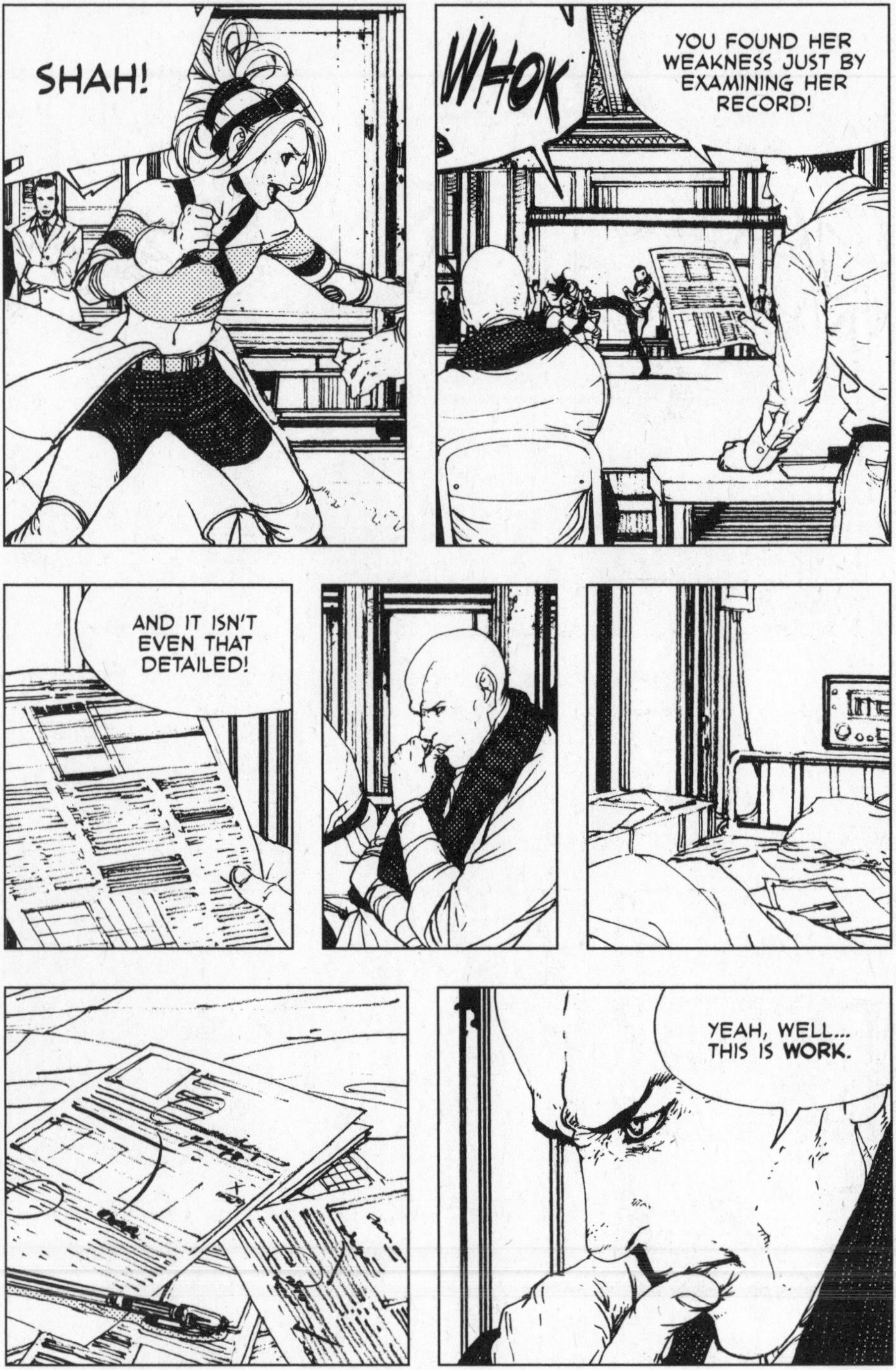
SHAH!
WHOK
YOU FOUND HER WEAKNESS JUST BY EXAMINING HER RECORD!
AND IT ISN'T EVEN THAT DETAILED!
YEAH, WELL... THIS IS **WORK.**

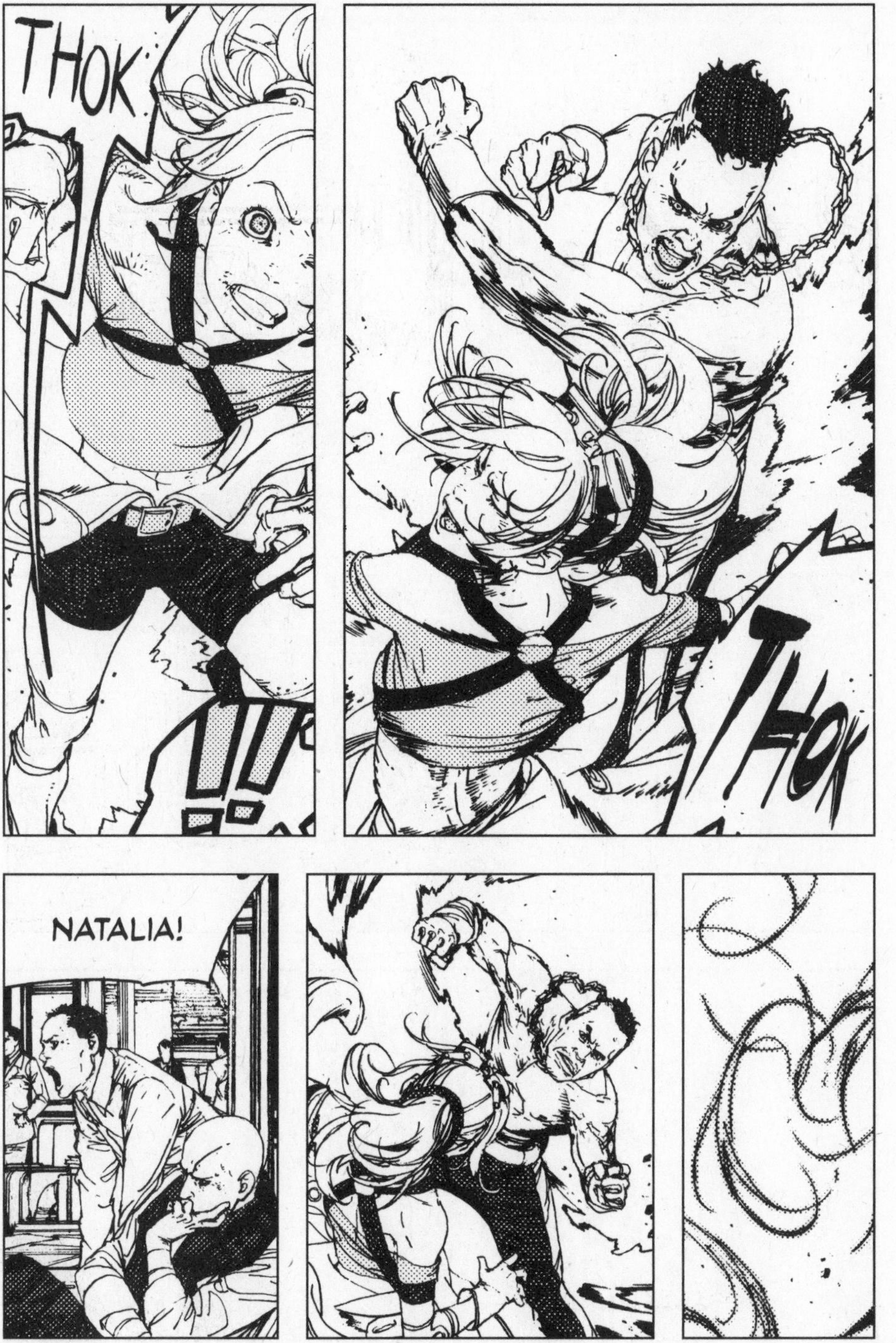
THOK
!!
THOK
NATALIA!

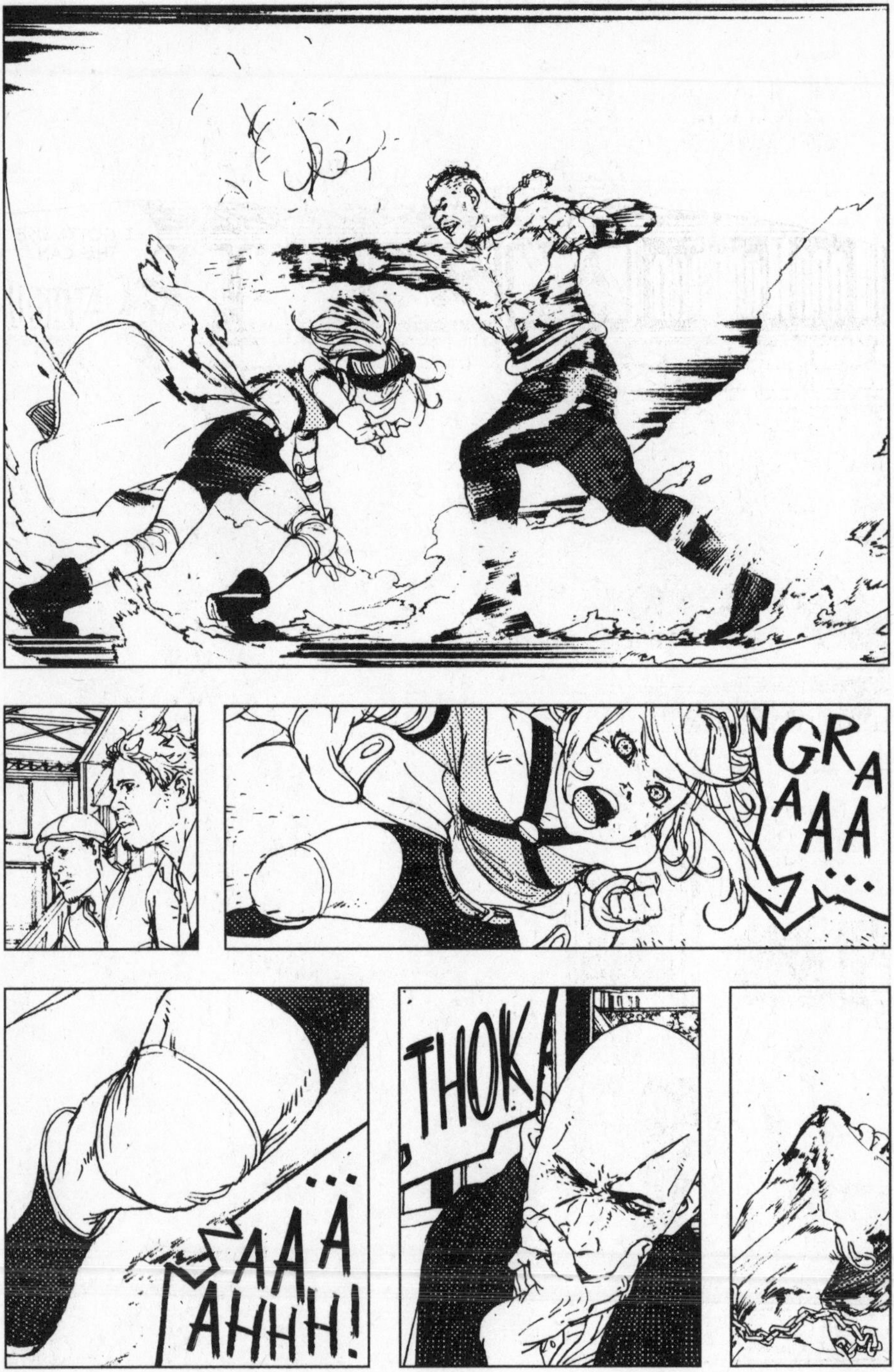
GRAAAA...
AAAAHHH!
THOKA

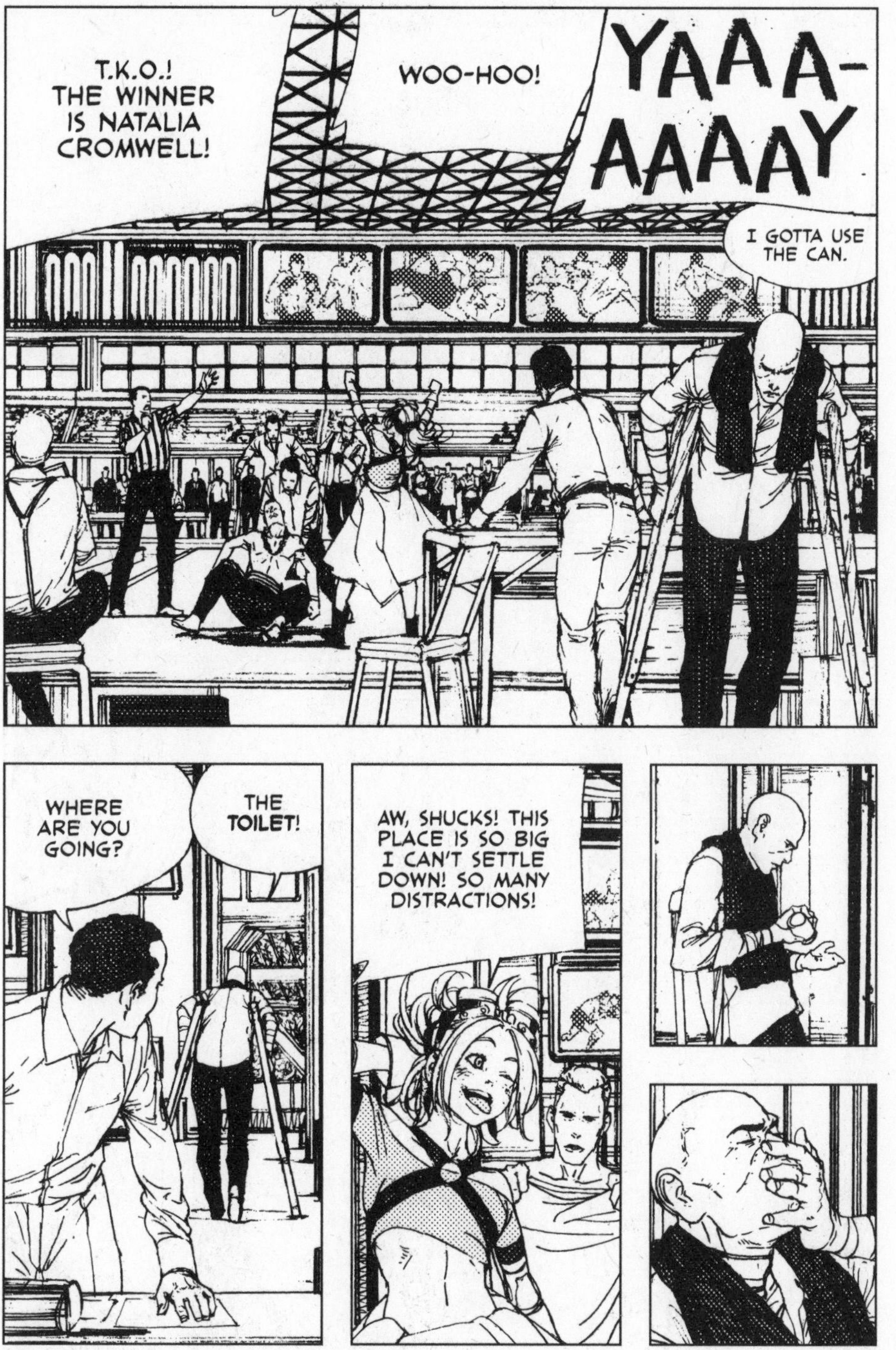
T.K.O.! THE WINNER IS NATALIA CROMWELL!
WOO-HOO!
YAAA-AAAAY
I GOTTA USE THE CAN.
WHERE ARE YOU GOING?
THE TOILET!
AW, SHUCKS! THIS PLACE IS SO BIG I CAN'T SETTLE DOWN! SO MANY DISTRACTIONS!

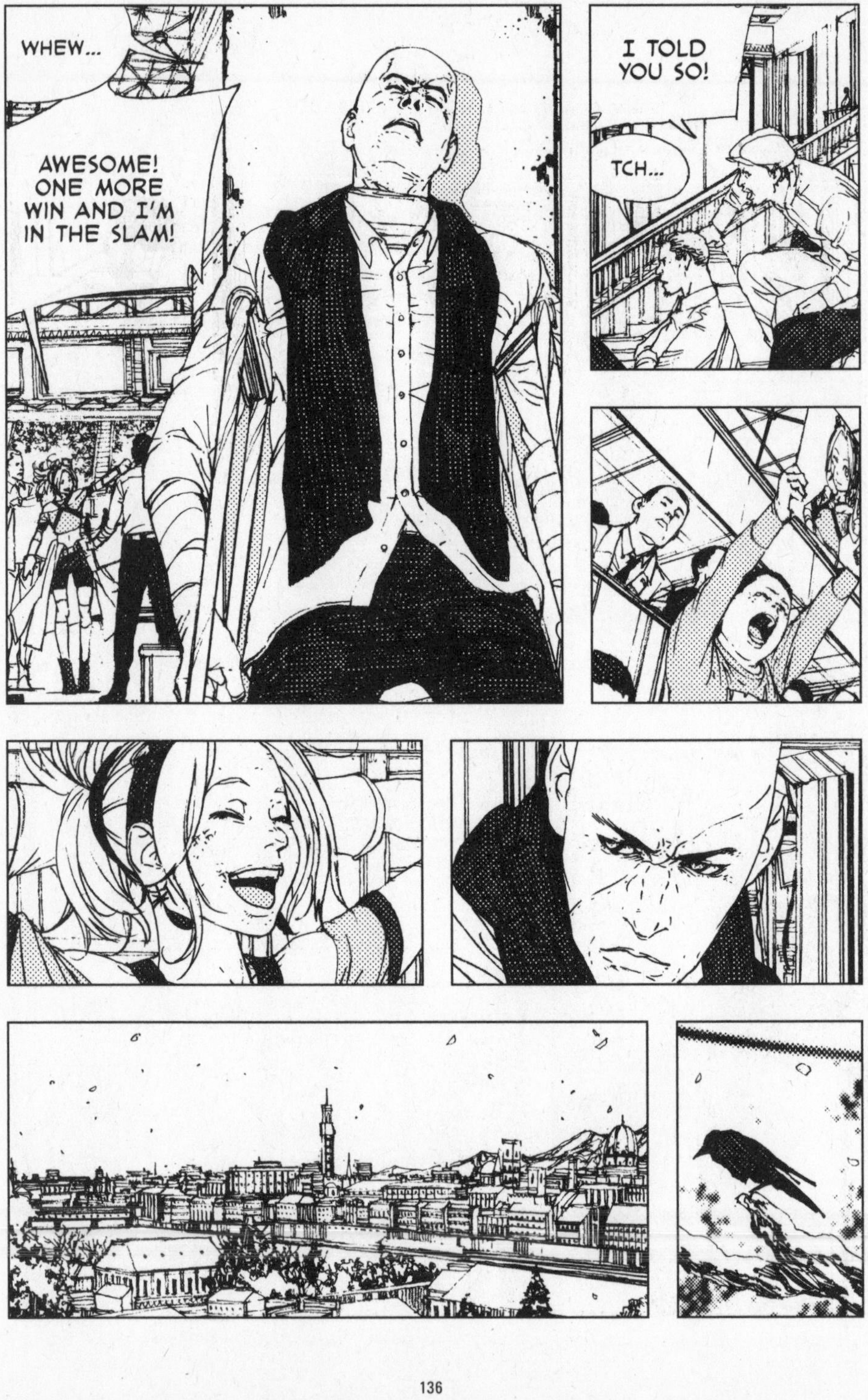
WHEW...
AWESOME! ONE MORE WIN AND I'M IN THE SLAM!
I TOLD YOU SO!
TCH...

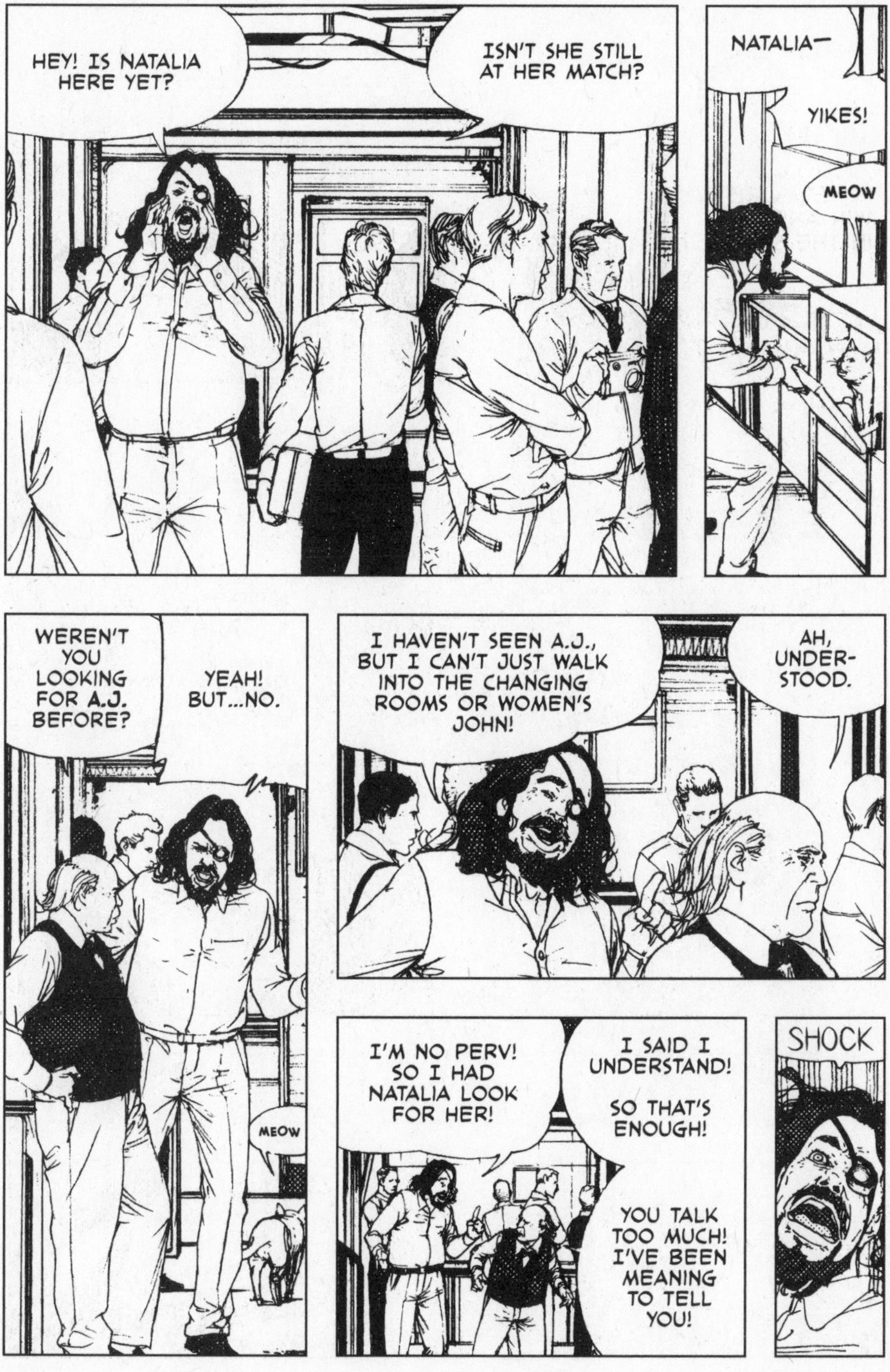

HEY! IS NATALIA HERE YET?
ISN'T SHE STILL AT HER MATCH?
NATALIA—
YIKES!
MEOW
WEREN'T YOU LOOKING FOR A.J. BEFORE?
YEAH! BUT...NO.
MEOW
I HAVEN'T SEEN A.J., BUT I CAN'T JUST WALK INTO THE CHANGING ROOMS OR WOMEN'S JOHN!
AH, UNDER-STOOD.
I'M NO PERV! SO I HAD NATALIA LOOK FOR HER!
I SAID I UNDERSTAND!
SO THAT'S ENOUGH!
YOU TALK TOO MUCH! I'VE BEEN MEANING TO TELL YOU!
SHOCK

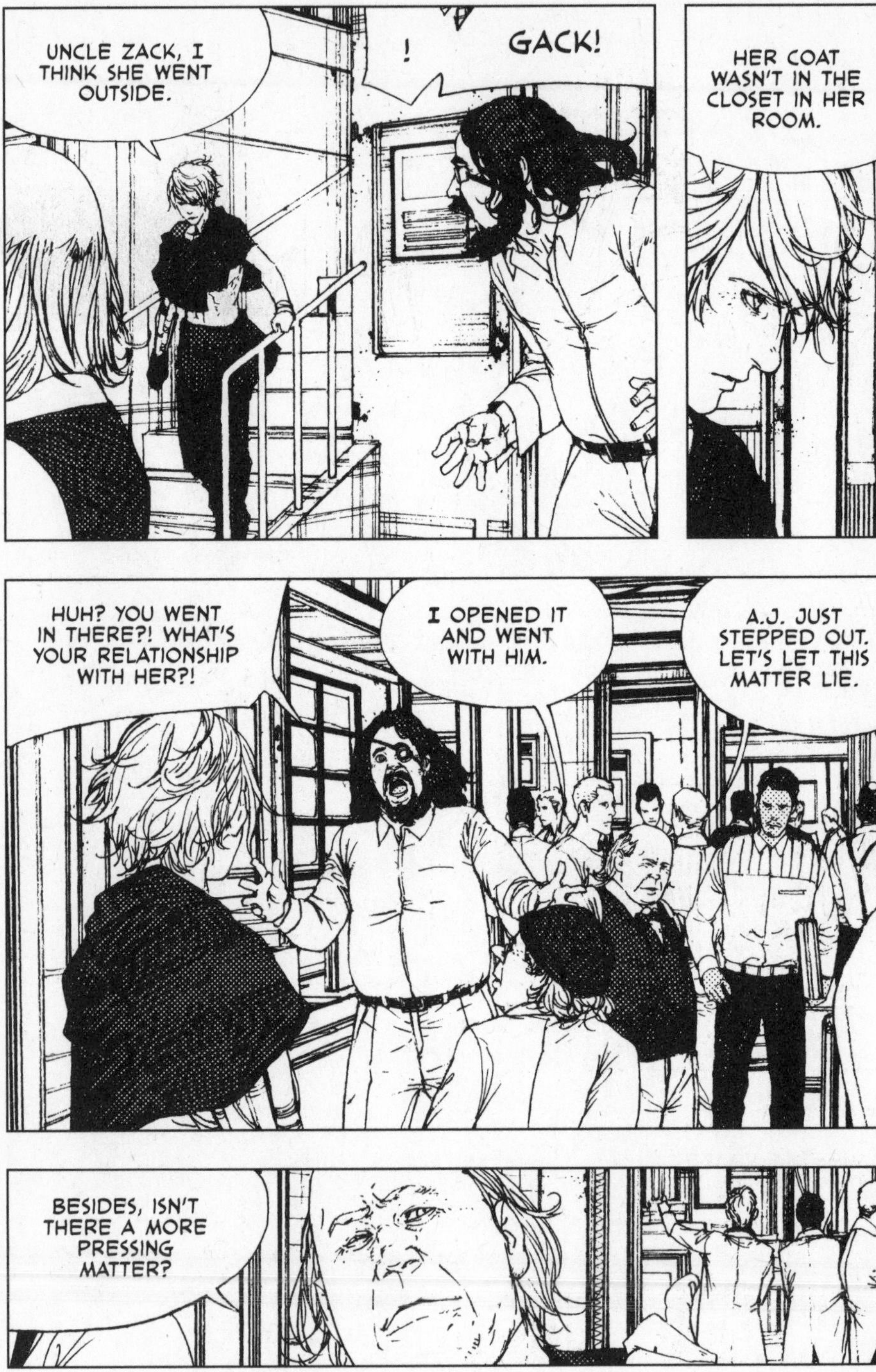
UNCLE ZACK, I THINK SHE WENT OUTSIDE.
!
GACK!
HER COAT WASN'T IN THE CLOSET IN HER ROOM.
HUH? YOU WENT IN THERE?! WHAT'S YOUR RELATIONSHIP WITH HER?!
I OPENED IT AND WENT WITH HIM.
A.J. JUST STEPPED OUT. LET'S LET THIS MATTER LIE.
BESIDES, ISN'T THERE A MORE PRESSING MATTER?

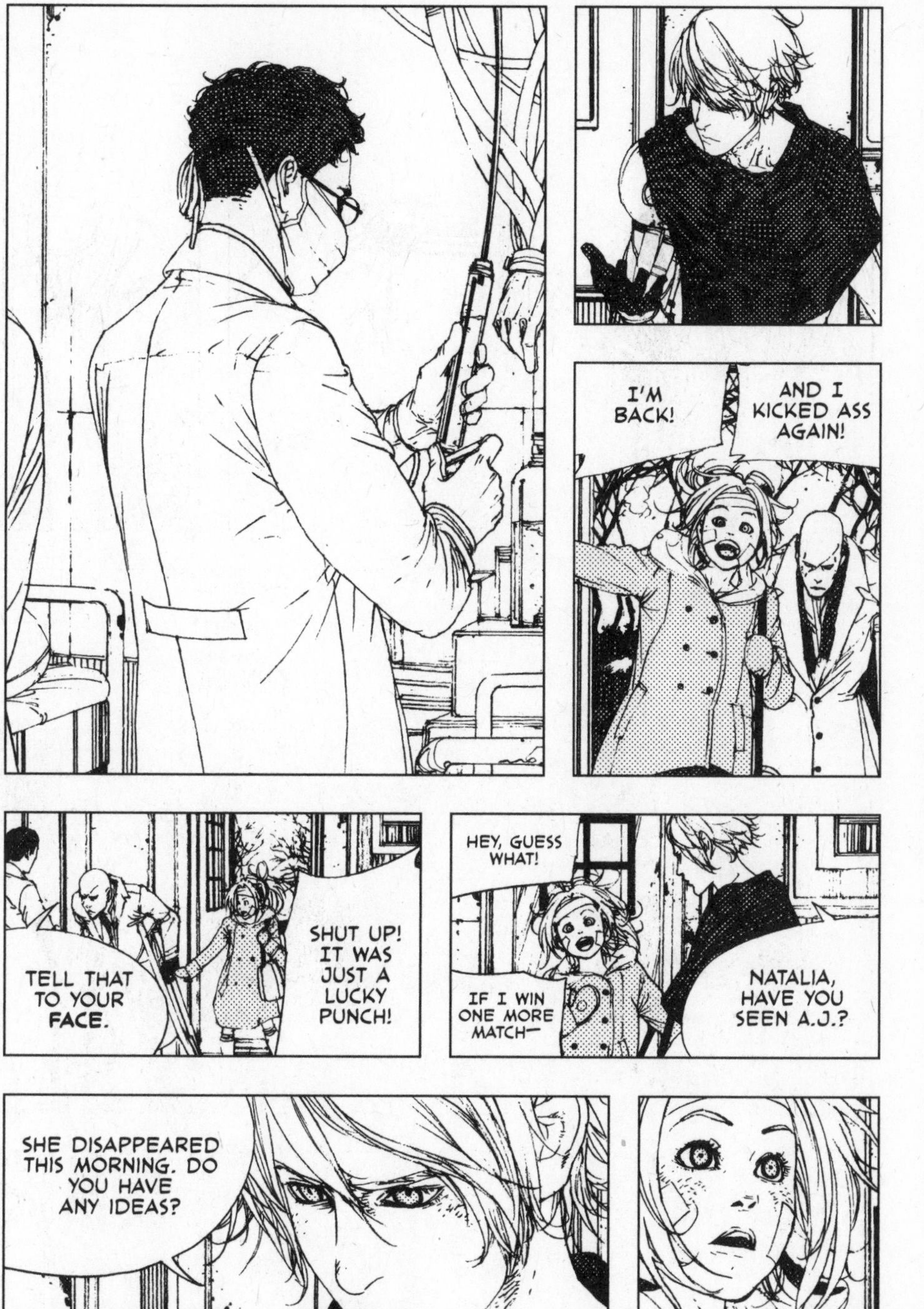
I'M BACK!
AND I KICKED ASS AGAIN!
SHUT UP! IT WAS JUST A LUCKY PUNCH!
TELL THAT TO YOUR FACE.
HEY, GUESS WHAT!
IF I WIN ONE MORE MATCH—
NATALIA, HAVE YOU SEEN A.J.?
SHE DISAPPEARED THIS MORNING. DO YOU HAVE ANY IDEAS?

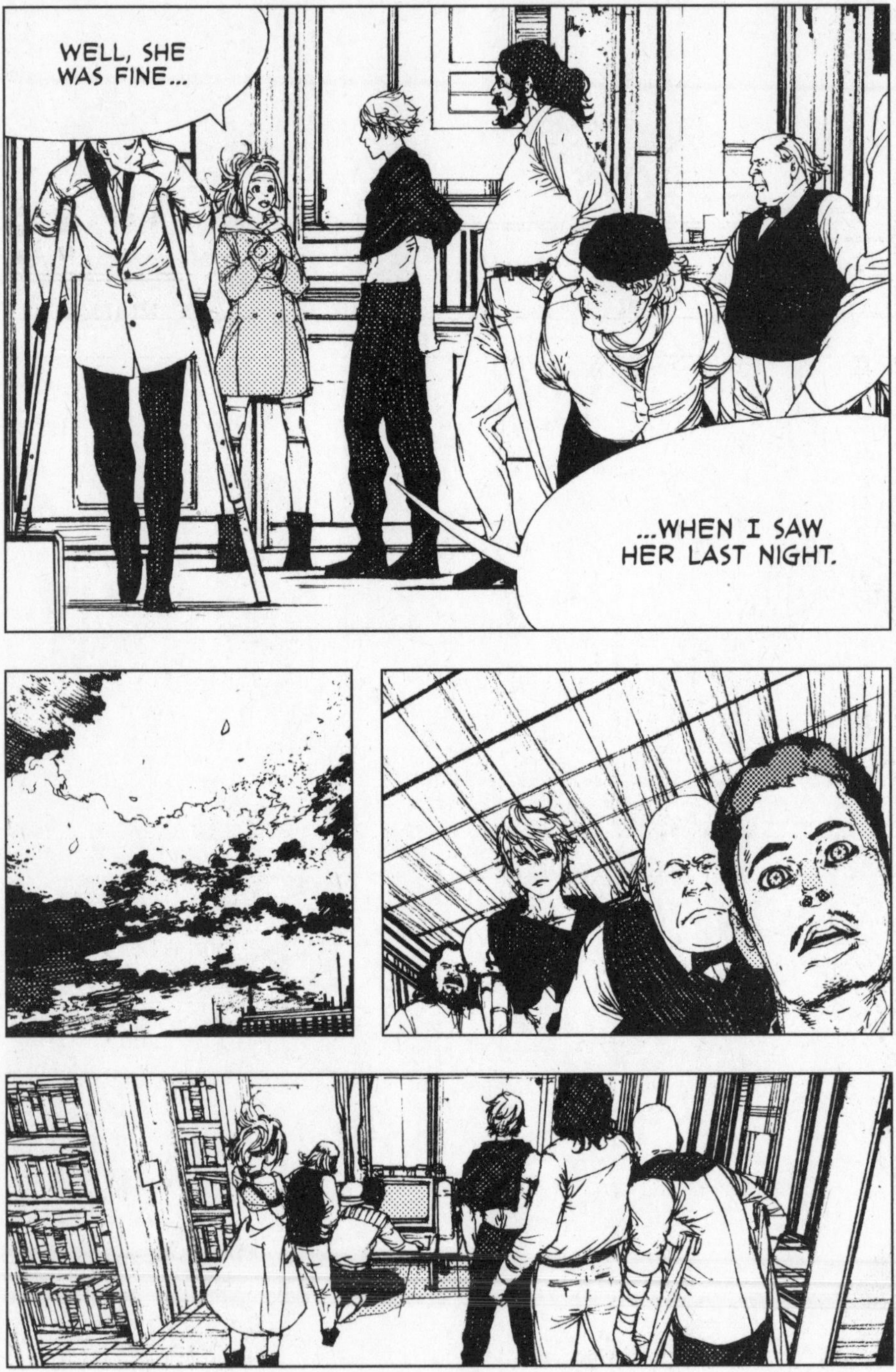
WELL, SHE WAS FINE...
...WHEN I SAW HER LAST NIGHT.

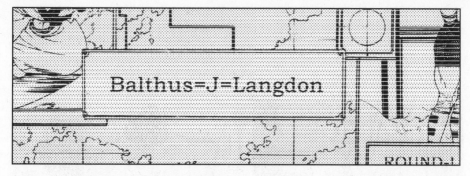

Balthus=J=Langdon

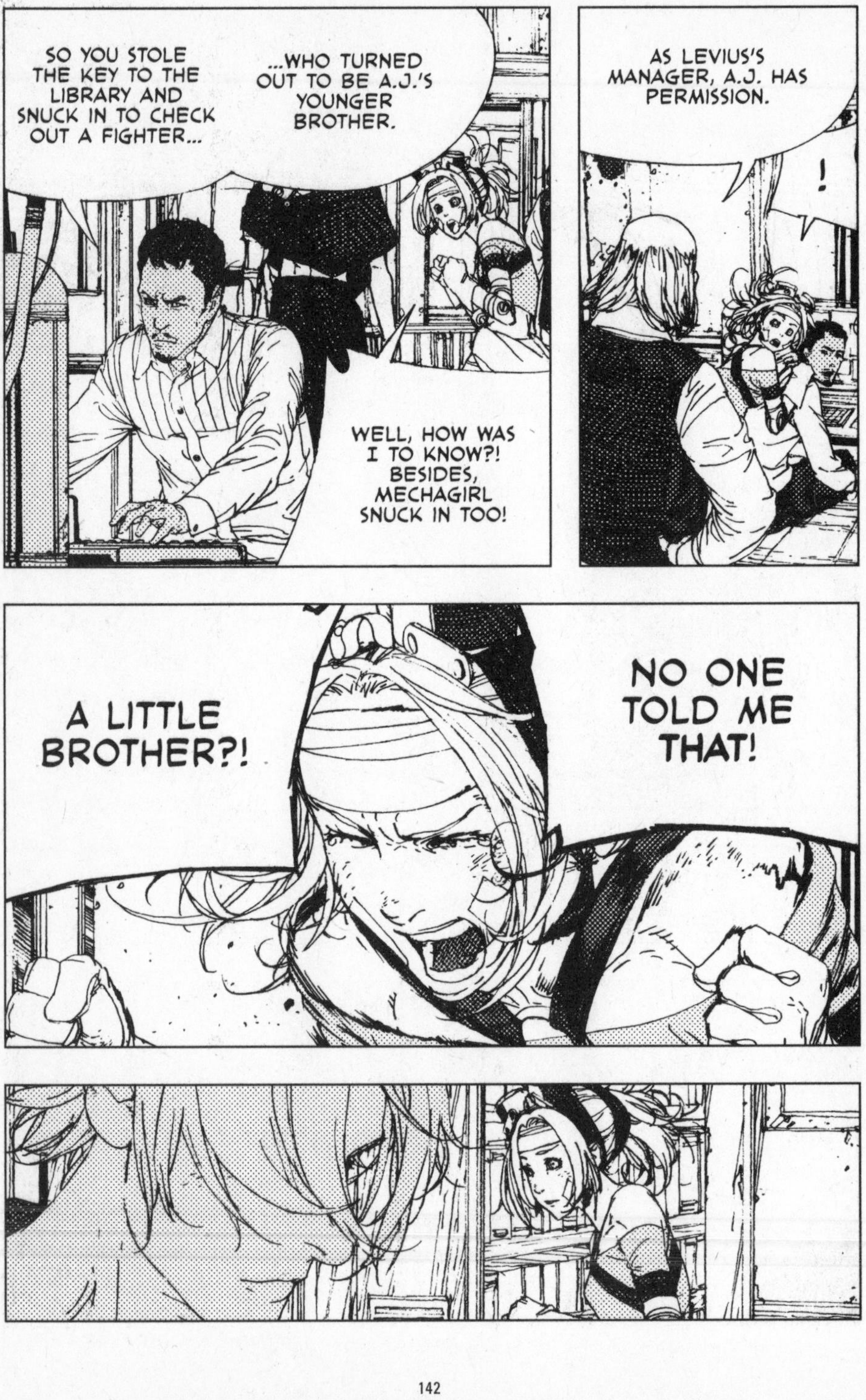

SO YOU STOLE THE KEY TO THE LIBRARY AND SNUCK IN TO CHECK OUT A FIGHTER...
...WHO TURNED OUT TO BE A.J.'S YOUNGER BROTHER.
WELL, HOW WAS I TO KNOW?! BESIDES, MECHAGIRL SNUCK IN TOO!
AS LEVIUS'S MANAGER, A.J. HAS PERMISSION.
!
A LITTLE BROTHER?!
NO ONE TOLD ME THAT!

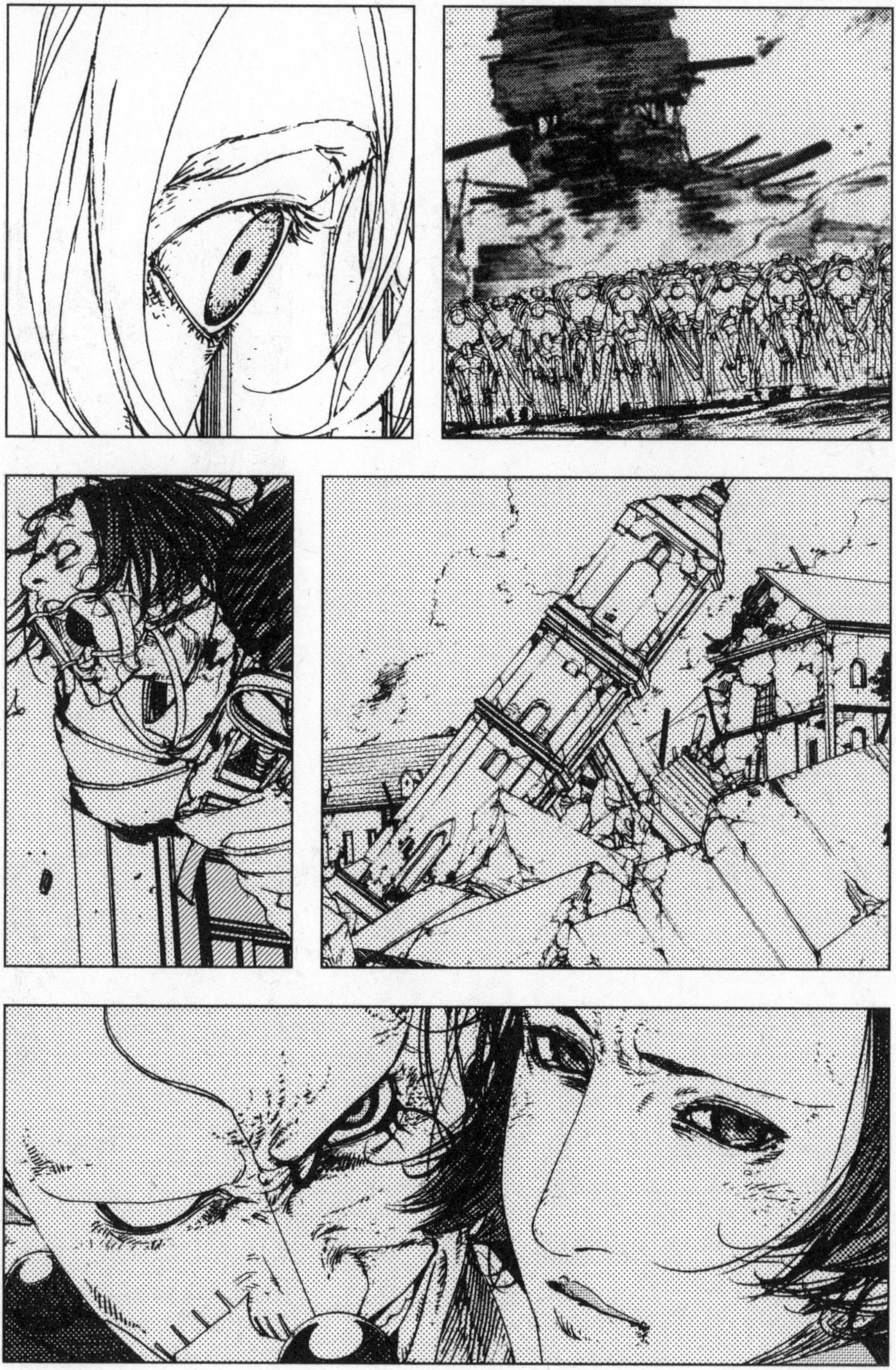

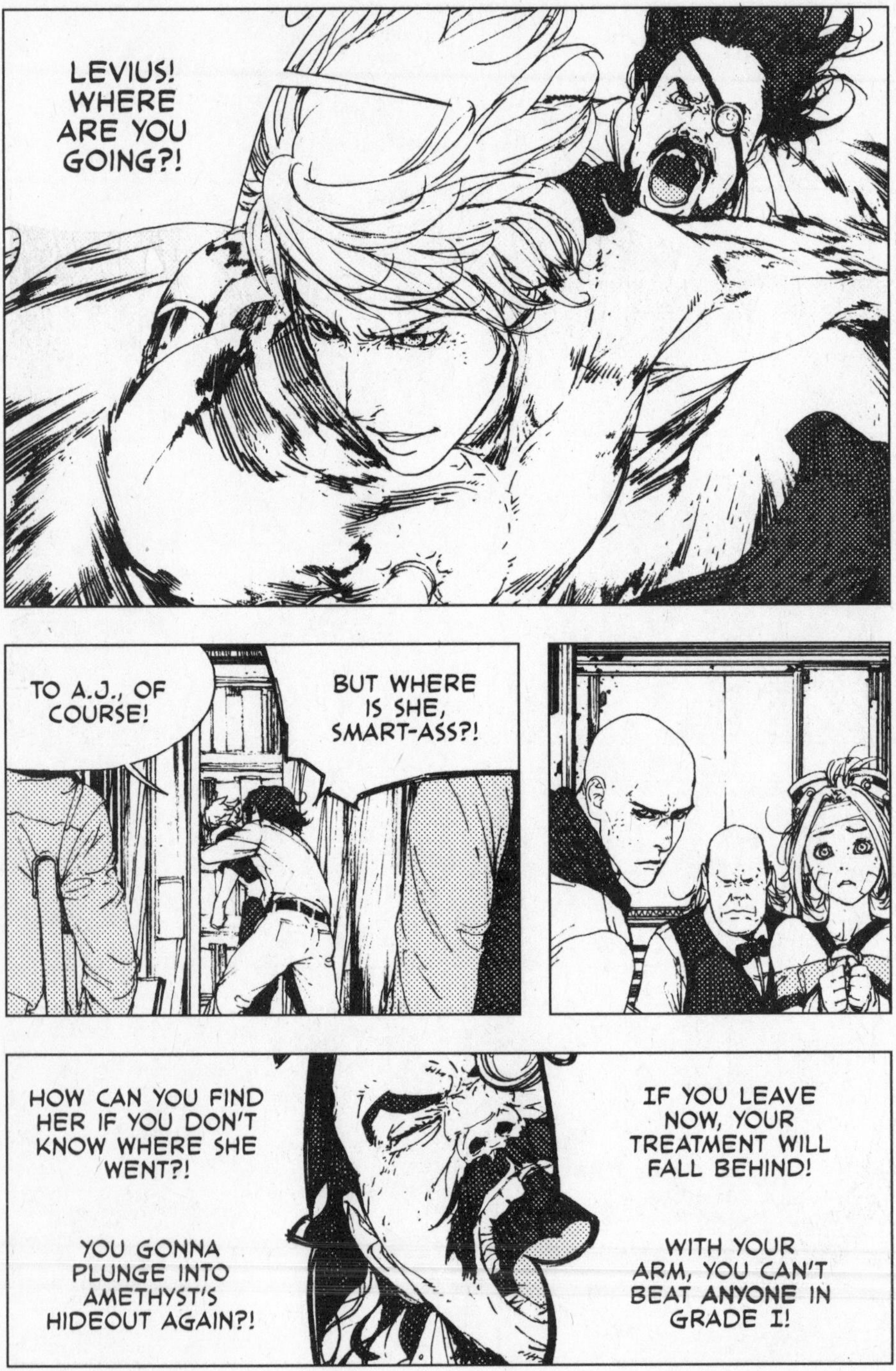
LEVIUS! WHERE ARE YOU GOING?!
TO A.J., OF COURSE!
BUT WHERE IS SHE, SMART-ASS?!
HOW CAN YOU FIND HER IF YOU DON'T KNOW WHERE SHE WENT?!
YOU GONNA PLUNGE INTO AMETHYST'S HIDEOUT AGAIN?!
IF YOU LEAVE NOW, YOUR TREATMENT WILL FALL BEHIND!
WITH YOUR ARM, YOU CAN'T BEAT ANYONE IN GRADE I!

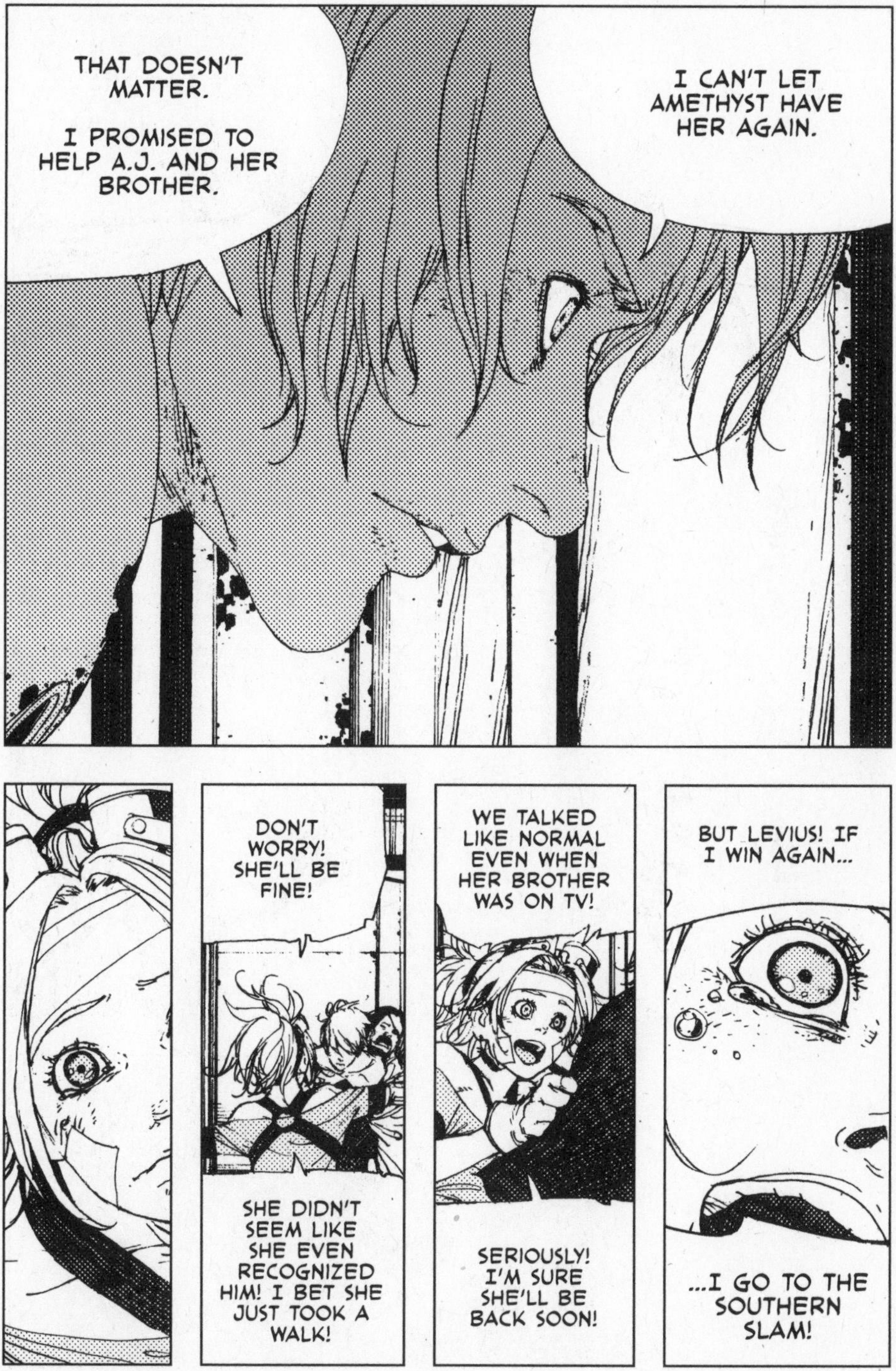
THAT DOESN'T MATTER.
I PROMISED TO HELP A.J. AND HER BROTHER.
I CAN'T LET AMETHYST HAVE HER AGAIN.
DON'T WORRY! SHE'LL BE FINE!
SHE DIDN'T SEEM LIKE SHE EVEN RECOGNIZED HIM! I BET SHE JUST TOOK A WALK!
WE TALKED LIKE NORMAL EVEN WHEN HER BROTHER WAS ON TV!
SERIOUSLY! I'M SURE SHE'LL BE BACK SOON!
BUT LEVIUS! IF I WIN AGAIN...
...I GO TO THE SOUTHERN SLAM!

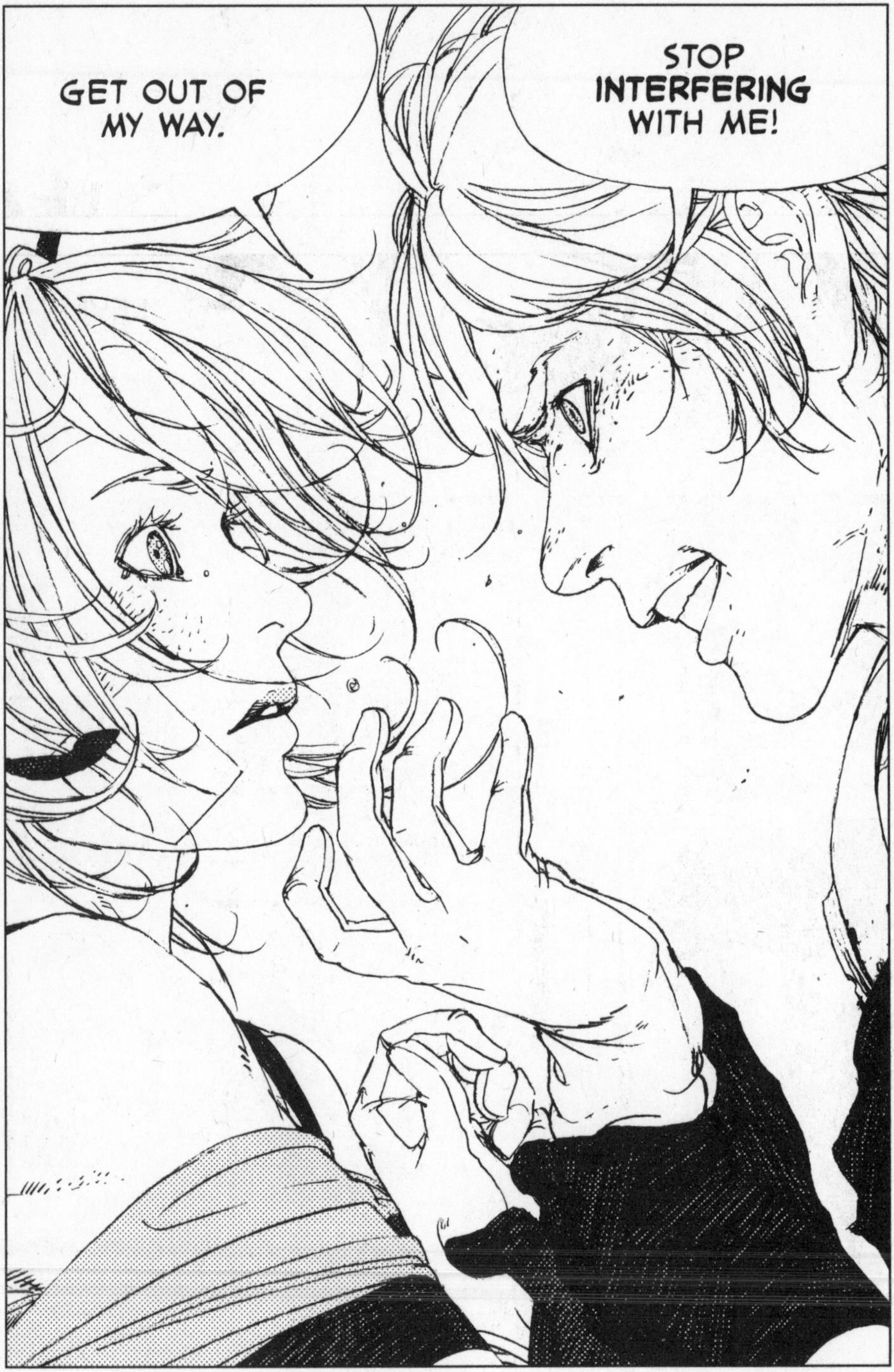
GET OUT OF MY WAY.
STOP INTERFERING WITH ME!

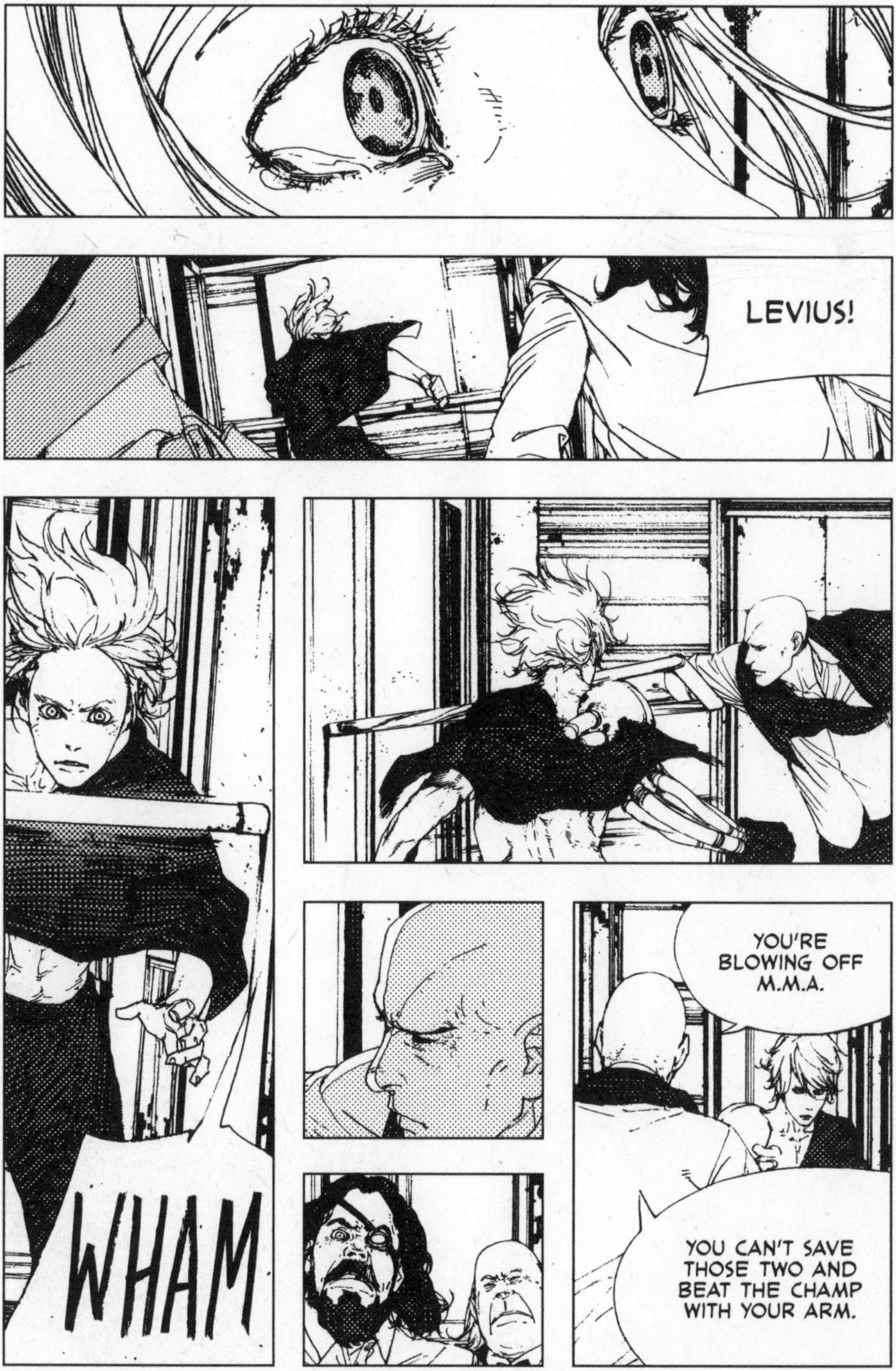
LEVIUS!
WHAM
YOU'RE BLOWING OFF M.M.A.
YOU CAN'T SAVE THOSE TWO AND BEAT THE CHAMP WITH YOUR ARM.

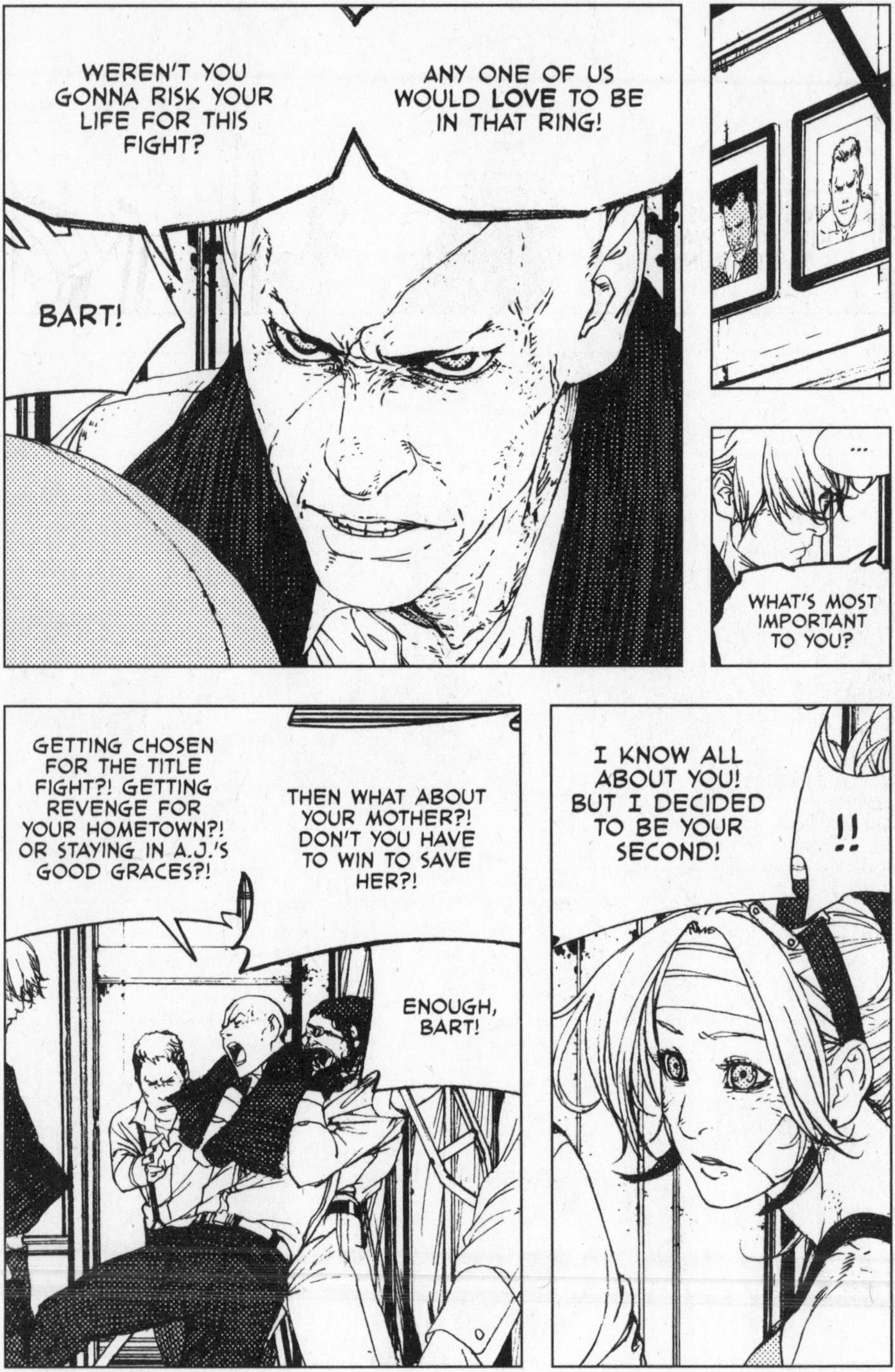
WEREN'T YOU GONNA RISK YOUR LIFE FOR THIS FIGHT?
ANY ONE OF US WOULD LOVE TO BE IN THAT RING!
BART!
...
WHAT'S MOST IMPORTANT TO YOU?
GETTING CHOSEN FOR THE TITLE FIGHT?! GETTING REVENGE FOR YOUR HOMETOWN?! OR STAYING IN A.J.'S GOOD GRACES?!
THEN WHAT ABOUT YOUR MOTHER?! DON'T YOU HAVE TO WIN TO SAVE HER?!
ENOUGH, BART!
I KNOW ALL ABOUT YOU! BUT I DECIDED TO BE YOUR SECOND!
!!

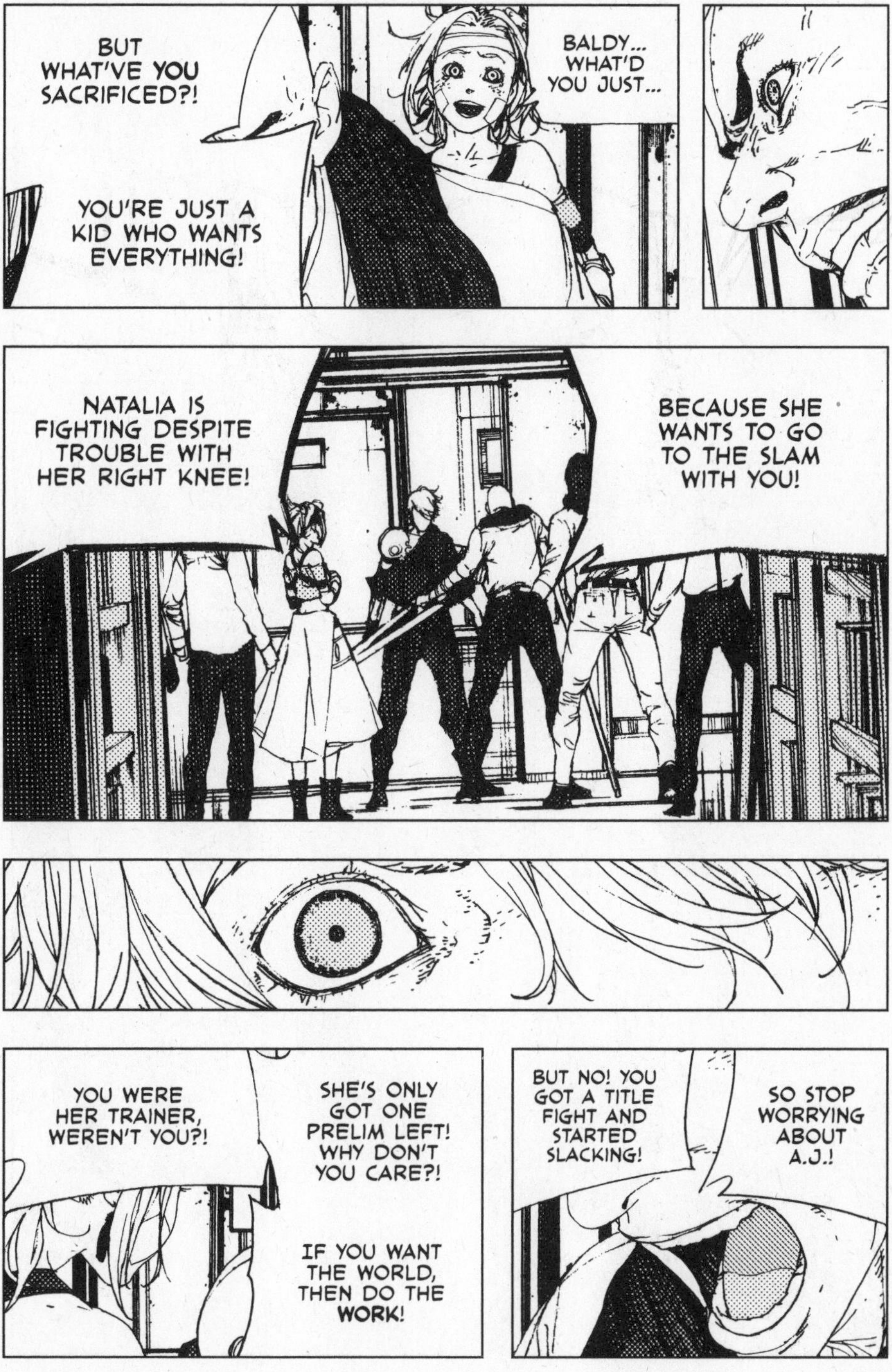
BUT WHAT'VE YOU SACRIFICED?!
YOU'RE JUST A KID WHO WANTS EVERYTHING!
BALDY... WHAT'D YOU JUST...
NATALIA IS FIGHTING DESPITE TROUBLE WITH HER RIGHT KNEE!
BECAUSE SHE WANTS TO GO TO THE SLAM WITH YOU!
YOU WERE HER TRAINER, WEREN'T YOU?!
SHE'S ONLY GOT ONE PRELIM LEFT! WHY DON'T YOU CARE?!
IF YOU WANT THE WORLD, THEN DO THE WORK!
BUT NO! YOU GOT A TITLE FIGHT AND STARTED SLACKING!
SO STOP WORRYING ABOUT A.J.!

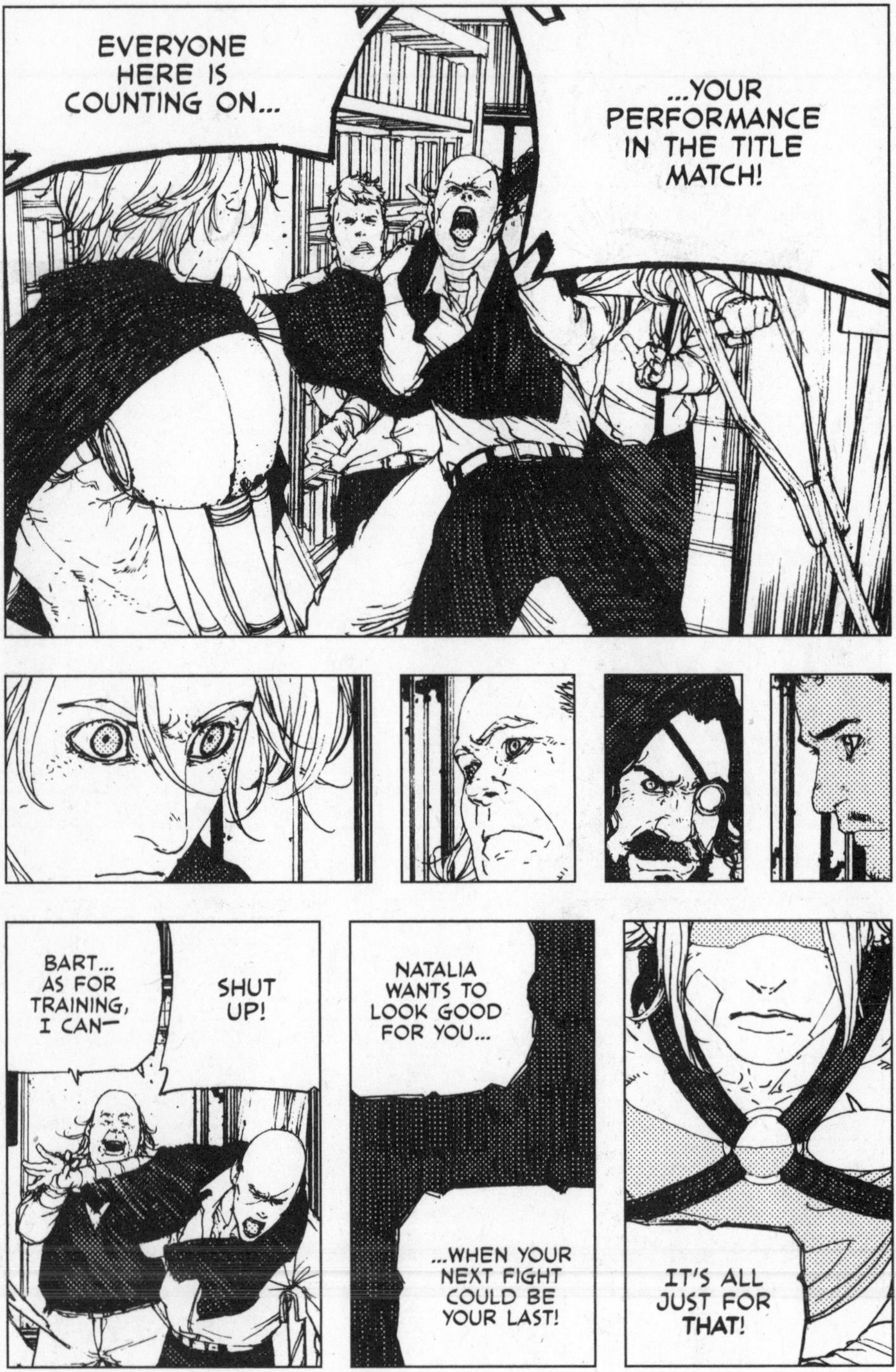
EVERYONE HERE IS COUNTING ON...
...YOUR PERFORMANCE IN THE TITLE MATCH!
BART... AS FOR TRAINING, I CAN—
SHUT UP!
NATALIA WANTS TO LOOK GOOD FOR YOU...
...WHEN YOUR NEXT FIGHT COULD BE YOUR LAST!
IT'S ALL JUST FOR THAT!

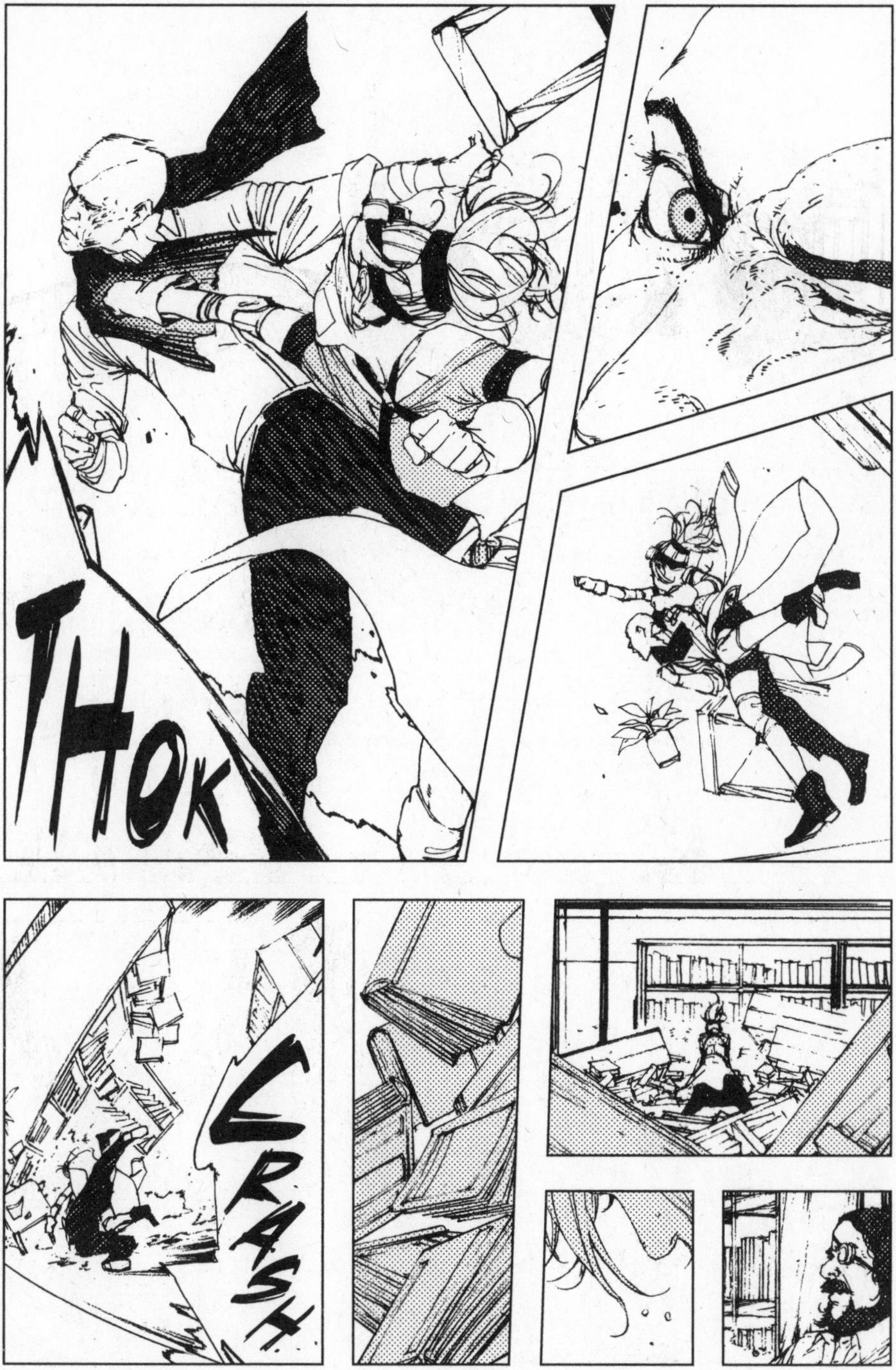
THOK
CRASH.

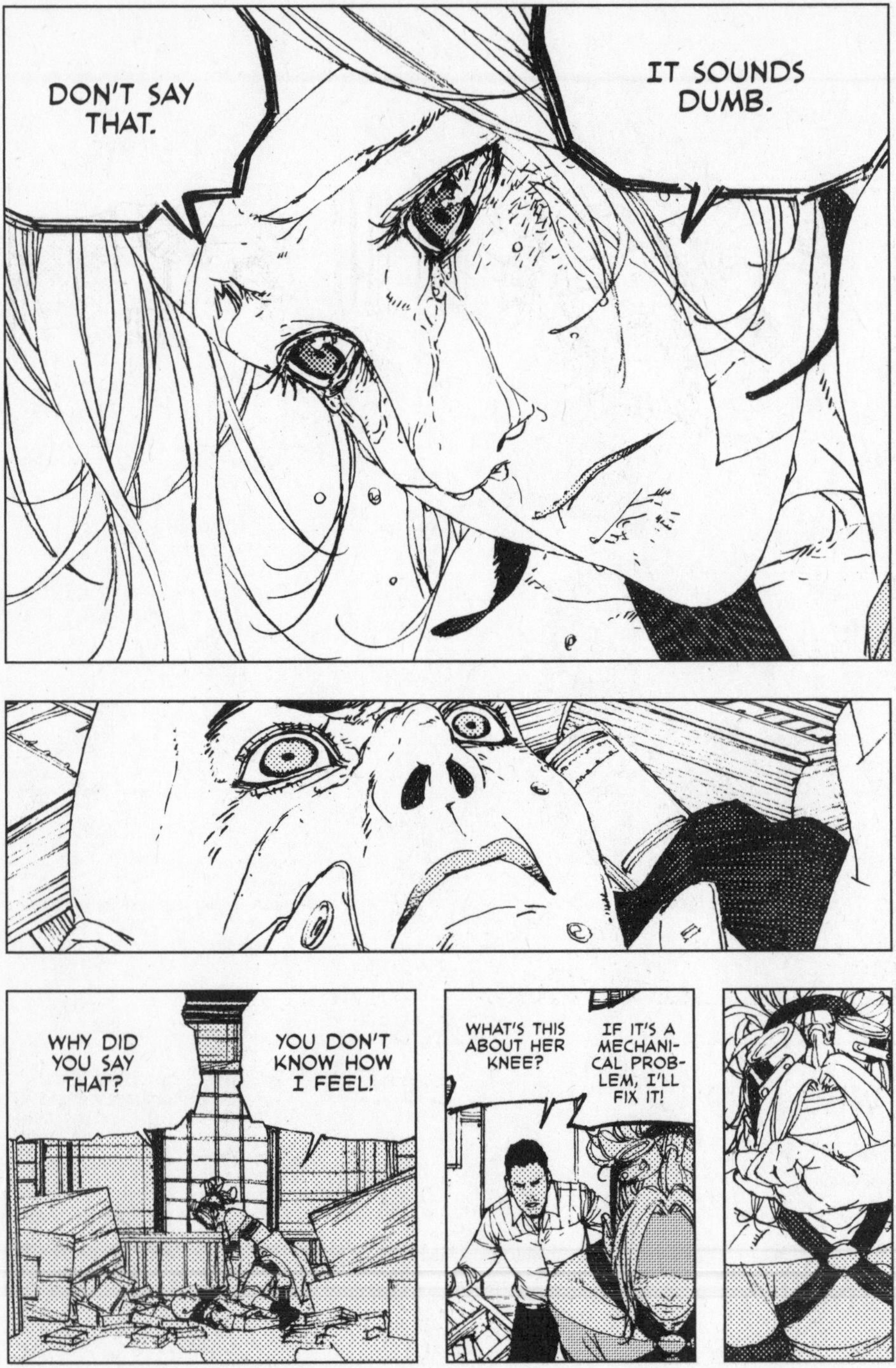
DON'T SAY THAT.
IT SOUNDS DUMB.
WHY DID YOU SAY THAT?
YOU DON'T KNOW HOW I FEEL!
WHAT'S THIS ABOUT HER KNEE?
IF IT'S A MECHANICAL PROBLEM, I'LL FIX IT!

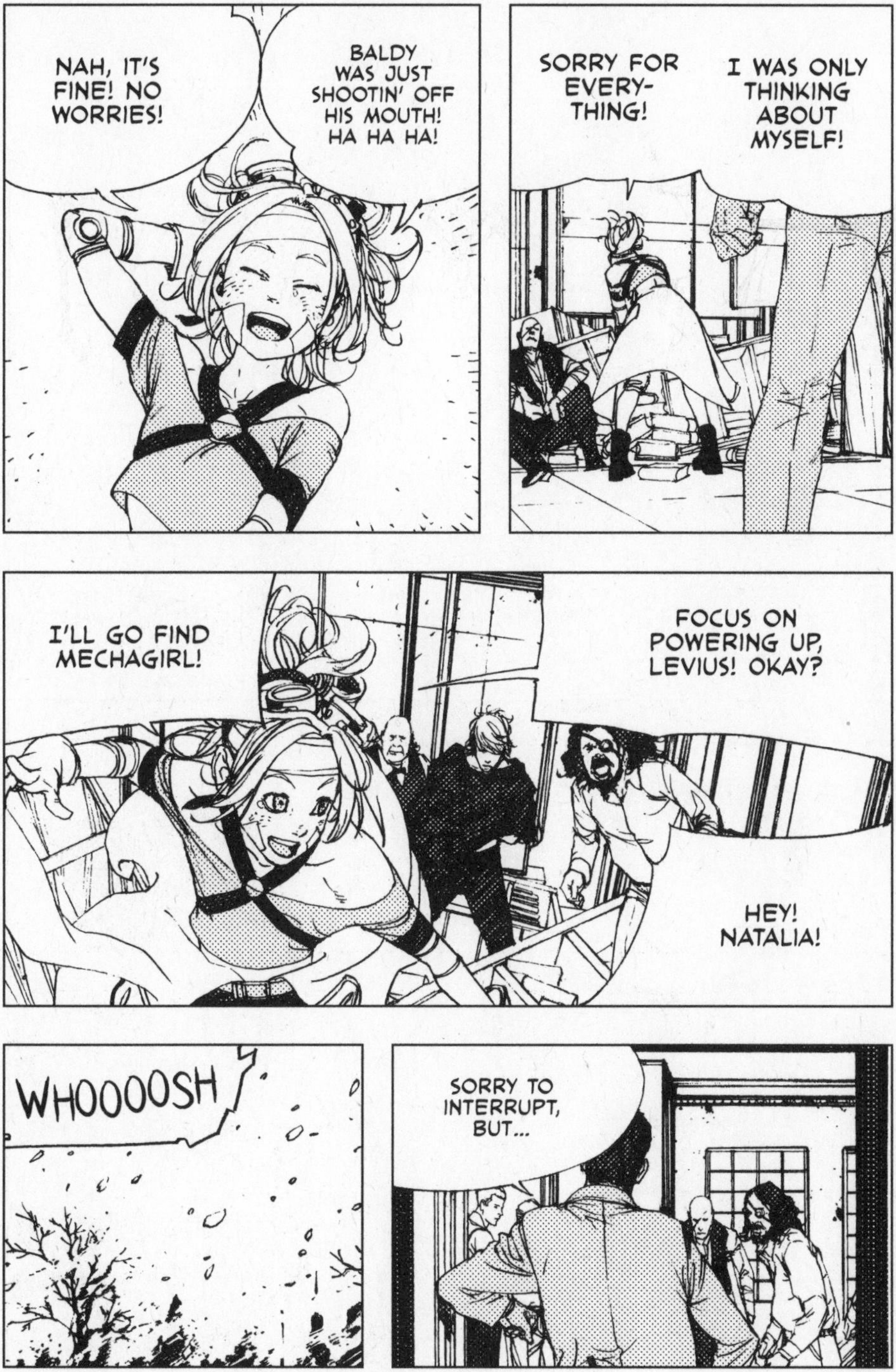
NAH, IT'S FINE! NO WORRIES!
BALDY WAS JUST SHOOTIN' OFF HIS MOUTH! HA HA HA!
SORRY FOR EVERY-THING!
I WAS ONLY THINKING ABOUT MYSELF!
I'LL GO FIND MECHAGIRL!
FOCUS ON POWERING UP, LEVIUS! OKAY?
HEY! NATALIA!
WHOOOOSH
SORRY TO INTERRUPT, BUT...

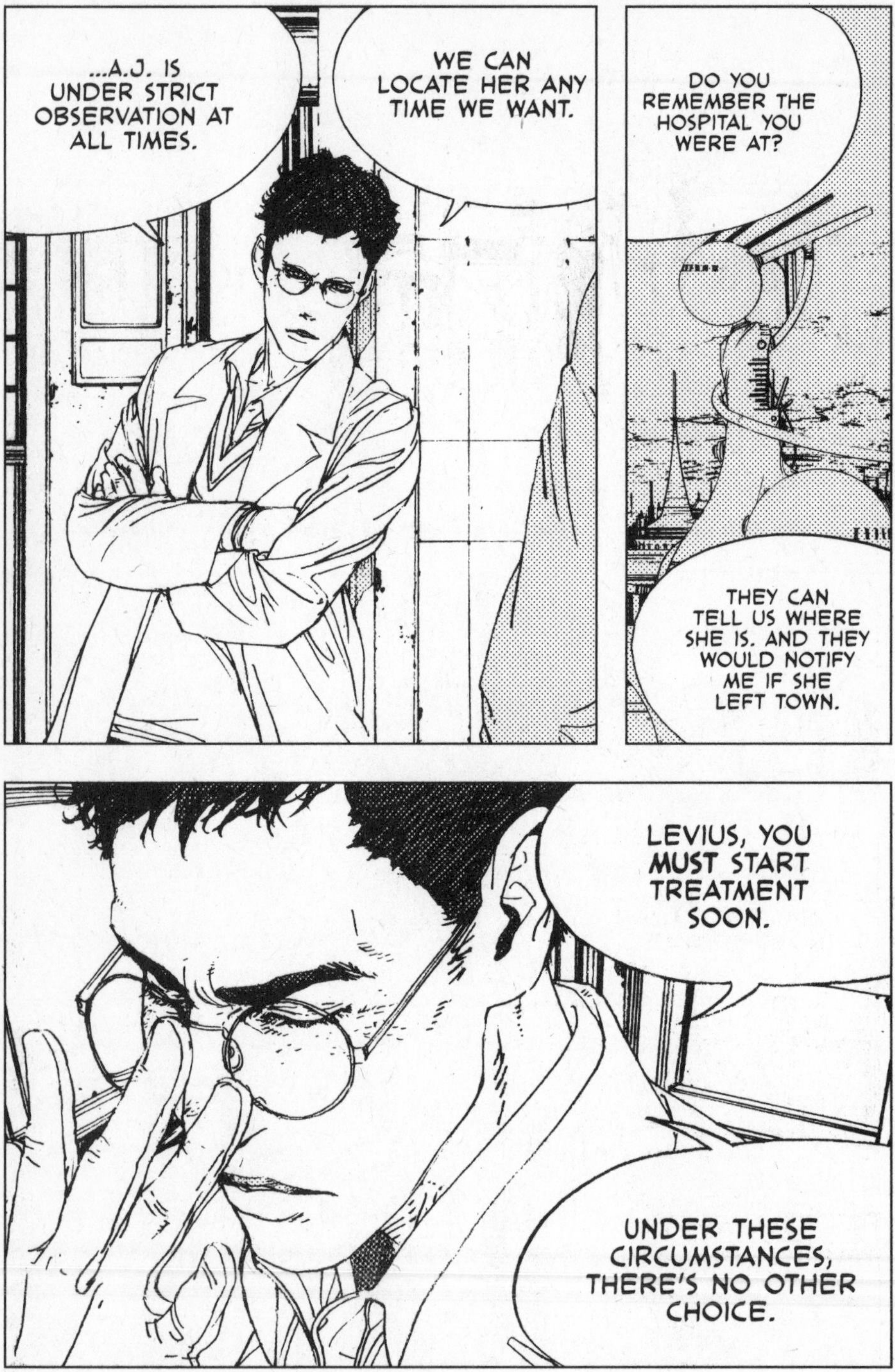
...A.J. IS UNDER STRICT OBSERVATION AT ALL TIMES.
WE CAN LOCATE HER ANY TIME WE WANT.
DO YOU REMEMBER THE HOSPITAL YOU WERE AT?
THEY CAN TELL US WHERE SHE IS. AND THEY WOULD NOTIFY ME IF SHE LEFT TOWN.
LEVIUS, YOU MUST START TREATMENT SOON.
UNDER THESE CIRCUMSTANCES, THERE'S NO OTHER CHOICE.

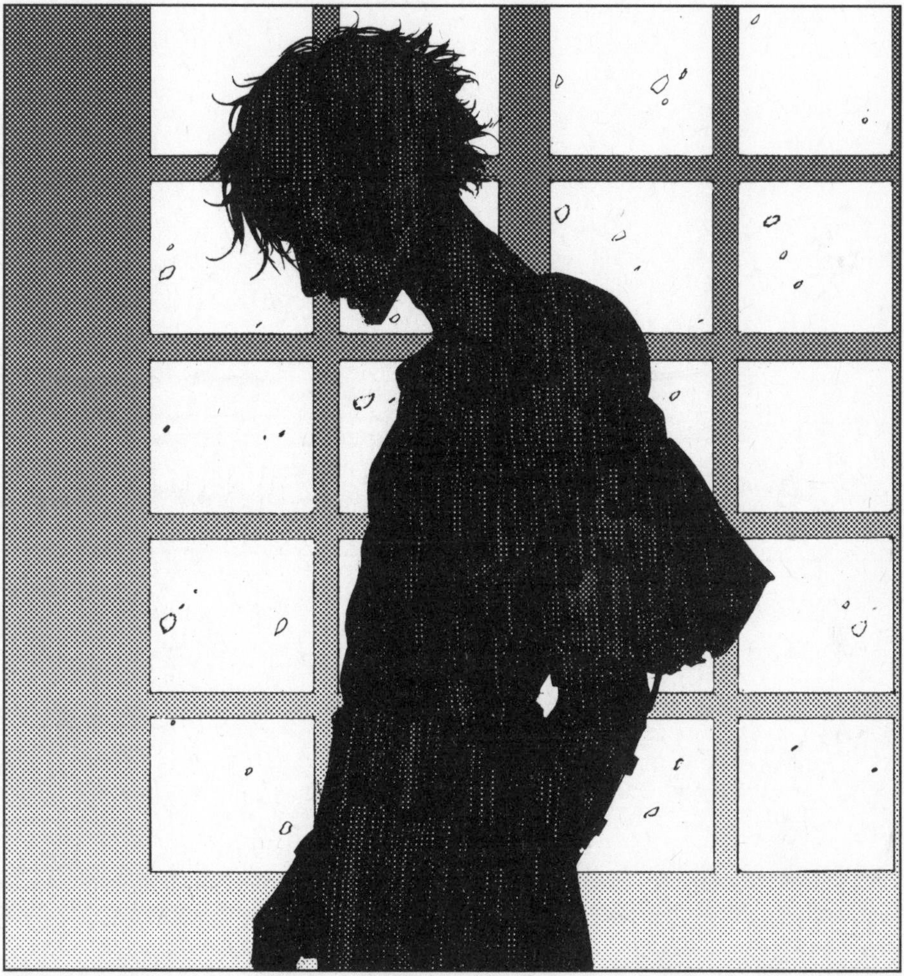
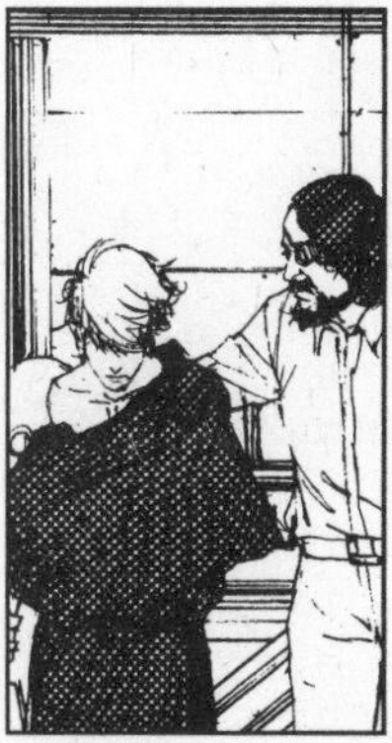
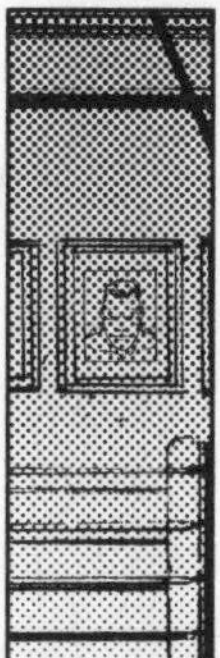
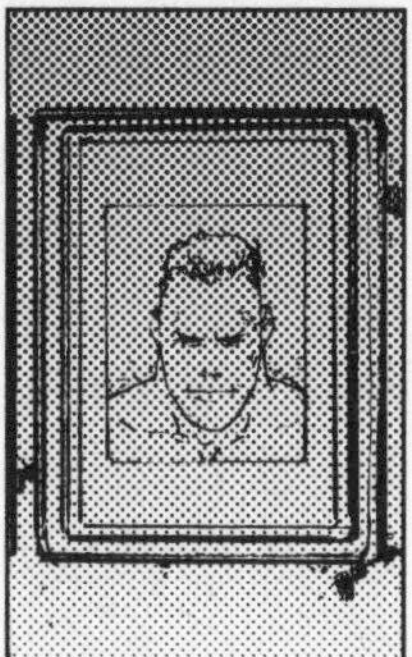
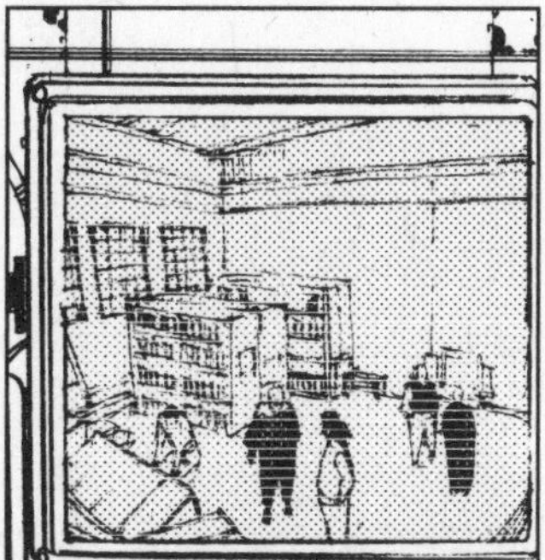

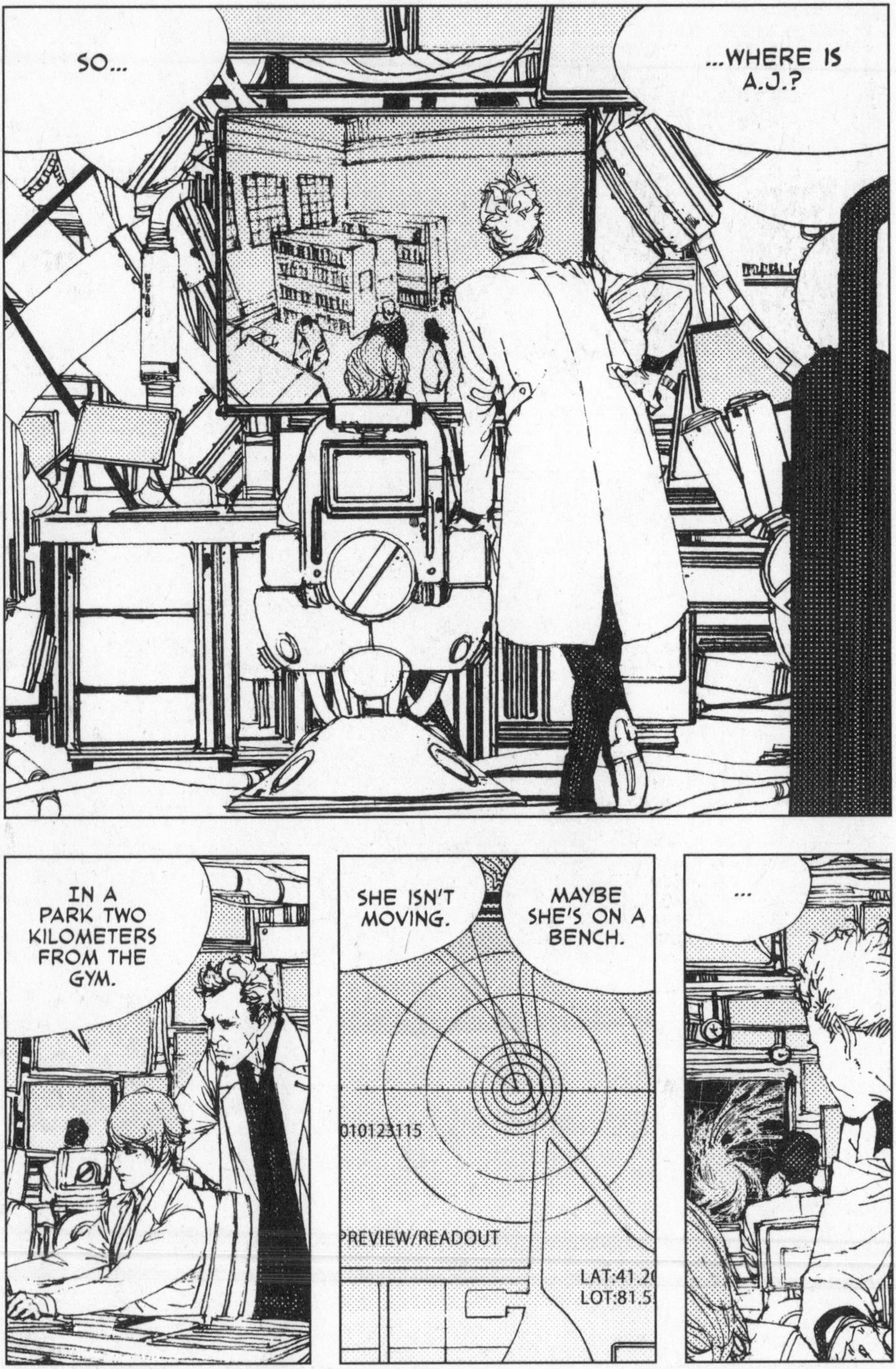
SO...
...WHERE IS A.J.?
IN A PARK TWO KILOMETERS FROM THE GYM.
SHE ISN'T MOVING.
MAYBE SHE'S ON A BENCH.
010123115
PREVIEW/READOUT
LAT:41.2
LOT:81.5
...

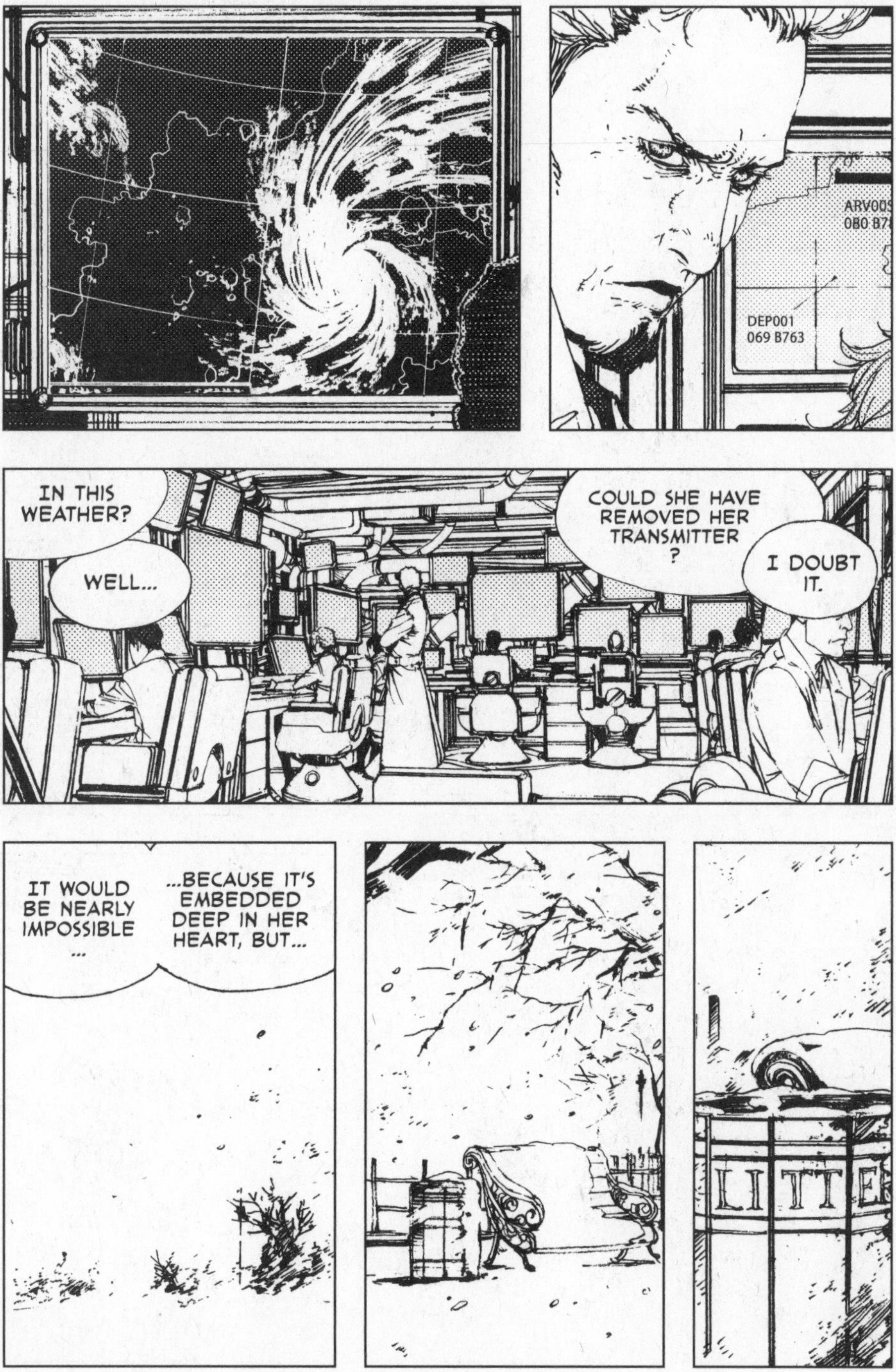
DEP001
069 B763
IN THIS WEATHER?
WELL...
COULD SHE HAVE REMOVED HER TRANSMITTER ?
I DOUBT IT.
IT WOULD BE NEARLY IMPOSSIBLE ...
...BECAUSE IT'S EMBEDDED DEEP IN HER HEART, BUT...

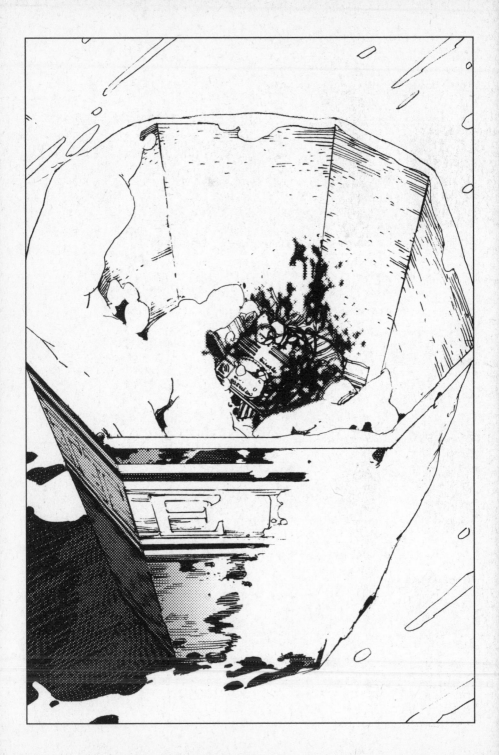

Levius/est
VOL. 3

Chapter 17

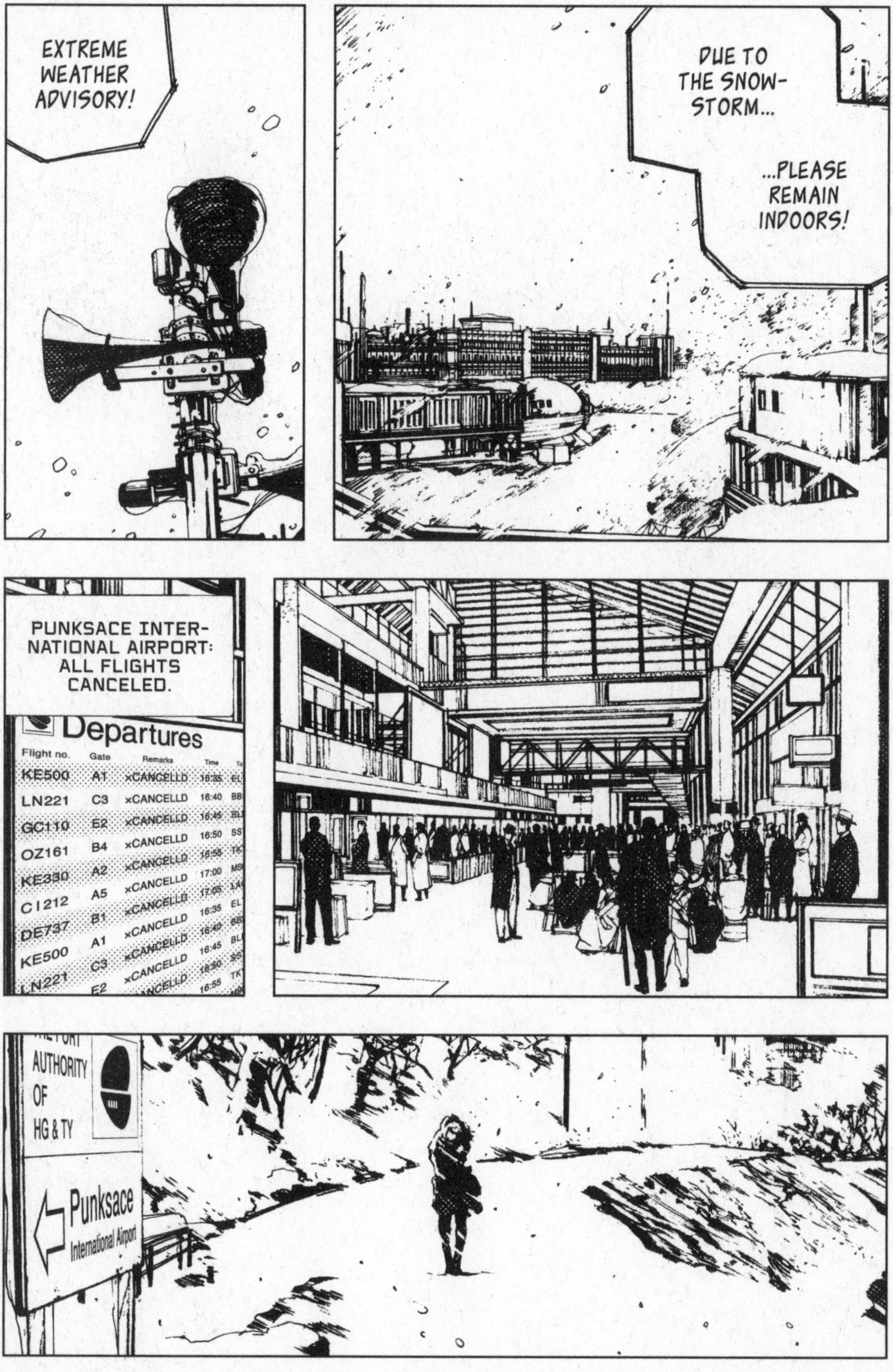
EXTREME WEATHER ADVISORY!
DUE TO THE SNOW-STORM...
...PLEASE REMAIN INDOORS!
PUNKSACE INTER-NATIONAL AIRPORT: ALL FLIGHTS CANCELED.
Departures
Flight no. Gate Remarks Time
KE500 A1 ×CANCELLD 16:35
LN221 C3 ×CANCELLD 16:40
GC110 E2 ×CANCELLD 16:45
OZ161 B4 ×CANCELLD 16:50
KE330 A2 ×CANCELLD 16:55
C1212 A5 ×CANCELLD 17:00
DE737 B1 ×CANCELLD 17:05
KE500 A1 ×CANCELLD 16:35
AUTHORITY OF HG & TY
Punksace International Airport

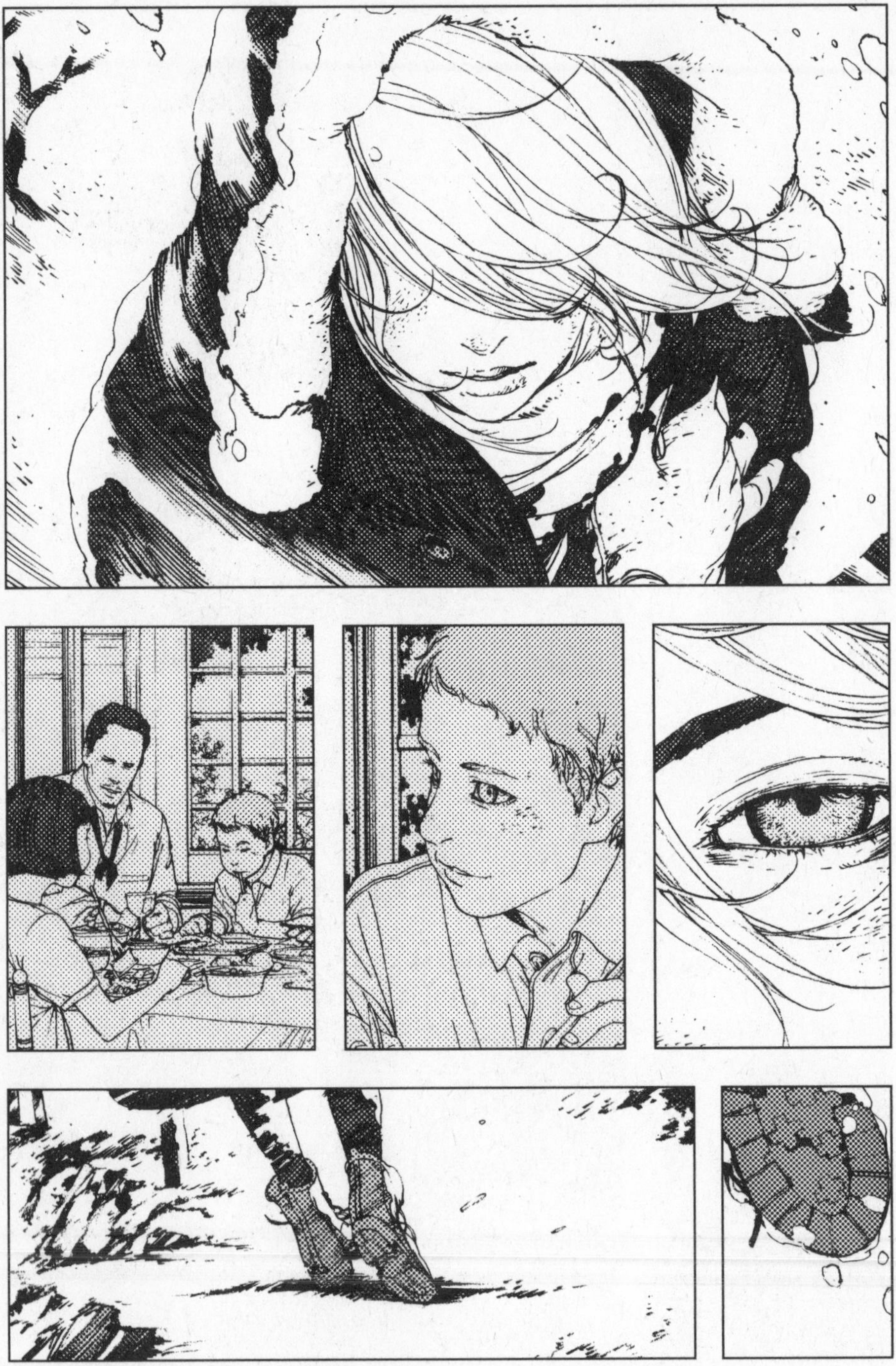

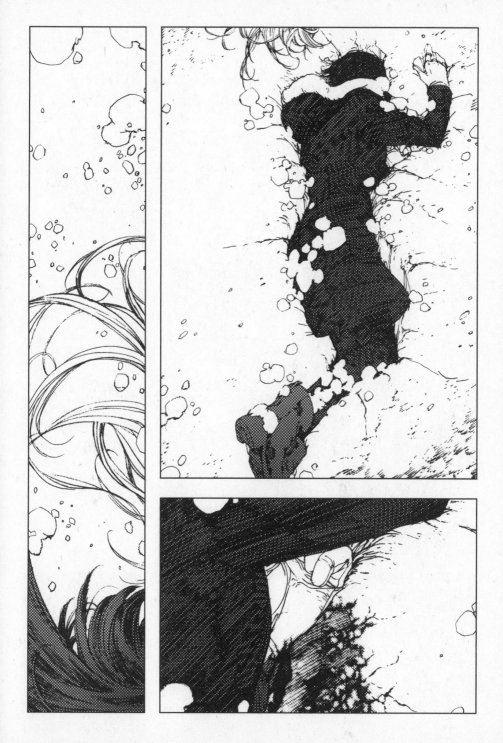

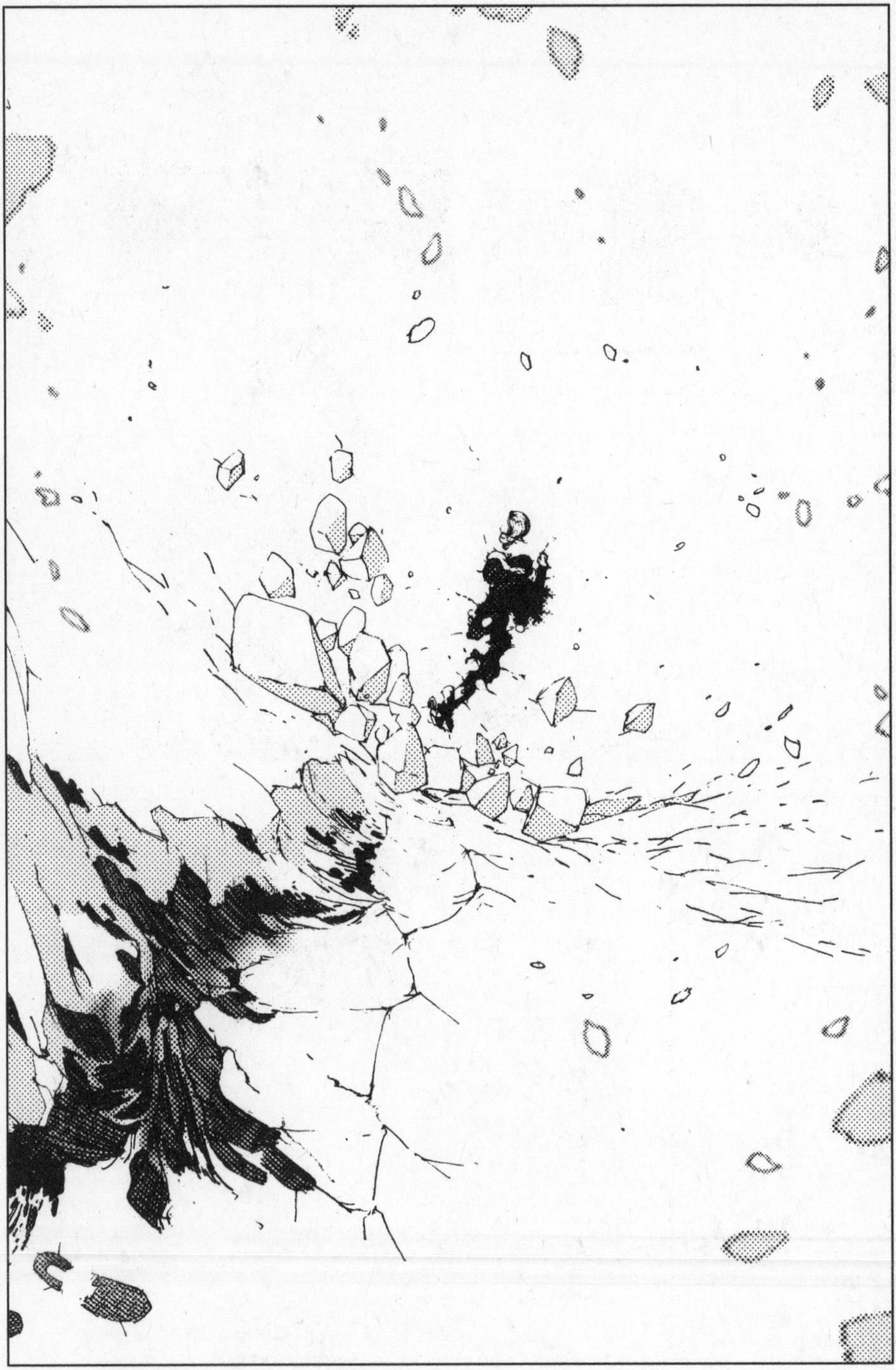

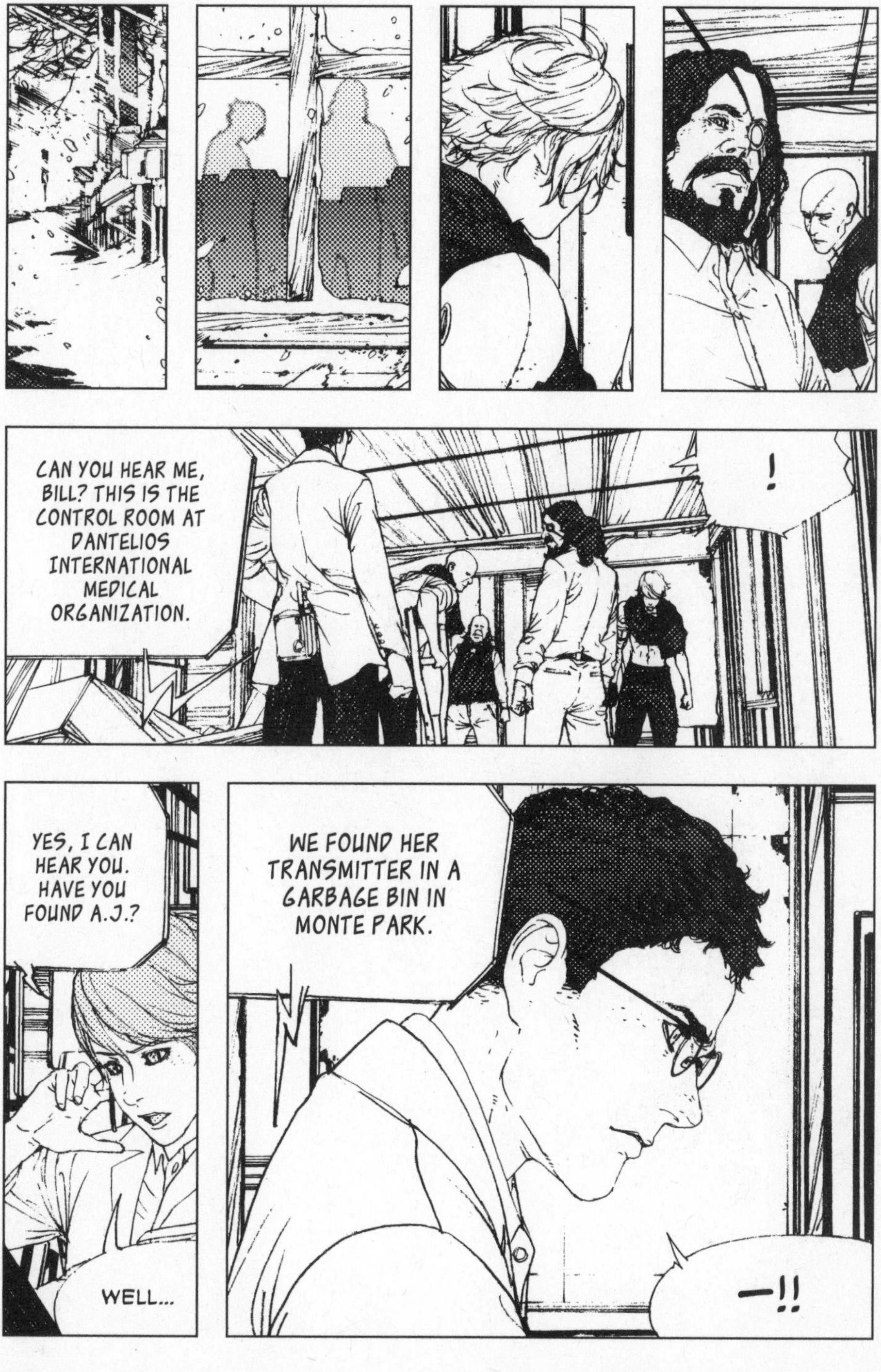
CAN YOU HEAR ME, BILL? THIS IS THE CONTROL ROOM AT DANTELIOS INTERNATIONAL MEDICAL ORGANIZATION.
!
YES, I CAN HEAR YOU. HAVE YOU FOUND A.J.?
WELL...
WE FOUND HER TRANSMITTER IN A GARBAGE BIN IN MONTE PARK.
—!!

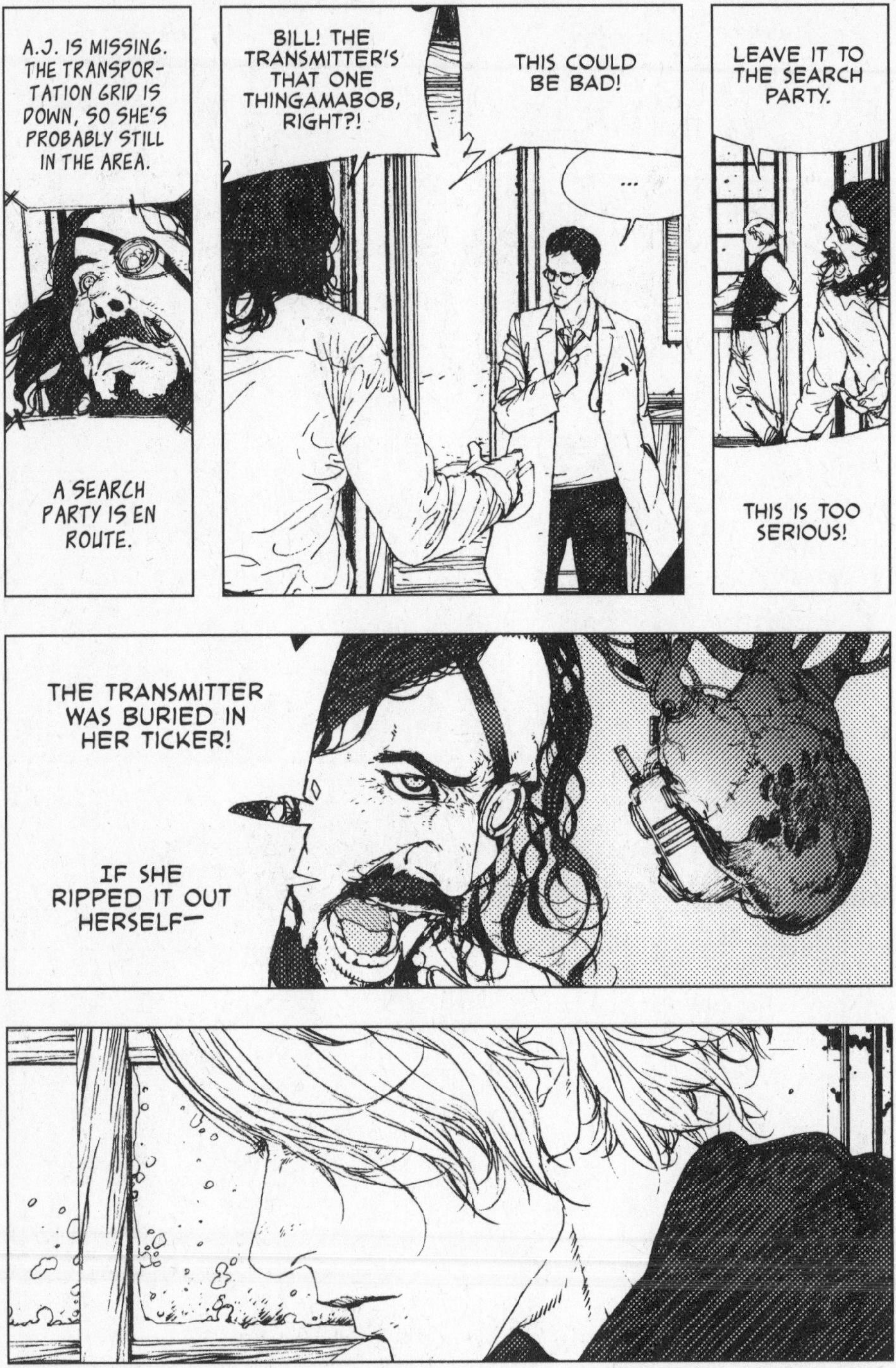
A.J. IS MISSING. THE TRANSPORTATION GRID IS DOWN, SO SHE'S PROBABLY STILL IN THE AREA.
A SEARCH PARTY IS EN ROUTE.
BILL! THE TRANSMITTER'S THAT ONE THINGAMABOB, RIGHT?!
THIS COULD BE BAD!
...
LEAVE IT TO THE SEARCH PARTY.
THIS IS TOO SERIOUS!
THE TRANSMITTER WAS BURIED IN HER TICKER!
IF SHE RIPPED IT OUT HERSELF—

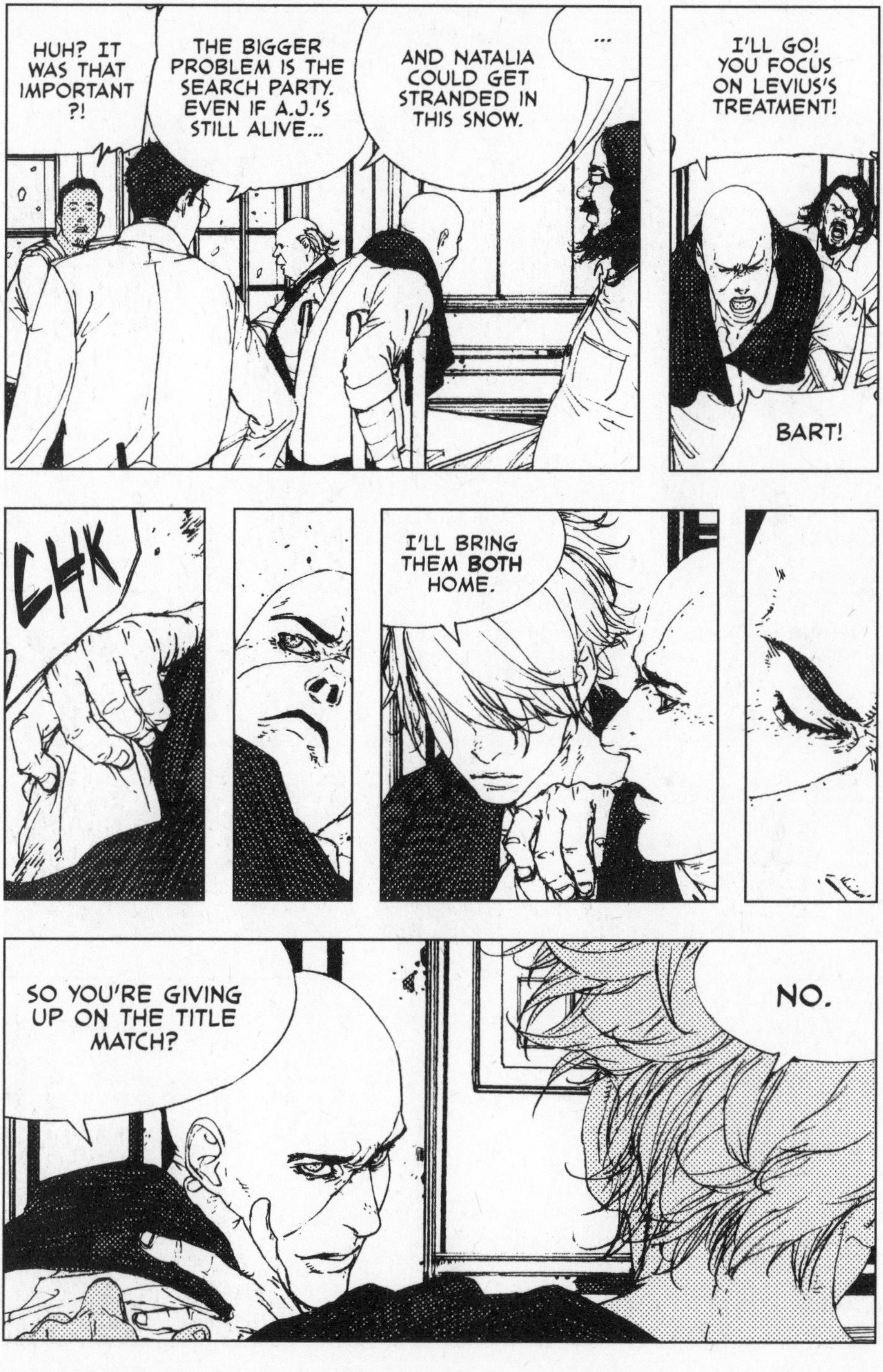
HUH? IT WAS THAT IMPORTANT?!
THE BIGGER PROBLEM IS THE SEARCH PARTY. EVEN IF A.J.'S STILL ALIVE...
AND NATALIA COULD GET STRANDED IN THIS SNOW.
...
I'LL GO! YOU FOCUS ON LEVIUS'S TREATMENT!
BART!
CHK
I'LL BRING THEM BOTH HOME.
SO YOU'RE GIVING UP ON THE TITLE MATCH?
NO.

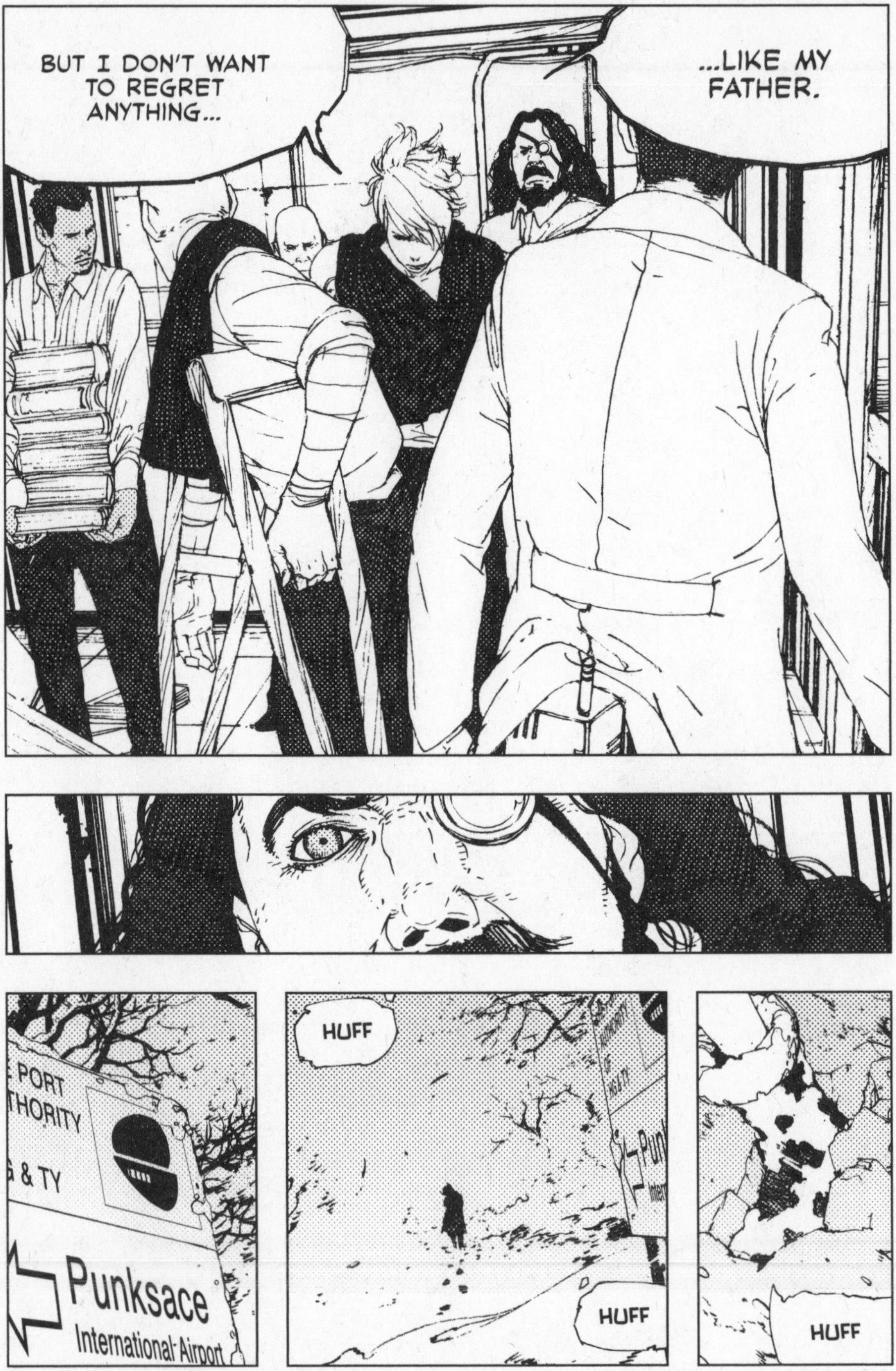
BUT I DON'T WANT TO REGRET ANYTHING...
...LIKE MY FATHER.
PORT
THORITY
G & TY
Punksace
International Airport
HUFF
HUFF
HUFF

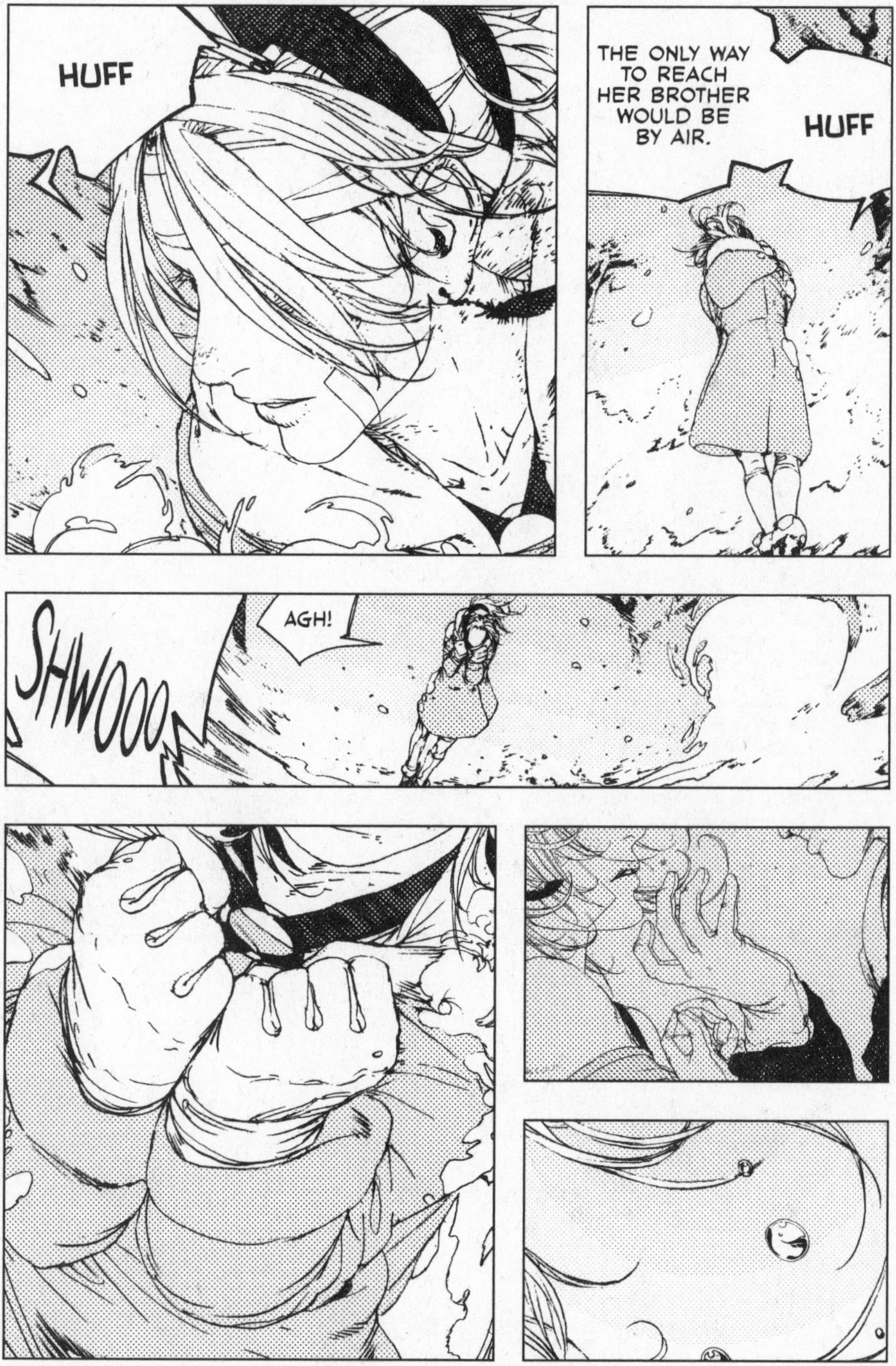
HUFF
THE ONLY WAY TO REACH HER BROTHER WOULD BE BY AIR.
HUFF
SHWOOO
AGH!

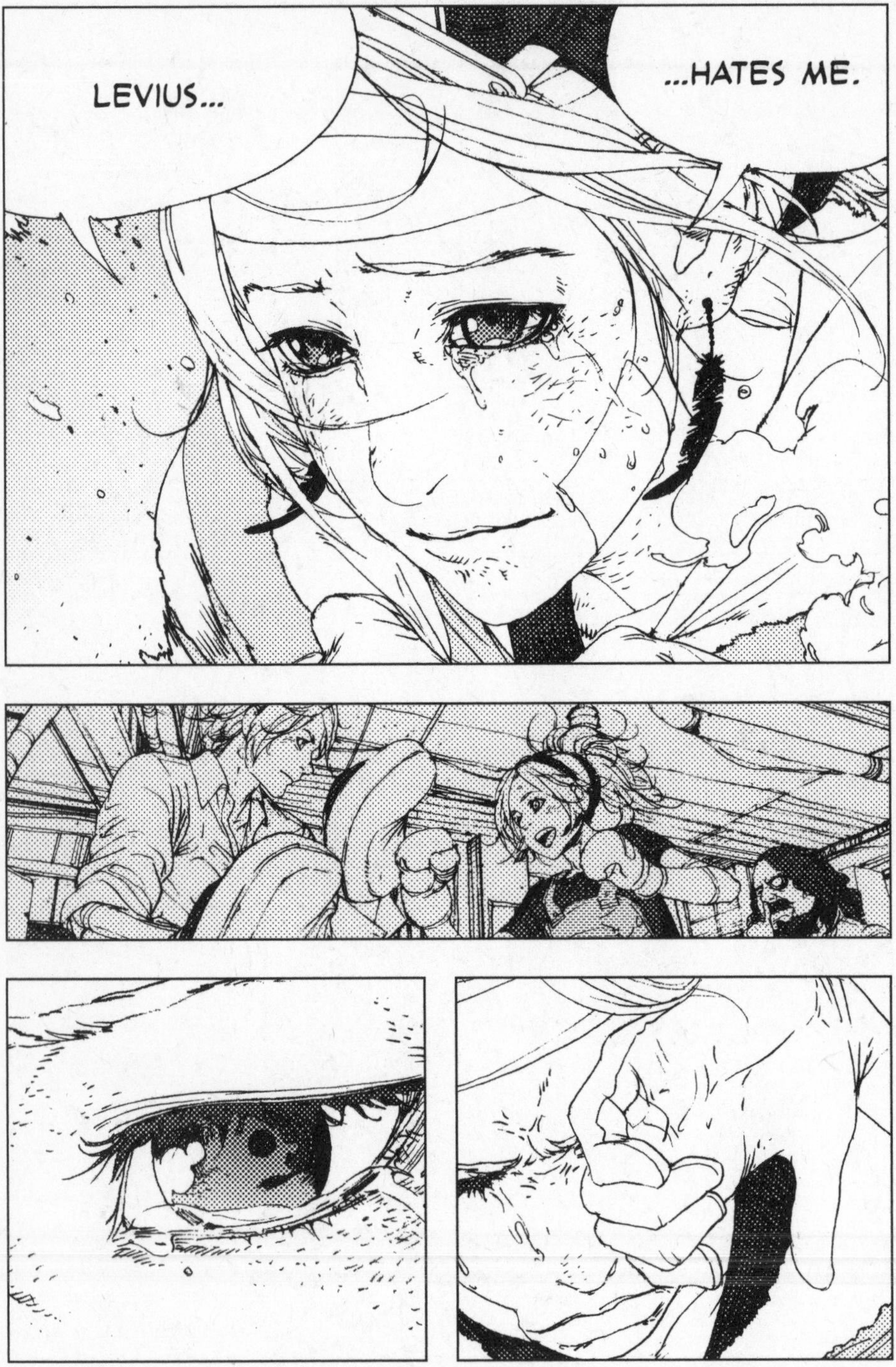
LEVIUS...
...HATES ME.

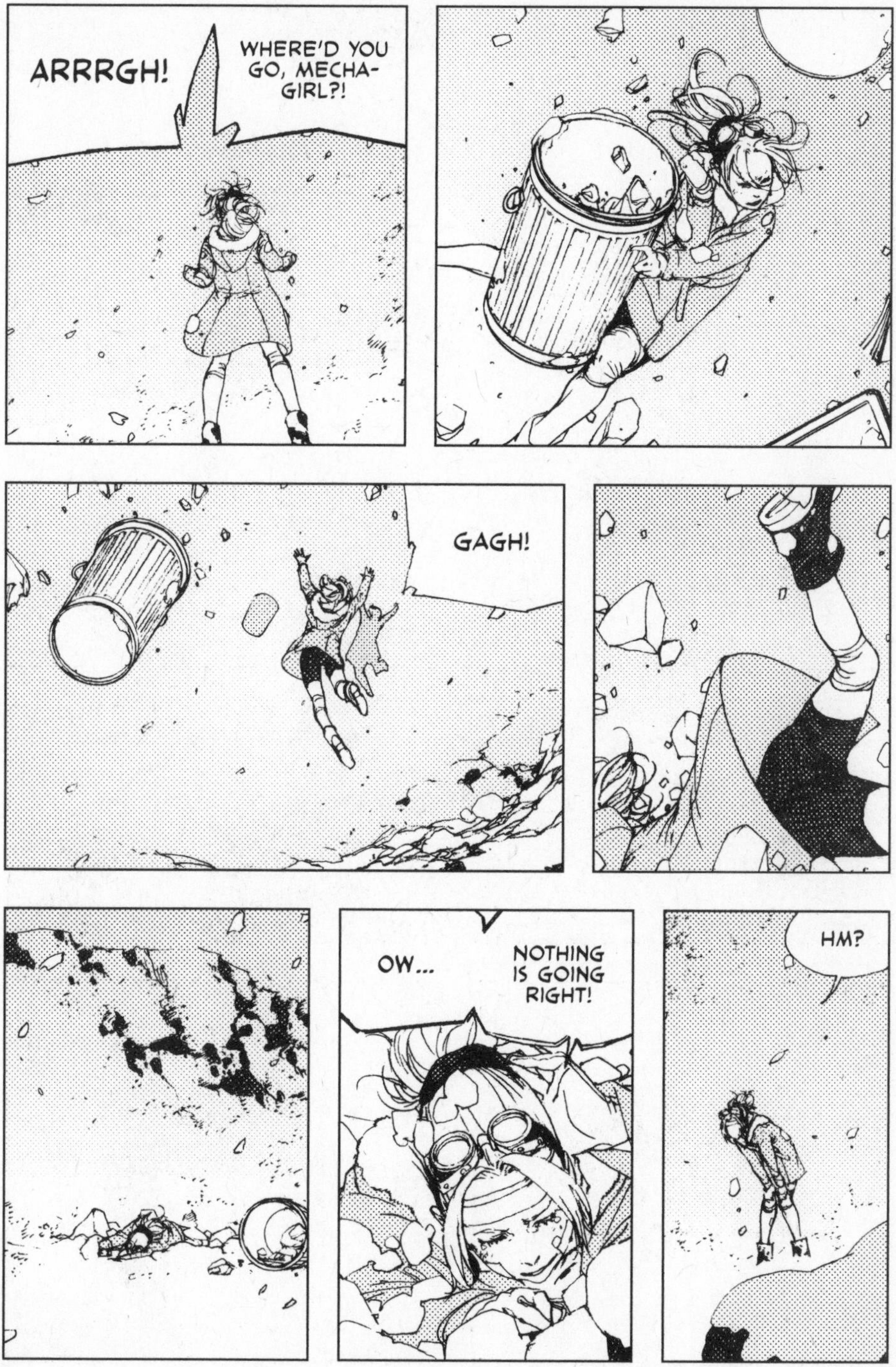
ARRRGH!
WHERE'D YOU GO, MECHA-GIRL?!
GAGH!
OW...
NOTHING IS GOING RIGHT!
HM?

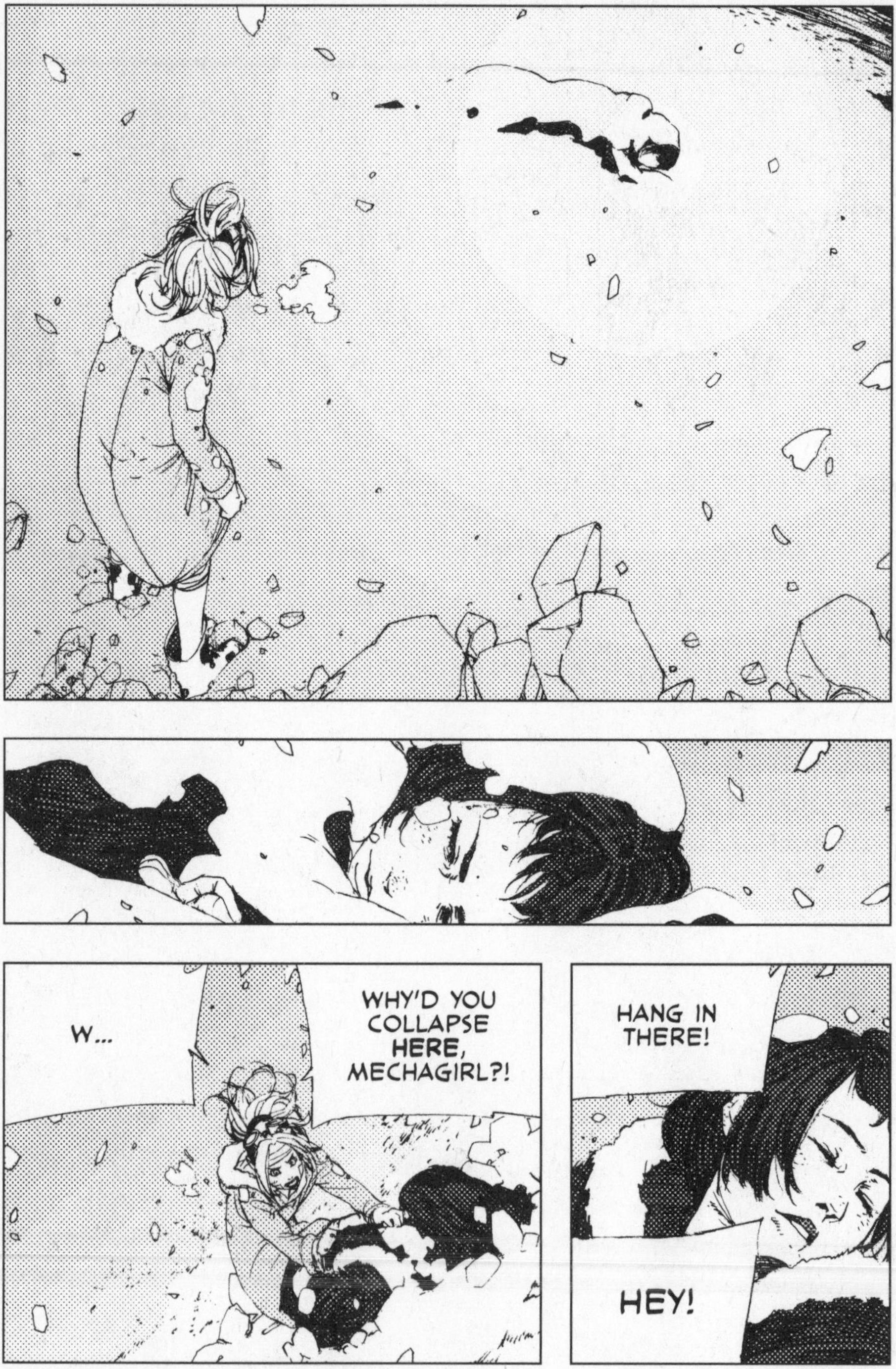
W...
WHY'D YOU COLLAPSE HERE, MECHAGIRL?!
HANG IN THERE!
HEY!

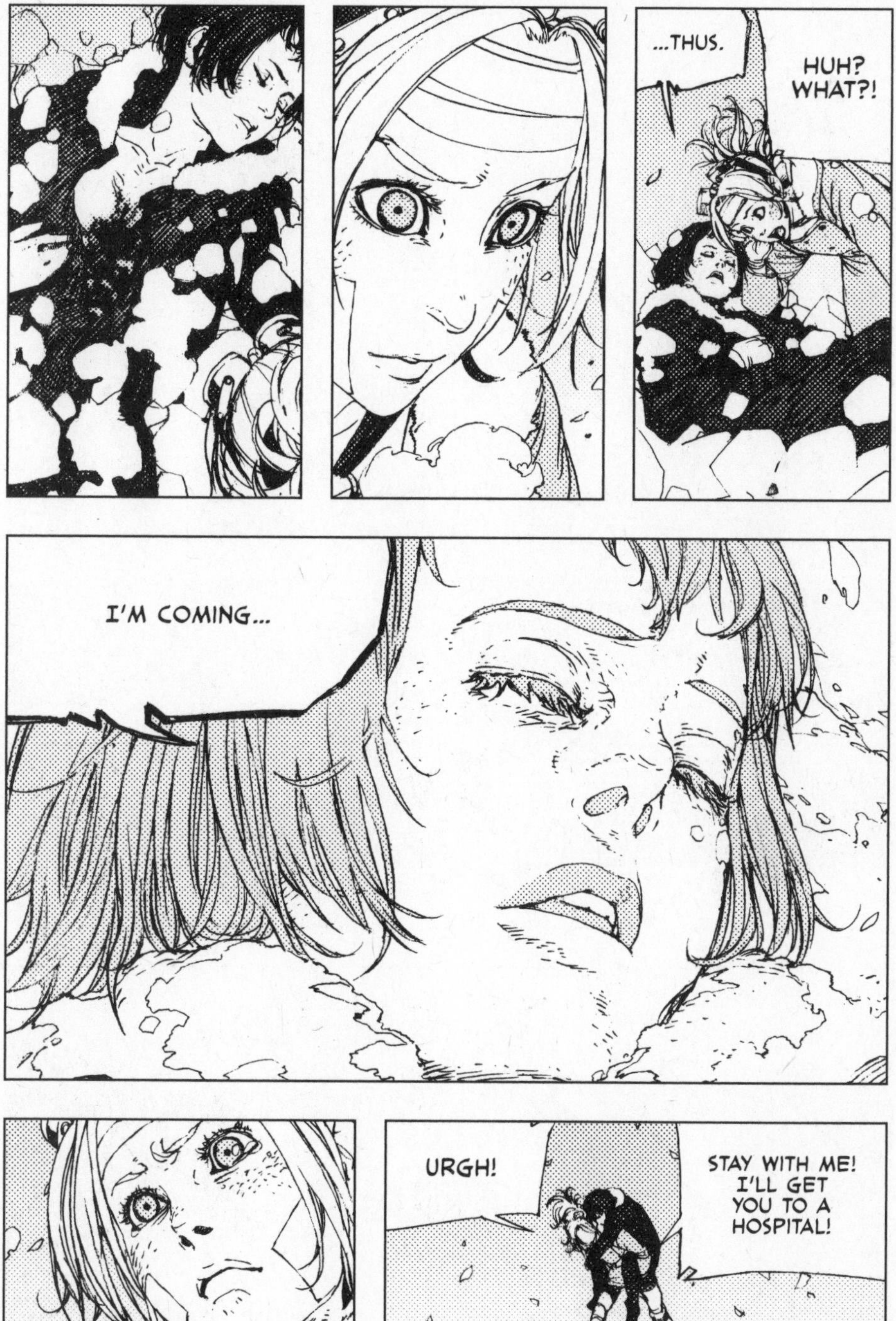
...THUS.
HUH? WHAT?!
I'M COMING...
URGH!
STAY WITH ME! I'LL GET YOU TO A HOSPITAL!

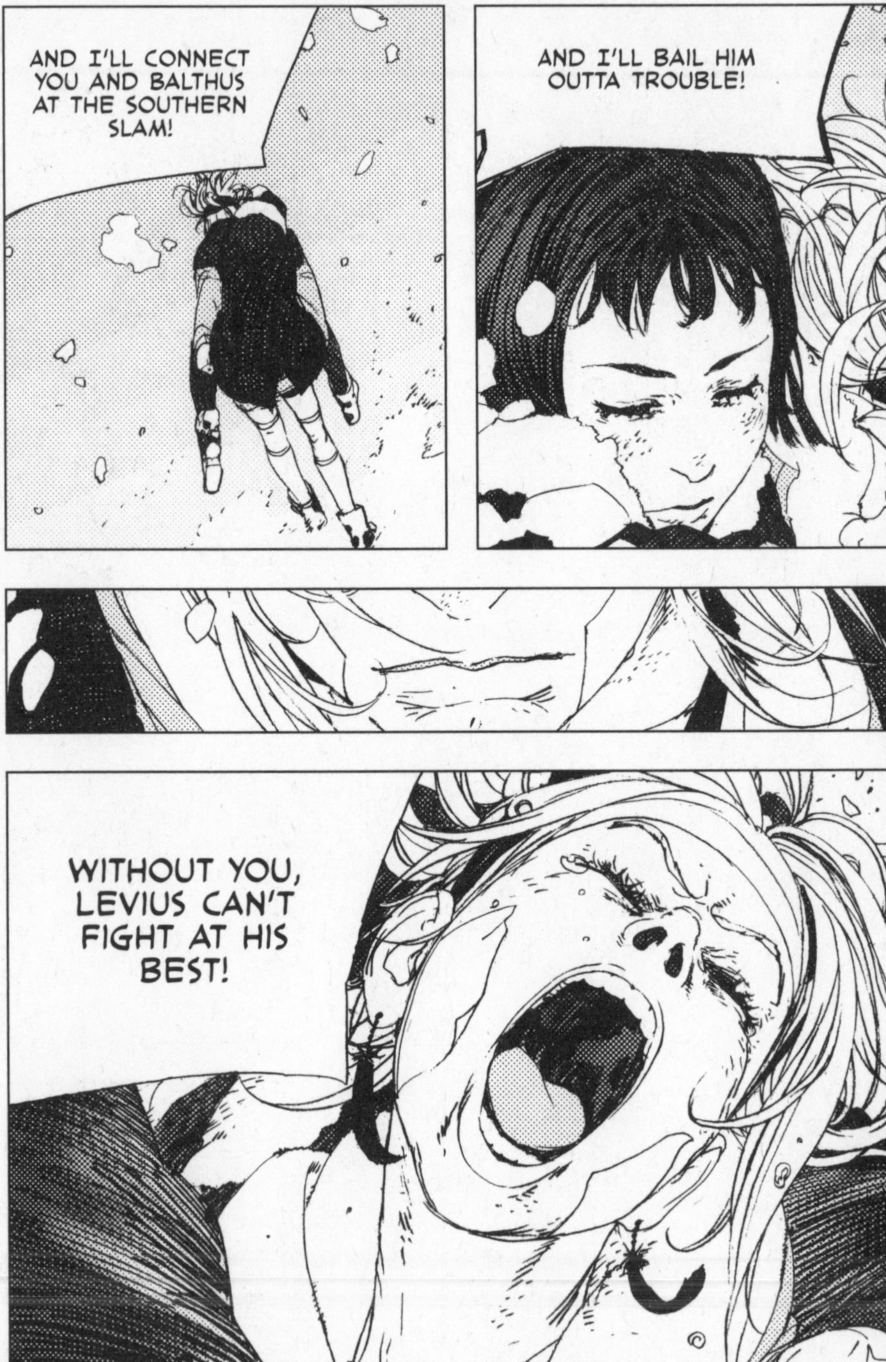
AND I'LL CONNECT YOU AND BALTHUS AT THE SOUTHERN SLAM!
AND I'LL BAIL HIM OUTTA TROUBLE!
WITHOUT YOU, LEVIUS CAN'T FIGHT AT HIS BEST!

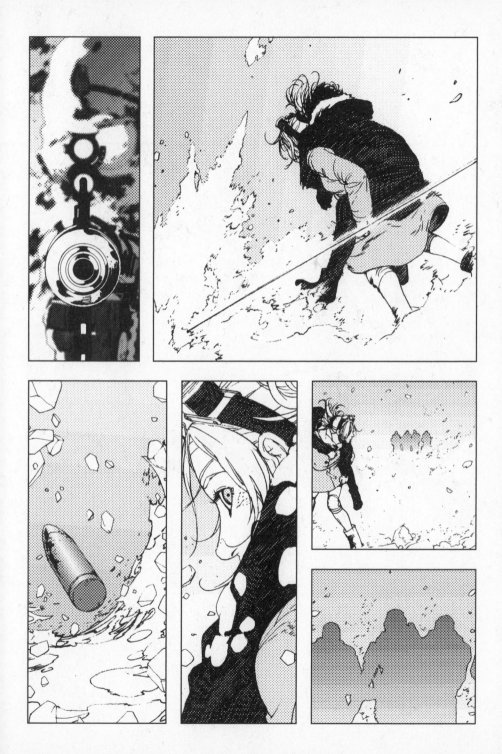

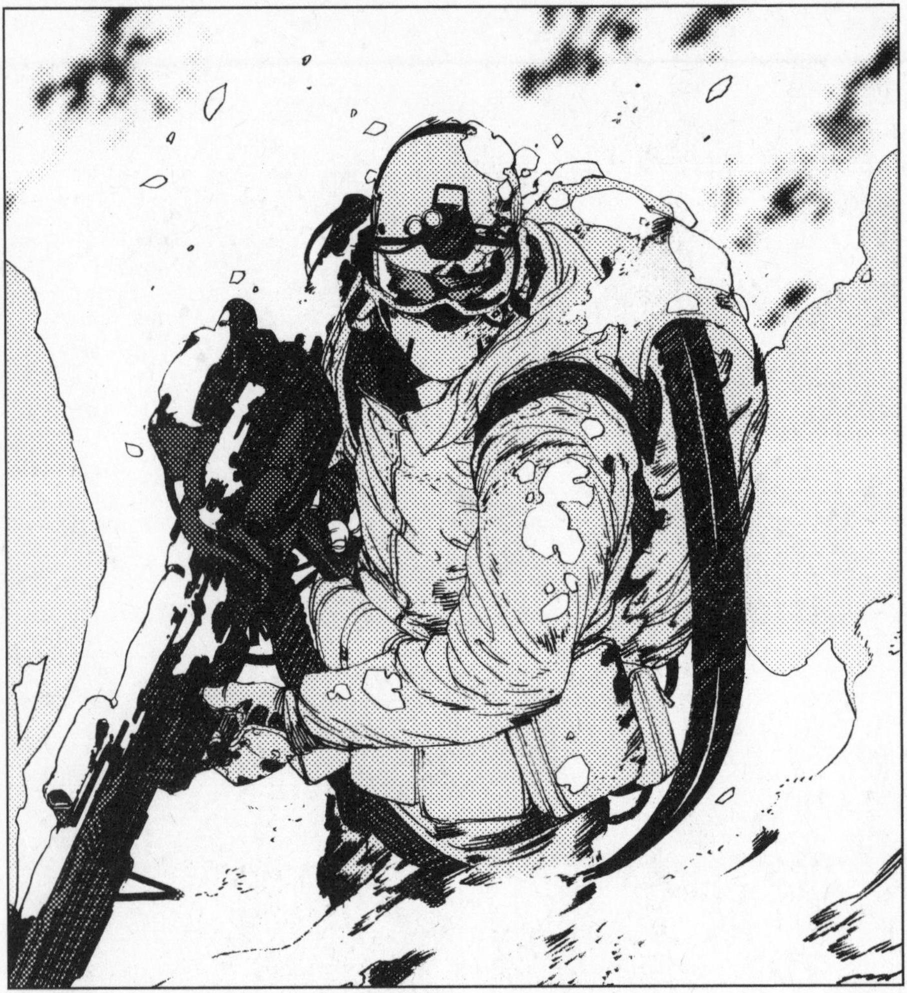

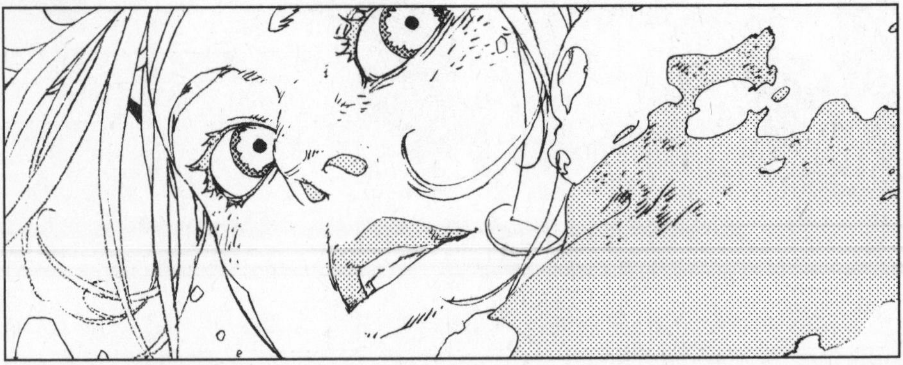

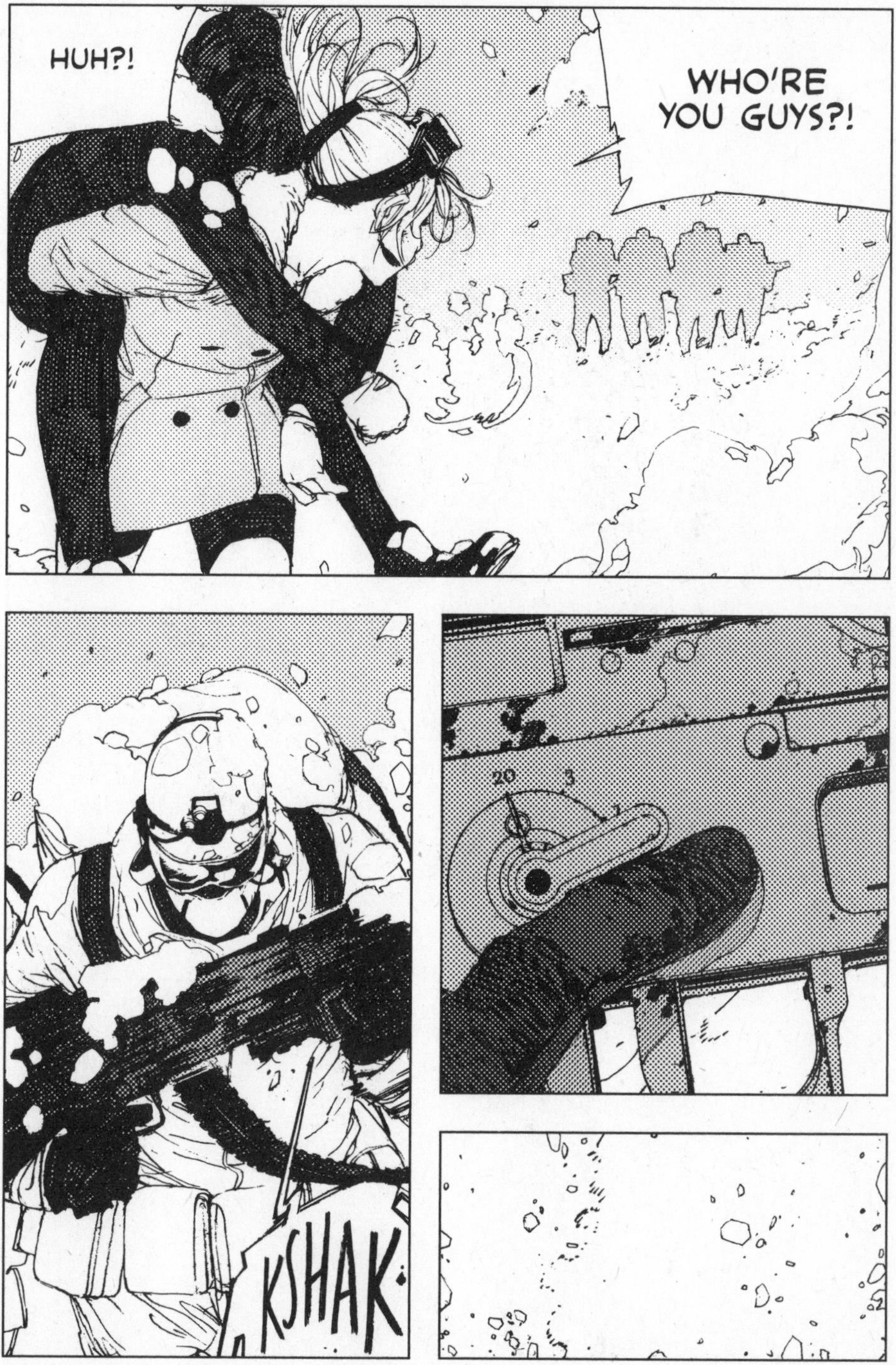
HUH?!
WHO'RE YOU GUYS?!
KSHAK
20
3

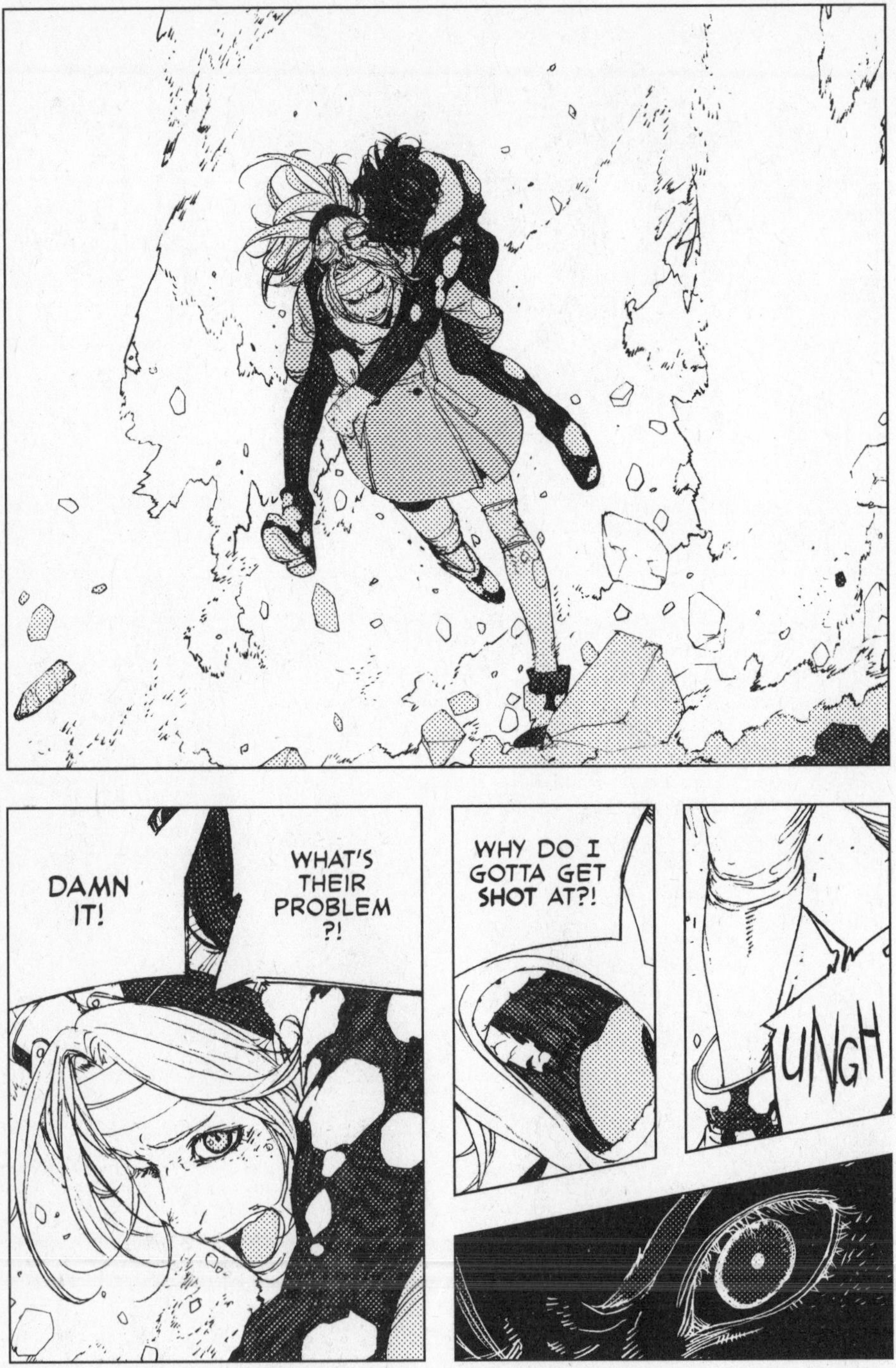
DAMN IT!
WHAT'S THEIR PROBLEM ?!
WHY DO I GOTTA GET SHOT AT?!
UNGH

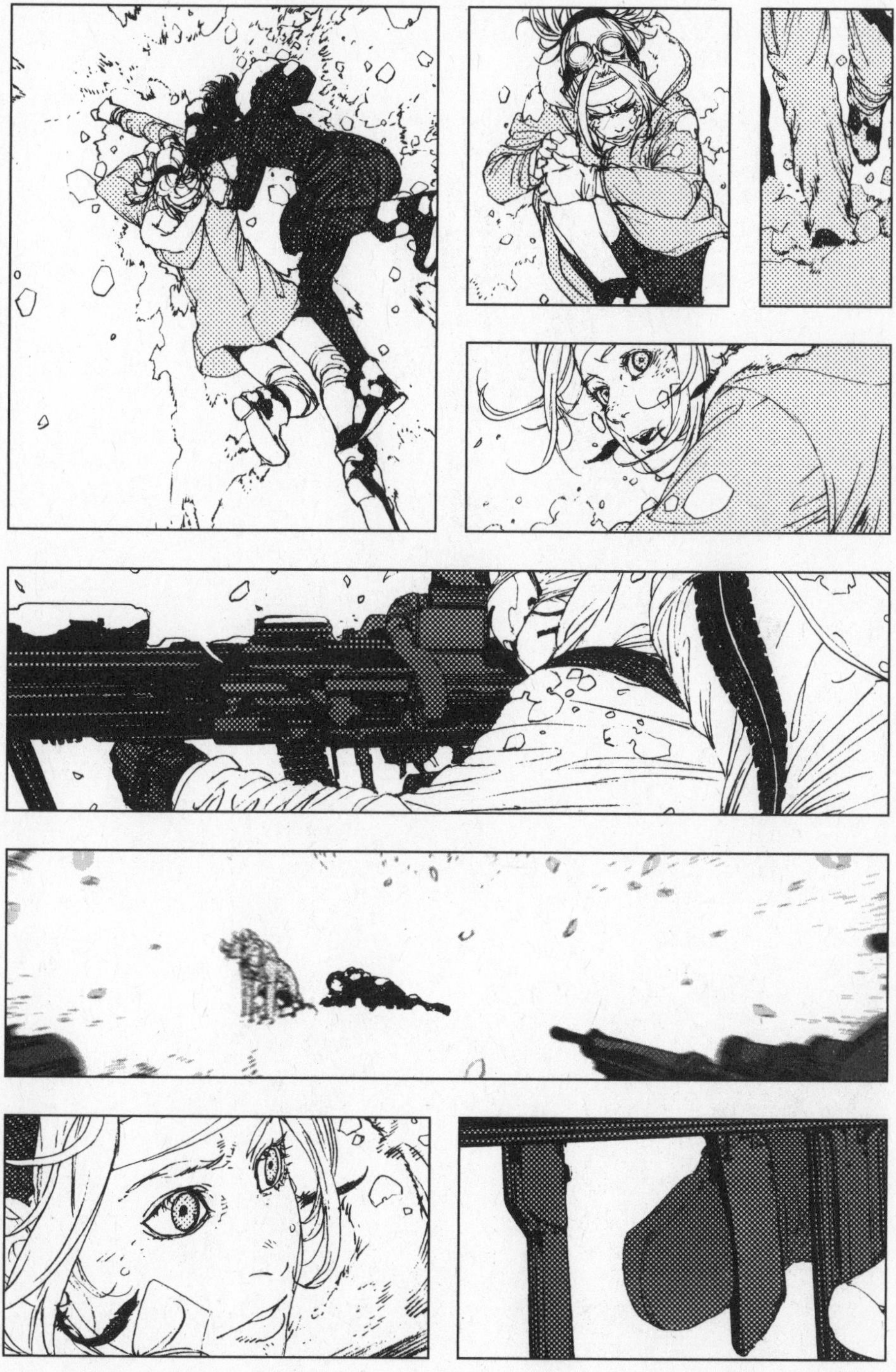

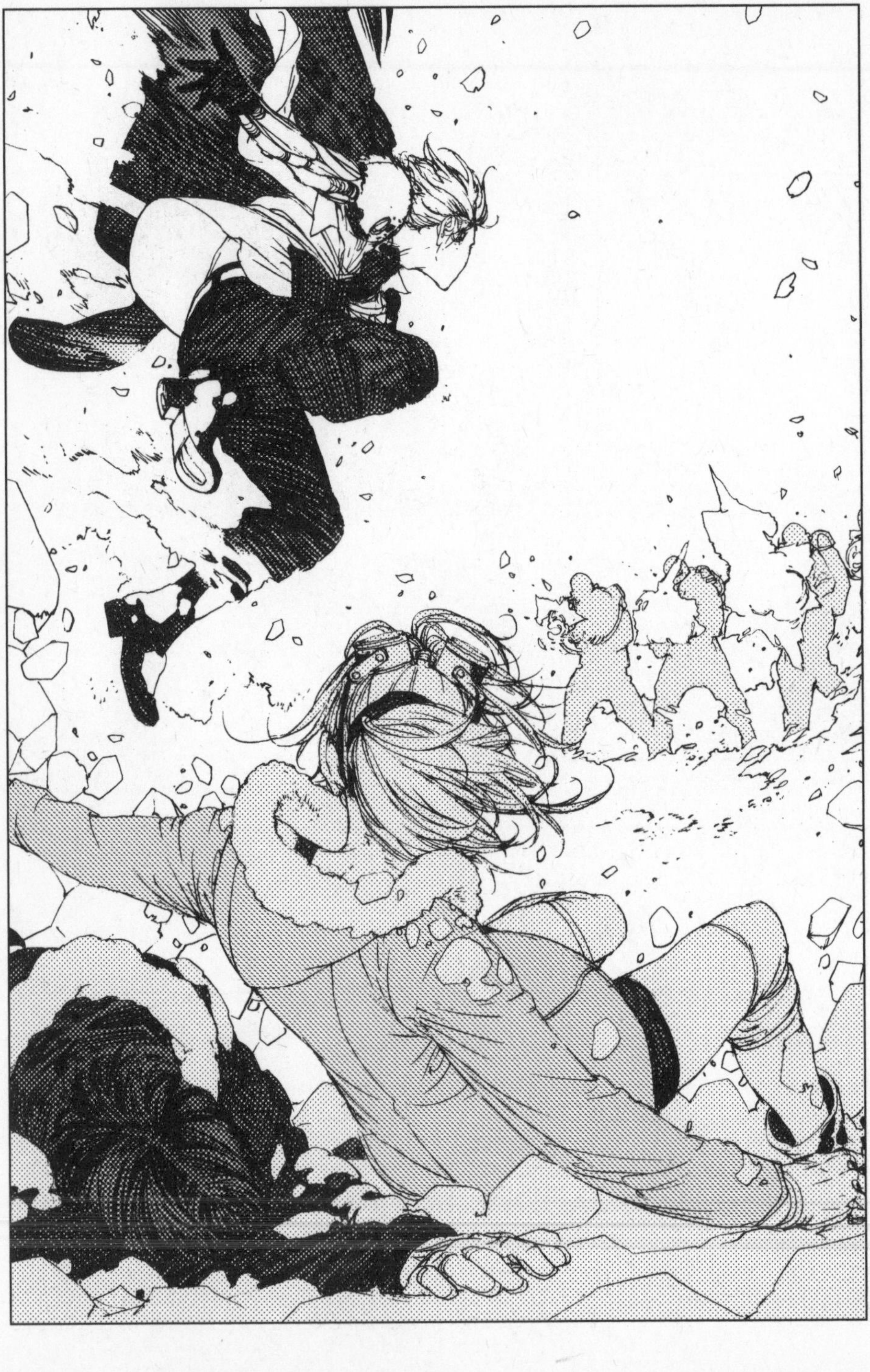

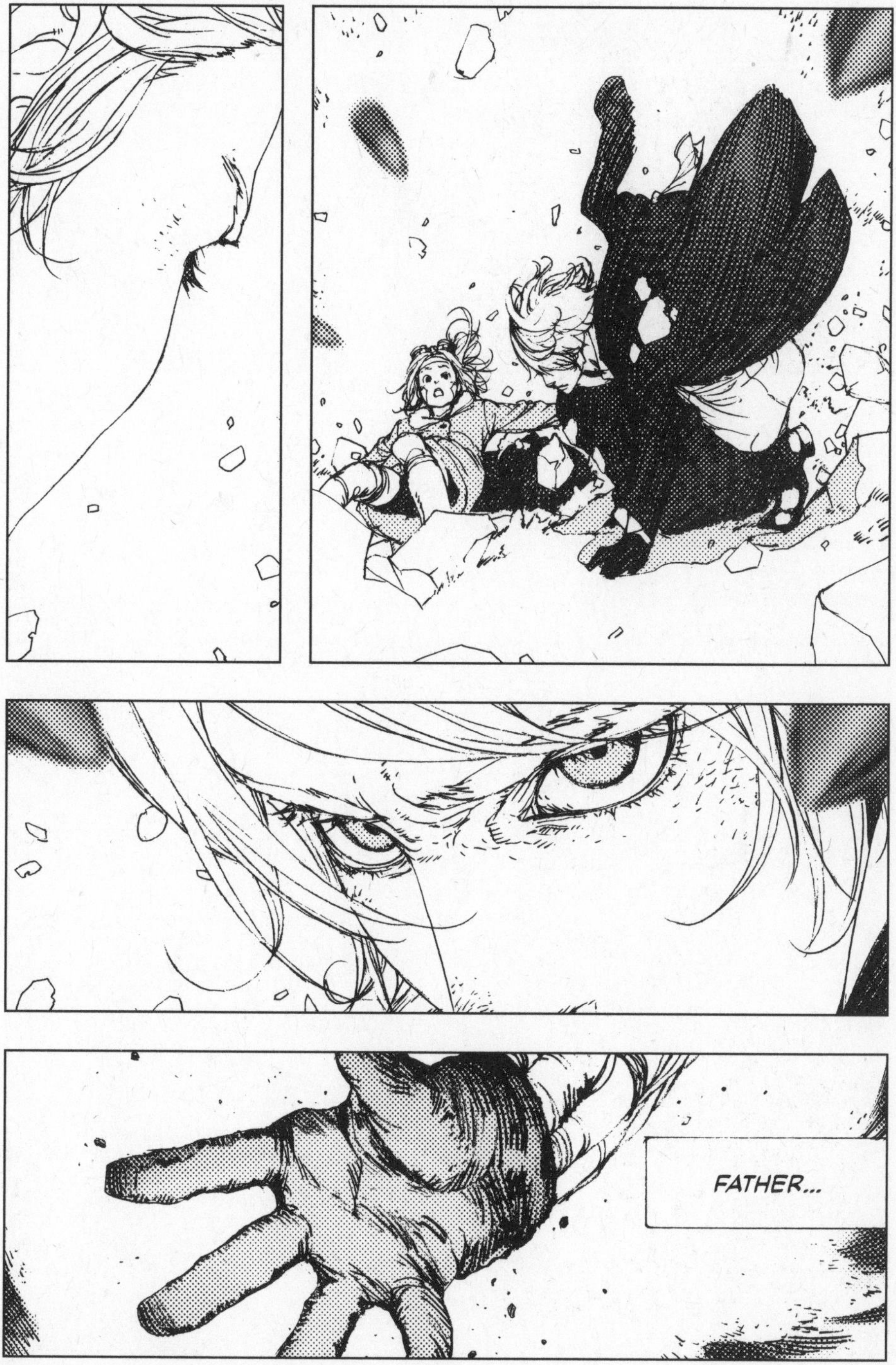
FATHER...

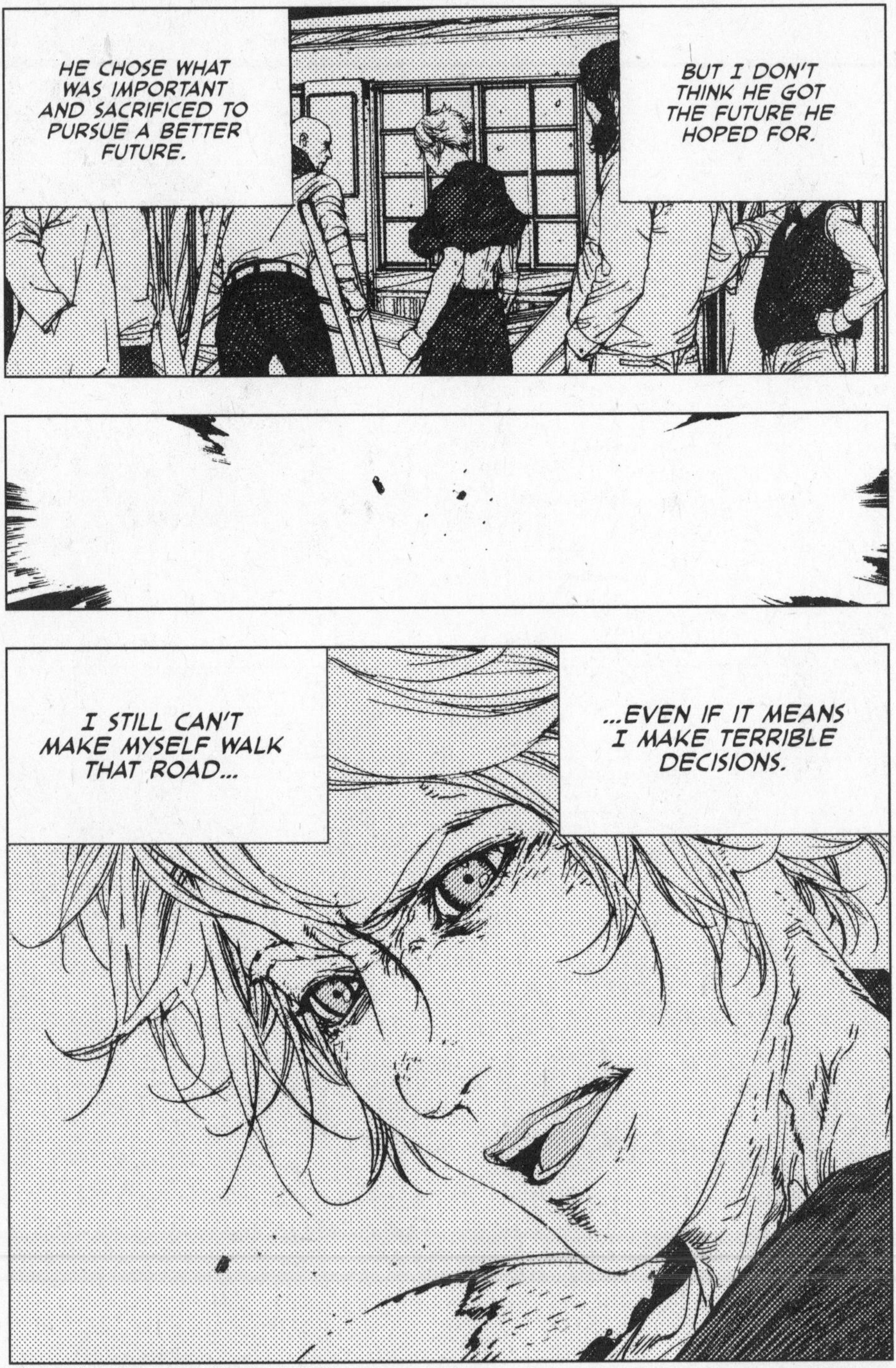
HE CHOSE WHAT WAS IMPORTANT AND SACRIFICED TO PURSUE A BETTER FUTURE.
BUT I DON'T THINK HE GOT THE FUTURE HE HOPED FOR.
I STILL CAN'T MAKE MYSELF WALK THAT ROAD...
...EVEN IF IT MEANS I MAKE TERRIBLE DECISIONS.

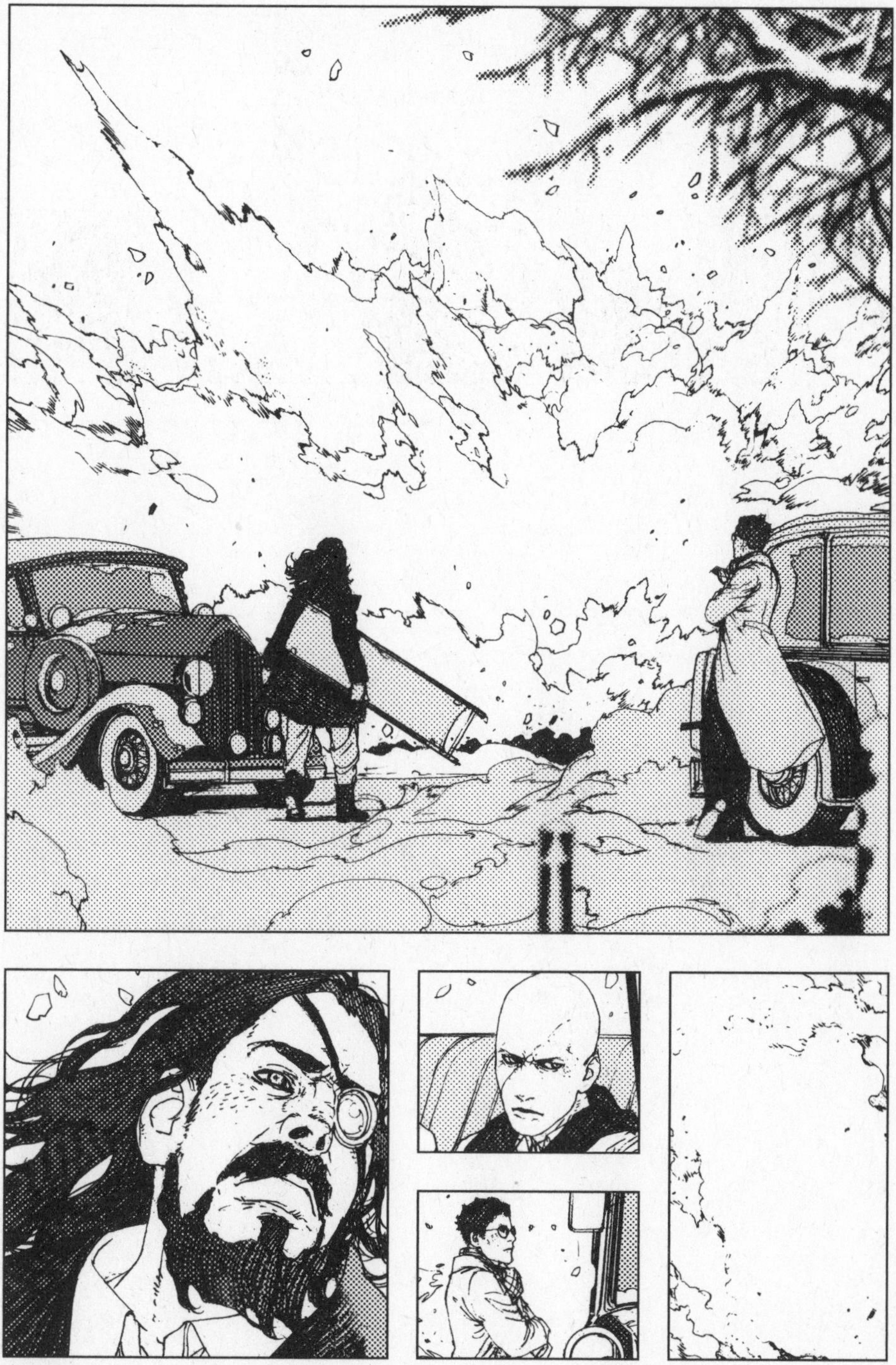

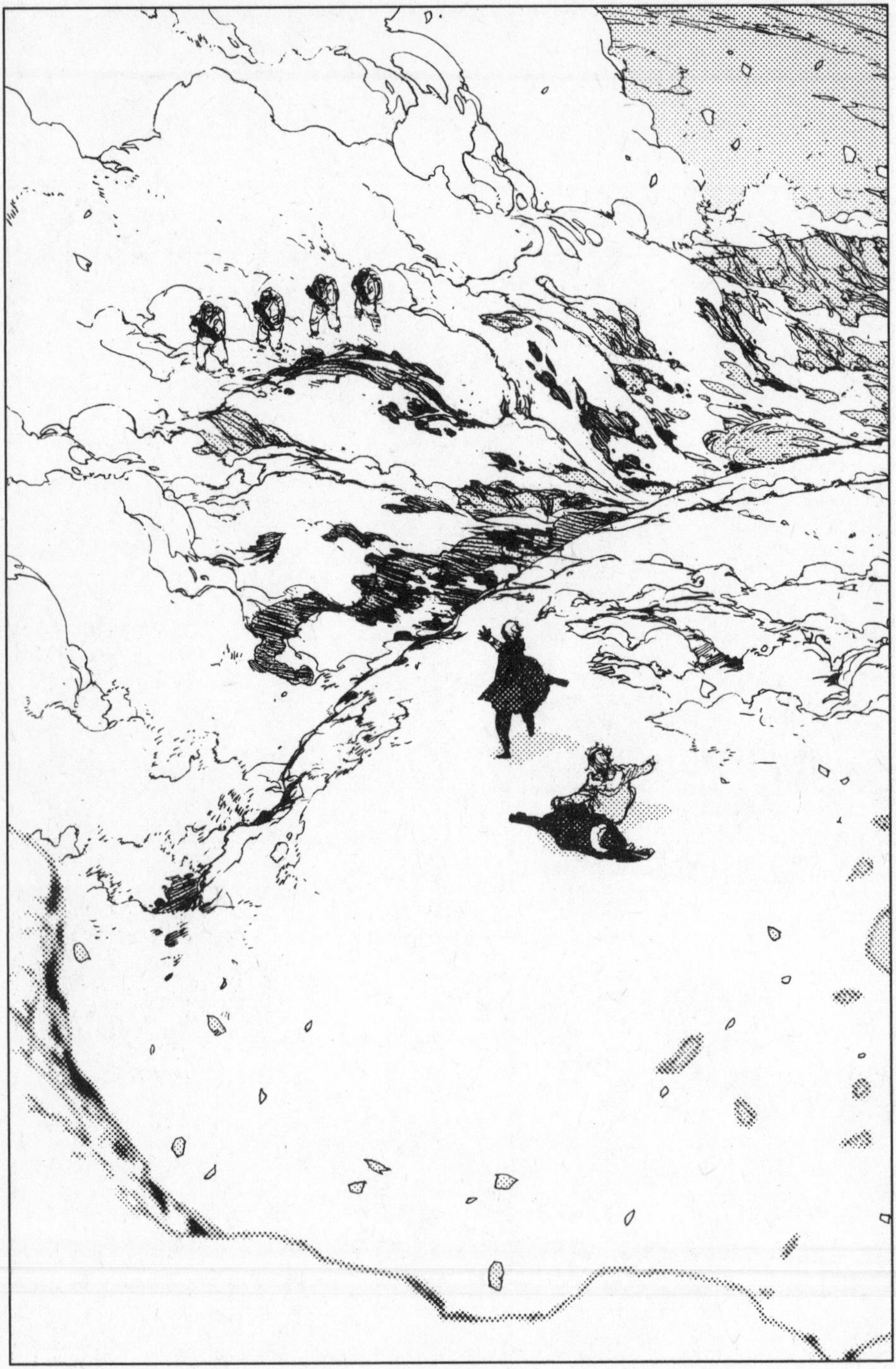

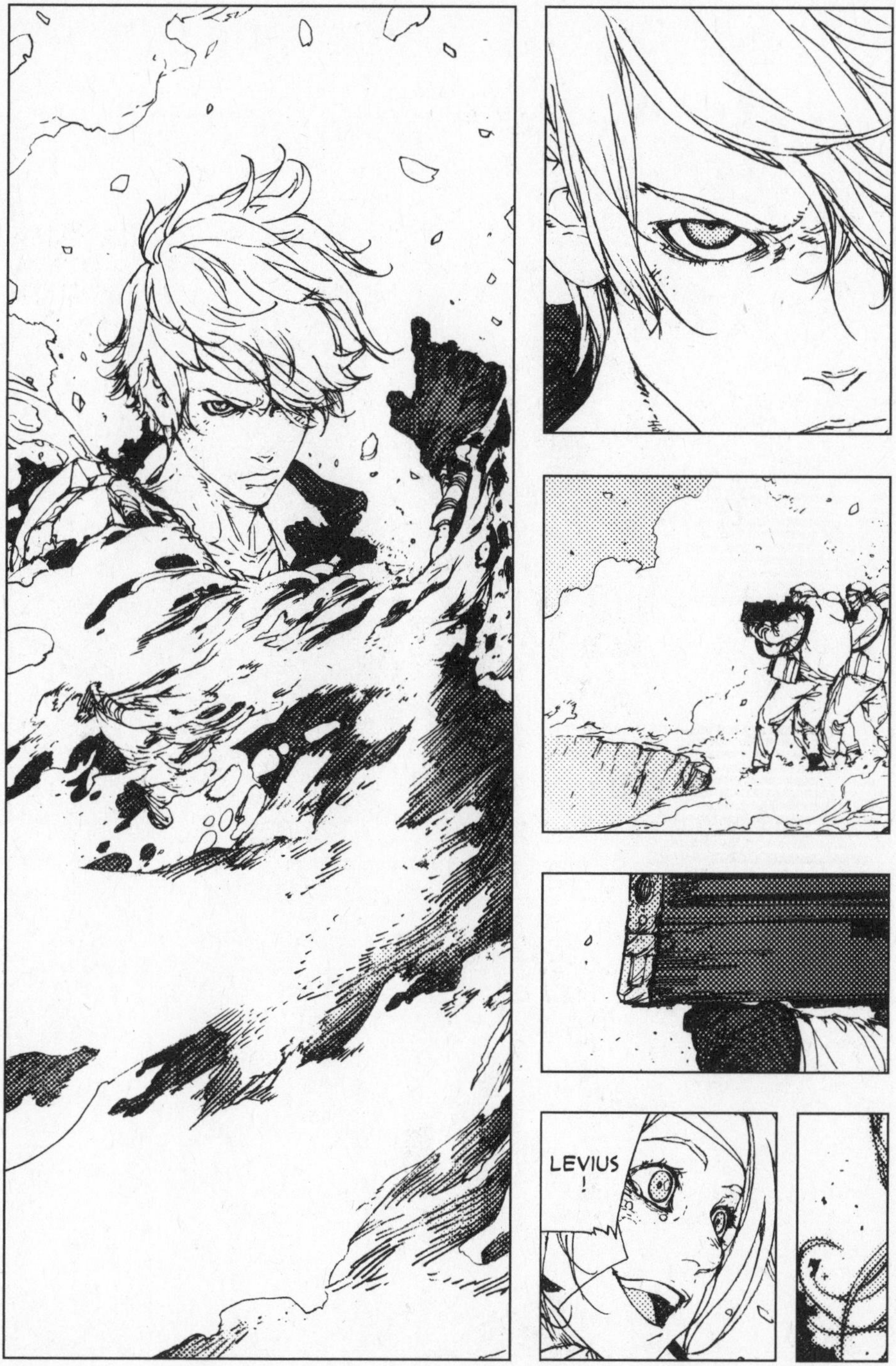
LEVIUS
!

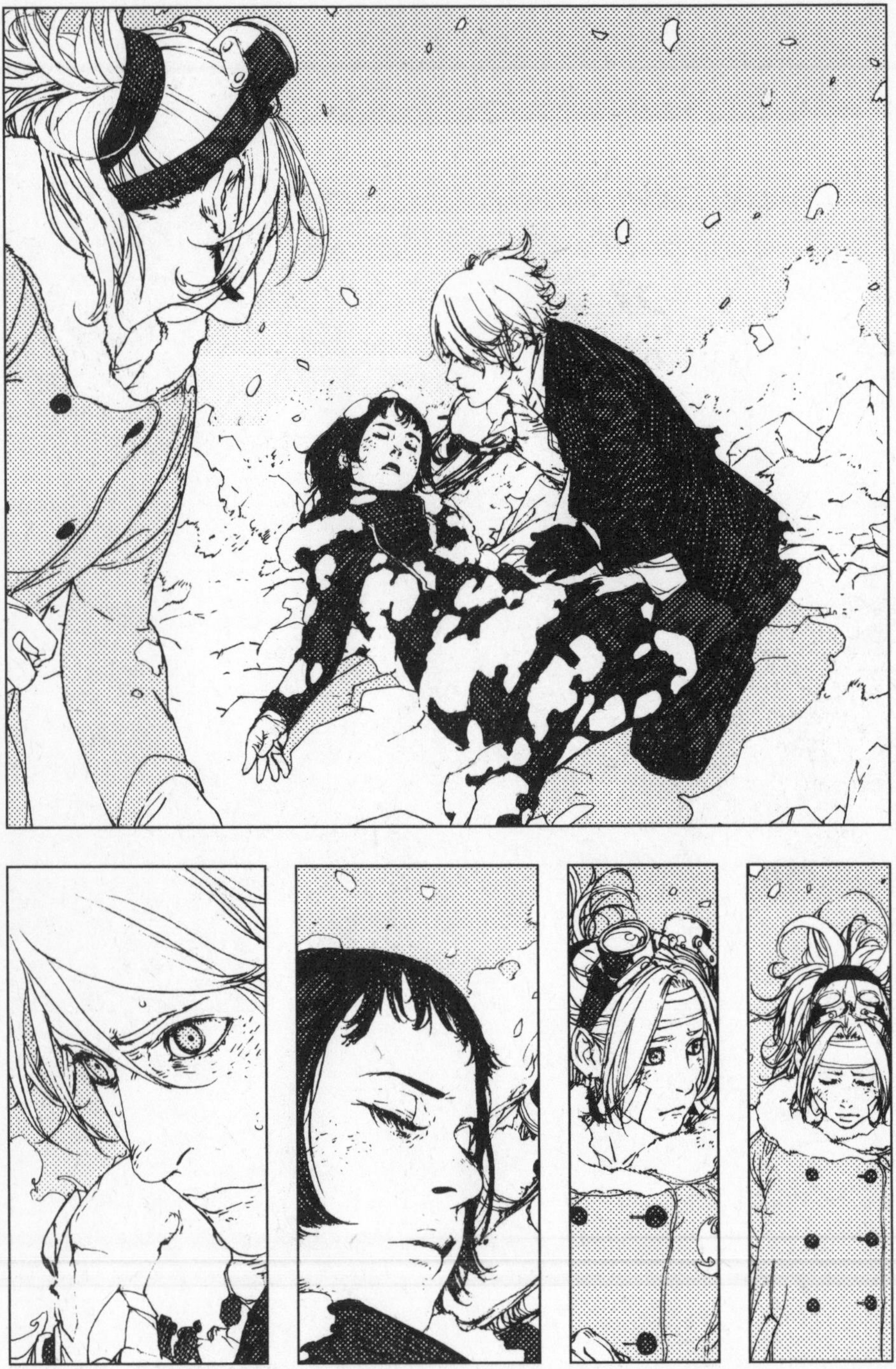

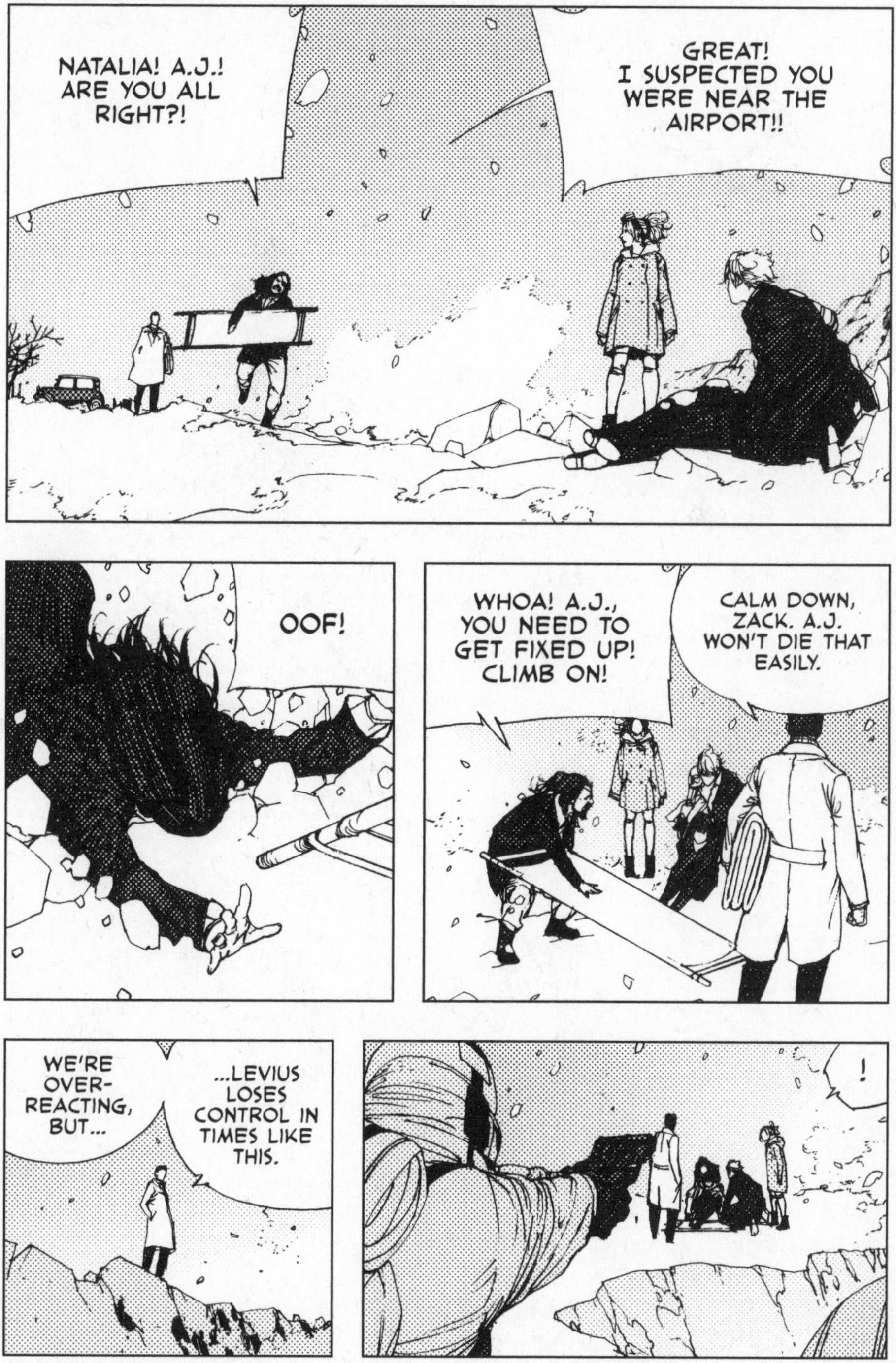
NATALIA! A.J.! ARE YOU ALL RIGHT?!
GREAT! I SUSPECTED YOU WERE NEAR THE AIRPORT!!
OOF!
WHOA! A.J., YOU NEED TO GET FIXED UP! CLIMB ON!
CALM DOWN, ZACK. A.J. WON'T DIE THAT EASILY.
WE'RE OVER-REACTING, BUT...
...LEVIUS LOSES CONTROL IN TIMES LIKE THIS.
!

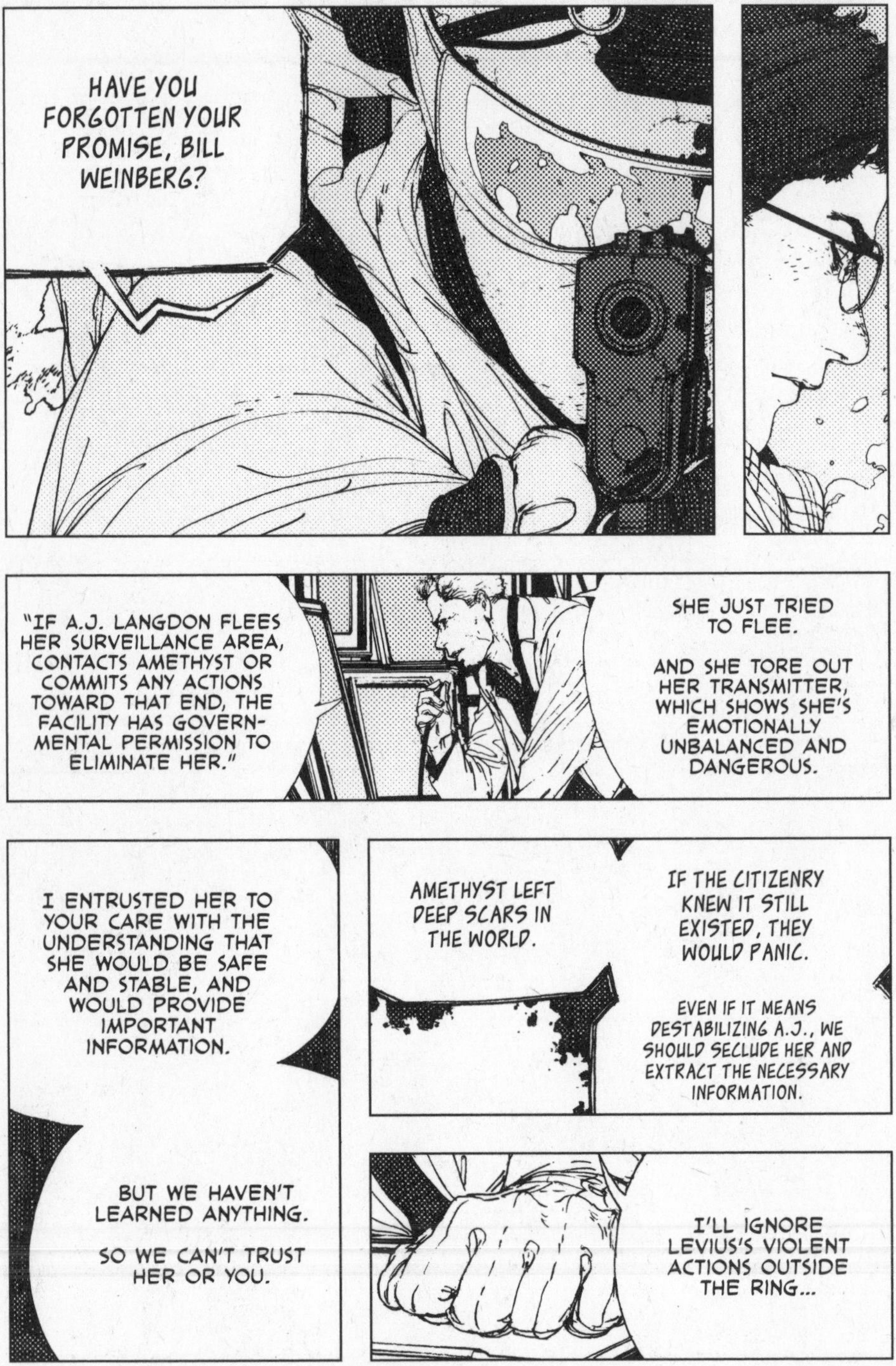
HAVE YOU FORGOTTEN YOUR PROMISE, BILL WEINBERG?
"IF A.J. LANGDON FLEES HER SURVEILLANCE AREA, CONTACTS AMETHYST OR COMMITS ANY ACTIONS TOWARD THAT END, THE FACILITY HAS GOVERN-MENTAL PERMISSION TO ELIMINATE HER."
SHE JUST TRIED TO FLEE.
AND SHE TORE OUT HER TRANSMITTER, WHICH SHOWS SHE'S EMOTIONALLY UNBALANCED AND DANGEROUS.
I ENTRUSTED HER TO YOUR CARE WITH THE UNDERSTANDING THAT SHE WOULD BE SAFE AND STABLE, AND WOULD PROVIDE IMPORTANT INFORMATION.
BUT WE HAVEN'T LEARNED ANYTHING.
SO WE CAN'T TRUST HER OR YOU.
AMETHYST LEFT DEEP SCARS IN THE WORLD.
IF THE CITIZENRY KNEW IT STILL EXISTED, THEY WOULD PANIC.
EVEN IF IT MEANS DESTABILIZING A.J., WE SHOULD SECLUDE HER AND EXTRACT THE NECESSARY INFORMATION.
I'LL IGNORE LEVIUS'S VIOLENT ACTIONS OUTSIDE THE RING...

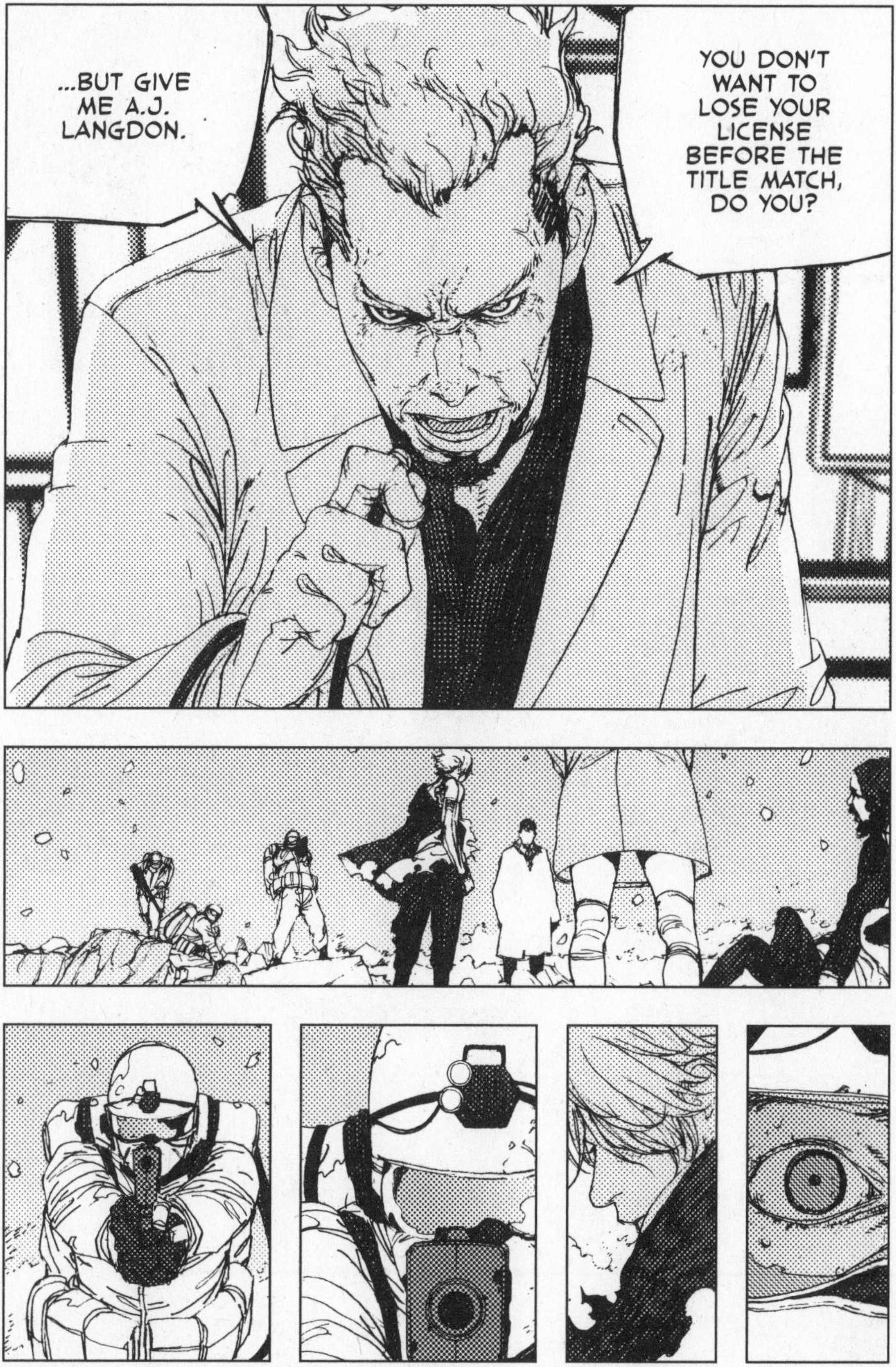
...BUT GIVE ME A.J. LANGDON.
YOU DON'T WANT TO LOSE YOUR LICENSE BEFORE THE TITLE MATCH, DO YOU?

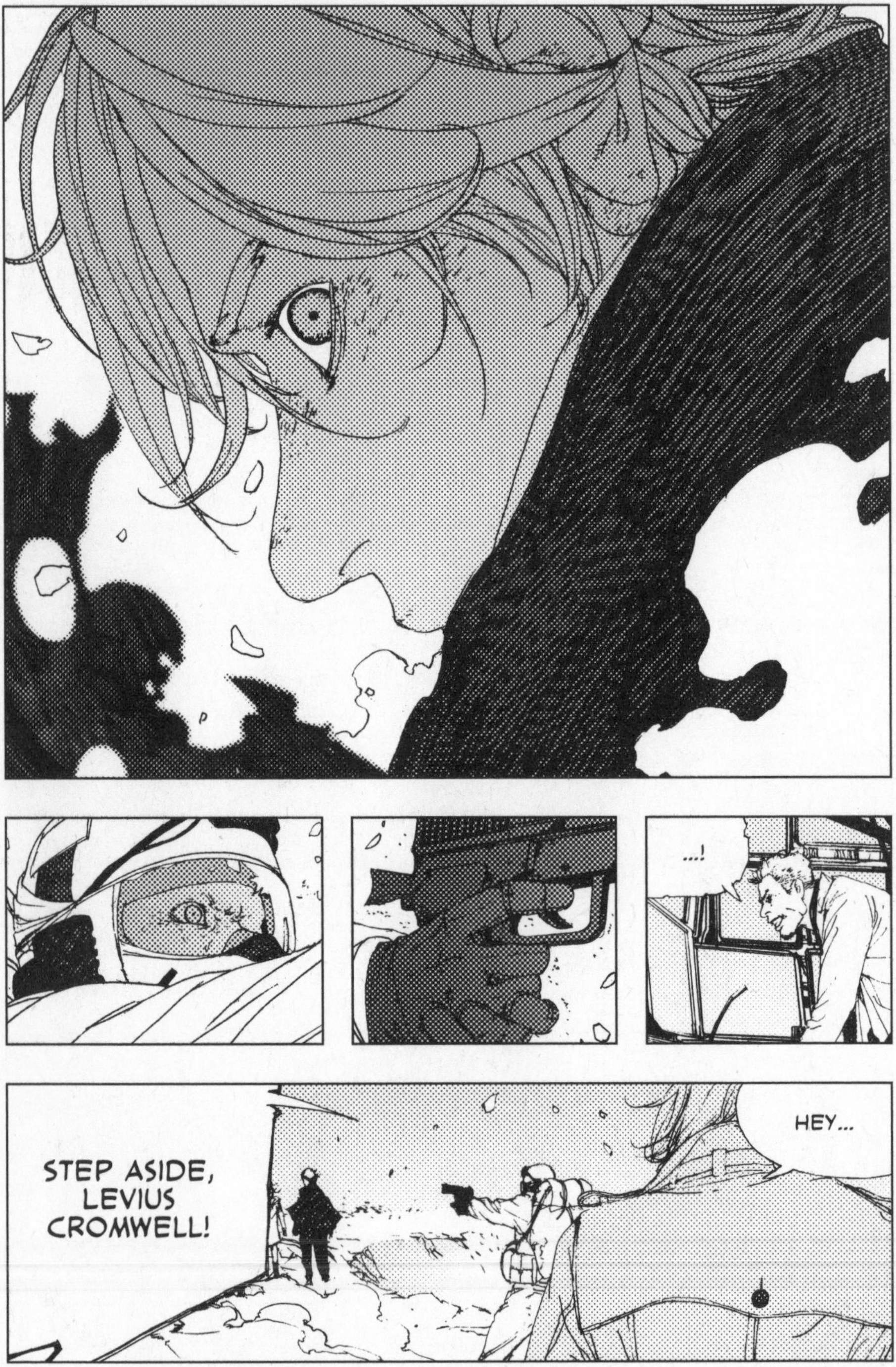
...!
STEP ASIDE, LEVIUS CROMWELL!
HEY...

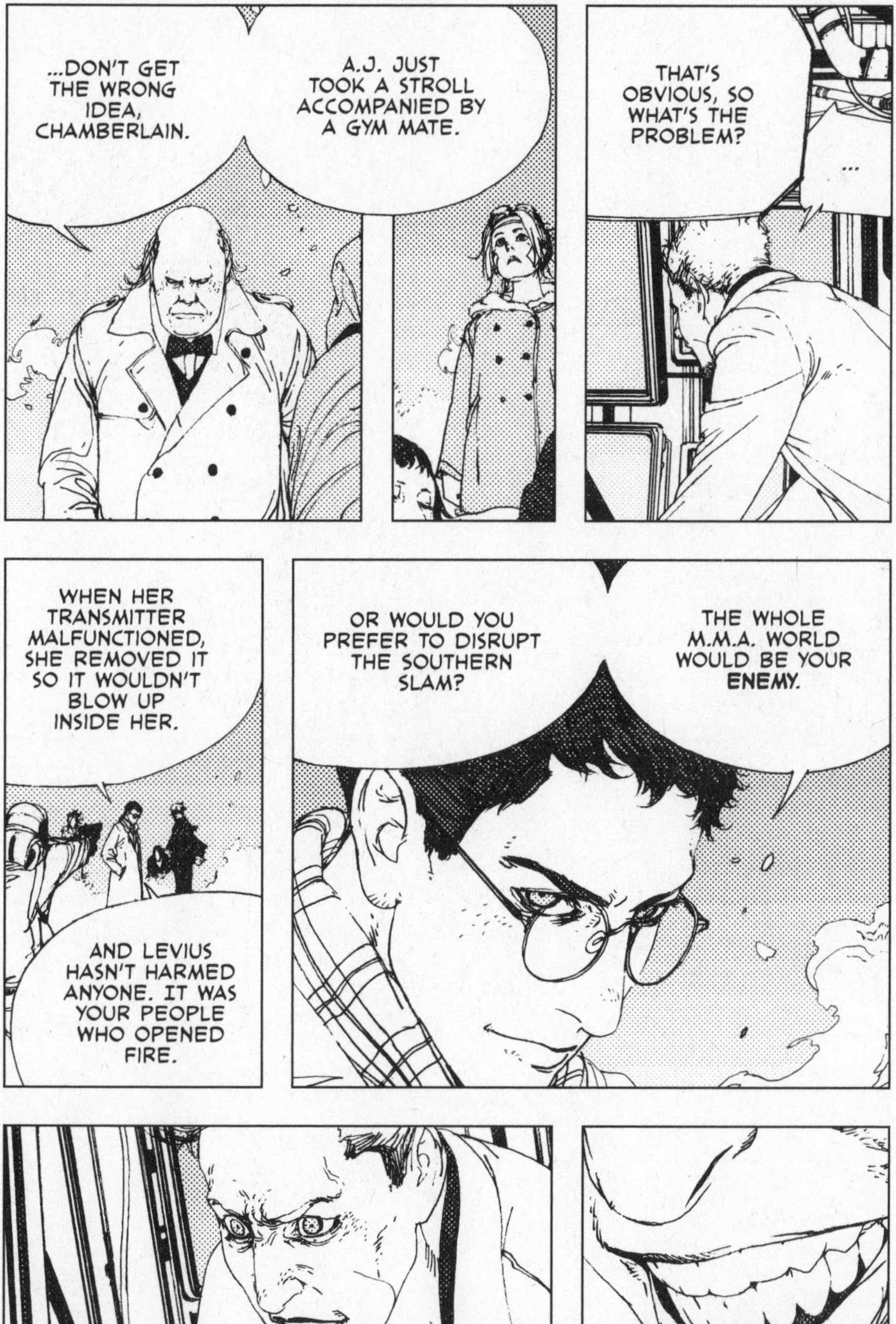
...DON'T GET THE WRONG IDEA, CHAMBERLAIN.
A.J. JUST TOOK A STROLL ACCOMPANIED BY A GYM MATE.
THAT'S OBVIOUS, SO WHAT'S THE PROBLEM?
...
WHEN HER TRANSMITTER MALFUNCTIONED, SHE REMOVED IT SO IT WOULDN'T BLOW UP INSIDE HER.
AND LEVIUS HASN'T HARMED ANYONE. IT WAS YOUR PEOPLE WHO OPENED FIRE.
OR WOULD YOU PREFER TO DISRUPT THE SOUTHERN SLAM?
THE WHOLE M.M.A. WORLD WOULD BE YOUR **ENEMY.**

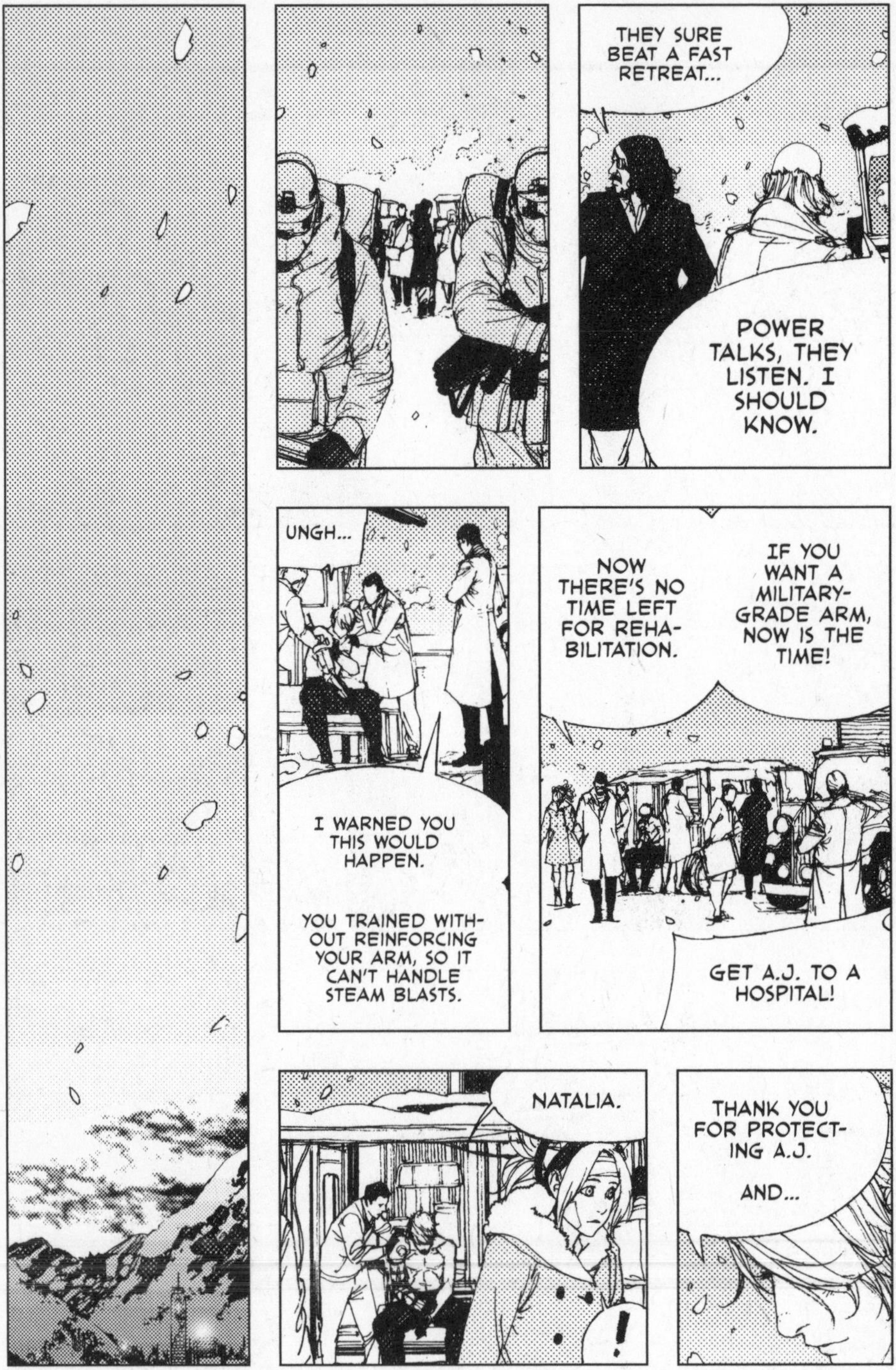

THEY SURE BEAT A FAST RETREAT...
POWER TALKS, THEY LISTEN. I SHOULD KNOW.
UNGH...
I WARNED YOU THIS WOULD HAPPEN.
YOU TRAINED WITHOUT REINFORCING YOUR ARM, SO IT CAN'T HANDLE STEAM BLASTS.
NOW THERE'S NO TIME LEFT FOR REHABILITATION.
IF YOU WANT A MILITARY-GRADE ARM, NOW IS THE TIME!
GET A.J. TO A HOSPITAL!
NATALIA.
!
THANK YOU FOR PROTECTING A.J.
AND...

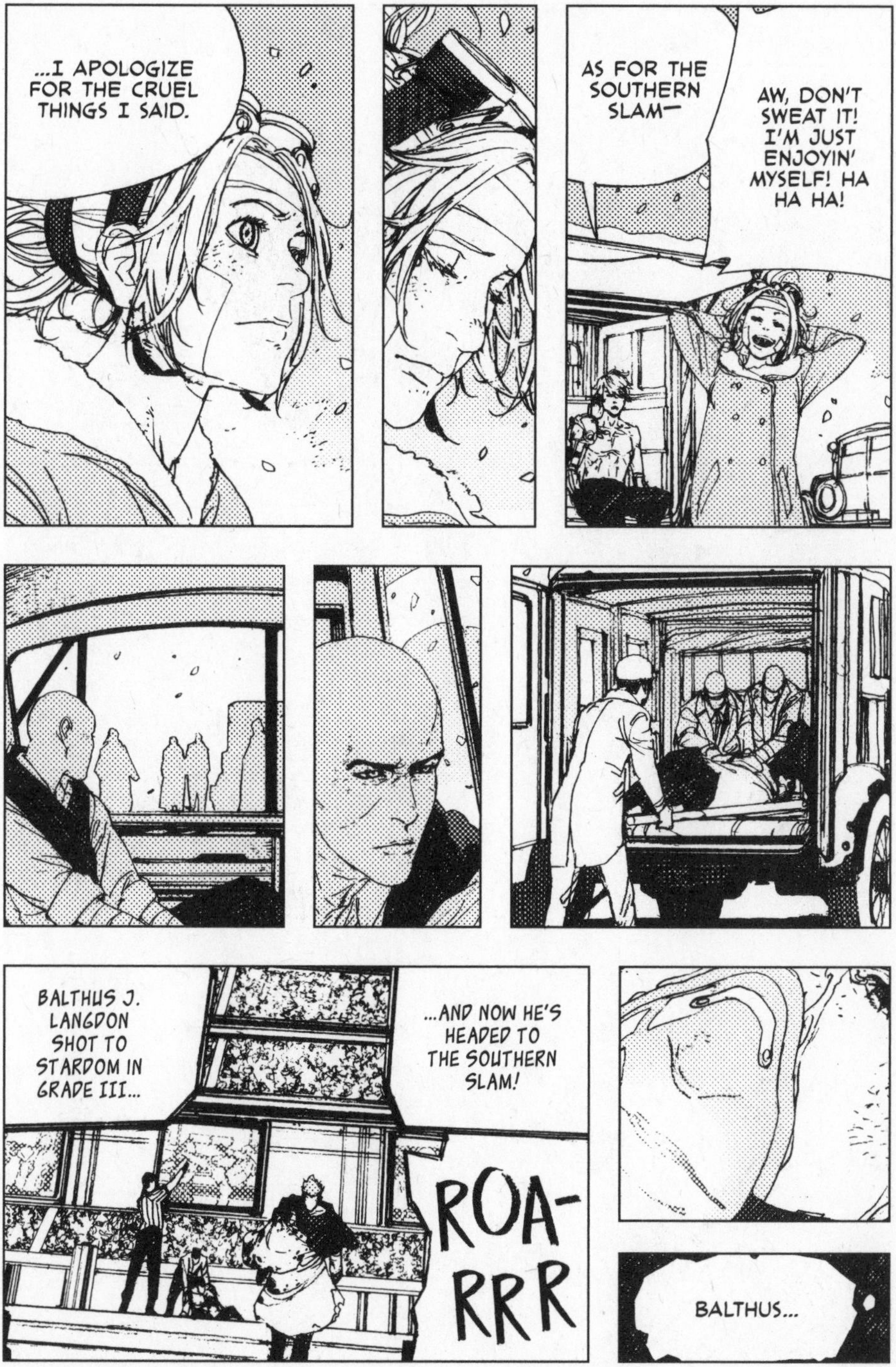
...I APOLOGIZE FOR THE CRUEL THINGS I SAID.
AS FOR THE SOUTHERN SLAM—
AW, DON'T SWEAT IT! I'M JUST ENJOYIN' MYSELF! HA HA HA!
BALTHUS J. LANGDON SHOT TO STARDOM IN GRADE III...
...AND NOW HE'S HEADED TO THE SOUTHERN SLAM!
ROA-RRR
BALTHUS...

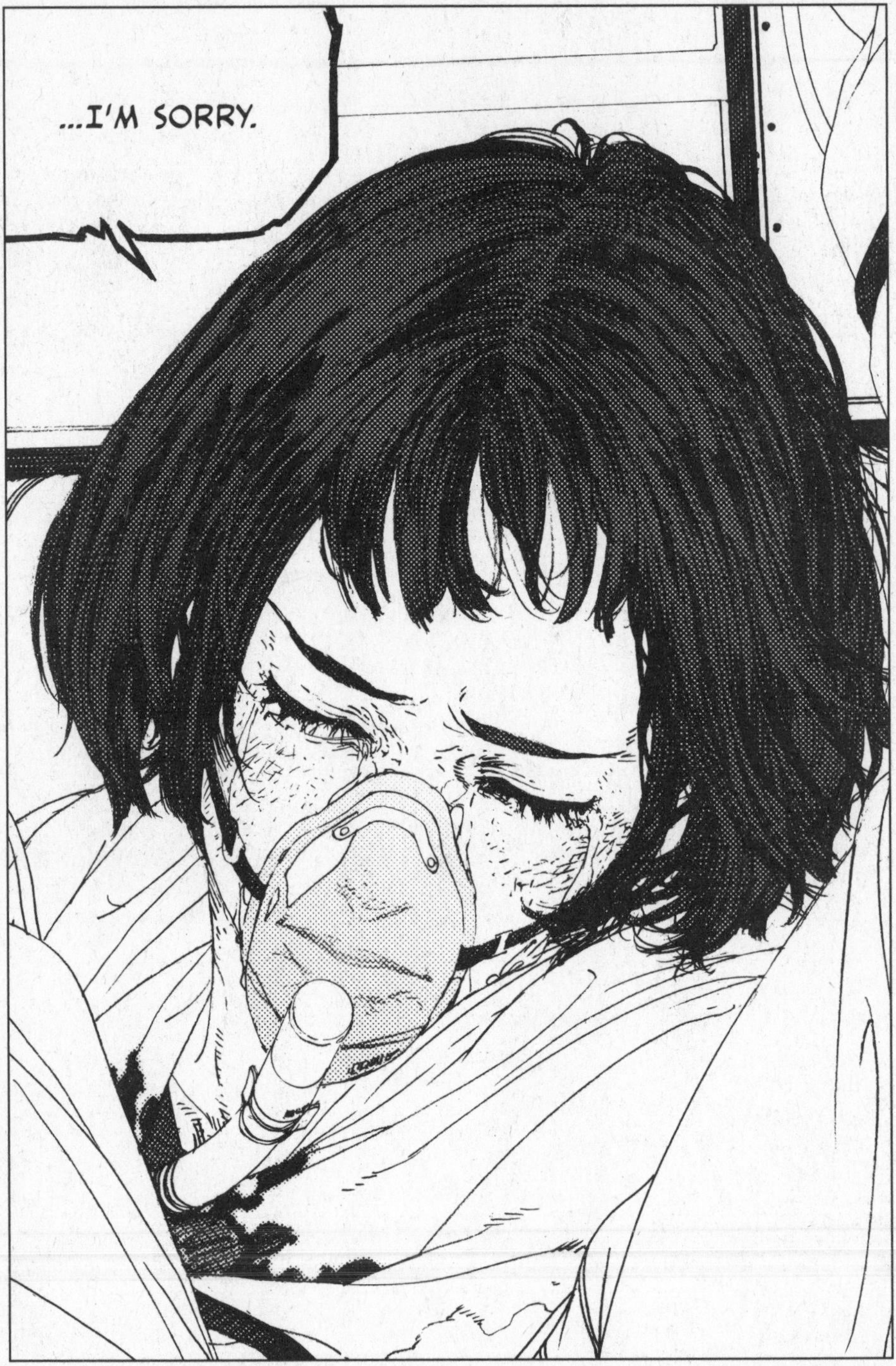
...I'M SORRY.

To Be Continued…

About the Author

Haruhisa Nakata began his professional manga career in 2010 with *Maureca no Ki* (Tree of Maureca) in *IKKI*, the same magazine where *Levius* began its serialization. In May 2015, Nakata restarted the *Levius* series as *Levius/est* in *Ultra Jump*.

LEVIUS/est

STORY & ART BY
Haruhisa Nakata

VOLUME 3
VIZ SIGNATURE EDITION

Translation — John Werry
English Adaptation — Jason A. Hurley
Touch-Up Art & Lettering — Joanna Estep
Design — Adam Grano
Editor — Joel Enos

Printed in Canada

Published by VIZ Media, LLC
P.O. Box 77010
San Francisco, CA 94107

10 9 8 7 6 5 4 3 2 1
First printing, March 2020

ratings.viz.com RATED T+ OLDER TEEN

PARENTAL ADVISORY
LEVIUS/EST is rated T+ for Older Teen and is recommended for ages 16 and up. This volume contains violence.

VIZ SIGNATURE
vizsignature.com

VIZ MEDIA
viz.com